Aberrations of Mourning

Aberrations
of
Mourning

Laurence A. Rickels

UNIVERSITY OF MINNESOTA PRESS

MINNEAPOLIS

LONDON

The writing of this book was sponsored by the Alexander von Humboldt Foundation.

The University of Minnesota Press gratefully acknowledges the financial assistance provided for the publication of the paperback edition of this book from the University of California, Santa Barbara Freshman Seminars program and the Foundation for International Art Criticism, Los Angeles.

Originally published as *Aberrations of Mourning: Writing on German Crypts* (Detroit: Wayne State University Press, 1988).

Published by the University of Minnesota Press
111 Third Avenue South, Suite 290
Minneapolis, MN 55401-2520
http://www.upress.umn.edu

Library of Congress Cataloging-in-Publication Data

Rickels, Laurence A.
Aberrations of mourning / Laurence A. Rickels. — [New ed.].
    p. cm.
Includes bibliographical references and index.
ISBN 978-0-8166-7595-1 (pbk. : acid-free paper)
1. German literature—History and criticism. 2. Authorship—Psychological aspects.
3. Psychoanalysis and literature—Germany. 4. Death in literature. 5. Authors,
German—Psychology. I. Title.
PT129.R47 2011
830.9'353—dc22   2011013910

Printed in the United States of America on acid-free paper

The University of Minnesota is an equal-opportunity educator and employer.

18 17 16 15 14 13 12 11   10 9 8 7 6 5 4 3 2 1

CONTENTS

PREFACE
INVITATION TO A REPRINTING

"Reprinting" was one of the analogues Freud used to illustrate transference; the other image was *haunting*. My book is back! My thanks to Douglas Armato for arranging its ghost appearance with the University of Minnesota Press. *Aberrations of Mourning* thus has another outside chance to circulate in its own writing and to reunite with its immediate context, the trilogy *Unmourning*. In addition to this book, *Unmourning* counts *The Case of California* (reprinted by Minnesota in 2001) and *Nazi Psychoanalysis* (which first appeared with Minnesota in three volumes in 2002).

In 1988 (twenty-two years ago as I issue this invitation), *Aberrations of Mourning* was way ahead of its time. Though I doubt its time has come, there is now a milieu of comps in the publications market that makes it a little harder to ignore a work of mourning. Literary and cultural studies of mourning, melancholia, trauma, haunting, and occult and technical media were not always topics of interest admitted by the university. While in the meantime it's all the range of what anyone in the academy could ever want to know, that's not because there has been a continuous history of scholars taking dictation and writing on crypts. A colleague (who many years later would write a ghost book that was welcomed as the height of the new—in sociology) asked me back then, as though in shock, how long it had taken me to write *Aberrations*. I guess most first books are cursory exercises, like dissertations probably should be. But I answered and then knew that I had spent all my young life writing this book.

Aberrations of Mourning had a vulnerable start. But that it appeared at all, very much before its time, I owe to Robert Mandel, who was director of Indiana University Press when I published what would become one chapter or case study in *Aberrations of Mourning* as a contribution to a centenary collection of essays on Kafka. Mandel is the reason Avital Ronell's *Dictations: On Haunted Writing* appeared from Indiana, out of context but at every other press at the time completely out of the question. Mandel moved to Wayne State University Press, and my manuscript followed him.

One of my senior colleagues then, sensing perhaps that I felt Wayne State wasn't all it should be, assured me that this press was known for keeping its list in circulation for the long haul. Jump cut: in no time *Aberrations* was abandoned as out of print. I can't imagine that this book was the biggest drag in the press's stable. I can imagine that intimate intrigue on the part of one of the academic series editors killed the book's young shelf life.

Aberrations of Mourning was the opening of all my resources for reformulation already inside its own looped discourse but then also beyond. (A review in *SubStance* characterized the book, very much to this point, as "overstimulating.") At a time when in the humanities you were expected to take sides with Benjamin and dismiss Adorno I took the latter of this law as my style consultant. I loved the way he used apodictic statement to make what I later learned to identify as a paradoxical intervention in the most transferentially loaded passages of our tradition of thought. He also created clichés (in the sense of printing and reprinting) out of syntactic asides on which I modeled my own recurring hieroglyphs to corral a following or understanding.

I was already writing *The Case of California* as I was just beginning to close the covers on *Aberrations*. *Nazi Psychoanalysis*, already well on its way, was all I could talk about in interviews held on the occasion of the publication of *The Case of California*. Between 1982 and 1995 I was writing "one" work that broke apart or was released in parts along the way. The separateness of the works, which I would never deny or abandon, is marked mainly by shifts in the specific manner in which I gave form to thought. But that is a major part of my task as writer.

For *The Case of California* I promoted as forced marriage the juxtaposition between teen idioms and the Germanic jargons of critical thought, but in *Nazi Psychoanalysis* I opened up shop at the borderline to psychosis. But there is already extensive commentary available (by me and by others) on the stylistic features of those works. Now it's time for me to stand by my first book.

How did a young man of good upbringing, to whom the chance had been given to live—really to live—on the Coast of unlimited opportunities for happiness, come to write such a monstrous book?

California wasn't all bad. The shock of it brought me back to Freud. I had turned to Freud already in adolescence, when, trying to think about mourning, I discovered that, quite simply, Freud alone addressed mourning directly or, to borrow Derrida's excellent formulation, without alibi. But in the course of my higher education I became convinced that a more abstract or overriding frame that would encompass Freud's thought among other discourses was what earning the doctoral degree ordered. OMG: I was on my way to becoming Foucauldian! But the isolation of UC Santa Barbara (especially in the early 1980s) delivered me of that contact high school of the academy's conformity to the one discursivity.

With the former world thus lost, I sought recovery inside Freud's "underworld of psychoanalysis," the corpus that had not even begun to be read yet. I am grateful to the gods that I was not situated in the academy in such a way that I had to become what I'm not in order to publish and perish. Friedrich Kittler confided to me early on that he had switched from psychoanalysis to Foucault in order to wage a career in the German university system. Please don't misunderstand my anecdotal indiscretion: Kittler managed just the same to offer, to my mind, the most original reading of Lacan in evidence to this day.

I was fortunate not to be left alone in my isolationism as California antibody during the time of this book's conception. Avital Ronell, with whom I had done time as fellow graduate student at Princeton, came to California to teach just a few years after my arrival. In our shared sense of the shell shock of life is a beach, we were close colleagues, preparing our classes and presentations together, when not in person then on the telephone. Once upon a field trip together to the amusement park Knott's Berry Farm ("not buried!"), we took a break from our on-location research assignment (before proceeding to the ghost town exhibit) to peruse the rentals section of the local newspaper. For all the carpeting included in the many apartments advertised we couldn't see the "crpt" as anything but another crypt to rent or tear open. We came to recognize that the "fun" the natives kept letting themselves have—while wondering whether they had started having it yet—had already been put back into "funeral."

But California is not enough. Here the Alexander von Humboldt Foundation came to my aid. What I needed was a year in Germany alone with Freud's collected words, out of range of all the paraphrase and explanation books back in the U. S. of A., which are here to serve you only as the prevention of any encounter at all with an original work, word, or thought. I'm referring here to my training prior to coming to California, but since it was all I thought I knew, I hadn't yet broken the habit, which the local campus bookstore supplied. I was able finally to break through my blocked relationship to writing (although I remain uncertain whether it was mine as much as it was institutional as usual). The breakthrough took place first as my sudden acquisition of a sense of audience. Like the fourteen-year-old Nietzsche I found out that to write a book you have to want to read it. I greeted the already copyedited manuscript with a frenzy of rewriting that didn't let up until I could recognize myself in its newfound excess.

Ten years after the appearance of *Aberrations of Mourning,* which was already off the shelf, John O'Neill first encouraged me to reissue the book with another press. I was following his counsel when I reassigned the portions of *Aberrations* dedicated to Freud's major case studies as parts of a "new" essay, "Digging Psychoanalysis," which appeared in a collection O'Neill edited, *Freud and the Passions.* My first footnote, in a context of gloomy forecast, advertised a reprint that I hoped would be coming soon: "To turn up the volume on *Freud and the Passions* and admit both melancholia and gadget love as the other two passions that get off together in Freud's name and corpus, a trip back into the crypt was required, into that double recess where my book *Aberrations of Mourning,* which first let roll the genealogy of media inside Freud's thought, was buried alive in the fast-food fields of one-stop researching."

It is wrong, however, to claim that *Aberrations of Mourning* was simply and surely buried alive or that it was one of the unread. The book all along had its own inside cult of strong readers. In his preface to *Der unbetrauerbare Tod* (the German translation of the Introduction, slightly expanded, followed by chapter 5 and a slice of Kafka—and not, as was mistakenly acknowledged, *Aberrations of Mourning* itself), Friedrich Kittler summarized my project with the perspicacity of the one it takes to know one:

> Freud's distinction between mourning and melancholia, that endless death cult, remains onset of a work of mourning that however falls back upon psychoanalysis itself. For the one who died and returned under the sign of Oedipus was always, as though there were no other dead, the father: guarantee of a logic to which his vacant position itself testifies. The counter reckoning is, because it must do without calculation, more difficult and subterranean. It demands a listing of all the dead who fell out of the semiotic order, all the corpses (or corpora) that disappeared without graves and rites (as ghosts have always been defined). The extinguished traces of children, siblings, and mothers promote at first a reading of Freud against Freud, but then with evidence that builds connections across the residues of psychoanalytic case studies and literary texts.

Kittler identified media theory as the science of such connections. And yet he also recognized that my book does not double, not even between the lines, as another history of machines.

> Only do not expect any history of such materialities or media. Even when it concerns historical connections like between book printing and the cult of the child, psychoanalysis and film technology, over and again Europe falls under an external gaze that traverses its self-historicization. That which is stored in unmourned crypts is older than any history and opens up Europe too (not to mention the American uncon-cept of a "Western Culture") to the fieldwork and grave excavation of ethnology. In order to decode why there is in Hollywood a mummy cemetery just like in Egypt right next to the film studios there is no more suitable science. Only ethnology can describe how the technical media fall as ghosts from the heavens upon their own culture in the Melanesian Cargo Cult, the secret and eccentric center of this book. The Cargo Cult in a book that addresses after all Goethe and Keller,

Nietzsche and Freud, Kafka and Artaud teaches us something. We too, among exploded transmissions and forgettings, become the aborigines of media technologies that more likely invented us than we them.

Aberrations of Mourning offers, then, a new history of "world literature," not as the academic novelty item that some legal clause might introduce but as endless missing persons report.

One reviewer back then when this book was first published characterized my style as Mannerist. Repetition, artificiality, and jarring juxtapositions are your friends at the frontier of haunting. It was also argued that I attempted working in ways analogous to musical variation. I show this hand in the last chapter, for which I selected, rather than another haunted corpus in which to immerse my reading, a single work, *The Tin Drum,* a novel without the depth charges of a case of melancholia but from which I could riff off a great many mirth-in-funeral leitmotifs both for the purpose of summary and to herald a new affirmation that would belong to the work next in line. What crossed my mind was the operatic and manic close of Goethe's Helena Act (in *Faust II*). While I sign in on location throughout *Aberrations,* the final chapter for the first time directly addresses the postwar era—and thus the book is allowed to get past the horizon of "final destination" that encloses the other chapters. And yet a postwar period's ready-made optimism can be as shallow as the graves catastrophe digs. It is one more proof of the trilogy's powers of augury that the grass grew over a buried secret that an entire society sought to keep undisturbed. But then out popped the Nazi teenager, a recognizable mascot of the works that follow *Aberrations of Mourning.*

Aberrations of Mourning

INTRODUCTION

For instance, the belief that there is a magical bond between a wound and the weapon which caused it may be traced unaltered for thousands of years. If a Melanesian can obtain possession of the bow which caused his wound, he will keep it carefully in a cool place so as to reduce the inflammation of the wound. But if the bow was left in the enemy's possession, it will undoubtedly be hung up close to the fire so that the wound may become thoroughly hot and inflamed.

Freud, *Totem and Taboo*

On the sidelines of German intellectual history—*Geistesgeschichte*—ghostbusters can find, tucked inside a supplement to "Documentary Reports," the inside view of vampirism as the work of the *Weltgeist*.[1] *Geist* is *Geist:* the intellect or spirit is, in German, always also a ghost. *Aberrations of Mourning* explores a phantasmatic *Geistesgeschichte* not addressed within the traditional framework of theories and histories that emphasize only Oedipal structures. The study accordingly involves a reconsideration and reshifting of certain basic tenets which inform the way we read literature, philosophy, and, in turn, psychoanalysis itself. As such it suggests a reading of both reading and writing that would go beyond notions of patricidal writing which continue, to this day, to receive so much currency.

In the ensuing chapters literary texts and their aesthetic and semiotic theories are read alongside the breakdown of mourning discernible throughout the name-bearing corpus. Since psychoanalytic hermeneutics, which remains inseparable from Freud's works, is the only context available for consideration of the place of aberrant mourning in a corpus, this critical perspective will be invoked to account for problems and peculiarities attending the interpretation at the same time that it is called to account for its own complicity in misinterpretations or misplacements of the corpse in question. Throughout this study it therefore proves necessary to interrupt readings of specific literary and philosophical tracts and, guided by the new blockages each course of aberrant mourning advances, to take yet another turn in what is ultimately, as Freud puts it, "the underworld of psychoanalysis."[2] In this way—and on the way—the precise contours, implications, and exclusions which the concept of mourning seeks to attain in psychoanalytic theory find a kind of archaeological desedimentation or deconstruction.

In "Transience" Freud declared mourning the central problem or riddle with which the psychologist must come to grips: "Mourning over the loss of something that we loved or admired, appears to the layman so natural, that he takes it for granted. To the psychologist, however, mourning is a vast riddle, one of those phenomena which can itself not be explained but to which other obscurities can be attributed."[3] And yet, as Freud instructs in "Our Relation to Death," the practice of these inscrutable mourning rituals remains indispensable, since the mourner's own survival—indeed, the continuation and growth of culture—would be imperiled if the period of mourning, approximately two years in duration, did not come to some definite conclusion.

Our first reaction upon the death of a loved one issues in the wish to die along with the departed. And yet already alongside this first spontaneous upsurge of solidarity, Freud adds, we also admire—and thus keep our distance from—the one who, in going on ahead, has accomplished a difficult feat. The original refusal to substitute for loss—which in turn reflects a deadlock brought on by sorrow's instant ambivalent supplementation—must itself find substitution; otherwise, the survivor is condemned to live without taking risks, without life. As Freud concludes: without proper burial of its casualties, life can only become shallow and insubstantial, "like an American flirt." The unbearable intensity of grief arising from paralyzing contemplation of irreplaceable relations would have barred man from engaging in "attempts at mechanical flight, expeditions to distant lands, and experiments with explosive substances."

The neurotic impasse reflects and reverses the outcome of its primal scene: the premier passing of a loved one. Unlike the slain

2

enemy, who bears the sheer target of exteriority, the dead loved one covers two registers to the point of bringing confusion to the distinction between life and death. Since the dearly departed is at the same time other, he remains alien and inimical; but he also takes with him what he always reflected back or embodied: the most cherished extension and part of the survivor. Following the original departure of someone close, primal man, doubled over with the first bout of ambivalence, conceived spirits and other forms of afterlife and thus anticipated, for the first time, the need to mourn. While primal man's terrible grief gave rise to the premier speculations of psychological thought, modern man's ambivalent reception of death produces, in isolation from any channel or outlet of occult or psychological reflection, only neurosis.[4]

Enter psychoanalysis, the exploratory allegorization of the psyche in terms of Psyche, bride of death. And yet, by all accounts, psychoanalysis penetrated the underworld only to excavate and commemorate the father, and never to the point of bringing back a lost object—an object which, since capable of being lost, would not be paternal. According to John Bowlby, while Freud recognized the part the urge to recover the lost object plays in healthy mourning, he overlooked its role in melancholia. One reason for Freud's oversight, says Bowlby, is the overwhelming emphasis which, in his conception of both mourning and melancholia, he gave to identification with the lost object.[5] On occasion this oversight almost became part of the definition; for, while Freud saw the unappeasable demand of bereaved longing as informing the painfulness of normal mourning,[6] he adopted almost the opposite view with regard to melancholia, where both the object and the longing for the object are thus doubly abandoned. With melancholia, Freud argued, the object is given up and the object-cathexis brought to an end; but the free libido, which is not displaced onto another object as the work of mourning demands, is withdrawn into the ego, where it serves to establish "an *identification* of the ego with the abandoned object."[7] Since the first or primal identification is always with the father,[8] even melancholia remains, for Freud, lodged inside that substitutive economy of symbolic positions organized around the father, who, according to psychoanalysis, is already his own shadow when alive and then, once dead, is broadcast live. This substitutive economy, which guarantees that death will introduce no loss into the family that adoption—of the name—cannot replace, accordingly finds its backup support in the work of mourning, which puts to rest and replaces what is already at rest. And yet, Bowlby concludes, Freud's conception of melancholia lies outside the "work of mourning" only as its outermost protective surround.

Even the most ancient theories of ghosts see the specter as a dead person who has been improperly buried, or to whom performance of mourning rituals and presentation of sacrificial offerings are still owed. The dead person's soul must be appeased; otherwise his phantom will return to take vengeance. Robert Burton was not alone in linking the imagination affected by melancholia to the legends of ghosts, vampires, and devils he collected as integral part of his *Anatomy of Melancholy*. But whereas Burton reserved in his vast compendium of theories and legends of melancholia but one subsection for discussion of mourning disorders, Freud addressed melancholia as in essence a form of mourning. Freud's divergence from the long history of speculation on the consequences and causes of excess of black bile is thus announced in the very title of his hallmark essay: mourning *and* melancholia.

At the same time, however, Freud disconnected the telepathic call from the phantom realm only to take and answer this call in zones of theorizing which did not directly address mourning and aberrations of mourning. By keeping the theory of ghosts separate from his theory of mourning, Freud did not accord a place in his redefinition of melancholia to that which is genuinely improper to mourning. In Freud's essay the catastrophe of another's death summons mourner and melancholic alike while turning them apart: the loss that afflicts the former is conscious, whereas the occasion for the latter's interminable grieving is kept in the unconscious. Which reception of loss will be available depends upon the channel of the original object choice. Thus Freud agrees with Otto Rank that whereas the mourner disengages his ego from an object loved for its separateness and otherness, the melancholic discards a narcissistic choice by consummating the ego's rapport with this cherished object through identification, internalization, and idealization. Hence the mourner feels impoverished but not degraded, such extraordinary lowering of self-esteem being precisely the melancholic's plight.

Acco[...] g works both to "conserve" the [...] cure compensation for the loss. M[...] he ambivalence which disturbed t[...] ect even before its departure no[...] only method available for dislodgi[...] lization of the lost object, whereby the hostile feelings the highly ambivalent mourner cannot help but address to the departed are directed against himself. Thus Freud's suggestion that normal mourning was devoid of ambivalence was, on Abraham's recommendation, discarded by Freud himself; in psychoanalysis, ambivalence-free safety zones are always somewhere else.[9] Melancholia, Abraham concludes, is, simply, an archaic form of mourning,[10] just as the narcissistic object choice—the hinge that keeps mourning and melancholia turning together but in different time zones—remains more ancient than any genuinely heterosexual attachment. Indeed, what is threatened with extinction during mourning is heterosexual libido itself: he who cannot stop mourning becomes the widow of his heterosexuality.

Behind this extreme of the analysis of mourning, Abraham loses the theory of ghosts among the disposable effects of repression; by assuming or anticipating that underlying the haunting of his patients is the always anticipated death—the divinization and murder—of the father, Abraham advances, in advance of any exhumation or burial to be performed, the interpretation of phantom possession as the displaced effect of repressed sexual research which can be conducted only as intercourse with ghosts at one end and, at the other, as simulation of, or in place of, sublimation.[11] This scenario corresponds, in Freud's work, to the place Leonardo da Vinci's unconsummated homosexual disposition holds: the study of da Vinci was Freud's first treatment of protracted or delayed mourning—in da Vinci's case, for his mother—already in terms of an inward, inverting turn identification takes in lieu of substitution.[12]

This phantasmic reading of the homosexual disposition, from which the theoretical pursuit of mourning and melancholia springs, finds a counterpart in Abraham's investigation of consanguineous marriages which occupy an intermediate zone of "compromise" between incest and homosexuality.[13] Viktor Tausk accordingly

libido Development *Introjection*

views melancholia—or melancholia-cum-paranoia—as the pathological application of detached heterosexual libido already shaped and shattered from within by the narcisitic position it occupied. Whereas detached homosexual libido is readily reabsorbed by the ego—which is already aggrandized because capable of making such investments in the first place—narcissistic libido installed in a heterosexual object cannot, once severed from itself, be recuperated by an ego which melancholia reduces and miniaturizes.[14] Thus, in Pausanias's version, Narcissus can enter into the suicide pact of melancholia only with his dead twin sister, whom he recognizes in place of his own reflection or double.

Freud therefore assigns work to be accomplished if libidinal investments are not to be lost; when loss of object disengages libido, substitution can be effected immediately or the detached libidinal cathexis "can return for a time to the ego."[15] Introjection and identification, the support systems of mourning which effect this return, accordingly have incorporation as corporeal, literal, or primal model: the ego "wishes to incorporate the object in a manner commensurate with the oral or cannibalistic phase of libido development, namely by devouring it."[16] Melancholia thus retains what is otherwise devoured, assimilated, and expelled by the mourning body.

mania

Mania in turn confirms by reversing this retentive tendency of melancholia. A "festival of liberation" according to Abraham, mania celebrates the ego's sudden triumph over both ego ideal and the once-loved, lost, and subsequently introjected object. Whereas in melancholia the ego is vampirized by the introjected object, in mania libido turns with ravenous hunger to the external world of objects; whatever appears before the manic's rapidly advancing probe is swallowed. But this pleasurable swallowing during the manic phase, which succeeds the melancholic's sense that he is excluded from the world of objects as though disinherited, corresponds to an equally rapid, equally pleasurable expulsion of the briefly retained objects and impressions.

In mania, then, incorporation takes over the controls of the perceptual apparatus it puts on fast forward, thereby animating the divergent "metabolisms" that keep mourning and melancholia apart. The speed and excess of mania thus anesthetize without terminating the pain of mourning. That the detachment of libido

6

from its annihilated objects should be such a painful process, and that the libido should cling to its objects rather than relinquish them when lost, even when a surrogate is available, remained for Freud the most puzzling feature of mourning.[18] "Mourning has a quite specific psychical task to perform: its function is to detach the survivors' memories and hopes from the dead. When this has been achieved, the pain grows less and with it the remorse and self-reproach."[19] And yet when pressed into the service of mourning, this "work of recollection," as Freud called it in *Studies on Hysteria*, which records only in order to erase, remains the most painful requirement of proper mourning. The separation from the object must be effected at each way station, before each niche within the memorial architecture.

> Mourning occurs under the influence of reality-testing, for the latter function demands categorically from the bereaved person that he should separate himself from the object, since it no longer exists. Mourning is entrusted with the task of carrying out this retreat from the object in all those situations in which it was the recipient of a high degree of cathexis. That this separation should be painful fits in with what we have just said, in view of the high and unsatisfiable cathexis of longing which is concentrated on the object by the bereaved survivor during the reproduction of the situations in which he must undo the ties that bind him to it.[20]

This inner topography of the lost object must be reassembled outside the mourner in the form of funerary rites and monuments addressed to the idealized dead. Otherwise, live burial in some internal vault must result for both living and dead. An example of successful building in the wake of death was delivered by Freud's son Ernst, who studied architecture before World War I. In a letter to Lou Andreas-Salomé dated November 9, 1915, Freud narrates Ernst's supernatural rescue in the war zone: "He happened to be away from the dug-out where the whole crew in charge of his gun had sought shelter during the battle on the Karst plateau and he was thus the only one to escape the fate of being buried alive by a direct hit." Nine days later, again in a letter to Andreas-Salomé, Freud can bring the story of accident and chance to a successful close: "The news from the front is good. My son has been invited to design the memorial for his troop; this will no doubt have been his first job as an architect."

Around this now external, now internal monument for which

war trauma

premature burial serves as the occasion or model, psychoanalytic treatment of countless cases of wartime traumatic neurosis began to push the theories of haunting and melancholia into alignment, though Freud continued to give them equal but separate time. The traumatic neurotic occupies the opening threshold of *Beyond the Pleasure Principle* because he in particular exhibits the compulsion to "repeat the repressed material as a contemporary experience instead of, as the physician would prefer to see, *remembering* it as something belonging to the past."[21] Thus Georg Simmel prescribes that, in each case of war neurosis, the "film" of the traumatizing incident must, in place of the missing recollection, be run again: "Through the hypermnesia to which the patient has recourse in hypnosis, the experience can be repeated. The 'film' is let roll once again; the patient dreams the whole thing one more time, the sensitized subconscious releases the affect which in turn discharges in an adequate emotional expression, and the patient is cured."[22]

On this side of Simmel's media-technical analogy, Freud introduces, in place of a link-up of his different takes on aberrant mourning, the death drive, which points to a beyond to the pleasure principle as to the work of mourning by following out a certain rereading of repetition. But on the other side of the analogy with film: only a theory of ghosts can anchor this paradoxical beyond, though in a ground that will always have slipped away from the psychoanalytic theory of pathological mourning. And yet Freud compares repetition compulsion to demoniacal possession, and those afflicted by traumatic neurosis to the haunted; because they seem to be under occult influence they are, in fact, "uncanny."[23]

In the midst of this set of analogies Freud also noted, but did not pursue, a certain resemblance of traumatic neurosis to melancholia. Both sides of the double connection that the study of traumatic neurosis thus anticipated returned with the survivors of concentration camps, who delivered to psychoanalysis concepts of delayed mourning under rubrics they themselves supplied and embodied: "the homeless dead," "the missing grave," "the imitation corpse." According to the post–World War II psychoanalytic view of traumatic neurosis, the continued suffering of these survivors could thus be ascribed not only to the persecution they had endured but also, and in large measure, to their having been

8

deprived of the possibility of mourning their dead. This deprivation had taken place under circumstances which, it was argued, could only have heightened those feelings of ambivalence otherwise dispelled, according to Freud, through the work of mourning: in the death camps the murder of another also always meant that one's own death had been deferred.[24] The continued insistence by these analysts on hostility and guilt in every evaluation of the haunted, itself participated in the guilty fantasy of restitution it would describe; indeed, the evaluations put forth by physicians and analysts were in fact claims addressed to administrators of the "restitution" policies instituted in Germany after World War II. In a context that is thus always and already one of double resentment, this assessment of the degree of suffering and psychic traumatization can only lead to the supreme ambivalent closure in which every position or identification which might be assumed or acknowledged remains false and ignoble.

Freud had accordingly already reserved for future discussions of traumatic neurosis an analogy doubly registered in the zone of the uncanny. Because this neurosis was always a delayed response to the impact of specific trauma—a train accident, for example, or shell shock—Freud found it fitting to compare the intervening period to one of "incubation."[25] But alongside its designation of the uncanny stealth of infection, incubation has another meaning. In Jones's monograph *On the Nightmare*, a work sufficiently present to Freud to pop up as a prop in one of his examples of thought transference,[26] incubation is examined at length in terms of its occult pedigree. Incubation is accordingly plugged back into the incubus it contains: the incubus who could assume the form of some animal to have intercourse with a living person sleeping in sacred precincts, was either the ghost of a departed ancestor or himself a god. The deep sleep that left one pregnant, often with prophecy though most frequently with the actual offspring of phantoms, was called incubation. To sleep near a spring or in a grove or temple consecrated to a certain deity was tantamount to requesting to be visited by the incubus of its inhabitant.

At the switches of this death cult of sexual congress we find the first call girls mediating the cross-over within sacred precincts of the divine and the dead into the realm of the living. The snake, the temple prostitute's cohabitant, was the impregnating incubus that carried the calls the prostitute put through. As Jones concludes, the incubating snake delivers the signs and semen of the dead only to the extent that it embodies the father's phallus or phantom.[27] Freud in turn kept at the limit of his interpretation of traumatic neurosis a disturbed rapport not with death—as in fear of death, which, according to Freud, never exists as such but always reflects dread of retaliation for death wishes directed, ultimately, against the father—but with the dead who, under wartime conditions, often cannot be properly buried and mourned.[28] Incubation thus represents the shutdown of corpse disposal; when loss does not yield to substitution, incubation keeps it in safe deposit. It is in this sense that the shell-shock victim resembles one who cannot stop mourning; like the melancholic he comes predisposed to take loss in, rather than, simply, to take it.

To describe the secret, internal repository and meeting place that takes the place of proper mourning, Nicolas Abraham and Maria Torok have set incorporation aside, at one end from cannibalistic identification with father, at the other from introjection.[29] Whereas introjection covers a metaphorical ingestion and digestion enabling the subject to internalize and comprehend objects that are discarded before they are lost, incorporation demetaphorizes this process, yielding the fantasy of an actual consumption of the lost object, which is kept not only isolated and concealed but even sealed off in a separate portion of the ego. Only in this way can the topography which loss would otherwise have displaced be conserved. The corpse thus remains inside the mourning body, though as a stranger, a living dead encrypted in a specific place in the ego.

Inasmuch as this internal crypt is haunted by the phantom of the deceased, who has not been laid to rest, it doubles as transmitter through which the phantom teleguides the crypt carrier, who guards with his life its undead remains. In Hitchcock's *Psycho*, for example, Norman Bates identifies with his dead mother only to the extent that this bond is forged with what remains of her, her corpse, which he has mummified, and her voice, which commands him via a ventriloquism he does not control. Bates's incorporation follows the migratory, nomadic trajectory of birds, ancient symbols of the returning dead. His crypt in turn is constructed within the resonance or depot of the word "bird," which also serves as

10

password: enter Miss Crane in flight from Phoenix. The mother—or rather, the mummy her son has created and animated—must safeguard against substitution within a laboratory of resurrection and mummification in which every bird ends up stuffed with recycled, irreplaceable nonlife.

Following his mother's departure, then, Bates recreates a separation between himself and a demon who performs all further separations. But the restless demon always seeks final repose and burial by going out of control. Faced with the collapse and exhumation of his condemned crypt, which the frenzied phantom has thus cracked open, Norman Bates in turn renders his whole ego a tomb, or transmitter, covering over the secret bond and bondage of his identification. Once the crypt cracks, becomes destabilized, lets in light and air, the carrier must divert attention away from the evidence of his incorporation by profusely mimicking always adjacent Oedipal structures, in Bates's case the signs and expressions of sexual repression. The vampire killers need only locate the crypt the vampire leads them to; they need only enter it and put to rest the undead remains which lie there utterly unprotected. It is this paradoxical openness of the crypt which its bearer must cover and contain.

Incorporation is always a maternal legacy. When in *Totem and Taboo* Freud attributes the haunted rapport with the dead—whose wind-carried seed, it is believed, remains responsible for every pregnancy—to societies governed by matrilineal descent, he names, though again in a context kept separate from his exploration of melancholia, the double agent who, in the midst of hardened survivors, also serves the interests of the dead.[30] The mother is always in a position to hide secret treasure in her child's body which she has trained, arranged, and mapped out; she can thus deposit the unmourned corpse of one of her children in the body of another little one who survives. The mourning that never took place is covertly and ambiguously entrusted to a surviving child who must carry a dead sibling and mourn in the mother's place. Whether on behalf of a dead child or in her own absence, the mother advertises a solution that is edible, not Oedipal. Right from the start the mother is her child's *Lebensmittel,* at once "medium of life" and "nourishment." Karl Abraham accordingly emphasizes that, whereas in most neurotic conditions the father is the focus and recipient of hostile tendencies, in melancholia it is invariably the mother who attracts the ambivalent cannibalistic impulse. Because the trauma of loss casts the melancholic back to the early age or stage to which he thus ever returns, repression cannot anchor him in an Oedipal past.[31] The mother alone can be received, in this stricken world, as the melancholic's premier and perpetual station of identification.

But Freud can render the death-wish bond with the father the model of all mourning sickness only by keeping the mother in the shadow—as the shadow—of the moving target. Freud's first mention of aberrant mourning can thus be found lodged inside his first rehearsal of the Oedipus complex, which emerges as an Oedipal theory of grief: "It seems as though in sons this death wish is directed against their father and in daughters against their mother."[32] Customarily repressed upon the death of one's parents, the death wish, Freud continues, can nevertheless assert itself as a substitute for mourning. The survivor who thus believes that he has brought about the death of his parents accordingly administers self-reproach and even self-punishment, which he effects through a form of "identification" enabling him to share their fatal illness.

The occasion for such identification is always an unmournable death. In Freud's case the question of mourning or not mourning had first been posed and deposited by an infant mortality he confronted in early childhood. When Freud was nineteen months old his eight-month-old brother Julius died; this death, Freud allows, installed in him his own tendency toward self-reproach. In Julius's departure he had witnessed the realization of hostile impulses harbored against his rival—and god.[33] According to *Totem and Taboo,* Freud's guilt or *Schuld* can be converted back to the effects of an original haunting of the young child or savage by his murder victim. And yet, the young child and the savage are not legitimate bearers of guilt: the fantasy of retrieving, recycling, and retaining the lost object, which underlies the so-called savage's animistic beliefs, is highly protective; it therefore also exceeds conversion into guilt, that standard of decidedly nonprotective pathologies.

Freud allows another interpretation of his rapport with Julius when, contemplating Goethe's rivalry with each of his doomed siblings, he declares Goethe's relation to Cornelia, owing to the minimal difference in their ages, immune from such murderous jealousy.[34] Within a series of primal recollections centered on his mother we find Freud, shortly after Julius's death, wounding himself in a fall.[35] *Trauer* (mourning) bears etymological association with falling, dropping, or casting down. The fall in the wake of Julius's departure left behind on Freud's face a permanent scar which heralded or outlined in advance the operations on his cancerous jaw. Thus the analogy with an "open wound" which Freud draws already in 1895 and later in "Mourning and Melancholia" to describe the way in which melancholia empties out the ego remains, as the legacy of a dead child and sibling, the most vulnerable point of articulation in Freud's corpus.[36] What rebounds from this point of impact are the sole *revenants* or phantoms Freud acknowledges to the extent that he finds them haunting, via transference, his closest friendships.[37]

But with regard to haunted forms of grief, even those openly addressed, in the first place, to dead siblings, Freud can see the analysis through to completion only by exchanging their occult or animistic value for the guilty currency of relations with father.[38] In the case of "A Seventeenth-Century Demonological Neurosis," Freud casts the hallucinated devil as double of the dead father.[39] Etymologically, devil embraces the meaning of double, while the morbid reception of the father's passing invariably installs in the surviving son a kind of double vision equally divided between willingness and refusal to accept a loss which, as this reception confirms, is not a loss. Thus the two men in "Fetishism" who happen not to be fetishists display instead a split in the ego resulting from their refusal to acknowledge the death of their fathers, which, paradoxically, they also accept. Hence their inclusion alongside fetishists who remain always only partially blind to the evidence of nothing there in the scanner of their desire: the bereaved sons deny that the object is lost—forever.[40] The dead father is thus locked into a return trajectory at either end of which there is neither loss nor retrieval: what returns, only to the extent that it is already in place as the ego's guilty relation to the superego, is the son's repressed death wish, which must be kept both intact and undisclosed.[41] Thus in *The Interpretation of Dreams* we find a ten-year-old boy's double take in the wake of his father's sudden death: "I know father's dead, but what I can't understand is why he doesn't come home to supper."[42]

13

Abraham and Torok turn to Freud's case study of the Wolf-man, in which Freud briefly turned to the other side of this ambiva-lent invitation to the dead father to come to dinner only to swerve, however; from the not yet Oedipal interpretation Wolfman's aber-rant mourning invites.[43] Freud kept this inability to mourn for a dead sister in focus long enough to uncover in Wolfman's tearful pilgrimage to the grave of a poet—to whom his sister had often been compared—the attempt to "substitute for the missing out-bursts of grief." Even though this episode seems securely anchored in the case history, where the sister's seduction of Wolfman in early childhood is already in place, Freud shifts to the Wolfman's father, whose specter must cover, under the aegis of ambivalence, every effort to cope with corpses. And yet Wolfman, too, invites his father to act as referee and referent of his relations with his sister, "the most dearly beloved member of his family." When she kills herself, however, Wolfman puts on a show of sorrow while coolly rejoicing "at having now become the sole heir to the prop-erty."[44] And yet this is too much: with respect to his beloved sister, Wolfman's calculations summon an interpretation they par-ody and empty out. Wolfman fakes not only sorrow but even hostility and guilt. The urge to recover and retain the lost object thus climaxes in the fantasy, articulated and camouflaged in the register of father and son relations, of having (had) nothing to lose.

The double displacement—by Wolfman and by Freud—of in-expressible sorrow over a sister's passing nevertheless emerges alongside Freud's remark in the *Introductory Lectures on Psycho-analysis* that "there are neuroses which may be described as morbid forms of grief."[45] Indeed, "Mourning and Melancholia" follows the case study of Wolfman almost, Abraham and Torok suggest, as a delayed response to the aberrant mourning only briefly admitted in Wolfman's case. Thus Abraham and Torok double and diverge from Freud in making their rereading of the Wolfman case the point of access to their theory of the crypt. The crypt, they argue, contains the objective counterpart of the loss reconstituted from recollected words or images; what is thus reanimated remains a complete per-son with his own topography, including the traumatic incidents and accoutrements which made incorporation necessary and intro-jection impossible. Wolfman witnessed not so much certain scenes as the emergence of words, names, or word-things which he could

14

not release because they doubled, in his case, as testimony against the father. Since the significance of these words could not be assimilated, they were instead incorporated, at once mutilated and preserved. The resulting cryptonyms cover up the incorporated verbal artifact only by garbling and thus also retaining—by gargling—certain of its material linguistic features. Wolfman's unspeakable magic words, though swallowed, nevertheless haunt other words and phrases in which they keep coming up as rhymes and stammered variants. The very keystone of his crypt is a secret desire which is at once a secret word or name, a summons which commands absolutely. And this key name or password covers the terms and conditions of the secret desire's incorporation.

Cryptology thus calls for inclusion alongside Freud's pursuit of Oedipus of Oedipus's daughter Antigone, whose undead bond with her "irreplaceable" brother at once mimics and exceeds the bond of and with parents.[46] In the context of literary analysis, cryptology forces inclusion of those relational relations which the biographical text can impose or dispatch but never reappropriate. Incorporation covers this contractual space of the crypt also to the extent that it possesses, in English, a technical legal meaning which invites, simply but subtly, a corresponding literary application. Incorporation, in this register, describes the process whereby, in forming a society or organization, large corporations "swallow" smaller businesses. The corporation thus created, renewed, or aggrandized has the status of a fiction. Legally, a corporation is a fiction which is entitled to act as a person, and is—except in the case of criminal acts—responsible in law as an individual would be. To create this fictional person, it is required that three or more "real" persons—signatories who are not or not yet corporations—join in its formation.[47] Cryptological analysis of a name-bearing corpus accordingly exceeds the literary relation to the text by summoning all the relations, all the signatories comprising the corporation in question.

Alongside Abraham and Torok's rereading of Wolfman, *Aberrations of Mourning* inserts as its mascot and point of return Freud's Ratman, in whose case the competing deaths of sister and father and the survivor's omnipotence of thoughts—which, via projection, underlies a certain totemic rapport with the dead—converge. Freud always addressed the phantasmic consequences of improper burial in the course of elaborating the mechanism of projection. And yet, like a projection, the concept of projection was never analyzed inside "Mourning and Melancholia." In *Totem and Taboo* Freud explained that the ghosts and demons which haunt so-called savages are dead people who have not been properly mourned; according to the interlocked logics of ambivalence and projection, the hostility the dead, while still alive, had aroused in the still living is attributed to the phantoms of the deceased who now persecute the survivors. Without any conception of natural death these savages, like children, cannot help but view the dead as murder victims who, because never at rest, must be avenged or appeased.[48]

Freud did not sustain the connection he briefly made—only to leave it missing—between this haunting of savages and children on the one hand and, on the other, aberrant variants of mourning in adults. The impediment blocking the connection is what Freud viewed as central: the bereaved's management of hostility and guilt. It is as though Freud inserted—as protection against their ghosts—the decidedly nonprotective pathology of guilt in place of its inconceivable bearers, children and savages. Freud's development of a theory of pathological mourning cannot bring into focus the children and savages who, in *Totem and Taboo,* are the premier projectors of ghosts; they cannot be tied with conviction to the charges of guilt which Freud makes stick in the case of melancholic self-reproach. This is where Abraham and Torok diverge, close-range, from Freud. The melancholic's self-reproach is, they argue, ultimately his way of reliving, as openly as is possible for the crypt carrier, that bond which was taken from him. Even the melancholic's grief is a detour taken to relive the bond with the unmourned dead. The melancholic's excessive mourning acts out the deceased's grief at losing him. In melancholia it is always ultimately the living dead or phantom who must thus perform the mourning rites. Only the phantom mourns—always to the point of not surviving the loss of the haunted melancholic. The melancholic never loses his dearly beloved. He only mourns in anticipation—of his own demise.[49]

These qualifications Abraham and Torok make of Freud are matched point by point in Mary Shelley's *Frankenstein:* the monster is created at the end of a trajectory of departure which takes Victor Frankenstein to his alma mater at the same time that it

Frankenstein

doubles the departure of the mother.[50] To counter this doubling or incorporation of the mother, which can only yield unnatural, monstrous creation, Victor's father invites his "melancholic" son to enter the "house of mourning."[51] But Elizabeth, the supernatural substitute the father holds out to Victor as enticement back to life, enters the melancholic's embrace only when—first in a dream and then on their wedding night—she becomes a corpse superimposable onto the dead mother. Before the final chase scene can commence, Victor visits the family plot: his rundown, in passing, of its inhabitants omits mention of the mother, who can thus only be found missing.[52] In what follows, Victor pursues a monster who in turn telecommands Victor, who follows. At the end, then, the monster mourns Victor, who is the first to go, and then, like a mother, puts herself to rest.

Only by tapping into the separate places occupied by Freud's theory of ghosts and his theory of pathological mourning can we begin to discern that which remains outside by substituting for mourning: the audio and video broadcasts of improper burial—analyzed in *Totem and Taboo*—which are transmitted via the crypts which—as set forth in "Mourning and Melancholia"—those who are incapable of mourning must build inside for the unmourned and, hence, undead. Projection is the doubly missing link between melancholia and phantom possession. Sandor Ferenczi originally introduced introjection as one end of transference opposite projection, which covered the other end.[53] This point of cohesion is also where, in Freud, the terms must billow apart: projection or counter-transference always already inhabits—haunts—the highly problematical frame of transference also to the extent that this frame, which comes into focus for Freud only by going out of control, harbors doubles and *revenants* from earliest childhood. Transference, which thus reflects back ancient projections, is accordingly anchored in introjection, even in the more literal or primal ground of incorporation.

A certain standard reception or edition of Freud's thought thus claims to join Freud in only projecting the full-fledged treatment of projection. In the case study of Schreber, Freud postpones the investigation of projection until some future occasion, which prompts an editorial footnote to the effect that there "seems no trace of any such later discussion." Only "one of the missing

projection – introjection – transference

metapsychological papers" might have been reserved for the discussion that never took place.[54] In the editor's introduction to the extant metapsychological papers we find, again, mention of Freud's dissatisfaction with his own preliminary treatment of projection in the Schreber study which had issued in the promise to return to its fuller elaboration: "This he seems never to have done, unless it was in one of these missing papers."[55] And yet the next major work to follow the Schreber study was *Totem and Taboo*, which turns on a far-reaching theory of projection developed alongside Freud's account of haunted receptions of the dead. The enigmatic force of the repression that keeps this central discussion of projection in some other—missing—place cannot help but find an unwitting accomplice in Freud: in "A Metapsychological Supplement to the Theory of Dreams" Freud interrupts another discussion of projection to "defer the full treatment of projection."[56] But is this the same deferral that he had earlier inserted into the Schreber study? The editor prompts from the corresponding footnote that this is in fact the case.

The point of conjunction between "Mourning and Melancholia" and "The Taboo upon the Dead" that has been thus excluded nevertheless returns via certain sets of analogy, which in turn invite the theories of projection and incorporation to conjoin by plugging into the technical media. In the margin of Tausk's presentation on projection and identification as the interlocked structuring principles of every sensorium, which thus finds its analogue, not only for the schizophrenic, in the cinematographic apparatus, Freud adds from the place of the missing paper the matching analogue for projected vision: the two-dimensional representation or projection of the body supplied by the cinematograph was also the aim and frame of mummification.[57] Freud's analogies to unconscious processes and psychoanalytic technique always shift between the technical media and the domain of archaeology. But Freud also always borrows these two sets of analogy from his patients whose delusional formations in turn already double as what Freud calls endopsychic perceptions, which always anticipate by reproducing his own theories of the psychic apparatus.

In his essay on Jensen's *Gradiva*, Freud explores the archaeological end of endopsychic perception which recognizes excavation and exhumation of ancient relics in place of the retrieval of some-

18

thing from the more recent, repressed past.[58] Upon expressing his satisfaction in *Totem and Taboo* that psychoanalysis had penetrated behind the screen to the projection booth of haunting, Freud is suddenly reminded of Schreber, who had found reflected in his own delusional formations the links and limits of his libido.[59] In that case study Freud had in turn been startled upon recognizing that, via the same endopsychic projection, his theory of libido also found reflection in Schreber's "rays of God," so startled in fact that he rushed to give evidence within his study—in a frenzy of anticipation that some might call paranoid—that he had developed his theory of paranoia before reading Schreber's memoirs.[60] In the endopsychic scanner, psychotic projections, psychoanalytic conceptions of the unconscious, and the technical media converge to the point that Freud can only put through or apply his discoveries by picking up a phone. Freud thus recommends right from the start that the psychoanalyst "adjust himself to the patient as a telephone receiver is adjusted to the transmitting microphone."[61] But Freud's telephone always also plugs into the occult. In the "New Introductory" lecture devoted to the occult Freud conceives of the telephone as telepathic medium to the extent that both the technical and the occult medium await hook-up to psychoanalysis, which alone can elucidate them. The telepathic process thus finds its analogy in "speaking and hearing by telephone": "And only think if one could get hold of this physical equivalent of the psychical act! It would seem to me that psychoanalysis, by inserting the unconscious between what is physical and what was previously called psychical, has paved the way for the assumption of such processes as telepathy."[62]

Endopsychic projection embraces a primal convergence of archaeology and the technical media at one end and, at the other, psychoanalysis. Psychoanalysis accordingly advances primal structures to the extent that these structures commence in the eighteenth century: on the one hand with the first impact of the advent of technical media, on the other with the premier articulation of the nuclear family and its reserve, childhood. The amalgam of technical media which Adorno and Horkheimer designated the culture industry lags behind childhood, which first held the place of this industry, to the extent that both in their respective places hold the place of our missing death cult. The child attained ontological status within the new habitat of literacy which the printing press, by the eighteenth century, had fully established; but this status had been attained too soon, in advance of any decrease in infant and child mortality; the death of the child thus continues to pile up for almost a century a massive occasion for and challenge to mourning.

This unmournable death of the child remains the trauma at the primal—or eighteenth-century—origin of culture as conceived and advertised by psychoanalysis. In closer range: we find in the case study of Ratman and in Freud's own case the motive force of the unmournable—and doubly unacknowledged—death of child and sibling: that unthinkable thing. The death of child and sibling is the rehearsal and, then, repetition of the death of the father, the guarantor of proper mourning. We mourn only for the one we have murdered: in turn, we mourn by killing off the deceased. As locus of testamentary substitutions, the father's death is that mournable death which, according to Freud, allows civilization itself to survive. Thus in many cases—Ratman, Schreber, and Wolfman, for example—Freud encountered difficulties on two fronts, specifically in superimposing the dead sibling onto the father's corpse. And yet both deaths, the mournable and the unmournable, must find simultaneous broadcast if psychoanalytic theory is not to founder on the two deaths on which it is founded. To this day the powerful logic, or strategy, of analogy makes psychoanalytic theory indistinguishable from its effects: has Madison Avenue read Freud before juxtaposing castration, death, and desire in its advertisement designs, or was Freud right all along?

Following this powerful delegation of analogy, the Melanesian Cargo Cult emerges, in the ensuing chapters, as the dramatization or coverage—with all the Freudian coordinates in place and intact—of the two separate deaths. A West German anthropologist, who has recently been spending half her time playing back tape recordings of her Melanesian hosts, encountered, shortly before recording the occasion for some recent issue of *Geo-Magazin*, the furious indignation of a mother mourning for her dead son.

You are able to see my son. . . . You can talk to him. But do you talk to us about him? Which is what he asked you to do? No! You hide your knowledge from us! . . . Not even our Big Men, our elders, achieve what is within the reach of white men. Yet the whites don't want to tell us anything. You! You know my son and all our dead. You meet them in your country Australia. That is where you receive the Cargo. But it doesn't belong to you! The clothes you wear, the cameras and radios, all the food you eat out of conserving cans! You whites did not produce any of these things! Black men, who are dead, did the work. . . . You came to us, because our dead told you: "Go back to our homes and give all the Cargo to our mothers, fathers, wives, and children." But you keep from us what is rightly ours.

The white man interferes with mourning by occupying, with respect to the dead laborers in the Land Down Under, the place of unmournable death. Between the living and the mourned dead, we find an amalgam of telecommunications and canned and manufactured goods conserving itself as living dead. Within the endopsychic perspective which thus emerges with this late arrival of psychoanalytic theory, we can begin to answer Adorno and Horkheimer's call, in *Dialectic of Enlightenment,* for a "Theory of Ghosts" that would exorcise that phantomization and posthumization of civilization's future which, from the eighteenth century to the period of Adorno and Horkheimer's exile in California, remains part of the culture industry's program. Thus at this end psychoanalytic theory goes beyond, while including, the standard emphasis on Oedipal structures. And it is to this end that *Aberrations of Mourning* is offered.

CHAPTER ONE
AVUNCULAR STRUCTURES
(Sigmund Freud / Friedrich Nietzsche)

THE DEATH CULT OF THE CHILD

The invention of the child

Lessing's childhood portrait which, according to his own wish, depicted him reading a book is the *Ur*-portrait of the child. The idea of childhood was among the effects of the printing press; the new standard of literacy summoned the pupil who, until he became a differentiating reader of print, was not yet an adult. As became increasingly clear the more he could be observed in his new habitat, this pupil had to be considered as something separate, as child. With the advent of printing-press culture the child received a proper name and image which could be reflected even beyond death; not only was the child's portrait now painted but even his place of burial was, from this time onward, marked and preserved. Only since the eighteenth century have there been special clothes, games, and even books designed just for children. In West Africa, where the advent of childhood today counts a late arrival, the miniature model of a chair is tied around a child's neck to offer the spirit of some ancestor a place of rest which will in turn keep the ghost with the child. And, indeed, the double but sepa-

Brutal construction of the child

22

rate world of the child has always had only one available model and analogue: the temples and cities of the dead where even the accoutrements and utensils of everyday life were counterfeit replicas constructed out of utterly flimsy and impractical materials.

According to Philippe Ariès, in the eighteenth century the new focus in the work of representation in mourning covered not some image of the living person but the moment or monument of his individual death. "Children were the first beneficiaries of this new desire for preservation," but not because they had benefited from any decrease in infant and child mortality, as Ariès miscalculates in assigning the advent of childhood to the child's increased chances for survival. The decrease went into effect nearly a century after the invention of the child, who thus attained ontological status too soon, only in time to deliver a massive occasion for mourning. The gap between the invention of the child and the era of its expected survival thus frames the onset of a certain history of the unmournable death of the child.[1]

The apotheosis of the printing-press-child shadowed by death is the beautiful soul, who is always also a niece. In Goethe's rendition, for example, who attains as her prime identifying mark the almost supernatural status of niece, is in turn reincarnated by her own niece who, all agree, is the true beautiful soul. The beautiful soul, eros in Kant, is, according to Friedrich Schlegel, a coquette and, according to Weininger, a woman who has introjected a man's soul—devoured a man's corpse. In Kant, Schiller, and Hegel, the discourse on the beautiful soul faces toward eros while pressing back annihilation: the beautiful soul ultimately attains and retains nonbeing, "an empty nothingness."

The beautiful soul in *Wilhelm Meister's Apprenticeship* occupies, as supreme leftover, the position of perennial mourning. In a culture where a high rate of infant mortality, including infanticide, is the norm, the beautiful soul would be the first to go. In the new culture of *Bildung,* however, she survives the various severe childhood illnesses which correspond to her basic inclement health. Kept artificially or supernaturally alive, she buries and mourns even her well-constituted siblings; she alone remains behind to argue with her uncle about the upbringing of her nephews and nieces.

The avuncular structure which attends the death cult of the

The Death Cult of the Child

child has not yet come into focus, though the specter of the niece has been sighted in certain cases. Flaubert's niece Caroline, for example, who covered over her namesake, the corpse of the sister Flaubert could not mourn, embodies a circuit of unmournable loss which becomes in many other cases the rule. In the corner of every secret transmission of the legacy or corpse, the niece was there.

According to Freud, every scene of legacy transmission—such as the survival of Moses' religion through what Freud also calls tradition—remains an instance of transference. Freud first discovered the mechanism of transference in the course of analyzing Dora, whom Lacan calls a beautiful soul.[2] However, when it turns out that Dora, following her aunt's death, reproduced in hysterical symptoms the appendicitis that had recently afflicted one of her aunt's children, Freud overlooks this mournful identification, as niece, with a diseased body; instead he tries but fails to shift her into the Oedipal zone of what would henceforward be called transference.

Transference reanimates the original, infantile rapport with the parents, *imagines* of the parents which lie buried in the adult. Freud also calls these childhood *imagines* carried within each individual "clichés" which, over time, are repeatedly "reprinted."[3] When Freud first defines transference following the miscarriage of Dora's analysis he refers to "new editions" of relations already established during early childhood; indeed, Dora's transferences, which ultimately overshoot Freud's capacity to define for her her every action and ailment, are always and already made onto the dictionary she consults on sexual matters. The control of the mechanism of transference, Freud would henceforth believe, is the guarantor of a successful analysis. It is by taking over the controls of the press that the ego, according to one of Freud's analogies, tells the id what to like and what not to like.[4] But the "control" of transference remains out of reach; Freud later rephrases his most fervent wish as the dread hope that telepathic transference of thoughts might one day be brought under man's remote control.[5]

Transference, an intermediary realm between illness and life, a kind of artificial illness, is also a "playground" where the patient is permitted to act everything out just so long as everything is kept in the analyst's view.[6] Transference requires, then, a map, a book, a cemetery—an at once visible and legible terrain. And transference requires introjection, the internal resurrection of originary object relations.[7] These relations, exploited in hypnosis (hence the "uncanniness" of hypnosis according to Freud), are disinterred and put to rest in the course of analysis, though, Freud adds, even following an otherwise successful analysis, scars and phantoms frequently remain.[8] Ever since the invention of childhood—of an unconscious—the annihilation of the remainder is, as such, impossible, unthinkable.

At the same time, however, the fantasy of annihilation directs that transfer of introjection, which ends up as melancholia.[9] Even during the two-year term of healthy mourning, the bereaved must, as Abraham, for example, argues, temporarily introject the deceased so as to safeguard the departed against the "threat of annihilation." Once the frenzy of sadistic vengefulness and self-torture has subsided, the encrypted object can be expelled from its hiding place and released into the outside world. In melancholia, of course, this release is held back; the "threat of annihilation" is greater since more closely encountered. The melancholic's wish remains the incorporation of his love objects: "In the depths of his unconscious we find the tendency to swallow, to annihilate the object."[10]

The threat of annihilation which always attends the disposal of a corpse can also appear, as in the case of one of Freud's near-telepathic dreams, alongside the arrival of two nieces in mourning.[11] According to Ernest Jones, the niece belongs to the first pieces of the kinship puzzle which Freud, in his own early childhood, summoned the premier psychoanalytic insights to interpret: doubled through the inclusion of step-relations, the family he would interpret proffered Freud a childhood structured from the start by an avuncular complex.

Born an uncle, Freud had as his first playmates and object-choices among his peers in age his own nephew and niece, John and Pauline Freud. The niece was later offered to Freud in marriage, allegedly to encourage replacement of his unprofitable intellectual pursuits with more practical ones. The offer of the niece represents a recurrent temptation, which Freud would always resist, to enter the death cult shaped by melancholic annihilation. Karl Abraham argues that the incestuous attachment to cousin or niece is the libidinally impoverished choice of the melancholic, the melancholic conceived, that is, as one who mourns his lost libido.[12] According to Abraham, in those families in which such intermarriage occurs perennial bachelors abound; to marry the niece, for example, is tantamount to not marrying at all. And yet the niece in particular is granted special powers by Abraham; in the marriage between uncle and niece the latter rules absolutely.

Though Freud withstood this considerable temptation to submit to the niece, the Pauline episode nevertheless belongs to his most profound erotic fantasies; according to Jones this episode rehearses and repeats Freud's first experience of love in adolescence, as well as, of course, his infantile rape fantasy concerning Pauline.[13] This primal fantasy regarding Pauline had been one of gang rape conducted together with John. It was talk of corpses and name effacement, however, that prompted Freud to recognize the reincarnation of his rapport with John in his relation to Jung. In addition to being, obviously, a way of sleeping with the person at hand, the dead faint which invariably followed Freud's recognition of John in Jung also represents, according to Freud, either self-punishment for a death wish or identification with an actual corpse.[14] The only corpse available in time to cover both John and Jung would have been that of Freud's younger brother Julius, who died in infancy when Freud was not yet two years old.

Freud first interprets the impact on him of Julius's death in the course of his correspondence with Fliess, another repeat of John as well as the recipient, at the time, of Freud's transferences. Fliess's dead sister was named Pauline. In a letter to Fliess dated October 3, 1897, Freud views Julius's death as having implanted in him a "seed of reproach." And to that day, Freud concludes and forecasts, both his nephew John, with whom he had pursued his niece Pauline, and his younger brother Julius, dead in infancy, continue to determine the intense though neurotic quality of his every friendship. Freud interprets Julius's death to Fliess as the death of a rival and, hence, as the casualty of Freud's own early death wish which, conveyed via the omnipotence of thoughts, places him—according to the logic Freud later develops in *Totem and Taboo*—at the disposal of the murder victim's phantom.

At the same time, however, Julius's phantom has been tuned out to the extent that this reception of a rival's death renders the dead sibling a mere prop in the main scenario, the death of the parent. This is made clear in an earlier letter sent to Fliess in which Freud first rehearsed the theory of Oedipus, which was formulated, moreover, as an Oedipal theory of grief. Freud writes on May 31, 1897, that mourning dead parents is a vulnerable undertaking precisely because the son has, at one point, harbored the wish that the father depart, the daughter that the mother do the same. Identification with the deceased is described at this time as hysterical adoption of the symptoms of the ailment which disposed of the parent.

And yet it was Julius's death which Freud commemorated by toppling from a chair. This fall, this enactment of an ancient meaning and interpretation of *Trauer,* left behind on Freud's jaw a permanent scar, which his beard would cover over. The beard was removed, however, for each of the countless cancer operations which would increase the reach around the mouth of wound and scar. In "Mourning and Melancholia" Freud uses the image of an "open wound" to describe the point of impact in the ego of unmournable loss. In a manuscript forwarded to Fliess on January 7, 1895, Freud first touched on the "wound" of melancholia.

On Freud's internal scanner the inward turn of the melancholic's psychic apparatus comes into focus as an "indrawing process" or "internal bleeding" which, "in a manner analogous to pain," "operates like a wound." The "open wound" of melancholia which Freud first discloses in his correspondence with Fliess—and thus alongside his only open reference to Julius's passing—is that indrawing process or suction effect of Freud's corpus that doubles, at another end of its inward turn, as uncanny harbinger of Freud's cancer. The beard that identification with the father always grows remains, in Freud's case, the excremental—and thus alternately disposable and returnable—deposit on Julius's death. This departure that leaves behind a wound that is also always a seed—of reproach—remains the primal model of Freud's theory of projection, which found its first rehearsal alongside explorations of media-technical delusions and their analogue or model: belief in ghosts.

The main prop in Freud's mourning over Julius was a *Kästchen,* a little box or casket. Freud fell for Julius while trying to reach this *Kästchen,* emblem of the womb, of course, but also, as Freud shows in the case of the third "mute" casket made of lead, cradle of death.[15]

The central tenet of psychoanalysis, the concept of castration, is also part of the *Kästchen.* In *Inhibitions, Symptoms, and Anxiety,* for example, Freud concedes that castration represents or contains that which cannot be conceived, namely, "annihilation of life." And since death is inconceivable as such, it is always a dead person who is death's delegate.[16]

As Stephan Broser has shown, the homonymic strands which ultimately combine to form *Kastration* were first collected in a box or *Kasten* which Freud confronted at the time his younger brother departed and his younger sister arrived.[17] In the letter to Fliess in which he first mentions the continued influence on him of nephew and dead brother, and in a follow-up report dated twelve days later, Freud addresses a proliferation of boxes within boxes. His brother Philipp, the younger of his two elder half brothers, was responsible for the incarceration of Freud's nursemaid; the expression Philipp most likely used would have also meant, Freud stresses, that she had been put into a *Kasten.* Philipp, little Freud surmised, must wield the power of the *Kasten;* the emergence from another box of his sister and new "rival" must also be Philipp's doing. At the time of her incarceration, Freud's nanny was already dispensable; Freud was by now infatuated with his mother, whose naked body he had only recently beheld when, in the course of a journey, Freud had shared her room. Back home Freud demands that Philipp open up the armoire or *Schrankkasten* and release his mother, who happens not to be around at the moment. When Philipp reveals that nothing is there within the frame of his desire, Freud is inconsolable until his mother returns.

Though it must also always pass through the relay and delay of an avuncular structure, the *Kasten,* which contains loss, is transmitted by the mother. Following Julius's death, Freud's mother takes him on a trip and shows him the box; Freud looks out the train window and sees smoke stacks which he takes to be souls burning in some underworld.[18] Travel has always conveyed death. Following Julius's death, Freud reaches for the *Kästchen.* Falling and mourning for Julius, Freud finds the *Kästchen* fit in his mouth, not in his hands. On March 27, 1895, Freud includes in his letter to

Fliess a citation that leaves out what Freud would ever keep in: "My heart is in the coffin here with Caesar." Freud signs the letter that thus does not bury Julius with his own mutilated, mumbled name: "Your Siegm." Alongside the Oedipus and Hamlet stories, that of Julius Caesar crowds Freud's writing. And yet, unlike Oedipus and Hamlet, Julius Caesar keeps too close to Freud to be admitted to psychoanalysis as its allegorization. As recounted in *The Interpretation of Dreams,* when nephew John—now the *revenant* of Freud's childhood playmate—returned to Vienna on a visit, he played Caesar to Freud's Brutus before an audience of children.[19]

In "Dream and Telepathy" Freud recounts the reappearance of the *Kasten* in his dream of July 8, 1915, which forecasts the death of his eldest son Martin, the death or castration of the father in Freud. Like the third casket in *The Merchant of Venice,* Martin is pale and mute; indeed, he stands on top of a stool in front of a box. This triggers Freud's recollection from childhood which centers on a box, a fall, a scar, the trace of which, he emphasizes, is yet visible. But the dream's prophecy that son and father must go was not, Freud concludes, fulfilled. And yet, although Freud points to the wound beneath his beard, the wound in his dream remains concealed, displaced with regard to Freud's recounting of the dream. The broadcast of the *Kasten* which prophesies the castration of the father is indeed pushed back; but, as Derrida points out, Freud leaves out of his essay on telepathy the transmission of the wound itself.[20] For Freud in fact receives three days after his dream a postcard in which Martin mentions an already scarred-over wound.

The vampire which leaves behind these wounds only taps into the Oedipal system of circulation; the casket to which the phantom must return is kept in some other place. The death of the brother, which Freud neglects to include in the interpretation of his casket dream, haunts the examples of telepathic communication he borrows from patients and correspondents. While giving the Oedipal interpretation of the recurring nightmare which pursues Freud's correspondent "like a ghost" and always prompts her to fall out of bed, Freud pauses to take cognizance of a brother's corpse. The only overtly telepathic material at Freud's disposal in this case—the dream itself is not telepathic—in fact concerns the correspondent's brother. She once heard her brother, who was far away in some war zone, call out for "mother," a call which, as was soon confirmed, had broadcast the news of her brother's death. But her telepathic communication, which, it turned out, was broadcast simultaneously to her mother, appears to have tapped into the mother's line. What remains, in place of the sibling's call, is the Oedipal call, placed by rivals for the mother position.

The ghostly recurring dream, which Freud's correspondent would like to have exorcised, shows her clinging to a palm tree, reaching down toward the waves, desperately attempting to help out of the water a faceless man swimming to shore. Only recently, she adds, did the swimmer acquire the face of the physician currently treating her at the asylum. Freud, who is familiar with this transference onto treating physicians, calls the faceless man the father, whose attempt to swim to shore betokens a birth or impregnation fantasy. And like the palm tree, the bird Freud's correspondent remembers being shown in early childhood, which returned her gaze with a human stare, is, Freud concludes, the phallic token of this childhood fantasy. However, Freud continues, the bird, like all small animals, also stands in for a young child, usually a sibling. And indeed the brother is always his sister's imaginary child. He is also her rival, however, the target of early death wishes. But the telepathic communication which transmits the death of the brother must tap into Oedipal lines of transference.

The Oedipal call issues from an internal transmitter: the superego is a kind of transmitter *Kasten* which stores and broadcasts early "parental influence." And, as Freud makes clear in his essay on Dostoevsky, the castration from which father and son must swerve is performed incessantly by the superego on the ego in the form of castigating commands. In the case of Dostoevsky's tendency to play dead, the *Kasten,* point of impact of repeated internal "castrations," transmits, in the wake of the father's actual death, a punishment which fits the fulfillment of death wishes the son has harbored against the father. The p-unitive fantasy which permits identification with the corpse can be simply put: You wanted a dead father—go ahead then and be the dead father. Though Freud borrows this circuit to explain his reception of Julius's death—the very fall or Dostoevskian faint he repeats alongside *revenants* of his nephew John[21]—in his occult research Freud

30

borders on another zone of transmission which is not linked and limited to identification with the father.

In "Dream and Occultism" Freud gives an example of maternal transmission of a corpse. One day during the session with her analyst, a mother brings up her childhood memory centering on a gold coin. That evening her son, who is also undergoing analysis, gives her a gold coin for safekeeping. On another occasion the mother, on the recommendation of her analyst, begins to write down her early coin memory, whereupon her son arrives to ask for his coin back so that he might show it to the analyst. Thus the transferential relation, doubled by telepathic rapport, secretly lodges a corpse in the child: the telepathically transferred thought regarding the coin does not correspond to any context specific to the son; it remains, as Freud puts it, a "foreign body" (*Fremdkörper*) implanted by the mother in her son.

The mother's Medusean head—her womb or box—which, according to Freud, reveals to the son the prospect of castration, is, in another context, a shield or emblem with which the ancient Greeks marked and protected the thresholds to their tombs. In Freud's double scenario the *Kasten* holds the place of the mother it holds in place. But the mother always also remains in a position to place into the river between life and death the little box or casket (*Kästchen*) that also bears Moses to his foster parents. In his revision of the story of Moses, Freud thus chooses, as always, the third casket, the one bearing death.

Freud's association with Moses was such that his essay on Michelangelo's Moses even appeared anonymously because, as Freud asked, "Why disgrace Moses by putting my name to it?"[22] Freud's identification with the Moses name also embraces a certain tradition of German authorship which always returned to Moses. Before he, like Moses, perishes in view of the promised land, Faust recognizes his death in the form of "the rhyme-word . . . death." When in *Moses and Monotheism*, Freud's final work and testament, this rhyme-word returns as the double of a name, Freud calls on Goethe for support of controversial claims regarding the name and identity of Moses. Freud notes that Goethe advanced in early essays a singular interpretation of the character and fate of Moses: in the essay "Israel in the Desert," for example, Goethe had already assumed the murder of Moses by the Jews. Moses, the leg-

31

endary father of the Jewish people, was in fact, says Freud, their resented stepfather, a conclusion Freud reaches by emphasizing—as had Goethe before him—that Moses' speech was marked by a speech impediment, a stutter, from which evidence Freud curiously concludes that Egyptian was probably Moses' native tongue. Goethe, by contrast, had concluded that since Moses' every word was confounded by a stutter, Moses was destined to concentrate on deeds—concluded, in other words, that, in this case, the stammer gave rise to the deed (*That*).[23]

In proving his claim that Moses was an Egyptian who used the Jews as carriers of the short-lived Egyptian monotheistic religion devoted to Aton, Freud shows that, even in name, Moses was plainly Egyptian. Moses, meaning "child," is itself the detachable, suffixal form of Egyptian patronymics; Freud attaches to this child a rhyme with the German word for death—*Tod*—when he speculates that Moses' name was originally Thotmoses. Though Freud hesitated before signing his own name alongside that of Moses, just as he waited till the end of his life to declare Moses to be Thot, already in his anonymously published essay on Michelangelo's statue, his writing on Moses had been guided by rhyme-words of death: Freud's every insight into the statue's significance had been prompted by Henry Thode, and his method of inquiry by Morelli.

MOSES AND THE MOTHER TONGUE

A blast of lightning—a stammer of light—illumines the scene of monstrous Frankensteinian creation of the first Thotmoses. In exchange for his having survived blasts of lightning near Stotternheim ("Stutteringhome"), Luther entered the local monastery; there he would fall into a frenzy upon hearing the scriptural words about a "son, which hath a mute spirit."[24] As Luther would later clarify: "a silent man compared with a speaking man is the same as dead."[25] The need to amplify what Luther feared was, in his own case, a "small voice with little resonance"[26] led, according to his testimony in the *Open Letter on Translation,* to his special rapport with printing. Once this amplification outdistances his control over

32

his works, Luther is beset by plagiarists as well as by demons and phantoms, against whom he recommends directing flatus. That this impulse to annihilate the specters of the printing press should find its final destination in Moses, whom Luther finally sends to the gallows,[27] indicates the terms of the race between Luther's "mute and weak voice" and "writing."[28]

In Luther's translation Moses has "a heavy speech and a heavy tongue." And this stammer requires representation and amplification by Moses' younger brother Aaron, who thus emerges as Ur-medium. This sibling relation guarantees that the candidates for playing founder in place of Moses will not be lacking. Luther's strategy, commemorated in Goethe's Faust, can be simply put: In the beginning was translation. In close combat Luther contested Moses's authorship of the Pentateuch.[29] But by launching the first German translation of the Bible which was not anonymous, Luther could claim himself to be, with respect to German letters, the first person in history—as opposed to the great prophet Moses—to sign his name to the Bible. "Now I realize what it means to translate," Luther confides to von Amsdorf, "and why no one has previously undertaken it who would disclose his name."[30]

Yet this relation of his name to his translation was also a source of dread: "Who is Luther? . . . How did a poor, stinking bag of worms like me come to have the children of Christ called by his wretched name? Do not do it, dear friends. Let us wipe out the partisan name and call ourselves Christians after him whose teachings we follow."[31] Luther pushes back the carcass that was in fact his patronymic; he brings it up only to wipe out—and preserve— the mark of his text. And yet within the chronicle of the Luther name-changes there remains the stammer of Moses.

Luther was christened Martin Luder, and within his own lifetime altered his name several times before settling on Luther, the name under which he published. Both in one of his lectures on the Book of Moses and in his remarks entitled "Certain German Proper Names Restored to Their Original Etymology," Luther explores the various and often random mutations which various proper names have suffered over the ages in the folk-etymological imagination of peoples. In the course of his remarks he does not fail to include speculations on the pedigree and multitudinous mutations of his own family name Luder—which he chooses to cite primarily in its plural form Lüder—associating this name now with the word *Leute,* now with the word *Herr,* but not with the potentially pejorative interpretations of his name as it resonates in the noun *Luder,* a noun whose literal meaning is "carcass used for bait" and whose extended and more common meaning is "scoundrel" or, in the case of a woman, "tramp." Luther claims to owe his name to Caesar, who had mentioned, in the *Gallic Wars,* a certain Lucterius. In the lecture on the Book of Moses Luther writes: "And in Saxony a famous name and family, *die Lüder,* was born from Lothar, or Luther, as the emperor calls him."[32]

In his offering a few revised etymologies of German proper names, Luther attempts to elevate the term *Marschalk* through mere association of its first element with its near homonym *mehr.* When dabbling with his own name, however, he appears to have made some effort to create a diversion by emphasizing such phonetic considerations as aspiration: "However, desiring through aspiration to render Ludher properly, Caesar found it propitious to pronounce this name Lothar."[33]

When, in accordance with the contemporary custom of hellenizing or latinizing one's vernacular name, Luther got around to adopting a so-called *Humanistenname,* he selected the Greek moniker Eleutherius, which not only partially translated his name—a name he now believed to be related to the German word *lauter* (pure, unmixed)—but furthermore and in contrast to *Humanistennamen* adopted by other scholars—Melancthon and Agricola come to mind—was even somewhat homophonous with his own name: with Luder, Ludher (the name he signed as early as 1501 upon first entering the university), and, in particular, with Luther. Luther's *Humanistenname* Eleutherius conveyed roughly the meaning of the "free one" or "free thinking one," and as an adjective in Greek bore the meanings "autonomous," "independent," and even "free of debt." Thus his awareness of the etymology of this Greek word—a word related to Latin *liber* (free) which stems from Indo-European *leudho* (people)—led Luther through a process of backward extrapolation to connect his own name with the German etymon *Leute* of this Indo-European root.[34] It remained a tribute to his conceived affection for his *Humanistenname* that Luther, even after his break with the Humanists, elected to retain the *th* of Eleutherius within his own name, formerly Luder, now Luther.

That Luther already heard this new name resound in his chosen *Humanistenname* is clear from his signature to a letter to Spalatin in the latter half of March 1518: he signed ÊLuther.[35] In transforming his name, now through translation, now through near rhyme, Luther performed these operations on what he took to be the underlying etymon or "true meaning" of his name—*lauter*—thus swerving from the meaning of *Luder* which was readily accessible to "mothers in the house, to children in the street," to those whom Luther designated the ideal recipients of his own translations into the mother tongue.[36] Instead he was inspired by the literal meaning of his patronymic to translate, beginning with his own name, according to the spirit rather than the letter of the mother tongue whose purity (*Lauterkeit*) thus inheres in his true name. In the translation scene in Goethe's *Faust* this spirit gives dictation:

> I can hardly value the word so high
> But must, if I am truly illumined by the spirit,
> Translate it otherwise. . . .
> The spirit helps me out! Suddenly I see the light
> And write with confidence: In the beginning was the deed [*Tat*].

By 1940, according to Valéry's *Mon Faust,* this spirit had become, quite simply, the dictator. The terms of the contract with and on Thotmoses had come due.

SPIRITUALIZATIONS

Even as he wrote it down, *Moses and Monotheism* "haunted" Freud "like an unlaid ghost."[37] Effects which Freud analyzed as belonging to the uncanny are everywhere in evidence in his final work. The study itself has been written twice, while the subject is double throughout. Moses comprises two historical personages, just as there are two Jewish peoples, two empires, and two foundations of Judaism.[38] Doubling, for Freud, always summons the specter of castration or death, the specter, that is, of a corpse. Enter the primal father, whose assassination the murder of Moses repeated.

Freud stresses the radical divergence of Judaism from the an-

35

cient Egyptian rapport with the dead; and yet, in his reading, the Mosaic prohibition against naming or representing the father-god— the injunction, that is, to commemorate the divine name with muteness, stammering, and mutilation—creates, for Judaism, its own transportable death cult. Circumcision, for example, which, Freud notes, leaves behind the most "uncanny" identifying mark of the Jew, is, like all initiation rites, a rehearsal of the ultimate initiation, the cross-over into the realm of the dead. It is, accordingly—like all ancient mourning practices—a form of mutilation whereby part of the living body is sacrificed to the deceased, who is thus diverted from taking, on his own, even larger portions. It was circumcision which served Freud as his leading clue or "fossil" in reconstructing the Moses story.[39] And Freud observes that "mutilations" of an account remain discernible as such in the dissembling text. The urge to annihilate every trace of a text's distortion or, Freud adds, of a crime, cannot outlast a certain tendency which retains loss and leaves behind clues.[40] But before Freud can call this retentive tendency "pious," he must first recast it as superimposable onto the disposable relations of paternity.

In Freud's account Moses instructed his adopted Jewish children to practice circumcision and paternal filiation; the idea of maternal connectedness had to be abandoned. Owing to the uncertainty and unverifiability of paternity, the paternal relation, which is always secured through adoption, is more spiritual than the bond with the mother; "for that reason the child should bear his father's name and be his heir."[41] In the paternal relation the possibility of adoption (of the patronymic) also prevents death from imposing irreversible loss. And yet even while the bearer is alive, the patronymic, as that which survives one's death, commemorates the bearer each time it is cited. But the death which occupies interchangeable places with the patronymic is the death of the father; and according to the logic of adoption, this is a loss which is not a loss.

The rule of the patronymic marks, according to Freud, an "advance in spirituality" (*Geistigkeit*). The first step forward, the invention of language, led to the premier conception of a "spirit realm" (*Geisterreich*).[42] Citizenship in this realm is always the father's pedigree. A visitor from the outside, the father pops up anywhere at any time.[43] This supernatural guest penetrates to the

36

inner psychic apparatus where his recorded voice commands absolutely. Even repression of the Oedipus complex only turns up the speaker full blast.

Freud hoped *Moses and Monotheism* would solve a "problem" which had "pursued" him his "whole life long."[44] But it seems that the "problem" was repeated, not solved. To account for the inscrutable uncanniness with which *Moses and Monotheism* confronts him, Freud allows that one's own work always reaches completion as best it can and then stands before its creator as something independent, even alien (*fremd*).[45] In discussing the mechanism of return repression which the Moses story dramatizes, Freud addresses another Frankenstein monster, in this case a portion of repressed material which has remained accessible to memory, and which consequently appears on occasion within consciousness, though even then it is kept in quarantine, like a "foreign body."[46] In this section on "Difficulties," Freud is attentive to apparent exceptions to the basic theory of repression and the unconscious. One such exceptional cross-over to another zone is effected when an unconscious process in the id is raised to the preconscious level and "incorporated" into the ego. What exercises phantom control over the one most in need of putting it to rest is a disturbance of the order of such "difficulties" as incorporation by the ego of a foreign body.

Though Freud first brings up the stammering attributed to Moses only to dismiss it as referring simply to Moses' Egyptian accent, stammering, it turns out, not unlike the mutilation of a text, gets pressed into service in place of annihilation of name and legacy. Since Jahweh was, according to Freud, the proper name of the "uncanny" primitive desert deity worshipped by the Jews in Aton's stead, the interpretation of Jahweh as a stammer significant of the Mosaic prohibition against naming or representing God arises, in Freud's reading, upon the return of Aton within the religion of Jahweh. But Aton returns only to the extent that Moses's speech impediment returns. In *Adonai* Freud accordingly detects a stammered variant of Aton: "If it is not merely by chance that the name of the Egyptian Aten (or Atum) sounds like the Hebrew word Adonai and the name of the Syrian deity Adonis, but if it is due to a primaeval kinship of speech and meaning, then the Jewish formula might be translated thus: "Hear, o Israel our god Aten (Adonai) is a sole god."[47]

In *The Psychopathology of Everyday Life*, Freud viewed stammering as the aborted result of the blocked "temptation to employ the artifice of a slip of the tongue for enabling improper and forbidden words to be freely used."[48] In "Parapraxes with an Overcompensating Tendency," Karl Abraham opens his reflections on cases that confirm Freud's *Psychopathology of Everyday Life* by bringing the stutter into focus as the lapsus that always "mutilates" only proper names which thus come to be invaded by the baby babble of forbidden words.

> The patient, a teacher, whose articulation is usually quite normal, tends to duplicate the first syllable of proper names by a single stutter. . . . It is hardly necessary to remind readers that baby talk nearly always consists of words of two similar syllables. These words are used for persons, animals, and objects familiar to the child, and particularly for the names of various parts of the body and bodily functions. These latter words often remain in use long after the child has adopted the language of adults and no longer says "bow-wow" but "dog."

According to Freud, stammering returns words to their origin as primal words. Freud, following Karl Abel, argues that, as evidenced by the Egyptian language, the oldest roots of words referred to two contrary meanings. Stammers, metatheses, lapses, and the like refer back to and derive from the original antithetical meanings of words. Every word was originally indissociable from its antithetical stammered variant; to this day, Freud notes, slips of the tongue, which make use of opposites, demonstrate that both a given meaning and its contrary still inhere in every word. Over time, the primal word that meant at once strong and weak, for example, or "strongweak," split off into two words differentiated by a slight modification in sound. As the twofold meaning of *sacer* still attests, the primal word is doubled by a death wish which achieves, only through the stammer, the stereo broadcast it anticipates. Through *fort/da*—the stammering differentiation which irrupts within the primal word *o*—the young child recuperates loss and separation by reversing their administration. The broadcast of death wishes covers over separation with the simulation of some terrible control the child exercises over all transit between life and death. *Fort/da* thus holds the magical place of the name. In this name game can even be discerned a stammered variant of Freud's own patronymic.[49] The stammer that mutilates the name also preserves it; the stammer is the name's internal support system.

The boomerang-like return, as Freud puts it, of Moses's legacy was cast by the primal father, native speaker of primal words.[50] Hence, among the examples Freud cites in "The Antithetical Meaning of Primal Words" is the word pair *stumm*/*Stimme* (mute/voice) which indirectly, through his association of *Stummheit* with death in his essay "The Theme of the Three Caskets," for instance, assigns to death a kind of voice, a stammer. In ancient Egyptian, Freud stresses, the name Moses means, simply, child; according to Freud's textual reconstruction, which he compares to excavation of a tomb,[51] the child Moses is shadowed by "Thot," the death, in fact, of the stammering primal father. Freud selects the term appropriate for the animal and near-animal realm when he refers to the head of the primal horde as *Männchen.* Another meaning of *Männchen* can be found in Freud's nineteenth "Introductory Lecture," where he supports his own use of such technical analogues as photography to illustrate, say, the unconscious by pointing to the electromagnetic model constructed by Ampère, which simulates and contains a *Männchen,* a little man, who swims in the electric current.

Freud generally reserves the tiny or small for oneiric representation of the genitals. But Freud also associates miniaturization with death: the ego bearing the open wound of melancholia shrinks, just as the melancholic considers himself to be, in every respect, "small" and inferior. When, with the advent of the printing press, dead children were included in representations of the family on tombs of parents, they were rendered slightly smaller than the children who still lived at the time the portrait was carved. Dead children are such dolls. And as is the case with Ampère's model battery, these dolls inhabit the vaults of the technical media which, beginning with the printing press, create them.

Childhood developed out of the printing press, just as, to follow out Freud's analogy, the *imagines* of childhood are printed and reprinted through transference. Only since the eighteenth century, however, has there been a special children's language. Part stammer or lisp, part private code, even that idiom of transference love—baby talk—dates from the point of the printing-press child's emergence. At Freud's end of this emergence we find the case of the patient who, locked into a "pleasant father-transference" onto Freud, shares with Freud a "secret language."[52]

The origin of printing-press culture borders on a more ancient province. Gutenberg built his original printing press out of a wine press which he incorporated into his new mechanism. The original press continues to induce inside its transferential analogues states of seeing double.

Jung first made Freud swoon following a bout of communal drinking which Freud had instigated. He pressed Jung, who was a teetotaler at the time, to go ahead and have a drink with him. But Jung, his tongue loosened, would not stop talking about mummified corpses, whereupon Freud fainted. Freud passed out a second time when Jung disagreed that Ikhnaton's sublime achievement could be explained in terms of patricidal impulse. Freud, who claimed to dislike the effect of liquor, attributed both his fainting spells to slight intoxication. In both instances of drinking and swooning, of taking communion and playing dead, Freud recognized in Jung the uncanny double or reprint of his nephew John. This avuncular relation, which embraced Freud's mourning for Julius, became, for Freud, the replacement and embodiment of melancholic annihilation of the corpse Freud himself would become each time the avuncular relation resurfaced.

Identification with siblings, who are always initially one's rivals, is, Freud argues in *The Ego and the Id,* the origin of social sensibility. Social sensibility is thus fueled by sublimated homosexuality, which breaks down when spirits are swallowed and shared. Cannibalistic identification with the father, the primal model of sublimation, is thus reversed. But this reversal is also the first rehearsal of the theory of identification which Freud offered, in his essay on Leonardo da Vinci, as explanation of one type of homosexuality. The replacement of libidinal attachment to an object by identification with and introjection of that same object describes the way in which a male homosexual can first adore his mother and then, upon identification with her, adore like or as his mother; it is his mother's adoration of him or of his brother, his double and god, which he relives from the other end. Freud allows that such inversion through identification is often the case when the mother has died. She herself need not go, but some loss must shadow her.

40

The mother with whom her son identifies is shadowed by a loss which she transmits to her son for safekeeping. The notion of the superego as that place of mournful identification with the father which contains and keeps eternally alive the Oedipus complex thus represents and carries out Freud's later "spiritualization" of what had started out as the exclusively maternal province of aberrant mourning.

According to Freud, sons and brothers eventually took over the controls of that matriarchal society which had first established itself and its legacy through avuncular relations in the wake of the primal father's execution. The mother, who thus occupies the place of mourning even in Freud's phylogenetic scenario, is dislodged by the "empire" shaped, ultimately, by the omnipotence of thoughts. The omnipotence of thoughts, which first gives rise to language and magic, summons the phantom father as more fitting mascot for its empire. But this empire also installs, in the place of the missing mother, uncanny substitutes for mourning: as Freud points out, even the modern technical media have their origin in the omnipotence of thoughts. Belief in the omnipotence of thoughts, which requires that the creditor take full responsibility for the fulfillment of death wishes, summons the vengeful phantoms of the dead which haunt the channels of telepathy and telecommunications.[53]

In the section in *Moses and Monotheism* entitled "The Return of the Repressed" Freud emphasizes that what two-year-old children experience and, of course, fail to comprehend need not be remembered except in dreams. But eventually certain experiences of the two-year-old will nevertheless invade his adult life in the form of compulsions which rule his every action, and force on him personal likes and dislikes even in the choice of beloved and friend. The analogy Freud uses here to explain how, given the weakness of the infant's perceptual and psychic apparatus, early eidetic memories can emerge is the somewhat delayed development of photograph out of imprint. The image Freud next uses, this time to illustrate the displacement whereby that which was repressed in early childhood returns in some other place in the form of symptoms, is that of a "repression scar" which blocks immediate outlet or gratification and thus makes symptom formation necessary.

This scar returns, full scale, in the place of the missing death cult which the coemergence of childhood and the technical media covers and conserves. What was thus projected in proportion to cities of the dead could also be contemplated in close up: eighteenth-century mourning lockets, which contained, locked up, miniature reproductions of the loved one's tomb or—in turn—a lock of hair or some other vestigial part of the deceased, came to hold the place of the memento mori, the distant object of piety. But this photographic miniaturization remains always interchangeable with yet another magnification or projection of the image and wound. What is always originally projected, according to Freud, is the death wish, our first occasion to share the omnipotence of our thoughts with an other, who must, however, go. This death-wish bond between survivor and departed is the underlying projective structure of every death cult.

The media-technical analogues that continue to keep mass media culture on this side of the Freudian system find their point of coherence in *Totem and Taboo* in the close encounter between projection of death wishes and cinematic projection. At the other end of these analogies, Freud's double theory of haunting and the technical media receives confirmation and realization in the Melanesian Cargo Cult, which also first appeared in 1913.

The Cargo Cult astutely interprets products of technology, in particular those in the service of telecommunication, as achievements of the dead. But even the cargo which dead persons have made for the living members of their tribe has been stolen by the white race, which keeps all cargo for itself. To intercept some of these products of their dead, one tribe sets out paper reproductions of birds to attract the cargo-bearing planes flying overhead, much as in contemporary West Germany—though in this case the purpose has been muddled by ambivalence—bird silhouettes clutter every larger window. White men, who are the rulers of the realm of the dead—some tribes call it Australia—and who remain, via magic transmitter boxes, in constant contact with their phantom laborers even across vast distances, also keep to themselves the messages from the dead intended for the tribe. Because he stands at the switches of telecommunications the white man is such a god. In *Civilization and Its Discontents* Freud calls modern man, whose every sense organ finds extension and amplification through the technical media, a "prosthesis god."[54] Since each prosthesis or

42

"auxiliary organ" extends and replaces a particular organ, it always effects castration by adding something on—Castration or death— that is, a dead person—already lies secretly buried beneath the point of impact in a body of each of its prosthetic devices. In certain African cultures lightweight reproductions of televisions are placed in graves alongside the departed. But this does not represent extension of material comfort to the dead; nor do these graves commemorate actual material possessions. On the contrary: if they had a television in every household there would be no need to practice their cult of the dead in some other place.

Avital Ronell has read the inscriptions on Freud's cancerous jaw as symptoms in a phantasmatic scenario where Goethe first discovers the most vulnerable point of articulation of Freud's corpus.[55] In the course of this investigation, Ronell draws attention to the operations Freud performed on his own given name, though he each time preserved the -*mund* or -mouth. "Words can do unspeakable good and cause terrible wounds," Freud allows; "No doubt 'in the beginning was the deed' and the word came later; in some circumstances it meant an advance in civilization when deeds were softened into words. But originally the word was magic—a magical act; and it has retained much of its ancient power."[56]

The given name is always the full name of the child. The scar Julius's death carved near Freud's mouth corresponds, then, to the mutilation and stammering of the name around a single mouth shared, it appears, by two childhood names and identities. If Freud's cancer can indeed be read as symptom formed by the displacing power of a scar, then in the treatments can also be discerned ancient or primitive, that is, childhood, mourning rituals. In certain primitive cultures, for example, the shaving of the beard and the mutilation and extraction of teeth are mourning practices. Mourners extract their own teeth which, in these societies, are considered to be carriers of the soul, and cast them, together with their cut hair, into the grave. Thus a part of the mourner's soul accompanies the departed. The corpse's teeth are worn by the mourner to retain the dead person's spirit which in turn offers protection. In Freud's case these rites continued in the form of countless operations which would make it necessary for Freud to install in his mouth a prosthesis, a *Kästchen* of foreign teeth.

43

RINGS OF RECURRENCE

To push back the complex which Jung recycled, Freud passed out rings. The members of the secret committee, for example, who were enjoined to "watch over" Freud's creation and "defend the cause against personalities and accidents" even after Freud's death, were united by the wearing of special rings, replicas of Freud's own ring.[57] With the secret committee, Freud returned to and lived out a full-fledged reference to the ring parable in Lessing's *Nathan the Wise* which had, as Freud reminisces to Martha Bernays in a letter bearing an epigraph from *Nathan the Wise,* even played a certain role in their engagement. For it was during his engagement to Martha that, owing to a series of mishaps with a ring, Freud was encouraged to allude to Nathan's ring parable, in which the patriarch, having "promised" his legacy, the single ring, to each of his three heirs, reproduces this ring only later to lose the original. Having been secretly presented by Martha with her father's ring, and after having had it copied for her so that she could still be seen by her family to possess it, Freud accidentally broke the original and replaced it with a copy (July 23, 1882).

With each ring, Freud rehearsed *Moses and Monotheism* by ringing up *Nathan the Wise.* The ring parable in *Nathan the Wise* allegorizes monotheism in terms of inheritance of the patronymic: hard-pressed to keep his promise that each of his sons be the sole heir, a father copies and multiplies his unique ring, which remains original only insofar as it is henceforward found missing. This loss or abandonment of the original ring promotes what Freud analyzes in *Moses and Monotheism* as the "spiritual progression" from the maternal relation, which is always verifiable through the senses, to paternity, which chooses or adopts to the extent that the patronymic is in turn adopted. And yet *Nathan the Wise* closes by embodying the terrible return of the discarded blood bond. It is not so much that Nathan's daughter is disclosed to be an adopted orphan—this shift only confirms the progression of the parable. But the adopted daughter also attains the status of niece. This revelation cannot be contained but doubles on contact until everyone in its range has been united within one avuncular blood line. Everyone but Nathan.

1977 saw the publication of the memoirs of Nietzsche's niece.

nice
Netzsche (?)

According to its dust cover, *Zarathustra's Kinfolk* focuses on a love story, "a love story in the shadow of the great tree."[58] The Nietzsche family tree (*Stammbaum*) shadows the niece's incestuous attachment to a young man who, as her anxious parents rush to enlighten her, is her half brother: he also becomes, by dint of this intervention, the gentile stepson of his Jewish father. The revelations summoned by the niece animate Nietzsche's nephew, her supernatural counterpart; the Jewish stepfather remains displaced with respect to the avuncular complex which excludes him.?

Every avuncular complex covers an unmarked grave. Enter the genealogist or ghostbuster who, consonant with Foucault's injunction, must look "in the most unpromising places, in what we tend to feel is without history."[59] It is always the very bottom of the process of handing down legacies that must be explored and sounded. The autobiography of Nietzsche's niece takes a walk across the night of nihilism, in the course of which Nietzsche and Freud, though both crying uncle, must meet.

By taking Nietzsche's school days at Schul-Pforta as her focus for the abbreviated images of the biography she centers around Nietzsche's Lou affair, the niece confirms Nietzsche's own inclination to include himself only in Pforta-graphs. The picture taken in Lucerne, for example, in which Lou brandishes the whip over Paul Rée and Nietzsche, can be seen as covering the range of Pforta. Nietzsche remains at the horse's end of the long haul of *Wiederholung*, of a repetition which reaches back to Rossleben, literally the "stallion's life," where Nietzsche's father attended the theological seminar, and forward to the photo-finish: Nietzsche, without a name, locked in embrace with the whipped horse.

Schul-Pforta, literally the school portal, served as aperture for the development or *Bildung* of Fichte, Klopstock, Novalis, Ranke, and the Schlegel brothers. At the other end there arrived, following Nietzsche, not only the father of the niece but even, and at closer range, Wilamowitz. At this end the niece receives from her father Nietzsche's essay on the institution of Pforta: *On the Future of Our Educational Institutions* (*Bildungsanstalten*). The portal, we learn in this essay, embraces and proffers access to the cultivation of the mother tongue, though only to the extent that it can regulate what Nietzsche calls *Bildungstriebe*, *Bildung*-drives. The students at Schul-Pforta, called *Pförtner*, gatekeepers, are ac-

45

cordingly trained to assume guardianship of the mother tongue and to superintend its course: "*Bildung* begins with the correct gait or tempo of language." Schul-Pforta is, according to Nietzsche, the "womb" of *Bildung;* as such it launches and regulates the flight and tempo of the "genius" of every Pförtner. The *Bildung*-drives must proceed, under control, in stately flotation: or else the mother tongue will die while a "glittering phantom" of *Bildung* emerges before the gates of the institution; like that uncanny guest nihilism, it waits at the portal.

While within the gates of Schul-Pforta, Nietzsche designed a satellite society of letters, which involved two additional correspondents in the "mutual surveillance of the *Bildung*-drives." In this society, called Germania, Nietzsche and his correspondents exchanged, through the gates of Pforta, letters and manuscripts which were returned with appropriate emendations. And yet this sending and receiving arrangement, which regulated its transmissions through Pforta, the portal of the mother tongue, cast off all but its founding member and genius. Unaware that the group had already disbanded, Nietzsche ended up sustaining this postal procedure for over a year with himself as sole participant. Though the society had been designed to include two or more correspondents, the Pförtner Nietzsche nevertheless played this Pfort/a game single-handedly on the threshold of a womb.

Nietzsche would find and found, around this womb, another society which, like Germania at Pforta, promoted through mutual superintendence the regulation and refinement of the *Bildung*-drives. This society—the Trinity—was commemorated in the Lucerne photograph: in Leipzig Nietzsche, Lou Salomé, and Paul Rée together attended a performance of *Nathan the Wise* to inaugurate their writing team in the ensuing exchange and emendation of separate takes on the Nathan problem. For Nietzsche this problem could be simply put: he was looking for an heir, a disciple to inherit and promulgate his thought. Though he was the acknowledged "father" of Rée's first book, Nietzsche turned around his reception of the "Réealism" of this book at the same time that he judged his own early work no longer equal to reflections he was now conceiving under the new rubric of Eternal Return. Even as the three of them were planning to live together in a major university town where Nietzsche would pursue studies aimed at elucidating and promoting the doctrine he was intent on handing down, it became increasingly clear that only Lou was to be Nietzsche's pupil, indeed his heiress. As Nietzsche confided to Lou in a letter drafted in December 1882:

> Back in Orta I conceived the plan of leading you step by step to the final consequence of my philosophy—*you*, as the first person I took to be fit for this. Oh, you cannot suspect what resolve, what determination, this took. As teacher I have always done much for my students . . . but what I meant to do *here, now,* given my continuing physical deterioration, went beyond everything earlier. A protracted building, building up! . . . I thought of you as my heiress.

During his single encounter alone with Lou in Orta—which he moreover commemorated by coining the expression "Orta-weather" to describe any particularly fine moment in terms of their special bond—Nietzsche first elaborated to Lou the Eternal Return of the Same. But Nietzsche's forecast was not quite accurate. Only when, after some delay, no reply to his letters to Lou was forthcoming did Nietzsche realize that he had put her off right from the start, and that the Trinity founded in Orta had, for some time already, retained only Nietzsche as correspondent.

Suspicious of the wedding ring of recurrence which Nietzsche had eagerly bestowed on her, Lou, looking back on the bond established between them in Orta, discovered a relentless return of discarded sensuality which continued to return in each of her post-Orta relationships until, in her relation to "father" Freud, this return subsided before its definition:

> Just as Christian (like every) mysticism passes into crude religious sensuality right at its highest ecstasy, so can the most ideal love become sensual again in its ideality precisely by the power of the great tensing of sensation. A disagreeable matter, this revenge of the human element—I do not like those feelings where they reconverge in their circulation, for that is the junction of false pathos, of lost truth and integrity of feeling. Is this what is estranging me from Nietzsche?[60]

Just as Lou found Orta-weather suspect, so she also suspected that the doctrine of Eternal Return turned—by recycling repressed feelings—on defective mysticism. But according to the logic she already embodied, her rejection of Nietzsche's legacy only guaranteed its transmission. Even as described in her commentary on the

Orta afternoon, the bond established between Nietzsche and Lou in Orta takes the form of a cycle which, at its apogee, links Nietzsche, through Lou, to Freud. Though she castigated Nietzsche's conceptions of Eternal Return even before he published them, composed them into a body, Lou—the father of Zarathustra, as Nietzsche saw her[61]—nevertheless doubled as secret bearer of the doctrine of Eternal Return.

The speculations which found their rebound in *Beyond the Pleasure Principle* were first released in the argument between Lou and Freud, in February 1913, over her poem "Life Prayer"—which Lou presented to Nietzsche, and which he himself set to music and continued to praise in *Ecce Homo*. When next Freud discloses to Lou, in a hushed voice, his discovery of the primal father alongside notions which would comprise *Beyond the Pleasure Principle,* she at first rejects the revelation, just as she had rejected the Eternal Return of the Same which Nietzsche, similarly in a hushed voice, had sought to hand down to her. Thus when it comes time to give an example of repetition compulsion in *Beyond the Pleasure Principle,* Freud inserts the return of the phrase "Eternal Return of the Same" into his example of the lover "each of whose love affairs passes through the same phases and reaches the same conclusion. This 'Eternal Return of the Same' . . . ."

"It was known that as a girl she had kept up an intense friendship with Friedrich Nietzsche, founded upon her deep understanding of the philosopher's bold ideas," Freud reports in his Lou eulogy:

> This relationship came to an abrupt end when she refused the proposal of marriage which he made her. . . . It was in Vienna that long ago the most moving episode of her feminine fortunes had been played out. In 1912 she returned to Vienna in order to be initiated into psychoanalysis. My daughter, who was her close friend, once heard her regret that she had not known psychoanalysis in her youth. But, after all, in those days there was no such thing.

Lou, who would claim to be "more Freudian" than Freud himself, was indeed "more than Freud" by having always been, already with Nietzsche, in the Freudian system. She returns the Eternal Return to the psychoanalytic model when, upon receiving it from Nietzsche, she interprets it as the return of the repressed. And she eventually returns the Eternal Return to Freud in person, to have it analyzed and to have her interpretation confirmed. Even Nietzsche returns to the psychoanalytic model, particularly when in *Ecce Homo* he suggests that, since he could not brook the thought of his mother's and sister's return, the Eternal Return would have to be selective or not be at all; indeed, as he put it, the whole maternal German side of his family posed the "deepest possible objection to the doctrine of Eternal Return."[62]

Freud was unable to come to terms with Nietzsche, to acknowledge any debt whatsoever to him, and what continues to attract our attention is that Freud's resistance seems so strong. In this context Lou is herself the return of the repressed. Lou was the link between Nietzsche and Freud, their only link, Freud claimed upon her death. This link even comes full circle: when Freud included her in the secret committee, Lou finally accepted the ring she refused in Orta.

Is Lou caught between Nietzsche and Freud in a tug of war, or is she holding the end of the line? Does Lou play *fort/da* with both of them, or is she herself the *fort/da* bobbin of each of the men, whose homosexual link—witness Freud's extraordinary jealousy of Nietzsche with regard to Lou—she would, then, guarantee. Lou is the messenger sent by Nietzsche to Freud, bearing the doctrine of Eternal Return which she thus rescued from that degenerescence of Nietzsche's name which in 1977 is embodied by his niece. A certain fear of contagion nevertheless accompanies this transfer. And though Freud's citation of Nietzsche's doctrine amounts to that insemination of Freud's corpus by Nietzsche which could only be accomplished by Lou, the father of *Zarathustra,* the very place of insemination is meticulously sealed off. It is within the context of a repression and of Freud's theory of repression that "the Eternal Return of the Same" is situated and contained in *Beyond the Pleasure Principle.*

The primal father was the superman, Freud corrects the teacher; Nietzsche placed in the future what belonged to the past.[63] Every father leaps out of the past to become the superego, the phantom over-and-out man. But there remains another type of phantom authority, Freud allows in the midst of his discussion of such uncanny phenomena as Eternal Return of the Same and return of the dead. Though he hastens to emphasize that this contrast does not hold the two mechanisms apart, Freud nevertheless goes ahead and offers another opposition. Uncanny experiences, Freud has already established, occur whenever repressed infantile complexes are reanimated through some current impression. Or, he now adds, they occur whenever long-overcome (*überwundene*) primitive convictions suddenly seem to receive new confirmation. The animistic convictions of primitive cultures have not been left behind by modern man but are in a precarious state of *Überwundensein*. The uncanniness of the double must also be charted back to a surmounted era of mental development. This ancient source of the uncanny's double aspect is still current today, Freud advises Jung, in the belief of many primitive peoples that the placenta is the baby's brother or twin which must, accordingly, also be fed and cared for, "—which naturally does not last long." Thus Freud postulates as part of the phylogenetic program that every child is born alongside a sibling who cannot be kept alive.[64]

In uncanny experiences which confirm surmounted convictions, it is belief in the material reality of a certain idea—the belief in doubles or ghosts, for example—which has returned. But, Freud stresses, it would press repression beyond the bounds of its definition to claim that this, too, belongs to the return of the repressed. The ghost hails from the tribal past, from childhood, but not from a childhood complex which can undergo repression.[65] The dead, child and savage alike believe, return as ghosts and vampires. Such a belief is not repressed but is overcome only to return whenever seemingly confirmed. As recollected in the essay on *Gradiva,* Freud once looked up from his desk and saw standing before him the look-alike sister of a deceased patient: the dead do return, Freud concluded. One's tribal past, including infantile or archaic beliefs associated with mourning, comes in, like a ghost, under and over the threshold of repression. But repression itself buries alive; the phantasm of live burial accordingly recycles and distorts the repressed wish that the womb return. Vagina dentata and vampire: as Freud allowed, in the realm of the uncanny, even the distinctions he would draw describe doubles. Yet in taking cognizance of the exceptional status of belief in ghosts, Freud touches on the wound of interminable mourning. Freud could never fathom what generally goes without saying, namely, why mourning should be so painful, why mourning should leave behind open wounds even as it

50

provides prosthetic replacements for each lost attachment.[66] With what may be Nietzschean pathos, Freud summons the great over-coming as well as, already secretly scarred over, the *Überwunde*, the superwound which, on telepathic channels, exercises the kind of control which is otherwise the superego's prerogative.

Freud puts the *Übermännchen* in its place, in Nietzsche's past, and leaves it there. There remains, however, another tele-pathic call to be put through.

In an aside in his case study of Schreber, Freud noted that Nietzsche's hymn "Before Sunrise" manifested Nietzsche's longing for his father. Shortly after his father's death Nietzsche received a close call from the father's ghost:

> In the church I heard organ sounds like those at a funeral. As I looked to see what the cause might be, a grave suddenly opened and out steps my father in shroud. He hurries into the church and soon returns with a small child in his arms. The grave mound opens, he climbs in and the cover sinks back down onto the opening. At the same time the organ sound falls silent, and I awaken. The next day little Joseph falls ill, convulses and dies within a few hours. Our grief was unbounded. My dream had been completely fulfilled.

In the dream the phantom father withdraws with an unidentified child, the double of the dreamer. Awakening, Nietzsche finds him-self still here, while the younger brother, as it turns out, soon goes. Both this dream and that reported by Elisabeth, in which Nietz-sche foresaw the death of his grandfather, another double of the dreamer, are telepathic prophecies that were each time fulfilled. Already as a child Nietzsche would seem to have possessed a new keen sense which enabled him to receive signals of impending death and degenerescence. He is able to receive these signals, Nietzsche writes in *Ecce Homo*, because he is his own double. And it is his double's departure which doubles Nietzsche and installs in him telepathic reception.

The formal epigraph to *Ecce Homo*, "Now I tell my life to myself," recalls the plan laid out in Nietzsche's autobiography writ-ten at age fourteen "to write a short book and then to read it," just as the claim to be his own double was rehearsed in his early novella *Euphorion*. In *Faust* Euphorion is engendered through the congress of rhyme-words; in Nietzsche's version he is another Dr. Franken-stein in search of his double, whose brain Euphorion would dissect.

51

Like the ancient mariner his albatross, Euphorion "carries . . . a rope called *Fatum.*"

Euphorion writes to and about his doubles in a place of double occupancy—at once crypt and alma mater—which Nietzsche already designated, as he first passed through its gates, as Pforta: "Seeing Pforta shining forth, I felt I recognized in it more a prison than an alma mater. I proceeded through the gate. My heart overflowed with sacred sensations: I was lifted up to God in silent prayer and profound peace settled over my spirit."[67] Inside this double aperture, at once "father womb"[68] and "mother Pforta," Nietzsche first conceived the doctrine of Eternal Return and amor fati (*Vati*). Pforta holds the place of the parents Pfort/a would hold in place.

Fatum is the principle of "unconscious action," writes the Pforta schoolboy; "the fatalistic principle," untempered by some notion of free will, would render one "an automaton." Free will without *Fatum* would transform one into "a god." But both free will and *Fatum* converge, Nietzsche advises, when we dispense with the reductive notion that unconscious action, allegedly programmed by "earlier impressions," covers only lifetime, only one lifetime.[69] We are part god, part automaton; we are godlike when armed with our prosthetic doubles.

Pfort/a must be played with doubles: enter Lou, whom Nietzsche explicitly named his "double" and "sister brain,"[70] and the typewriter, which Nietzsche, who was the first philosopher to type, celebrated as prosthetic part and portrait of himself. The typewriter, which first circulated as a writing and even reading device for the blind, was originally conceived as an extension of the field of vision. The typewriter is thus one of those supplements which, having taken the place of the dead eye, cannot help but be dominated and contaminated, in turn, by the evil eye.

The evil eye always projects the revenge of the murdered. The slain animal, which could still kill with its dying glance, had to be blinded by the hunters who, like Perseus in the face of Medusa, kept their glance averted. Amulets representing or reflecting eyes were worn to ward off the evil eye, just as mummy coffins displayed painted eyes to annul evil influence on both fronts. To reflect back or contain evil-eye effects, the shield of Medusa was fastened by the ancient Greeks to the entrances of their cemeteries.[71]

As Abraham points out, blindness also always conveys invisibility, as in the designation of hidden passageways and passengers as being blind.[72] Among the Bororo, glasses frames are worn by actors who, during mourning spectacles, represent the young soul of the deceased; like the black paint that covers the young soul's body, his glasses render him invisible.

The typewriter is a Mystic Writing Pad or *Wunderblock* which, with its styluslike keys, rips into one surface—the typewriter ribbon or unconscious memory—so that another surface can be printed upon. This *Wunde-block* leaves a wound which blocks the emergence of one inscription so that imprinted text can emerge in some other place. The "open wound" was typed; in a letter dated May 4, 1915, Freud announces that he is having "Mourning and Melancholia" "typewriten" so that Abraham can receive a carbon copy.

According to Abraham, blindness confers on the casualty of the Oedipus complex a zone of invisibility, a safety zone to which the father's sunlike stare cannot penetrate. In Nietzsche's case blindness blocked the other "selves" which spoke to him through books only to block his writing. Blindness thus bestows on Nietzsche the maternal gift of philosophizing, the ability to become a woman and conceive such works as *Zarathustra*. In lieu of reading, the typewriter granted Nietzsche an extra sense, a kind of automatic writing which specialized in spontaneous, almost childlike rhyming. The ultimate rhyme forged by Nietzsche as he typed hailed the typewriter as being "something like" himself; "delicate little fingers" are required when using either Nietzsche or his writing instrument.[73] And Lou, Nietzsche's declared double, occupies interchangeable places not only with the problem of Eternal Return, but even with Nietzsche's typewriter. In a letter to Elisabeth, Nietzsche complains that his typewriter, forwarded to him by Paul Rée, has arrived damaged, "like everything that people of weak character have in their hands for a time, whether typewriters, problems, or Lous."[74] According to Friedrich Kittler, the scene of writing which the typewriter introduces is new precisely to the extent that it admits women who henceforward mediate and take the place of every new prosthetic telecommunications device. Woman becomes Perse-phone putting through calls in the underworld, reinscribing the vampire's bite with typewriter keys.

The circulation system centered on typewriter and dictaphone cannot help but confirm the belief in vampirism it also helps to overcome.[75] The advent of typewriter and telephone renders the structure of human work independent of any job to be done. What remains is an empty circulation of information in which every possible memo is included and preserved, and yet disappears without remainder.[76] Down to Dracula's "child's brain" typewriter culture commemorates the Count: the typewriter introduces into writing a voice which babbles in rhyme and stammers in typos.

In 1928 Lou and Freud reminisced about their 1913 dispute over her poem "Life Prayer." Suddenly she realized that Freud had ended up accepting what her poem had praised and proffered: life's boundless pain. Mumbling and sobbing she touched on Freud's open wound. The typewriter-like *Kästchen* in his mouth rendered Freud's speech thick and clumsy. He put his arm around Lou, the good niece.

FRIEDRICH NICHTE

Nietzsche's dead brother installs in him a certain Pfort/a frequency that cannot be tuned out by the superegoical broadcast—always an admixture, according to Freud, of early parental criticism and public opinion. The Melanesian believers in cargo place unmournable death at the controls of a cult that keeps communication with their mourned dead pushed back. Thus that other cargo cultist Ratman does not know, owing to the interference his unmourned sister embodies and provides, that his every thought is known by his dead father. But the father, Ratman realizes, must continue to pay in the underworld for his son's death wishes. Like Ratman, Nietzsche does not know that his Oedipalized past nevertheless knows his thoughts and watches for the chance to return. According to the Cargo Cult: by the day lines of communication with the mourned dead are restored the believers must have annihilated everything that would remind them of their former lives. Total annihilation thus greets the return of the mourned dead.

It was upon sealing the breach between Nietzsche and Lou

that Elisabeth initiated the process whereby she would accede to the patronymic. A year after the dissolution of the Trinity group Elisabeth, a recent convert to anti-Semitism—her latest "distraction"—paid Nietzsche back for his own distraction with Lou by entangling him in a frenzy of retribution against Lou and Rée. "I belong to both of you with my warmest feelings"—Nietzsche had earlier written Lou and Rée to mark the end of their Trinity association—"as I mean to have proven through my departure more than through my *nearness,*" though one year later, together with Elisabeth, Nietzsche produced a second or simulated end to his affair with Lou, denouncing her now as "that scraggy dirty smelly she-monkey (*Äffin*) with her false breasts."[77] It was at this point, then, that Elisabeth dispatched the Nietzsche name, departing for South America to found together with her husband, the prominent anti-Semite Förster, Nueva Germania, a satellite society of the true fatherland, Germany having become, they felt, through increasing Jewish influence, a "stepfatherland."[78] And through the portals of the new Germania society Elisabeth continued to advise her brother to dissociate his legacy from the likes of Brandes, Rée, and Lou, lest his thought end up a Jewish science. By now, at the very latest, Nietzsche knew that he had risked and lost his name. Did Nietzsche only now recast his legacy, handing down, in *Ecce Homo,* "dynamite" set to go off in the midst of *Zarathustra's Kinfolk?* Is there not some relation of correspondence here—between Nietzsche's knowledge that the part of him that signed as his mother, that signed F. N., would live on, on the one hand, and—on the other—his desire for the annihilation of the name?

Though the resultant "birth" of his name would lead in the ensuing controversy over *Birth of Tragedy* to his being declared "academically dead," Nietzsche had interpreted as a good omen the circumstance that his name rhymed with that of his publisher Fritsch.[79] Once Nietzsche commences rhyming, *Nichts* and Nizza take on unsuspected value and force. A good deal of Nietzsche's thought was always born again within a zone of paronomasia or punning on his name.[80] Nietzsche invites us to give a closer hearing to the enigmatic force of nomination at work, for example, in *Schopenhauer as Educator,* in the play on words "zwischen Ichts und Nichts" ("between I and nothingness") as well as in his Dionysian dithyramb beginning "Jetzt / zwischen zwei Nichtsen /

eingekrümmt" ("Now suspended between two nothingnesses"). Though elsewhere in *Schopenhauer as Educator* Nietzsche characterizes "uncanny" deceptive speech as "stammering," it would in fact owe to stammering that he could not help but overhear the *Ich* in *Nichts* or, for that matter, the *Nichts* in *Ich* as a tension operating within his own name.

As the excursus on Nietzsche's typewriter has already confirmed: the genealogist philosophizes with a stammer. Every received concept has always already coincided with that drifting movement of contagion and association which the genealogist's stammer puts on fast forward. But does Nietzsche remain in some other place or niche, which he might have reserved for himself, when unscrambling the stammering associations to which nihilism always and again owes its emergence, or does he in turn succumb to what Freud in a letter to Fliess called "philosophical stammering"?[81] Stammering juxtaposes "Nietzsche" to the *Nichts* and to the will to *Nichts* or nihilism against which Nietzsche militated in identifying and attacking resentment, declared in the final section of *Genealogy of Morals* to be the only will on earth.

"The great nothingness," we read in Nietzsche, is also that which is nameless (*das Namenlose*). Though it has, in Nietzsche, no ontological status, existing as it does solely as negation of the other—like a parasite—without powers of affirmation, without voice or proper name, the will to *Nichts*—or *ressentiment*—nevertheless holds the place of the proper name, the place between self and otherness, between *Ichts* and *Nichts*. This place can be termed a principle, the stammer principle of the name. Each time the name is cited, is called by name, it is made to stand alone and expressionless on the one hand, while on the other it attracts, through rhyming, a new context of similar names.[82]

The stammering of the Nietzsche name always drifted toward the maternal side, at once the greatest objection to the Eternal Return of the Same and the embodiment of life.[83] When in a letter to Carl von Gersdorf, dated December 13, 1875, Nietzsche punningly inaugurated the adjectivalization and institutionalization of his name, he left his sister equal rights to this leftover; it is life together with Elisabeth which renders everything around him "wholly Nietzschean" (*Nietzschisch*). Already in a comedy written at age ten Nietzsche envisioned his own apotheosis by Jupiter as independent of his sister, whom he leaves behind weeping at her brother's grave while father and mother are raised by Nietzsche to heaven. And this arrangement, which also accords the parasite hosted by the patronymic the role of sole survivor and heir, continues to count late arrivals.

The dust jacket to the 1977 autobiographical novel *Zarathustra's Kinfolk* announces that the author—a certain Miss Sigismund—is none other than Friedrich Nietzsche's niece: Nietzsches Nichte. Tucked inside this novel we find:

> In this novel, any resemblance to real persons is by no means coincidental. Nietzsche's Nichte brings astounding things to light, things which hitherto had been guarded family secrets. What she divulges—about Nietzsche and his sister, about herself, her brother, and unusual sibling relations—she packs into an ingenious, delicate story which takes the curious reader into confidence and keeps him entertained. Here is Elisabeth, who once moved to Weimar with her sick brother Friedrich Nietzsche in order to profit from Goethe's city. Residing high above the city in the Nietzsche archives— designed by Henry van de Velde in the classical *Jugendstil*—she rules over the family and over her brother's literary remains and legacy, which she, as we now know, managed in her own way. Under her supervision Ursula, the narrator, grows up. Of Ursula's siblings one brother will become, in his not always philosophical manner, quite controversial. She makes his acquaintance in Sweden at the home of his alleged father, a rich banker who worships Nietzsche and his sister. Few know, as Ursula does, that the young man with the unkempt hair and unkempt thoughts is the son of someone else entirely. Even the aunt, who would like to couple the Nichte with him, suspects nothing about this nephew. . . . a love affair "in the shadow of the great tree."

> Ursula Sigismund, born in Danzig, raised in Weimar, is a Nichte of Friedrich Nietzsche. After her marriage she remained for a time in Weimar till, in 1955, she moved with her husband and five children to the German Federal Republic. Today she lives in Darmstadt. Following the appearance of a volume of short stories ("German Author Prize" 1963), her novel *Bordergoer* appeared in 1970, and, in 1971, the travelogue *Forward March, Madame*, which depicts her encounter with Robert Neumann.

Born twenty-one years after her uncle's death, Nichte was raised in close range of the most potent Dile-TANTE of our time—her aunt Elisabeth. And yet Nichte claims greater interest in what her aunt does *not* say ("was sie *nicht* sagt") than in what she does say (149). Within the conclave of ascetic priests, knowledge that does not know conducts secret assassination attempts.

One day our German teacher asked me to give an oral report on Nietzsche, and after his remark "For you that really shouldn't be difficult" I agreed to do it. Then I dared to criticize the great man—his aloofness, his Zarathustra style, his animosity towards women, his lust for war, his arrogance towards petty virtues. And yet at the end of my contradictory talk I cited the lines:

Yes, I know wherefrom I stem! [*Ja! ich weiss, woher ich stamme!*]
Unsated like the flame
I glow and consume myself.
All that I touch turns to light
All that I leave behind to coals:
Indeed I *am* a flame.

—and afterwards I almost started sobbing, which is why I quickly had to take my seat. (139)

Nichte thus claims her place, and, like Nietzsche himself, knows wherefrom she stems: the stammer attaches her to the *Stamm*. Though she mutilates and mumbles this *Stamm*, she also carves into it its secret name. Interpreting the destruction wrought by World War II as Nietzsche's legacy—the legacy of nihilism—Nichte concludes: "The war—we hadn't yet gotten out of the habit of personifying it—had destroyed, bombed out, and annihilated [*hatte zerstört, zerbombt, und zunichte gemacht*], and yet we could live, and like life, simply because we were there [*einfach weil wir da waren*]" (288). The war, Nietzsche's alleged legacy, amounts, as personification, to another name of Nietzsche: "Nietzsche" has made everything *zunichte,* into nothingness, into naught—into Nichte. In 1977 Nietzsche thus lives on as Nichte, a distant relative of his mother. Nichte is that double of Nietzsche forged out of Elisabeth's Oedipalized past. Thus the double that Nietzsche was, was in turn doubled—simulated and repressed. Nietzsche ended up double to the extent that he died within his own archives, within his sister's institution of the Nietzsche name. "Die ewige Wiederkehr des Gleichen" names the return of the double, at once the "same body" and the "corpse" (*Leiche*). In 1977 Nietzsche lives on not as the same—*gleiche*—name, but as its corpse, the *G-Leiche.*

Upon witnessing at the close of World War II the exodus of inmates from the neighborhood concentration camp, as they wandered about the streets of Weimar "like ghosts" and "dressed improperly" (287), Nichte comes to a conclusion. Watching her children vigorously sled down the hill dubbed "Death's Track," Nichte feels reassured about the capacity of her kind for survival. This could be the end of Kafka's *Metamorphosis* or a certain end of Nietzsche. In fact it is always only the beginning, the vigorous downhill slide of Nietzsche into Nichte.

POSTSCRIPT

It has recently come to my attention that Hitler's rise to power was accompanied by the suicide or murder of his own Nichte, Geli Raubal, his mistress at the time. The rules of haunting render Hitler, with redoubled force, the transmitter of "Nichte."

CHAPTER TWO

THE FATE OF A DAUGHTER

(Gotthold Ephraim Lessing)

If the plastic arts were put under psychoanalysis, the practice of embalming the dead might turn out to be a fundamental factor in their creation. The process might reveal that at the origin of painting and sculpture there lies a mummy complex. . . . The first Egyptian statue, then, was a mummy, tanned and petrified in sodium. But pyramids and labyrinthine corridors offered no certain guarantee against ultimate pillage.

Other forms of insurance were therefore sought. So, near the sarcophagus, alongside the corn that was to feed the dead, the Egyptians placed terra cotta statuettes, as substitute mummies which might replace the bodies if these were destroyed. . . .

No matter how skillful the painter, his work was always in fee to an inescapable subjectivity. The fact that a human hand intervened cast a shadow of doubt over the image. . . . The personality of the photographer enters into the proceedings only in his selection of the object to be photographed and by way of the purpose he has in mind. . . . All the arts are based on the presence of man, only photography derives an advantage from his absence.

André Bazin, "The Ontology of the Photographic Image"

LOOK NO HANDS

"A painter without hands who wanted to express the picture distinctly present to his mind by the agency of song," Nietzsche wagers in "On Truth and Lie in the Extra-Moral Sense," "will still reveal much more with this exchange of spheres, than the empirical world reveals about the essence of things."[1] Nietzsche summons here, from Lessing's *Emilia Galotti,* a painter's affirmation in spite of the always disfigured reach of artistic creation:

60

Ha! that we cannot paint directly with our eyes! On the long way from the eyes through the arm to the brush, how much is lost! But the way I say that I know what has been lost, and how it was lost, and why it had to end up lost: I am just as proud of this, indeed prouder than I am of all that which I did not let go. Because in the former I recognize more than in the latter that I am truly a great painter; but that my hand is not always one. Or do you not agree, Prince, that Raphael would have been the greatest painter, even if he had unhappily been born without hands?[2]

What Lessing's painter calls the long way from eye to hand to brush, Nietzsche designates as a series of transferences (*Übertragungen*) from nerve impulse to image, from image to sound-shape, with each metaphorical transference representing a leap between alien spheres. Our relation to language is, accordingly, illustrated by the deaf artist who discovers the sound effect of tone by examining Chladnic sound shapes in the sand.[3] By this "aesthetic relation" Nietzsche ultimately means "an allusive transference, a stammering translation into a completely alien language." The stammer alerts the ghostbuster that he now traverses friable ground; soon it will invade the name that summons it. A funerary structure emerges in place of these stammering translations: out of the residual remains of primitive, intuitive metaphors, mankind has erected a conceptual construct which can be compared now to a "cemetery of intuitions," now to a Roman columbarium, that tower of niches containing ashes of the dead.[4] Friedrich Niche.

Nietzsche opened his essay with yet another reference to the Lessing corpus. Lessing's dead infant son had already confirmed Nietzsche's view of the intellect: it inflates porter and philosopher alike "like a hose" and lands the blown-up creature on center stage where all eyes are "telescopically directed upon his actions and thoughts." Nietzsche concludes: "It is remarkable that this is accomplished by the intellect, which after all has been given to the most unfortunate, the most delicate, the most transient beings only as an expedient, in order to detain them for a moment in existence, from which, without that supplement, they would have every reason to flee as swiftly as Lessing's son."[5] These allusions to Lessing haunting Nietzsche's work on metaphor center on the loss of creation or fatherhood. Upon his father's death Lessing returned to— resurrected—*Emilia Galotti,* which he had conceived as turning, thus at both ends, on the absence of the father. In *Emilia Galotti,* as Friedrich Schlegel observed, every trace of that Lessing so garrulously present in *Nathan the Wise* seems effaced;[6] instead, at the end of the series of removals and retreats, of safety spacings, which characterized Lessing's search for the "true father," we find a daughter who, alone in Lessing's works, achieves through her suicide mission the father's corporeal resurrection.

But *Emilia Galotti* could not conclude Lessing's mourning for his dead father; in the summer following the play's publication, Lessing, still severely depressed, proceeded as head librarian in Wolfenbüttel to reorganize some one hundred thousand volumes. A tower built of embalmed metaphors and transferences is always the tomb with which a son commemorates his father. This work of metaphor and mourning towers over a stage of melancholic reflection Lessing referred to, in his own case, as *Wortgrübelei*, brooding on words.[7] Lessing accordingly pressed *Wortgrübelei* into service now to effect "Rescues"—a series of pieces Lessing wrote to protect certain authors from the effacing strategies of academic resentment—now to construct an etymological dictionary. One of the few actual mistakes or lapses in this dictionary remains his entry on *Sarg* (coffin), which he detached from *sarcophagus* and its meaning of "flesh eating" in order to append it instead to the more general sense of "vessel" (7:395). By concluding the entry with a final association of *Sarg* with *Arche* (ark), he enlisted melancholic cannibalism as stowaway on yet another rescue mission.

Lessing considered his attempt to control and apply metaphorical conversion of arbitrary signs into natural signs as his "original sin" (13:150). Metaphor, according to Lessing, simulates natural signification through "another similarity" whereby two things are associated and subsumed under one concept which remains renewable (14:429). But "the highest genre of poetry is that which completely transforms arbitrary signs into natural signs. But that is drama; for here words cease to be arbitrary signs and become instead natural signs of arbitrary things" (17:289–92). In closer range, the *Wortgrübler* saw every word as preserving, as its original metaphor or *Sinnbild,* the original coupling of *Sinn* and *Bild,* of sense and image, to which it owed its conception.[8] Drama thus reanimates what metaphor tends to preserve: the *Wortgrübler* raises the curtain to reveal the primal scene of concept and image, in which Lessing could make out the concept to be the man, the sensual image of the concept to be the woman, and the words the offspring which the couple produced (18:190). But in the coupling Lessing ceaselessly dramatized, the man only holds the place of the "true father," who, like the mother, is nowhere to be found. The woman in this staged scene is always the daughter who asks her father to create her anew—and to recreate himself as the missing "true father."

In *Emilia Galotti* the daughter's dying request to kiss the hand of the father she has reconstituted emerges at the end of a series of exchanges and removals of hands which in turn remains coextensive with the play. Hands have always supplied the first sacrificial substitutions in the wake of death: in place of burnt widows and other human sacrifices, hands were decorated and abbreviated. On the Marquesa islands women by age twelve had to bear mourning tatoos at least on the right hand if they were to be admitted to the preparations for mummification of the dead. The most ancient mourning practice, which reaches back into prehistory, is that of mutilation of fingers of the second hand, the left hand, which is always the maternal, inverted, and grieving side of coordination. Each finger can be viewed as holding the specific place of a loved one who takes the place-holder with him when he departs. The thumb, for example, is the oldest finger, the father of the hand. Leftish lack of hand-to-eye coordination—the state of being all thumbs—can thus commemorate the loss of the first condition of all proper exchange.

Rather than invalidate the presence of an absent vision, the painter in *Emilia Galotti* would cut short the mediation of both hands. Lessing in turn looks forward to a related sacrificial exchange: "But should it be the case that as long as I had the physical eye, its sphere would also be the sphere of my inner eye, then I would, to free myself of this limitation, deem the loss of the former to be of greater value" (9:91). In *Emilia Galotti* Count Appiani thus paints with his eyes—like yet another Raphael without hands—an image of Emilia that cannot vary. When Emilia informs him that she will wear on their wedding day the dress she wore on the day he first saw her, Appiani can assure her that, already from his end, each time he has seen her since that first day, she has not appeared otherwise (2:404). The shutdown of the outer sensorium guards an inner vision that keeps Emilia always in her wedding gown.

Outside the marriage ceremony, the bridal gown is worn in anticipation of Death's arrival. Karl Abraham examined this neurotic ceremony as practiced by women patients who, before going to bed, deck themselves out as virgin brides. In one case, a woman puts on the attire appropriate to the time zone when her father was still alive. Positioned on the bed like a corpse, she dreads the arrival of what she calls the "big snake," but which Abraham views as the incubus of her dead father. "At the conscious level she of course awaits not the father but Death. The analysis shows, however, that the two conceptions are identical. In fantasy, especially in the dreams of the patient, surprise attack and violent assault play a big role. She adopts in her fantasies a masochistic position; she awaits death from the man's—the father's!—sexual assault. She experiences in fantasy the fate of the Asra 'who die, when they love.' "[9]

This ceremonial of the bride of Death frames what Lessing placed at the center of the visual arts: the "pregnant moment." Upon receiving the "immutable duration" conferred by pictorial representation—which in the corresponding ceremonial or tableau vivant the daughter must deliver and embody—only the "pregnant moment" can withstand "repeated viewing:" "the painter's works are made to be beheld, beheld at length and repeatedly, and not simply glimpsed." Thus the perspective ultimately of Death or the dead father governs the selection of moments to be embalmed. The intensely transitory moment cannot be both repeated—swallowed—and held down. "All such phenomena"—Lessing is contemplating the libidinal outburst of laughter—"receive such an unnatural appearance through the prolongation of art that the impression grows weaker with every repeated viewing such that in the final analysis the whole object inspires dread and disgust" (9:19–20).

The moment pregnant with death marks a turn in the reception of death and the dead which, in the context of German letters, Lessing was the first to take. In his essay "How the Ancients Depicted Death," Lessing argued that the skeletons found in works from antiquity represent not death as such, as would be the case in Christian iconography—though even there, he stressed, they must first be armed with some allegorical attribute like the scythe—but rather instances of violent dying. Death was represented by the ancients as the twin brother of Sleep (9:23). Lessing's essay thus represents a certain secularization and individualization of mourning which, beginning with the Enlightenment, required the banishment of fear of death along with its accoutrements, skeleton and scythe. Death is natural; soon it will be declared beautiful. But death was recast as natural to the extent that it was now interpreted as disease; thus this natural death had to be separated from the living for hygienic reasons. In a move that found its model in antiquity, the dead were buried no longer in the polis but outside in separate zones. The already buried were accordingly relocated; in Paris twenty thousand corpses were exhumed and dumped into outlying stone quarries.

But the move to naturalize death on the way to its aesthetization ran up against the tomb of what had at the same time been repressed. As the direct result of evidence of premature burial uncovered during the mass exhumations required by the new segregation of the living from the dead, there arose in place of the fear of death attributed to medieval Christianity a new dread fear of being buried alive. The niche the exquisite sleeping corpse was to occupy thus turned out to be the defective keystone of the new improved conception of death. Beginning, then, with the Enlightenment, death becomes uncanny: an indeterminate zone of close-range doubling which, to the extent that sleep is its model, now more than ever can be kept in some other place only via repression, whereby it returns. At one end a whole bureaucracy of death watch and certification had to be inserted between death and burial to ascertain on which side of death each doubling of death and sleep transpired. At the other end we find a renewed interest, on the part of German scholars, in vampirism, the subject between 1728 and 1734 of seven major treatises.

Insurance first emerges in place of this doubling of death. But before it became the premier insurance firm, Lloyd's of London was a coffee house. By the time the wine press had been pressed into the service of printing, coffee substituted for the "wine" it translated: "Dear, melancholy coffee," we read in Lessing's *Minna von Barnhelm* (2:227). Ever since Aristotle, wine has been the drink of melancholics; but black bile thus acquired another analogue and agent when, just in time for the advent of the Enlightenment, coffee was introduced in Europe. Lloyd's of London accordingly holds the exemplary place of transit between

65

conceptions of melancholia. From a humoral disorder which strikes selectively, either giving rise to genius in the one so inclined or incapacitating a certain physical type always predisposed to the illness, melancholia became the specter of uninsurable loss which endangers even innocent bystanders. Beginning with the utopia Burton interposed in *Anatomy of Melancholy* as his plan for the deliverance of the state from the paralysis of melancholia, excess of burnt bile has posed a threat which must be outlawed from future societies. According to a nineteenth-century projection of some future utopia, telephones would be a required part of every household because the call of the phone always banishes the idle, harmful thoughts of incipient melancholia. Even in the future, then, melancholia threatens, between phone calls, to penetrate and paralyze systems of insurance and defense.[10]

In a culture ruled by insurance and propelled toward nihilism, even the most marginal existence must seek the cover of equal status. Enter the unborn fetus which, according to certain eighteenth-century tracts, occupies interchangeable places with the melancholic. When his mother, still pregnant with him at the time, received the shock of terrible fright, the melancholic blood and compressed heart of a certain Adam Bernd were already in place.[11] The precedent for this maternal transmission of injury was set when another expectant mother, upon observing a criminal being tortured on the wheel, later gave birth to a child with a broken arm. While watching the torture, the pregnant woman had, on empathetic channels, imagined her own arm being fractured. The internal vital spirits summoned by her threatened limb arrived in such force that the fetus, which was not yet distinguishable from the mother, received the fracture.

The melancholic remains as helpless as this injured unborn. A terrible image can "imprint" itself indelibly onto his brain such that the melancholic, who cannot help but take it to be real, is at its disposal. Once damaged, the pneumatic machinery of the soul will always turn itself on whenever a violent image strikes; the mechanism then torments the melancholic's tender conscience, his maternal legacy. In Bernd's case the idea and image of a knife pressed against his throat suddenly and unexpectedly entered and overwhelmed his mental mechanism. Involuntarily he thought of suicide; the more he retreated, horrified, from the unanticipated and unwelcome thought, the more deeply it "imprinted itself." The vital spirits, which rush to each trace that the image of suicide engraves and leaves behind, reanimate the image or idea even as the melancholic rejects it; Bernd cannot glimpse a knife without seeing and being overwhelmed by the scene in which he must turn the knife against himself.

In *Emilia Galotti* Count Appiani is strapped into the machine of his melancholia: at the other end we find the "machinery of dramatic events" which claims him as its first casualty.[12] The instrument of his imagination is accordingly "disposed to take in sad pictures" (2:404): pearls that metamorphose into tears, goals and clocks that either expand inside him or swallow him whole. Since, according to Appiani, "just one step away from the goal, or to have not even started out yet, is essentially the same" (2:405), he must race against the internal hand of a clock: "Yes, if time were only outside us! If one minute by the hand of the clock could not expand in us to years!" (2:404).

When melancholia is at the controls, the imagination efficiently retraces every terrible image or thought it can no longer leave out of the picture. According to Marshall McLuhan, this reflects a phantasmic reception of the merger of two media, clock and print, which together rendered both time and time's messenger, language, visualizable. As is the case in *Macbeth*, the future could now be seen to proceed "to the last syllable of recorded time."[13] The laterna magica already reserved a place for the phantom thought control which, in certain paranoid delusions, clock and camera would administer. Thus it was recommended that the first demon shows be performed every night and in every household to keep sinners in check; at the eighteenth-century ghost and mummy attractions, those in attendance would consult the commands of their dead in occult settings supplemented by electro shock. In between the haunted contexts that thus frame it, we find the craze current at the end of the seventeenth century: projection via laterna magica of the face of a clock. Abstract time, according to McLuhan, built man-the-machine, which it then put on automatic. The visualizing agencies of print and measured time replaced the sense of smell—the natural partner of memory—and programmed man to eat when it was time to eat.

Adorno and Horkheimer argue that the sense of smell always

admits the closest rapport with the other: "When we see we remain what we are; but when we smell we are taken over by otherness. Hence the sense of smell is considered a disgrace in civilization, the sign of lower social strata, lesser races and base animals." According to Freud, loathing of the body commenced when man walked upright at a distance from the smells of the other, with the result being that today, according to Adorno and Horkheimer, the despised body is now the corpse that must be disposed of in a lifetime of rehearsals: "personality scarcely signifies anything more than shining white teeth and freedom from body odor and emotions."[14] In these dress rehearsals we dress the wound inflicted by the *Uhrphänomen* time. Revenge, which Zarathustra defines as ill will against the "it was" of time,[15] emerges as surrogate and reversal of the lost smell bond with the other. In German "to seek revenge" shared its old participial form, which was occasionally yet current in the eighteenth century (see Schiller's *Don Carlos*), with that of the verb "to smell": *gerochen*.

When smell beats another retreat, man's sensual center has moved even further away from the mother on all fours—from periodicity in sex according to the menstrual cycle—and ever closer to the genitals, the visual center of the upright body. This shift, which must be repeated over and again, marks, Freud argues, the foundation of the family.[16] What lies outside this family is the maternal blood bond: just as maternal deities were banished, together with their fertility and death cults, by the monotheisms, so the mother, everyone's premier deity, is deposed by the father-god. But when we smell the stink of the vampire, a whiff of the blood bond with the mother returns and retreats. A contraption of blood that reproduces and recycles only blood, the vampire, indeed every monster, circumvents semen. Every monster is mummy.

At the end of Le Fanu's vampire tale "Carmilla," Laura, who has only recently been rescued from cross-over into the undead realm, joins her father on a sight-seeing tour through Italy, as though this upright view could put her back on her feet, away from the image of the vampire sniffing at the door. Every vampire is constrained to rest in some genuine burial ground which has at the same time been deceptively or improperly used. In the case of Countess Carmilla, the vampire is condemned to hold onto all the letters of her name Mircalla, which she can rearrange as Millarca or Carmilla, for example, but only within the confines of the given letters. So too her place of burial cannot be removed but only displaced within the family vault, and even the letters on this tomb which has been shunted to the side must remain legible.

Carmilla bears one living dead name in the wake of another name's extinction: the last bearer of her surname Karnstein long ceased to exist. Another patronymic, which Carmilla's host shares with his daughter Laura, is never revealed in the story; it is some English name, a foreign body in central Europe. Another unsayable word or foreign body, this time in the context of the English text, is the apparently untranslatable *schloss* which, like a proper name, cannot vary. It is this *schloss* which holds the little-known "resources" and recesses of "life and death."[17]

The ban on translating *schloss* turns up the volume of its literal meanings, the most prominent of which traverse *schliessen,* "to lock up." Carmilla's nocturnal habit of locking her bedroom door is soon adopted by Laura, who even keeps a light flickering in the vault that gives her "rest in peace."[18] And yet Laura soon discovers and concedes that "dreams laugh at locksmiths." Laura's dreams feature a deep female voice which speaks from a distance, though one night a sweeter voice, at once more tender and more terrible, resounds at close range: "Your mother wants you to beware of the assassin."[19] Taking the warning to signal that her guest is in danger, Laura rushes to Carmilla's room but finds the door locked. The door is forced open: Carmilla is gone.

Carmilla and Laura share an eidetic memory in which Carmilla tries to soothe or seduce little Laura crying in her crib. But the transition from crib to crypt comes to a deadlock. When Carmilla proposes that each "sweetly die" into the other's "warm life," or that each be the other's torment and rapture, Laura remains on the other side of ambivalence: "In these mysterious moods I did not like her. . . . I was conscious of a love growing into adoration, and also of abhorrence." Laura, who responds to Carmilla's "murmured words" as though they were "a lullaby,"[20] lost her mother at such an early age that she cannot remember her. In place of the missing souvenir she finds Carmilla, sealed in but gone. Carmilla, who first appears to Laura and her father as she is being lifted out of an overturned carriage—emblem of birth—and placed alongside her mother, in fact returns out of Laura's mother's dead past, Laura's mother having been maternally descended from the now extinct Karnsteins. Laura alone sees that among the family portraits which had been in her mother's possession the icon of Countess Mircalla is the double of Carmilla's image. The Karnstein line, Laura's multiply maternal lineage, thus retains the "mysterious state"[21] and power of return which the portrait, in Laura's eyes, has already vouchsafed. Ghostbusters first discern tremors emanating from a crypt in the stammering of a name within the frame of the name's unvarying portrait—its untranslatable *schloss.*

ANAGRAMS OF MADNESS

Cultural rereadings of eighteenth-century structures of thought have found, already in place, certain Freudian primal structures. Psychoanalytic hermeneutics thus begins with Wilhelm Meister, who, in order to understand Hamlet before he can perform the role, reconstructs Hamlet's past or childhood and his future: what he could have become. Freud in turn interprets *Hamlet* as though it were this *Bildungsroman;* in order to uncover or supply Hamlet's unconscious, Freud must locate the erotic relation to the mother in early childhood. Set apart from the psychoanalytic interpretation of *Hamlet,* psychoanalytic praxis, however, finds its rehearsal and repetition not in Goethe's *Bildungsroman* but in Lessing's bourgeois dramas, which chart the vicissitudes of what Freud called the mechanism of transference.[22]

In these scenarios the child's transfer of love for parents to others is vouchsafed by the father: Sara Sampson, for instance, can connect love for father to her fiancé's incoming demand for affection only to the extent that her father has already given the go ahead. "Fate" (*Schicksal*) thus did Sara a good turn by letting go that which does not let go: having died in giving birth to Sara, her mother was not around to tyrannize her with a mother's love. To fate, then, she is grateful for supplying her with a father who never gave her any cause to yearn for the missing mother (2:317). Lessing's transferential scenarios, which thus dispense with the

money??
fairy tales?

70

mother entirely, literalize the father's status as substitute for the object of the child's most original desire. Within this order of substitution, which the father introduces and embodies, the father does not, however, take second place, nor does he make any lasting demand on the child's devotion, as the other parent apparently must. Although all the conditions necessary for successful transference are thus satisfied in *Miss Sara Sampson,* the transfer is nevertheless impeded or haunted by the mother's fiendish return. According to the nightmare which afflicts Sara at the beginning of the play, Marwood, who poisons Sara, occupies the place of that tyrannical mother Sara had, in her role as "matricide," deposed: "through no fault of mine" (2:316). In the nightmare, which Sara herself sees as finding fulfillment in Marwood's vengeance, Sara was rescued—given life—only to be stabbed to death by someone she describes as "a person resembling me" (2:275).

In the transferences Freud recorded—those of Ratman, for example—the absence of the mother, specifically the death of Freud's mother, is, in one of Ratman's dreams, conveyed in a letter which, though legibly addressed to Freud, contains the cryptic message p.f.: *pour féliciter* in lieu of *pour condoler,* of course, but also *pour Freud.*[23] In the case study of Dora, where Freud first discovered and demarcated the context of transference, the mother is "nothing"—to husband, daughter, and Freud. Freud thus attends a bourgeois father-daughter drama where the mother has been shunted aside to reveal the encyclopedic and typographic terrain of what Freud hopes will have been Dora's transference neurosis. Dora's description of a painting depicting "Nymphae" reveals to Freud that Dora has explored and penetrated a vast female body which she reconstructed out of terms taken from the encyclopedia. Dora protests that she had consulted the encyclopedia only once, when, upon receipt of a letter from her uncle informing her that her cousin's appendicitis made it impossible for her to come visit, she sought the meaning of her cousin's ailment. Dora's beloved aunt, who had also been kept out of reach by her cousin's inclement health, soon died, whereupon Dora developed appendicitis.

This hysterical symptom formation confirms Freud's earliest conjectures regarding melancholia, though the ambivalence toward parents central to these conjectures has been displaced or circumvented in the avuncular context of aberrant mourning. Nevertheless, there remains something which exceeds or drags behind this episode and signals to Freud its underlying Oedipal context. The niece in mourning holds onto a single symptom left over from her false appendicitis. Like Fräulein Montag in *The Trial,* Dora drags one foot. She commences dragging her foot exactly nine months after her rejection of Herr K.'s proposition. Freud is eager to find a childhood rehearsal of this foot symptom in Dora's history, and soon stumbles on the missing recollection: while yet a child Dora had in fact injured the same foot in a fall down stairs. Once fallen, Dora is left with a swollen foot, an "Oedipal" foot, which Freud translates into Dora's *Fehltritt* or faux pas. Her unconscious has thus made restitution for her seeming rejection of Herr K. by giving birth, once again, to her Oedipus. Though Freud concludes that he and Dora meet at last in one pregnant moment of transference, Dora next shuts the case and departs, still dragging a foot which does not, however, correspond to some secretly desired transgression with father and father substitute. What follows Dora's departure is a footnote in which Freud acknowledges that he had overlooked Dora's homosexual bond with Frau K., who, above and beyond any encyclopedia, was Dora's main source of sexual knowledge.

This footnote is dropped in the midst of Freud's belated recognition of the role which transference should have played in his treatment of Dora. In general, Freud later admitted, he had not taken the <u>mother-infant relation</u> into theoretical account because the father-transferences made onto him always blocked his view.[24] In "On the Dynamics of Transference," however, Freud allowed that a patient's transference onto the treating analyst need not always take the father as model but could also be the result of a <u>mother or brother imago</u>. And yet the primal transference could only be made onto the father, the father of psychoanalysis: when it came to female homosexuality Freud would advertise that he never accepted mother-transferences.

In Lessing's dramas those declared demented—the "delirious women," for example, to whom Emil Staiger first directed attention[25]—though situated on the periphery of the transferential precincts, yet superintend the very switches of an extra-familial system of transfer: the post, at once a place of loss and the refuge of overinterpretation. In *Emilia Galotti,* as Goethe observed, each time fate (*Schicksal*) intervenes, the Countess Orsina is the agent of its sending and receiving operations.[26] First it is the coincidental absence of a response to her letter to the Prince which prompts her to undertake her, as it turns out, premature journey to Dosalo. Then once at Dosalo it is her knife, though not in her hands, which cuts short the Prince's intrigues. When Odoardo Galotti searches his cavernous pockets muttering, "Nothing! nothing at all! nowhere!" Orsina gets the message and loans him the missing knife (2:436). In *Miss Sara Sampson* it is through the post that Marwood, in a letter to Sara's father, first aimed to derange Sara's marriage plans. Having served instead to bring Sara and her father back together, Marwood, taken unawares by this father who could render "poisonous" missives remedies, must give Sara literal poison, which she now calls "medicine" (2:338).

Marwood represents, to the point of bearing a "barb," the phallic mother—a veritable "Medea"—who returns from the other end of the pre-Oedipal bond with the nursing mother to dispense poison, the nourishment that sickens.[27] Poison can be administered only close-range: hence in place of the poison she also carries with her, Orsina must take aim with a knife which can be conveyed only by proxy. In the place of this knife's target there emerges a pregnant moment which engenders father and daughter "a second time." Orsina inhabits the murderously engendering trajectory of these missives also to the extent that she bears "rigid Medusa eyes" (2:382). Orsina thus becomes *Urszene:* Medusa embodies, according to Freud, that primal scene—the sight of the mother's genitals—which instills in the boy a terror of castration which he commemorates with rock-hard erection. Through her own erect Medusean eyes, Orsina joins Abraham and Freud in adding to the mother in this scene the phallic attribute: the Medusa figure, like the spider symbol, thus emerges, even at this end of her reception, as phallic mother.[28]

Dora's mother is granted a comeback as Frau K., the mother who owes her admittance to the footnote to the text of her exclusion. According to Freud, the female homosexual couple plays mother and child as much as man and woman:[29] the phallic mother remains their center of attraction. Even in heterosexual love, which Freud sees as being always out of phase, it is the man's Oedipal fixation on his mother which is attracted to the woman's pre-Oedipal bond with the phallic mother.[30] As Freud instructs in his essay on Leonardo da Vinci, the so-called androgeny of certain ancient goddesses worshipped by men and women alike in fact refers in each case to a mother who comes fully equipped.

To receive funerary inscriptions the mourner puts his best foot forward, though other extremities are also offered: hence vampires suck blood as often from the soles of feet and the ears as from the throat. The appendage chosen for ritual mutilation bears association with the mother, in particular when the left hand, foot, or ear is marked by mourning tattoo. According to Freud, foot fetishism, which is predicated, however secretly, on the primal urge to smell all the sources of body odor, always recalls the maternal phallus. It is always in a footnote—in the underworld—that Freud equips the mother to claim equal rights alongside the father. In the footnote to his claim that the primal and primary identification is always with the father, Freud allows that the premier identification can also be with the phallic mother, in which case, however, Oedipal resolution would remain indefinitely postponed. Thus in Freud's study of female paranoia, just as the paranoid prepares to transfer libido to the man who courts her, the maternal bond returns, in this case as a shrouded photographic *Kästchen;* although her gentleman friend assures her that the ticking she hears must come from a clock, the paranoid, who cannot trust the words of one in league with her mother-substitute, knows that a camera has recorded evidence that will make her yield to impregnation.[31] The paranoid is always the superreader. As Freud explains in "Some Neurotic Mechanisms in Jealousy, Paranoia and Homosexuality," the paranoid projects cognizance he will not take of his own unconscious onto the unconscious of the other, which he reads with unmatched and unending exegetical skill.[32]

To overread and overinterpret is to abandon oneself to reason's automatic course unchecked by paternal guidance. True paternity (*wahre Vaterschaft*), we learn in *Nathan the Wise,* results not from any direct blood connection but rather from that "pure semen (*Samen*) of reason" which Nathan pours into the soul of his adoptive daughter by administering oral instruction in place of books and their "dead signs" (3:130). By instilling this semen into her soul, he insures that she will not be the "nothing," the *Nichts,* which would otherwise have been her lot (3:148). Nathan's strug-

female paranoid

74

gle to push back her *Vernichtung* is characterized by such opposi-
tions as medicine and poison or everything and nothing, opposi-
tions which, however, ever verge on mutual contamination since
they share the same domain. Language itself can be either poison
or remedy, Nathan instructs, its remedial course remaining contingent upon such fragile safeguards as his own benevolence and
adroitness. Without the safeguards only the true father can administer, the semen of reason engenders a tyrannical ego ideal which
censors and simulates the sensorium: "Imperiously [reason] prescribes what is fit for our senses, / renders itself ear of the ear, and
eye of the eye."[33]

In *The Education of Mankind* Lessing maintains that the solo
flight of reason (*Vernunft*) spirals down to disintegration and distraction, specifically, as he argues, with regard to the itinerary of
monotheism:

> If even the first human being came equipped with a concept of a unitary
> God, then this concept, imparted, not acquired, could persist in its purity for
> an impossibly long period of time. As soon as human reason, left to its own
> devices, began to refine it, it segmented the one and only immeasurable into
> numerous more measurable parts, and gave to each of these parts a distinc-
> tive mark (*Merkzeichen*). (13:416)

Spoken dialogue with the true father—the father or father-god
who is essentially an instructor—is the alternative to this parcelling
out and multiple stamping and addressing of a pure concept or
unique plenitude. Beyond this transference, reason and madness
become interchangeable. Enter Countess Orsina, the "philosopher" (2:428) who has been deranged by overreading (2:387). Her
very name is at once the anagram of *raison*.

Orsina, Herder observed, embodies reason in the midst of
utter madness.[34] To borrow terms of diagnosis from Kant's *Anthropology*, Orsina is mad with reason: this incurable derangement
leads the afflicted to interpret otherwise indifferent actions and
circumstances as menacing messages directed expressly against
them. The cause of Orsina's affliction, again in Kant's lexicon,
would be distraction: the reading of novels is particularly condu-
cive to the fragmented thoughts characteristic of distraction, for it
invites the reader more to digressive invention or visualization
than to the conjoining of ideas according to the unity of understand-

ing. Women, who are, Kant remarks, customarily not given to distraction, will, however, become distracted and ultimately insane if they devote themselves to learning.[35]

A certain transvestism of reason afflicts the man "buried beneath his books" and the man who spends recklessly what is his own, since both come under the rule of, or comparison with, woman, who by definition spends what is not her own. Without legal representation women are, Kant continues, rightly bereft of any legal status, though their power at home is for this reason aggrandized and their learned husbands even take pleasure in deferring to them in all domestic matters. This feminization of the household is accordingly most complete in the case of spendthrifts, men who lose their legal status and are classified, like women, as children or imbeciles.[36] Though Kant is otherwise quick to disclaim any injurious effect of too much learning on a young male pupil or student—unless, however, he has, because already damaged, a predilection for "mystical" books[37]—his examples of excessive reading and of its manic counterpart, overspending, describe a risk of derangement, even of crossing over into the other gender.

Orsina fears that she has become so masculinized by overreading that she comes across as a dandy: "A woman who thinks is as disgusting as a man who wears make-up" (2:428). In certain ancient and contemporary cultures we see what make-up originally and always was: a mourning mask, made up of ashes, excrement, and blood, which women must wear in the face of death. The men of the tribe keep apart to conceive and execute plans of vengeance directed against rival communities or inimical spirits. Through dark make-up the mourning woman identifies with the livid spots of the corpse, or, when white is chosen, with its paleness. In some cultures the practice of burning the widow of the deceased thus comes to be replaced by the make-up put on by mourning women who, by scratching themselves, supply the ingredient of blood. The mourning mask is also a blood offering which pays protection to the ghosts of dead tribal members ever in search of new victims.

The man who cannot stop mourning and the woman who, thinking, must take revenge both end up mourning for lost heterosexual libido.[38] The woman who worries that in contemplating revenge, indeed a veritable philosophy of revenge, she ends up

resembling a made-up man calls for a shut down of *Lust.* Like the
hypnotist who effects a trance through the surprise fright of a
sudden yell—a technique Ferenczi compares to the paralyzing effect of Medusa's head[39]—Orsina sets about "poisoning" and de-
ranging Odoardo so that he will "speak" to the Prince with a knife:
"You have understanding (*Verstand*); and it will cost me only one
word—and you will no longer have any" (2:435). The specter of
the single word immediately takes hold. Odoardo must beg her to
deliver the single sense of her words, and not dribble her "poison."
At last Orsina complies: "Here then; put the letters of it together
yourself! This morning the prince spoke to your daughter at
church, this afternoon he has her at his pleasure–pleasure palace
(*Lust-Lustschlosse*)" (2:435). The last word spoken by Orsina on
her way to enlightening Odoardo with a "single word" is characterized by a gap in articulation—*Lust-Lustschlosse*—a stammer which
fulfills Orsina's assurance to Odoardo that with a single word she
will rob him of his judgment and sanity. Driven mad by Orsina's
single word, the stammering irruption of the madness of *Lust,* and
aspiring now to effect a closure of pleasure—a *Schloss,* a *Schliessen*
of *Lust,* a *Lust-Schluss*—Odoardo discovers that he is at a loss: he
searches his pockets only to find "Nothing!" on his person. The
delirious phallic woman thus loans him the knife with which she, a
veritable "Bacchante" in the company of "the entire army of abandoned women," imagined cutting out the heart which the Prince
had promised to her and to the other "Furies" (2:436–37).

Denatured woman drops the mourning mask and plunges
into a blood bath which is also always a sacrificial offering to the
spirits which operate from behind the mirror. Only blood offered
to the phantoms of the reversed world of the dead empowers them
to speak and requires them to answer questions. The mirror from
which Conti allegedly stole Emilia's image (2:383) will not give
back Orsina's image. Orsina is first represented in the play not by
her portrait, which, according to the Prince, fails to show her true
character, but by her bitter words, which the painter quotes: "Oh
the true original," the Prince confirms (2:382). Another Countess,
the historical exemplar of the vampire legend, Elisabeth Bathòry,
sought to propitiate the spirit behind her mirror, which she believed was taking her looks away, by bathing in the blood which

Furies - Bacchae — women
who seek blood, Vengeance - dont
give aun blood @ mark; act insane

had shown astringent properties when it accidently spurted onto her face from the maid she had slapped. By bathing in the blood of 650 virgins, Elisabeth offered sacrifice to the mirror spirit to whom, during menopause, she, doubled over the mirror, addressed incantations two hours each day. The mirror is an ancient medium: it contains and opens onto the realm of bloodsucking ghosts. In Transylvania the mirrors were always covered over when someone died; otherwise the deceased's spirit would exit through the mirror from which it could only return as that vampire which shows its pedigree by casting no mirror reflection of its own. In the face of the mirror's ghostly power both Countess Bathòry and Countess Orsina become frenzied, murderous readers of omens.

Orsina enters the *Lustschloss,* the stricken zone of the Prince's "indifference" (*Gleichgültigkeit*) toward her, to regain her mirror image within the zone of its loss. First she broods on the very word *Gleichgültigkeit* which conveys not only indifference but also, literally, equivalence and interchangeability. Orsina defines *Gleichgültigkeit*—which, in having supplanted the Prince's love for her, as Marinelli suggests, would have replaced "something" with "nothing"—as an "empty word, a mere noise which corresponds to nothing, nothing at all" (2:427). "The soul is indifferent to that about which it does not think," Orsina reasons; "only to a thing which for it is not a thing. And indifferent only for a thing that is not a thing, —that is the same as being not at all indifferent" (2:427–28).

To assuage the anxiety Emilia feels following her encounter with the Prince in church, her mother Claudia assures Emilia that the Prince's "language of gallantry" is but an "unmeaning language": "Nothing in this language sounds like everything, everything amounts in it to nothing" (2:402). Yet at the end of the drama Emilia has only two interpretations of her plight: "Either nothing is lost: or everything is" (2:447). For Emilia's recognition of the power of the empty and indifferent word is such that she can view a dagger and a hair pin as equivalent and interchangeable:

EMILIA: Me, my father, give me that dagger.
ODOARDO: Child, it is no hair pin.
EMILIA: Then let the hair pin become a dagger! —It's all the same [*Gleichviel*]. (2:448)

As attested by the laughter of even the first audiences, Emilia's equation of her hair pin with her father's knife belongs to *Lustspiel* (comedy)—just as *Emilia Galotti* as a whole, according to August Schlegel, reflects transfer of the cool eavesdropping attitude of comedy to the tragic realm.[40] The comedy of sexual difference, of that meeting of gender traits in transit which excessive reading and interpretation always summons, was Lessing's first or primal dramatic conception.

In the preface to the first collection of his early plays, Lessing reflected that his own acquaintance with the sort of folly that results from an excessive absorption with reading had led him to write such comedies (*Lustspiele*) as his first full-fledged dramatic work *The Young Scholar:* "Already in those years when my acquaintance with people was restricted to books—he is to be envied who never gets to know them better—I was occupied with imitations of fools, whose existence did not concern me. . . . How I long to have those years back; the only ones in which I lived happily." In *The Young Scholar,* the overreader Damis retains and preserves a postal destination which, in between books, he repeatedly formulates as the question which in fact opens the play: "Has the mail (*die Post*) not yet arrived?" His father fears that Damis, who has no proper disposition (*Gemüthsart*) but adopts a new one with each book he reads (1:300), has, through overreading, already ingested some transsexual enzyme: "You have read enough dead books; look at a living one for a change" (1:287). The father thus takes Damis's unwillingness to exchange scholarly solitude for marriage to be an affront to Damis's dead mother, who was once alive: "your mother is turning in her grave. Keep in mind that she too was a woman!" (1:290). Following to the letter his father's analogy between books and women, Damis has access to his mother, who is not now a living woman, through the overreading of dead books. When the family gathers together to celebrate and seal Damis's acquiescence in his father's marriage plans for him by eating a common repast and past, Damis does not eat, exchange glances or words, but continues to read and overread.

Shortly after the premier performance of *The Young Scholar*—in which, as in his subsequent dramas, the mother was absent—Lessing received word from his father summoning him home to the mother's death bed. As it turned out, his father had lured him home under false pretext to reprimand and reform him, horrified as he had been by the news of his son's association with actors and the like. There followed a scene of reconciliation, in the corner of which Lessing's sister, in a frenzy of religious fervor, burned her brother's poems. Had Lessing in fact found his mother dying, he would have found, on the rebound, the primal scene of his writing, which thus had to be left out. Yet the fiction of a mother's death, which he had already employed to frame the relation between father and son, he now found already secretly reinstalled by his father within their relationship.

To Lessing's bevy of delirious legendary phallic women properly belongs Salomé, middle name of both Lessing's mother and sister. Salomé recalls a scenario in which Lessing was framed: Salomé, the stepdaughter and sexual obsession of a king, demands and receives the head of John the Baptist, the focus of her own obsession. At the other end of the castration which Salomé thus commands, her stepfather achieves consummation by having her in turn executed. In his marriage to Eva König, the widow of his close friend, Lessing also served as stepfather to her adolescent offspring—after whom, it was rumored, he lusted. At the close of their first year of marriage, Eva König died upon giving stillbirth to Traugott, Lessing's sole child and proper heir, to whom Lessing thus gave the same name his parents had given two of his brothers, who died in infancy. In place of the deaths of Eva König and Traugott, Lessing found himself alone with stepchildren.

God was Lessing's father's middle name: Johann Gottfried Lessing. Lessing's father's first born, who bore the father's name, died in infancy, whereupon the name was never again recycled. And yet Traugott was given twice more, first by Lessing's father and then by Lessing himself, after it had already acquired association with fatality. Trust in god (Traugott) became the bond between Lessing and his father when the latter used the fiction of the mother's death to communicate with his son. Rather than break this trust, the father's deception demonstrated that the absent father—the true father and father-god—could always tap into a son's phantasms of unmournable loss, and recast the mother shadowed by death as a mere prop in transferences under the father's remote control. This trust in god already counted casualties when Lessing again chose Traugott, this time to name his dead son, the second death of Lessing's father. The father's customary route of return had irrevocably closed. The detour left open had been rehearsed or anticipated in countless dramatic representations: the resurrection of the trust required one last live performance.

Lessing had been left alone with Eva König's children, including the sixteen-year-old Amalia. He thus found himself—at last—in the position the father already occupied in his dramas. During the last few years of his life Lessing was forced to defend himself in letters to friends against the rumor that after his wife's death he was holding on to Amalia as object of his not entirely reputable devotion. Dying in the home of the wine merchant Angott, Lessing delivered his desperate bid for incorporation. Bent over with grief just outside the door of the sick room, Amalia witnessed Lessing emerge stoically to pay his compliments to visitors. According to Amalia's recollection, Lessing mutely but with "an inexpressibly soulful look"—his countenance indicated "heavenly transfiguration"—pressed Amalia's hand. He then greeted his guests, whereupon he collapsed, dying with a smile on his face. The loss of such a father! On this and every other stage of Lessing's death-cult drama, we find that part of Lessing which, though afflicted, had been unable to reconstitute or retain the father. And this resurrection drama had been rehearsed and was now being repeated, always already using the secret name Amalia/Emilia.

The only time Emilia is not simply the mute medium of parental ventriloquism, according to Norbert Haas, is when, in the process of recounting to her mother her encounter with the Prince, she describes the way in which a certain "something" or "it" had placed itself close behind her in church.[41] Though she could not hear, and though she begged her guardian angel to smite her with deafness so that she would not hear, her narration to her mother of not hearing and not wanting to hear nevertheless amounts, according to Haas, to the stammering of Emilia's name in the accumulation and acceleration of vowel sounds: E-I-A/E-I-I-A. "*E*ben hatt' *i*ch m*i*ch . . . denn *i*ch k*a*m zu sp*ä*t . . . *E*ben f*i*ng *i*ch *a*n . . . *a*ls d*i*cht h*i*nter m*i*r *e*twas s*ei*nen Pl*a*tz nahm . . ." (2:399): E-A-I-I/E-I-A/E-I-I-A/A-I-I-I-E-A-EI-E-A-A. As she stammers out her name, Emilia relates that she had been immobilized, paralyzed. And what does she finally hear? "The name of your daughter" ("den Namen Ihrer Tochter"), Emilia defers to her mother, and then: "My name" ("*Meinen Namen*"; 2:400). When her mother asks her who accosted her in church, Emilia can only refer to *ihn selbst,* at once "him himself" and "it itself"; not until her mother presses her further can Emilia answer, "the Prince"—not Hettore Gonzaga, but *den Prinzen,* that is, *ihn selbst,* that is, *meinen Namen.* For whatever the Prince first says to her in church, all she hears is E-I-A/E-I-I-A: *meinen Namen.*

While glancing through petitions at the start of the play, the Prince glimpses the signature "Emilia" and at once takes it to signify "Emilia Galotti," though this is not in fact the case: "An Emilia? But a certain Emilia Bruneschi—not Galotti. . . . But her name is Emilia. Granted!" (2:379). If the signifier "Emilia" is not as compelling as Conti's portrait of "Emilia Galotti," then this reflects the completion "Emilia" finds in the portrait as the full signature "Emilia Galotti."

The Prince compares to a knife the deictic "She's the one" ("Eben die"), which can only point out and confirm that the Emilia whose portrait and signature are before him will soon marry: "Utter your accursed 'She's the one' again," the Prince exclaims to Marinelli, "and stab the dagger into my heart!" (2:388). Yet, once uttered, this knife-word, the very name Emilia, which the Prince conjures, does not stab him. The Prince deflects all danger directed against him, while the trajectory of this deflection leads to Emilia. Just as the dagger Orsina gives Odoardo at the end of the tragedy, though intended for the Prince, ends up in Emilia, so the Prince's knife-word strikes not him but Emilia; the Prince reacts to the knife-word intended for him by casting down the portrait of Emilia.

The knife-name Emilia travels the same route and is in a sense the same instrument as the dagger Orsina hands to Odoardo: Emilia thus achieves immolation by her own name. Indeed, this immolation amounts to emulation, to the literal enactment of the meaning of her name. It is by invoking the Virginia story that Emilia, true to the etymology of her name—"the emulating one"—compels her father to kill her. Emilia accuses Odoardo of not being a complete father, not the father he should be, not father enough to stab her and thus save her from disgrace: "In former days there was a father, who, to save his daughter from infamy, plunged the first, the best weapon into her heart—and thereby gave her life a second time. But

82

such deeds are past! Such fathers no longer exist!" (2:449). To this Odoardo immediately replies: "Yes they do my daughter, they do" (*Doch meine Tochter, Doch*)—yet it is the *Dolch* (dagger) with which he stabs her which enacts his *Doch,* his affirmation that such fathers as would wield a knife against their own daughters do in fact yet exist. Like Marinelli's *Eben die* to the Prince, itself an emphatic affirmative, Odoardo's exclamation harbors and conceals a knife-name, *Dolch,* and affirms an absence, that of the paternal knife. Thus this dagger—"the first, the best weapon"—returns in the form of the letter l which distinguishes *Dolch* from *Doch.* Emilia dies, then, by a graphemic knife-shape, the letter l, indeed by her own knife-name. What will mediate and separate the affirmative—together with the notions of identity, origin, and phallus which Odoardo's *Doch* involves—will be the phallic l shape, the *Dolch.*[42] Emilia's "pregnant moment," her insemination through *ihn selbst, den Dolch, den Prinzen,* that is, *meinen Namen,* always and already transpires in the name of the name and of nothing else—of everything and nothing.[43] The language of equivalence and indifference remains at once "mere noise" corresponding to "nothing" and the conduit of the sheer knife-name which "says everything" though in some former time.

In dying at her father's hand, Emilia reconstitutes the absent father, rendering Odoardo such a father. And in receiving what she takes to be her father's knife, or its synonym, her hair pin, Emilia creates her father anew by herself being created a second time. Essentially about the "fate of a daughter" (17:133) according to Lessing, *Emilia Galotti* presses toward that destination which all the sons or daughters in Lessing's dramas ultimately reach. The father thus must survive, the only alternate survivor being, according to *Nathan the Wise* and *Minna von Barnhelm,* the niece or *Nichte.* The father, who, to the extent that he occupies interchangeable places with death, is guarantor of the family's cohesion beyond each loss, cannot himself die. Instead the suicide mission of the daughter, which in turn detonates the nuclear family, achieves his continued existence. Thus Emilia's emulative death cannot help but engender, from pregnant moment to pregnant moment, tragically spectacular emulation. When Goethe's Werther takes his life, bowing his head before *Emilia Galotti* opened up on his desk, he also commemorates his own failure to become, like Emilia, the

83

true father's daughter. At the same time, however, this double failure proceeds to survive in place of Emilia Galotti's murderous telecommand, which Werther's own copycat suicides outdistance.

GOETHE PASSES LESSING ON THE *AUTOBAHN*

Subsequent to his brief analysis of *Hamlet* in *The Interpretation of Dreams*—an analysis which, as Freud acknowledged, he owed to Goethe's *Wilhelm Meister's Apprenticeship*—Freud again made reference to *Hamlet* in his 1905 essay "Psychopathic Characters on Stage" where he closed his discussion of Shakespeare's play with a citation from *Emilia Galotti:* "they who, under certain circumstances, do not lose their reason (*Verstand*), have none to lose." In book 5 of *Wilhelm Meister's Apprenticeship* we find tucked away in the extreme corner of the celebrated description of a *Hamlet* performance once again a brief reference to *Emilia Galotti,* specifically, as was the case with Freud, a reference to the Countess Orsina. Aurelia, who in the performance described in *Wilhelm Meister* plays the part of Orsina, exchanges madness for the indifference of her disenchanted lover. In her case, however, distress leads her, following the performance of the play, to summon suicide without herself committing it. As she withdraws into encroaching illness, Aurelia leaves behind a letter addressed to her unfaithful companion.

Both Goethe and Freud place *Emilia Galotti* alongside *Hamlet* where the ear—which, as is advised, should be lent to everyone while reserving the voice for a select few—nevertheless doubles as locus of the dissolution of Hamlet's legacy: Shakesp-ear. The plight of not being able not to hear resonates within *Wilhelm Meister* to the extent that Aurelia—*oreille*—assumes the role of the discarded Ohr-sina. It is in the ear that the madness of *Lust* irrupts. This is where Freud's citation fits back in: to rob Odoardo of his reason, Orsina points to that primal beyond of pleasure—that *Lust-Lustschloss*—where words and letters are interchangeable with knives.

84

In *Magic and Schizophrenia* we find this interchangeability of words and things etched within the cannibalistic delusions of certain patients. As Westerman Holstijn writes: "Often the patients declare that they themselves eat other people, or parts of other people. . . . A considerable part of their delusion may be summed up in the formula: they eat and are eaten." Géza Róheim comments: "Their persecutors appear most typically in cafes and restaurants; and patients of this sort attempt to sublimate their oral drives by studying philology or by inaugurating food reforms."[44]

A text is always also a tablet that invites swallowing: in certain cultures the medicine man or shaman writes down designations and paraphrases of his client's complaints alongside their corresponding diagnoses and cures. The prescription is washed off the tablet into a bowl from which doctor and patient drink the ink. Freud interprets *The Sorrows of Young Werther,* in a letter to Fliess dated May 31, 1897, as just such a tablet: it granted Goethe relief from suicidal proclivities which Werther's suicide thus kept in some other place. The course of treatment is preserved in Goethe's *The Triumph of Sentimentality* where the robot queen, once opened up, contains, deep in her insides, a copy of *Werther.* To blot up the close-range suicidal consequences of his own edible Oedipal past, Goethe had, at the same time, to swallow Lessing's *Emilia Galotti:* which is the first modern work of German letters also to the extent that it conducted the suicide mission it enacted and contained all the way to the other side of literature or performance.

Jerusalem, whom Goethe took as model for Werther upon learning of the circumstances attending his departure, killed himself with *Emilia Galotti* opened up before him on his desk. And *Emilia Galotti* continues to lie open before Werther as he carries out his suicide. But this utterly open and illegible reference also commits texticide. Thus Goethe would later claim that Lessing had used one of Goethe's texts to perpetrate murder. Friedrich Jacobi's account of Lessing's approval of Goethe's "Spinozistic" poem *Prometheus* literally caused, Goethe concluded, Moses Mendelssohn's sudden death.[45]

Werther and the suicidal frenzy the novel induced in its vast readership take over, over the corpse of its first casualty, the *Emilia Galotti* effect, which would henceforward proceed in Goethe's name. The series of emulations which Emilia's emulative

85

death engendered was blocked and appropriated by *Werther,* which in turn launched, as its own, a veritable genealogy of sui- cide by imitation. Frankenstein's monster is instructed in the means of self-destruction by *Werther,* which, as one of the three books the monster ever reads, is, like the android replica of the queen in *The Triumph of Sentimentality,* an actual ingredient of monstrous *Bildung.*

According to Goethe's mother, *Werther* accomplishes proper burial for actual events in Goethe's life which are thus commemo- rated and put to rest. But Goethe was haunted by *Werther.* The copycat suicides alone would introduce the ghost appearances of the discarded past. But Werther's improper burial at the novel's close, which was doubled in turn by Goethe's originally having published *Werther* anonymously, covers yet another improper burial: the incorporation or plagiarism of one of Lessing's effects. Goethe thus later compared *Emilia Galotti* to a mummy.[46] And yet that deflective trajectory Lessing discovered in *Emilia Galotti,* whereby the knives and knife-words destined for one body always end up in another's, also characterizes the murderous dispatch *Werther* embodies, which, even though its orbit remains between Lessing and Goethe, was first directed against a brother. *Werther* haunts him, Goethe reflects, like the unlaid ghost of a murdered brother.

In his essay on the childhood recollection Goethe recorded in *Dichtung und Wahrheit,* Freud unpacks the little one's antics at the window as enacting his bond with mother to the point of magically expelling all rival siblings back through the window womb. It is this relationship—Freud refers to it in short hand as Goethe's rapport with his mother—which, Freud concludes, is the source of Goe- the's great success. And yet Freud is moved to list those missing in action: the four dead little ones who found no place in Goethe's autobiography. The first fulfillment of Goethe's death wishes was thus the departure of his younger six-year-old brother Hermann Jakob, whose death was also the original occasion for Goethe's legendary refusal to mourn.

In the wake of his first cancer operations, however, Freud emerges in his Goethe essay from the footnote underworld to add that Goethe does in fact accord Hermann Jakob passing, but conclu- sive, reference. It is thus Freud who can recognize the death wish against a sibling only in the absence of any outward manifestation of its casualty's inclusion in the corpus. This inclusion always opens onto a mummy's tomb. As Freud notes in the original record of the Ratman case, the one who refuses to mourn believes and practices omnipotence of thoughts, especially in the form of its primal application—the death wish—to the full extent of entertaining ideas about survival after death which "are as consistently materialistic as those of the Ancient Egyptians."[47] Although in the case study proper Freud judges endless mourning for the father to be at the bottom of Ratman's obsessional neurosis, again in the footnote underworld Freud grants a dead sister "epic" significance in Ratman's fantasies.[48] And yet, Freud concludes, the terms and conditions of the analysis had precluded exploration of the sibling's crypt. In the original record, however, the dead sister Katharine rules absolutely: "What is the origin of his idea of his omnipotence?" Freud asks: "I believe it dates back to the first death in his family, that of Katherine."[49] In the corner of every primal scene presided over, according to the public record, by Ratman's dead father we find, in the original record: Katherine was there. "He had a memory that he first noticed the difference between the sexes when he saw his deceased sister Katherine (five years his senior) sitting on the pot, or something of the sort."[50] Another pot containing two rats which penetrate into or out of the anus first sends Ratman to Freud. As he listened to the officer recount this torture Ratman saw the ground heave in front of him as though there were a rat under it.[51] Under the case study a footnote allows that rats are chthonic animals that convey the souls of dead children.

Ratman is the name Freud bestows on his patient in a case he has recast as centering on a patronymic which emerges only to slip away like the rat out of the father's grave. Ratman's siblings call him *Leichenvogel*, carrion crow. In the original record, we find *Leichenvogel*, shortly after Katherine's departure, playing with a stuffed bird from his mother's hat: "As he was running along with it in his hands, its wings moved. He was terrified that it had come to life again, and threw it down. I thought of the connection with his sister's death . . . and I pointed out how his having thought this (about the bird) made it easier for him to believe afterwards in his father's resurrection."[52] But the father's resurrection cannot subsume his son's "necrophilic phantasy":[53] *Leichenvogel* heaves as though there were a rat inside him. "It is worth recalling in this connection," Róheim interjects in his case study of a hebephrenic pursued by the death wishes he launched against siblings, "that, among the Pitjentara of Australia, every second child is eaten by the siblings and parents in order to give them a kind of double strength; but if the baby survives until it acquires a name, the period of danger is over and it will not be eaten."[54] Thus it is dangerous to eat the sibling after it has acquired a name, the ticket entitling little one to proper mourning.

As his transferences attest, Ratman allows his dangerous past to emerge only by tapping into Freud's own: Ratman imagines Freud and his wife with a dead child between them. "The dead child can only be his sister Katherine, he must have gained by her death."[55] But Freud, thus charged with proper burial of a dead sibling, only discerns Ratman gaining—on him. Freud thus registers this gain on the other side of his own resistance, which emerges spectacularly at the start of the original record: "I have not mentioned from earlier sessions three interrelated memories dating from his fourth year, which he describes as his earliest ones and which refer to the death of his elder sister Katherine. . . . (It is curious that I am not certain whether these memories are his. . . .)" In the next entry Freud continues: "My uncertainty and forgetfulness . . . seem to be intimately connected. The memories were really his. . . . (They were forgotten owing to complexes of my own.)" "Once when he was very young," Freud now remembers, "and he and his sister were talking about death, she said: 'On my soul, if you die I shall kill myself.' "[56]

Suicide is always committed in the office of the other: according to Freud, suicide is always a pact that allows some internal other to exact retribution for death wishes, though only to the extent that both must ultimately stay or go.[57] The suicide pact covers that relationship to the dead Freud pursued under the rubric, borrowed from Ratman, of omnipotence of thoughts. The death wish, magic, the name, and the technical media are all applications of omnipotence of thoughts only to the extent that omnipotence must in each case be shared with a dead person. Because omnipotence of thoughts always turns around into a death wish, this pact between the dead and the living intercepts by phantomizing the rebound of hostile feelings.[58]

88

The force of nomination was, according to Freud, the premier stimulator and simulator of omnipotence of thoughts: the return trajectory of this force always and originally carried phantoms.[59] Thus the psychotic witnesses what is always the case: the name's dispatch and ghostly rebound. Words and objects accordingly billow apart for the psychotic only to the extent that both occupy, as always, interchangeable places. According to the delusional fantasies Freud, Jung, and Róheim have recorded, the psychotic must restore the connection to the outside by picking up the telephone. Words are thus treated as objects. Like the condemned man in the penal colony's torture apparatus—Kafka's primal representation of the telephone—the psychotic has a gag inserted into his throat. As Róheim's hebephrenic N.N. puts it: "When I say the word 'shoe,' a shoe would form itself in my mouth. . . . when I said 'street,' the whole street would be in my mouth, and it would be difficult for me to pronounce it. . . . I am talking and eating through some other part of my body than I ought to."[60] The name thus circulates only as gag, pun, or paronomasia. "My real name is N.S.N. But I have different variations of my last name. Sometimes my last name is N-x, or N-y, or N-z. I have finally decided to change my last name to 'Athol.' That is the name of a carpenter's drill. It is also the name of the cough drops you are eating."[61]

It is the taboo attached to the name on which Freud's theory of ghosts hinges: while other taboos would appear to offer the dead commemoration and even protection, the taboo on the name could only mean, Freud realized, that the living must in turn find protection from the vengeful return of the dead.[62] Because the call of the name would wake and summon its dead bearer, the name itself must be dismembered and concealed. Mourning costume accordingly turns out to be less a show of reverence than a retreat into camouflage; mourning rituals would then amount to desperate attempts on the part of the living to render themselves unrecognizable to the vengeful dead. Freud thus discovers in the scrambling of names the projective flight pattern of the death wish, which always brings back the dead.

The pact omnipotence of thoughts thus forges between the living and the dead takes the form, in each case, of prosthetic supplementation, which in turn always castrates that which it amplifies and extends. But castration and death cannot be represented but only embodied by their effects. Castration and death, which thus emerge only as some corpse to be exhumed, are always apprehended, however, as mutilation. According to the logic of doubling that gets Freud this far, mutilation is also always multiplication. Freud thus comes full circle by returning to the prosthesis. As is the case with any primal word, mutilation and multiplication converge only to the extent that they are linked and separated as a stammer. Róheim's patient Y.Z. speaks of multilation, a process which emerges from the other side of death:

> The people who are after the others put them in rocks or make the rocks freeze around them, and then they use the multilated ones as slaves to make gold. The sun, moon, and trees all must have people to make them and to keep them from freezing in the winter. These are the people who live in tombs and in statues. . . . The people who have the privilege to make children are those who have their *state right* or *ritual state right*. This means that they can *stay* the children, keep and hold them. I have this privilege. . . . they send children to me from Europe so that I should *stay* them. They have tried to multilate me and to kill me by sending two thousand people in a rock who were afflicted with pneumonia and full of phlegm to infect me. This is done by contact, by binding them together and then they would be bound to me. I wiped them all off my skin with a brush in a bath, and by sheer force I liberated them from the rock and liberated myself.[63]

Y.Z. thus describes the suicide pact with the dead which he calls multilation: at one end children are addressed, at the other the weather. Rainmaking emerges as the first ritual to focus on the child shadowed by death. In certain cultures changes in weather were summoned by pouring water over a small child. In other cultures the child selected for the rainmaking ritual had to be an orphan who was decorated with bushes and plants and with two desiccated frogs which were suspended from the child's ears. At the end of the singing and chanting the frogs were buried. Between the weather and missing children, the Goethe-effect, discovered by Avital Ronell, achieved its premier broadcast. As Ronell writes:

> The vapors . . . and the weighty yet invisible atmospheric pressures which at one time fascinated [Goethe] are quite similar to the development of the Goethe-formation itself. . . . To a certain degree, Goethe has grounded a concept based on the possibility of estimating or calculating in advance. . . . The sensible, invisible thing that Goethe thought to compute, to know in advance, as it advances . . . in the meantime has been assimilated to the delicate science of the Weather Forecast.[64]

In the long range, weather forecasting, by only anticipating its possible confirmation, follows out or succumbs to a certain logic of the signature which is always signed in the office of an other who can only be anticipated. These meteorological conditions of the signature dictate the terms of a suicide pact which Goethe, upon learning of the circumstances of Jerusalem's suicide, dramatized on both sides of what he called *Werther*.

Goethe's name was subjected to tampering right from the start: Herder detected in Goethe *Gott, Gothen,* and *Koth* (God, the Goths, and excrement), while Lenz divinized and adjectivalized the name as *das* Goethe-*liche*. Goethe in turn stages, in *Götz von Berlichingen,* the apocalypse of a name which also resonates his own. As his enemies close in, Götz comes to the end of the line where the name must be signed and countersigned. But without any heirs, he withdraws as sheer embodied name: "they have gradually dismembered me, my hand, my freedom, possessions and good name."[65] Goethe thus attaches this variant of his name—a variant which amounts to the superlative of the adjectivalization of Goethe, Götz-te—to that end of a line where the name is dispatched in isolation from its handing down. The name lifts off of the *Stamm* as stammer.

Already in the course of revising *Götz,* the first work to bring him acclaim, Goethe starts taking over by overtaking the *Emilia Galotti*-effect; he complains to Herder that already his first version of *Götz* appears, prior to *Emilia Galotti,* just like *Emilia Galotti. Götz* was right from the start, according to Goethe, so strictly thought out that one could, as with *Emilia Galotti,* guess the outcome of every scene, even anticipate every word. This notion, in effect, of sheer immediate thought is invoked in *Emilia Galotti* always as that which withdraws each time the hand intercedes in the execution of the eye's thought. In *Götz* hand and name embrace the series of their prosthetic supplementation: it is, in short, his right-hand man who ultimately betrays Götz and mutilates his good name.

Werther's every reflection on the disparity of eye and hand also originates in *Emilia Galotti.* In *Werther,* however, this incommensurability of eye and hand attends the handing down of legacies. Within the first fifteen pages of *Werther* we find no less than three legatees in pursuit of securing the equitable disposition of their respective inheritances. The double staging of some primal scene opens onto and surrounds Werther's own pursuit, in his expulsed state, of a patrimony: on the one hand, the "spectacle" of Lotte equitably dividing a loaf of bread among her younger siblings, giving to each an equal share apportioned according to age and appetite; on the other hand, the nightmarish vision of a phantom father returning to his ruined castle. The uncanny side of Werther's spectacles comes into focus as the legatees dispatched in the opening pages in pursuit of their inheritances return empty handed. Immediately following the news of multiple legacy derailments, Werther is overwhelmed by the impression that some puppeteer has been invisibly controlling his every move and choice right from the start: "As soon as one turns a hand, things are different with me." Or again: "I am being played like a marionette."[66] When Werther fills in for Lotte in the spectacle of equal and total distribution of bread among children, he can identify himself, in this scene of identification, only by telling the story of a princess invisibly served by hands.

Every choice (*Wahl*) Werther makes to advance to some other place repeats an earlier scene of departure. Werther arrives in the environs of Wahlheim as his mother's delegate in an inheritance dispute. When he chooses to take a detour on his way back, once again, to Wahlheim, he makes a pilgrimage to the place of his birth, which he and his mother left behind upon his father's death. To the extent that "there" and "here" are, Werther claims, interchangeable—"And ah! when we rush forward, when There becomes Here, everything before is the same as after" (29)—there can in effect be for him no departure from an earlier state. Even the dead, Werther pledges—thereby giving the layout of his repetition compulsion—return to the extent that they meet again. Suicide grants Werther audience with Lotte's dead mother and with God the father; but it also secures his return. Suicides were often buried at the crossroads outside town to prevent their phantoms from finding the way back home to prey on the living.

Sent by his mother to the scene of his father's departure, Werther encounters the spectacle of a mother who, in the absence of a father, divides the legacy without remainder. The bad news follows: the phantom father haunts the site of the squandered, ruined inheritance. Within this Oedipal scenario, Lotte's betrothed

92

occupies the place of the father since he alone among the sons in *Werther* receives a patrimony. Albert is accordingly in Werther's way, in such a way that the very thought that he might profit from Albert's death conducts Werther over and over again to the border of an abyss, a dash mark along which his thoughts are torn (122): "And you see, what oppresses me is that Albert does not seem to be as fortunate as he—hoped—as I—believed to be—if—I do not like to use dashes [*Gedankenstriche*], but here I cannot express myself any other way—and it seems to me plain enough" (82).

The calamity of a neighbor's empty-handed return from a legacy dispute is doubled by his youngest son's death. This passing of little Hans coincides with the onset of Werther's haunting—by little hands. And little Hans had, accordingly, presided over Werther's single satisfactory portrait. Werther emphasizes that he added nothing of his own to this portrait; instead he included everything surrounding little Hans and his brother. Though irreparably poor hand-to-eye coordination keeps Werther from rendering the perfect portrait—that portrait which Lotte, as the double of her dead mother, embodies for Werther (117)—the portrait of the brothers points the direction of Werther's art, which yields only silhouettes (*Schattenrisse*), dashlike outlines or hieroglyphs. In each of his moves away from some limitation and impediment—from the city to its natural environs, for example, or from the representation of Lotte to her silhouette—Werther is locked into an orbit that outlines that which he can neither leave behind nor bring into focus. The perfect portrait—the double or animated corpse—remains out of focus and out of reach: hand and eye attain synchrony only in the making of silhouettes, which in turn occupy interchangeable places with the dash marks punctuating and ripping Werther's thoughts whenever another death wish goes without saying. Werther has always only seen silhouettes; he acknowledges the affinity between his perceiving heart and a laterna magica, that painter without hands which generates silhouettes, of course, but also, as Werther calls the lantern's projections, "phantoms" (39).

At the time Goethe wrote *Werther* he was an adept at the physiognomic science of making and reading silhouettes. At a time when silhouettes were dispatched and exchanged through the post, like snapshots or postcards, even Goethe's love for Charlotte von

Stein commenced when he became infatuated with her silhouette, which preceded her. But while Lenz and Roderer jointly declared in a letter to Lavater that physiognomy allowed one to look on God face to face, Herder disparaged silhouettes as being mere "dead images."[67]

In accordance with the preeminence granted the hieroglyph as original inscription, the silhouette was deemed in the late eighteenth century the origin of the visual arts. Lavater and Winckelmann believed that the earliest attempts at drawing figures had aimed not to represent the actual bodily appearance of a person but rather to capture that person's essence, the outline of his shadow, that most ancient representation of the soul. This renewed interest in the silhouette as primal representation in turn resurrected Pliny the Elder's account of Dibutade outlining on the wall the shadow thrown by the lamp of the face of her departing lover. The silhouette accordingly delivers a perfect but finitizing portrait: one's silhouette is always and already the shadow of one's departure.

The shadows and dash marks intervening among eyes, ears, and hands finally afflict Werther's name, which is stammered on several occasions. For example: "The world for them had vanished. He . . . covered her trembling, stammering lips with frenzied kisses. 'Werther!' she cried out with smothered voice" (115). We can only speculate as to what the stuttered variant of Werther might be. *Wetter* (weather), for instance, comes readily to mind, a phenomenon with which Werther in fact entertains a secret identification. While dancing with Lotte for the first time, Werther is transformed: "I was no longer human. To have the most delightful creature in my arms and fly about with her like weather such that everything around us vanished" (25). The very rate of this "vanishing," which spins off Werther's silhouette, the shadow of his passing, is described in terms of weather-velocity: everything is driven into an eternally open grave, Werther forecasts, "since everything passes away with the speed of weather" (*mit der Wetterschnelle;* 52). The weather velocity that accelerates his passing also permits Werther—and Goethe—to keep guilty indebtedness in some other place. "Oh that I could be moody," Werther reflects, "could blame the weather" (*könnte die Schuld aufs Wetter . . . schieben;* 84). Upon learning of Jerusalem's suicide, the idea of *Werther* immediately crystallized, resembling in its preliminary state a glass of water so nearly frozen solid it required only the slightest shock to turn into ice. What had thus been conceived as a meteorological phenomenon was written down while Goethe was in a virtually unconscious state, as if sleepwalking. To control and apply the occult effects of the elements, themselves "colossal opponents" which reflected "caprice incarnate,"[68] Goethe always pursued the accurate weather forecast.

Goethe's conception of weather extended according to coordinates and associations which only Werther's phantom could have recognized. Whenever Goethe writes about weather—for example, in "Theory of Weather" and "Tribute to Howard"—he renders cloud formations and gale winds the phantoms they also conduct. By encouraging the establishment of weather stations throughout Germany, Goethe grants these phantoms a veritable telecommunications network. Goethe's meteorological analysis or application of occult phenomena gives the close-range *Werther* forecast in an essay entitled "Weather Conditions of the Literary Horizon" ("Meteore des literarischen Himmels") where cloud cover is secured for the rerouting of one writer's effects so that they might proceed in another's name.[69] Enacted at varying rates of velocity, now in reverse, now in anticipation, the weather conditions on literature's horizon are, in fact: Priority, Anticipation, Preoccupation, Plagiarism, Possession, and Usurpation.

Priority is a sensation nurtured in or as childhood which Anticipation, in turn, counters and subverts when evidence appears that one's own discovery was already made by some precursor. The English, Goethe notes, have aptly entitled this reversal Mortification, humiliation that kills off the self. "One sees oneself against one's will doubled, one finds oneself in a relation of rivalry with humanity and thus with oneself." The English accordingly introduced patent rights which, like logogryphs in the past, protect ideas not yet fully formulated from those who would bring them to market more expediently. Shifting from one market place to another, Goethe derides, under the rubric Plagiarism, proper citation as the weakness of most scholarship. As with the painter, who is never and always a plagiarist, Goethe stresses, the scholar, whose medium is inevitably another's ideas, should convey these ideas to a higher level rather than drop down always to the footnote of the other. Goethe marvels that plagiarism always circumvents detection precisely to the extent that this brand of occupation proceeds completely openly.

The worst mortification, however, results when a contemporary conceives independently the same idea one also contemplates. The contemporary precursor unleashes the most terrible rivalry, reflected in a vaster context by wars between nations. And yet, Goethe allows, certain thoughts and dispositions are simply in the air, as he actually puts it, such that they are accessible to many at the same time. Because air fills everything like a common collective soul inhabiting and uniting everyone, there are always several clever minds or spirits (*Geister*) who can pick up through the air what another man is thinking. Goethe recasts this observation in what he calls less mystical terms: "Certain conceptions ripen according to schedule. Even in different gardens fruits fall from the tree at the same time." Organic metaphors thus provide Goethe with a less mystical translation of air waves linking and separating *Geister*.

Weather prophecy always and originally issues from and interprets the stammering to which it owes its range of forecast. In turn, as Derrida has demonstrated, we always sign with our ears.[70] The signature, which fulfills its destiny only by being cast out and forecast, stammers out the name. It is along the pathway of the signature that Goethe outdistanced Lessing. Lessing always refused to engage his own name in his writing, in fact was consistent in his deprecation of the proper name as being but another arbitrary sign: "What miserable curiosity, this curiosity about a name! about a couple of letters, which are ordered this way or that" (8:198). Or again: "A beautiful title is more necessary to a book, than is a beautiful Christian name to a person" (16:90).

It is, appropriately, in a work fully organized around a single given name that we find Goethe's final passing reference to *Emilia Galotti*. In *Elective Affinities,* where the name Otto commands absolutely, both tombstones and names, which can be removed or changed, nevertheless assert themselves at the other end of every exertion or movement that would leave them in some other place. To these epitaphs, which thus always circulate as doubles, can be added the perfect portrait. To describe the execution of this perfect portrait, Goethe summons *Emilia Galotti* one last time and, for the first time, tampers with the sense. In *Emilia Galotti* the painter described the pathway from eye to hand in terms of the irreplaceable loss incurred along the way. In Goethe's version:

> Even those faces which the architect was left to paint alone gradually showed a very special quality; they all began to resemble Ottilie. The proximity of the beautiful child apparently had made such a lively impression on the soul of the young man that, by and by, he lost nothing on the long way from the eye to the hand, such that both, in the final analysis, worked together entirely harmoniously (*ganz gleichstimmig*).

As is clear from the way in which Ottilie's handwriting comes to be identical with Eduard's handwriting, the primary meaning of *Hand* in *Elective Affinities* is the signature,[71] that handwriting which, since it must ever be executed under visual superintendence, remains unaltered even by the advent of typescript. Eye and hand always work "harmoniously" (*gleichstimmig*) when the name is being signed, such that the signature is always a perfect portrait. The name at the center of *Elective Affinities* is at the same time one of Goethe's signatures or signature-supports inasmuch as Otto would be that skeletal outline, silhouette, or ear (*oto*) of Goethe's name, which had allowed such stammerings as *Gott, Gothen,* or even Galotti. Eduard's attachment to Ottilie, to her name as to his own names, had, he felt, been prescribed by the digraph OE etched onto a glass dating from his childhood; the digraph OE can thus be seen as the point of cohesion for this oto-biography. And yet, elsewhere, inaccessible to the ear, OE had already served as defective keystone. For OE is in fact that highly vulnerable center of Goethe's own name—vulnerable since, owing to the early uncertainty of its orthography, it could also be spelled with an O Umlaut, and even Goethe at first alternated between OE and O Umlaut signatures. As Benjamin emphasizes, *Elective Affinities* marks the commencement of Goethe's self-monumentalization. Goethe accordingly signs *Elective Affinities* with his name's perfect portrait and autograph: G-O-E-T-H-E.[72]

To close within the resonance of Goethe's names, it proves instructive to take cognizance of something that lay in Goethe's future, though in a sense he participated in its arrival—for example, as director of both the road construction and war committees, those two institutions which would together invent the *Autobahn.*

Indeed, that Goethe outdistanced Lessing along the pathway from eye to hand, along the very course of the signature, raises the issue of their respective velocities. Lessing had early on commenced composing a Faust drama which, he claimed, would revitalize German literature, and in which he claimed, in effect, that in the beginning was speed. When he got wind of Goethe's Faust plans Lessing at first took up the challenge, declaring that while the devil may well take his Faust, Lessing would take and overtake Goethe's. Later, however, in a mail coach somewhere between Dresden and Leipzig, Lessing's complete *Faust* manuscript, contained in a casket, was lost.

In closing, then, one final phantasmic stammer or rhyme: a certain Mr. Otto, born in 1832, contributed to the invention of the Auto, the operation of which, like the signing of the name, requires the simultaneous action of hand and eye. Driving and signing indeed remain the two ways—at least in California—in which identity is vouchsafed. And it is on this long way of signing or driving, on this Auto/Otto/Oto-bahn that Goethe is joined by Róheim's hebephrenic N.N., who concludes: "I called myself 'Race Track' because I would have liked to be on a race track going fast in a car."[73]

CHAPTER THREE
THE FATHER'S IMPRISONMENT

(Wilhelm Heinse)

According to *Geistesgeschichte* Wilhelm Heinse was a popular writer who, in his own lifetime, became the widow of his reputation and acclaim. And yet his untimely predictions of future achievements of the popular—the musical and military—*Geist* render Heinse one of the ghostwriters of the modern era. This secret reverberation, which can be conducted all the way to Nietzsche's Dionysus, commenced as the resonance Heinse's works found with Hölderlin, who dedicated his elegy "Bread and Wine" to Heinse before being beamed back to another time zone. Goethe, Schiller, and Wilhelm von Humboldt had witnessed only the ladies line up for this ecstatic cult of reception; at the other end of this line they accordingly dismissed Heinse's work as feminized celebration of "canine love." In terms amounting to a tentative definition of pornography, Goethe charged that Heinse had merely combined distinguishing and compartmentalizing thought with rank sensuality.

But what the greats of German letters thus took to be the investigation of a dog was conceived within Heinse's rapport with Hölderlin as the sublime departure from—and yet projection of—Kant's third yet "middle" critique. Hölderlin praised Heinse as that consummate traveler along the "eccentric track" who combined "boundless intellectual refinement" "with childlike innocence."[1] Heinse in turn lauded Hölderlin's apparent refusal, in *Hyperion,* to follow Kant on that trip in situ surrounded by stage scenery which Heinse saw as the sole trajectory mapped out by the first two critiques:

> Hyperion's letters are replete with lively sentiment and profound feeling. He is an apostle of nature. There are passages therein from p. 86 on which are so warm and penetrating, that they should move even old Kant and convert him from his mere appearance of all things. It is astonishing how the nordic philosopher has made so many learned persons believe that they could be content on the journey through life with painted wine and bread and ham, as long as one carries with one a certain talisman which he commissioned to this end, and for which factories could easily be laid out.[2]

Not only had he ostensibly refrained, like Hölderlin or Hyperion, from including among his travel provisions the painted victuals of the *Critique of Pure Reason* and the talisman of the *Critique of Practical Reason,*[3] but Heinse also steered clear of the goal of Kant's scenic tour, the "bridge" supplied in the *Critique of Judgment* between the two earlier critiques. Here Kant erected between understanding and reason a third faculty, a central or middle member (*Mittelglied*), in order to explain their reciprocal influence. A certain destiny of the *Mittelglied* was forecast when, in the third critique, Kant argued that in order to regard the beautiful or sublime in the human body, each limb (*Glied*) must be taken in isolation from the whole. "We must, in short," Paul de Man comments, "consider our limbs . . . in themselves, severed from the organic unity of the body. . . . We must, in other words, disarticulate, mutilate the body."[4] This cluster of limbs or members, severed from purpose and use, in which the sublime or the beautiful may yet be discerned, immediately calls to mind, de Man reminds us, Kleist's marionette (*Gliedermann*). The detached *Glied* which, on the rebound, links the body to the automaton according to certain conceptions of the beautiful and the sublime, remains outside as the distinguishing mark of scenes of resurrection from Osiris to Heinse.

Heinse departed from Kant by taking that premier trip or detour through Italy which would henceforward be constitutive of

Germanicity, Germany being, by all accounts, without eros. Henceforward the trip to *Italien* would remain a German genre of journey always conducted in search of *Genitalien*.[5] Kant never traveled; according to Otto Weininger this reflects Kant's lack of eros. "Kant lacks sensuality (*Sinnlichkeit*) in every respect," Heinse declares; "Therefore the sensual expression of perfection tells and explains to me here as in all cases infinitely more than his *Lust* and *Unlust*." On the one hand, Heinse admonishes that "Kant's system" denies truth its integrity: "Truth is a whole, which has everything that it must have" (8.1:6); on the other, Heinse rejects this system as being "too tyrannical for life on earth": "Here man's eyes are gouged out, his nose trampled under foot, his ears knocked deaf, his tongue burned, and all sensation hardened" (8.3:213).

In an aside which the reader is asked to leave outside the *Critique of Judgment,* Kant turns his attention to the fine arts in order to distinguish among them. He applies or develops a conception of the sign which is in effect a hierarchical interpretation of the body as a communicative medium.[6] What Kant nevertheless leaves out of the picture, according to Heinse, is the body itself and its pleasurable extensions. This range of bodily sensation Heinse calls *Gefühl:* "*Gefühl* differs from the other senses in that it senses without medium. The other senses must in addition always carry a medium in themselves; otherwise one would be able to taste with other parts than just the tongue" (8.3:59). As the technical media would come to confirm, *Gefühl* resides inside the body it doubles; this double can be released only by tapping into the nervous system rather than some discrete sense organ which always remains displaced with regard to its representations. To turn on this bodily amplifier Heinse turned away from the visual sense to the oral/ aural circuit. Heinse's closest friend, the anatomist Sömmering, turns the oral/aural circuit full circle when, on August 22, 1795, he broadcasts the news to Kant: "Heinse and I were overjoyed to discover, once we were reunited after the war, that, even though we had not been in contact, we had both arrived in our respective labors at the same conclusion: Hearing is the most important sense. He had come across this finding through speculation and I was able to give him the anatomical explanation why this is the case."

Heinse's conception of the arts can thus only begin to be received and find acknowledgment when the two German heralds of mass media culture, Ludwig II of Bavaria and Richard Wagner, come to read Heinse with great interest and respect. At this end of its delayed release Heinse's text becomes for the first time effective, indeed modern; it is modern to the extent that it distinguishes itself from the past by moving outside of literature; it overflows the boundaries between literature and history by turning to such phenomena as warfare to determine the common, though shifting, ground on which both art and spontaneous action transpire. At closer range, however, Heinse began composing his understanding of the arts over and against the alliance emergent in the course of the eighteenth century between semiotics and literature. This alliance ultimately legitimized what Lessing called the "fruitful" or "pregnant moment," that primal incursion of history into literature which was thus made to conform to the semiotic boundaries keeping the arts apart and in check. And yet, as Heinse discovered, *Emilia Galotti* remained proof and guarantor that even Lessing would never be able to carry to fruition his conception of a pregnant moment (8.2:384–85).

Lessing had put historical consciousness on stage only to transgress against, in imposing them, the limits of this encounter between history and literature. To effect this encounter, in contrast to classical tragedy, which essentially stages its own formal principles, *Emilia Galotti* transferred one discourse to another, mixing discourses belonging to different registers. The resulting historical trajectory—the "long way" from nature to culture, from country to city—conveys Emilia all the way from her father's country place to the Prince's pleasure palace, where her vulnerability to seduction by the Prince poses what remains the most unsettling problem of the new bourgeois drama: Emilia cannot withstand the Prince's "language of gallantry," a discourse from another time zone. Both Heinse and Lessing thus address a certain complicity or contamination of art and history, though Heinse, less fearful than Lessing, would push this complicity beyond the semiotic limit drawn between art and history. While Lessing always draws back, like Emilia, from "the true force" of "seduction," Heinse seeks to elevate this power, making it the guiding impulse of his inquiry into the arts.[7]

Heinse brought back from Italy *Ardinghello and the Blessed Isles,* the first self-reflexive novel in German letters which tested and transgressed against its own formal limits in the office of another medium. En route to this work Heinse had kept journals which covered not only the cultural rereading he would parcel out among *Ardinghello,* a subsequent novel on music, and his ultimate work on chess, but also theoretical notes inspired by the semioaesthetic tracts which, in place of travel guides, received a tourist's scrutiny. In *Ardinghello* Heinse once again pays tax to Lessing's *Laocoön* in the course of leaving it behind; the philosopher in attendance announces, echoing Lessing's views, that tenable positions in aesthetic theory will become available only once the limits of each art form have been ascertained or erected. These boundaries are necessarily semiotic in character: according to the painter Ardinghello, "all art is, in the final analysis, nothing but signs" (4:176).

In the final analysis: semiotic concerns are thus pushed to the forefront only to be pushed over the edge. Lessing's take on the arts had focused on the either simultaneous or consecutive mode of copresence of the constituent signs. But the measure of pleasure art elicits and recalls is in no wise contingent on taking in signs in their preset order. "All art is nothing more than a monument to the memory of bygone pleasure, mainly for the artist himself, and then for those who have enjoyed the same" (8.1:496). "Lessing's basic principle of poetry is, then, a sophistry. With each pleasurable sensation we seem to be eternal, and seem no longer to have a sense of time" (8.1:505). "Beyond pleasure and the recollection of pleasure there is no truth" (8.1:16). Conceived thus as the placeholder of a pleasure it does not so much represent as reproduce and conduct even in the absence of matching source or context, the artwork appears in direct connection and correspondence with the organs of perception, and not with the depicted object or action, as in Lessing's view. Conceived therefore as media, as the reproducers of sensual data as such, and as the extensions of physiological functions, the arts correlate directly to the materiality with which they deal, while in the traditional sense which Lessing's *Laocoön* yet embodies, the arts entertain only symbolic relations to the sensual fields they presuppose.[8]

When Goethe in turn returned from Italy he was instantly put off by the nature of *Ardinghello's* success: the novel dominated the literary scene through and as *Rumoren,* a term which embraces in German that mockery of fame which lends its ear to sheer "noise, rumble."[9] Goethe thus picks up the noisy static that lies in the future—in the background—of Heinse's conception of the arts. Such noise always sounds out some primal scene—of murder. Heinse summons this primal beyond of pleasure when he thrills to the omnipotent thought of his death wish: "To slay one's enemy is the greatest *jouissance*" (8.3:138). In *Ardinghello,* not only are certain innovations in pictorial composition—the depiction of crowds, for example—attributed to the impact of warfare, but the eponymous hero produces his best work only after he has experienced the exhilaration of warfare. Ardinghello exchanges his first visit to the combat zone for its eidetic souvenirs, which he sketches, including, notably—and in accord with a certain dialectic of Enlightenment—his slaying of the bastard Adorno.

The self-proclaimed "savage" (9:3) was accordingly haunted, though only to the extent that he anticipated the media-technical rebound of his death wishes. Already at the close of the eighteenth century Wilhelm Heinse had his ears on. That part of Heinse's primal rereading of culture which was dedicated to phantom possession received Goethe's secret acknowledgment. The tribute is paid in *Torquato Tasso,* where Goethe's conception of the haunted genius corresponds to Heinse's earlier reflections on Tasso. To be a genius, according to Heinse, was to be beset by feverish seizures and to be accordingly constrained, confined. Once locked up, Tasso encountered up close his phantom projections in ever increasing intensity: "His melancholy grew darker, his nerves weaker, he had feverish accidents, had visions, saw phantoms" (3.1:259). It was to underwrite his voyage to Italy that Heinse translated portions of Tasso as well as Petronius's *Satyricon,* which includes tales of werewolves and striges, female vampires who, upon assuming the form of ravenous birds, would attack the corpses of children. This time of translation embraced manic and melancholic phases (9.1:239, 243). Heinse would equate the essence of authorship with "screwing" (*vögeln*) (8.1:17), only to shift down to the recognition that he himself was but "a mute person, a stuffed bird" (9.1:240). While writing down, profusely and too quickly, his translations of Tasso,

Heinse was tempted, in his desperation, to cover his tracks by changing his name to Heinze, the change of one middle letter seemingly sufficing to veil or empty out his identifying mark (10.2:93).

In the course of fighting off phantoms, Heinse came to see every book as being always and originally a form of inoculation with "dead ideas" whereby the reader's own feeling (*Gefühl*) was weakened (8.1:25). The werewolf springs out of this laboratory-archive: "After Harvey had discovered the circulation of blood in the previous century, one of his countrymen, who also wanted to invent something, came up with the idea that through the infusion of foreign blood a different species, at once animal and man, could be grafted. At least he thought he had found the panacea for many diseases. Experiments were made: the rumor of this spread across mountains, sea, and land, and penetrated to the outermost corners of the scholarly world" (8.1:34). But these corners are not that far off: "the whole world is a living death. . . . This is as far as we have gotten with our philosophy" (8.1:63).

THE NAKED LUNCH

During his Italian trip Heinse crossed over from the vampiric conclave of literature and philosophy into a realm of *Rausch* where immortality is secured at the other end of extension and amplification of the senses. "Man, the endless creation, is made, according to my system, to pass through zone after zone, taking possession with his soul of everything that is good and beautiful" (9:261). In the midst of everything good and beautiful Heinse always evokes and privileges *das Nackende*, which covers, up front, nakedness as practiced by the ancient Greeks.[10] In Heinse's conception of the arts, however, *das Nackende* also derives unique motivation: having at least the appearance of a present participial form, the term suggests an active ongoing agency, and yet, as a substantive, it ascribes immobility and a certain permanence to the sensual and instantaneous. Thus *Nacken*, the back of the neck, from which, by metonymy, the voice resounds, is found in the background of *das*

Nackende, where it can be overheard; this erroneous semantic link resonates in Grimm's dictionary where *nackend* and *Nacken* are treated as etymons.

Although the embodiment of *das Nackende* is hailed by Heinse as the premier degree of pleasure successfully attained and transmitted by painting and sculpture, it also doubles as the measure of his despair: visual representation leaves *das Nackende* bereft of all motion and life. The ancient Greeks would have come to this conclusion if it, in turn, had not come to them; Heinse imagines them always on the verge of discarding their statues of naked bodies to rid themselves of the unbearable rigor mortis of arrested life (4:194). In rendering the beauty of the naked form, the visual arts stimulate the eye but cannot increase its power; they engage the spatial sense of vision but not that permanent inner force which Heinse equates with movement and life, a force attainable only in the more fluid media of poetry and music (4:182). But poetry is constrained by the history of its medium. In its origin language was, according to Heinse, already music, the first words having been amplifications through tones of sensations and things; in its degenerescence language clothes music, from which it must be stripped. It is, accordingly, in the "tone of voice" that Heinse discerns "something characteristic which points to the particular kind of nerves which constitute man."[11] This tone or "pure sound" is, as Heinse writes in a letter to Jacobi, dated November 22, 1780, "the most sensual thing that man can grasp from life"; the painted or sculpted image, by contrast, remains "dead." Heinse thus dismisses Herder's view that sculpture appeals to the sense of touch: it is the musical tone alone that penetrates to the so-called inner feeling, the extension, according to Heinse, of the tactile sense (3.1:65). When music plays: auditory vibrations play on the nerves such that the entire body is traversed by tones (8.1:65). Feeling itself is music, says Heinse; feeling is an ongoing oscillation of the nerves (5:24).

When the composer Lockmann gazes through a telescope at the bathing singer Hildegard, we witness, at one end of magnification, the only visual embodiment of *das Nackende* admitted within Heinse's music novel *Hildegard von Hohenthal.* Thus the name von Hohenthal already vouchsafes and summons what is less vision than projection of its "high valley." Lockmann observes that with every singing performance the singer is as though stripped naked (5:237); but nakedness on stage does not cover Heinse's shifting conception of *das Nackende,* which, on the other side of the simile, equals the sheer singing voice, unaccompanied by instruments (5:13). Heinse thus must peel away from the vocalic component of voice the consonantal element which he sees as "imitating the surface of things" (5:243). Colors are but fragments of the total light spectrum; tones, by contrast, have their own integrity (8.2:299). Every visual vestige of the voice which thus marks a deletion must in turn be deleted so that the pure vocalic tone, the highest instance of *das Nackende,* can emerge. But this tone is dis-clothed only to the extent that it penetrates through. While traditional conveyers of information such as words and images can be transmitted and arrested at will, sound alone remains capable of penetrating every attempt to shut it out. Heinse thus reminds us that the ear cannot readily be closed: whereas the eye is capable of giving and taking, the ear and the articulatory mechanism are always open to irresistible influence (5:23). "So when it comes to passions, music is in its right place; especially with strong passions, where one no longer thinks of words, but rather is penetrated by the things themselves. We expel a part of that which is in us" (5:243). This scene of sound is accordingly repeated and rehearsed in sexual relations, which provide discharge of an excess which stretches and strains the nerves (8.1:450).

And yet Heinse is also after another meaning of sense or *Sinn.* Upon identifying *das Nackende* with vocal music, Heinse celebrates the immediate response and release that music affords at its highest moments, when its sound resounds not with the word, nor even with the music, but with the sense: "namely the sense of the words enters the auditors in its entire strength and volume, without their noticing the music, or even the words . . ." (5:14). With the most engaging song, the music goes unnoticed; with the best poetry, the language; and with the foremost visual art, the sign (4:244). The best song allows one to take in only the sense of the words; it is thus the purest and most *nackend* presentation (8.2:497). *Das Nackende,* conceived as pure vocalic tone or as sense, paradoxically in both senses, penetrates beyond the attributes of semiotic systems.

According to the logic of simulation which subtends Heinse's lexicon of *Sinn* and *das Nackende,* only once the sexual component has been abnegated can the voice emerge all the stronger, more sensual and seminal: the absolutely supreme—most *nackend*— sung-out music accordingly achieves realization and climax only in the "fully developed castrato voice," which carries away the auditor's soul as though in a stream (8.2:357).[12] The castrato singer emerges as mascot for Heinse's conception of aesthetic pleasure as always suspended between the amplification of the senses and their auto-amputation.[13] To cut it short: all art is substitute for something lacking (8.1:543).

The conjunction of plenitude and lack thus serves as double origin; originally one and the same, music and language came to be separated and linked through a series of amplificatory supplementations. Before music could be adjoined to language for purposes of amplifying words and extending their range, it was first necessary to establish the independence of music from language. Thus with the invention of musical instruments, the potential strength of each of the original components of language came to be recognized (5:229). Music, now separate from speech, could be pressed into the service of transmitting commands: "The first music probably took the form of an address to a crowd by a leader, a Tyrtaios, who, to make himself understoood, spoke in tercets, quarter notes, and fifths" (5:242). The primal arts thus carry out—amplify or extend—that which commands absolutely: "the highest manifestations of life," featuring sex, murder, and natural catastrophe (4:196). Art amounts in essence to expressing again in the absence of an object that force which issued earlier from one of life's highest manifestations: "The arts are the surging of the seas after a storm, when winds no longer rage. When the force in the highest manifestation of life has expressed itself, has been effective, and then expresses itself anew in the absence of any real object: That is art. For this reason the arts have always flourished after great wars" (8.2:115). Or again: "Whenever forces are unleashed, and no longer find anything real in their path, then imitation, art arises."[14]

But art can never call forth or recall anything in such a way as to satisfy the imagination's demand for totalization: "the first and most passionate longing of the soul remains perfection or destruction of things" (4:178). Art is, on the one hand, the representative of a total image to the imagination while, on the other, it remains a fragment treated as a whole. Despite the urgency with which art rushes to meet the demand of the imagination that totalities be rendered, each artwork always only points to its own fragmentary status, the limit beyond which it cannot give back or represent wholly anything outside itself (4:178–79). Thus the greatest art form is always the one that is "quickest in introducing a totality into the soul" (8.1:542). The speed race between act and expression—and this is the speed Heinse refers to here as essential to the greatest art—seems won only in the crying out or singing out of tones. Whereas words either precede or follow a given act, the exclamation of joy (*Jubelton*) is coincident with the act (5:243): "the cry of joy (*Jubelschrey*) in the instant of sexual union . . . surpasses any other language."[15]

The development of the voice as the organ best suited to accelerate beyond the race between act and expression accordingly takes off from the advent of automata that play chess, sing, and speak. Just as these early robots were originally contrived for the purpose of serving in the office of some absent sense organ, so every stage in the development of the voice appears contingent upon some perceived deficiency. In Heinse's account the human vocal apparatus cannot rise above analogy with machine parts; in turn the body is deemed a more powerful amplifier than water, owing not only to its greater density but also to the cavities it bears (5:24). The supreme victors in this body-building contest are thus the castrato singers: they are "instruments playing themselves" (10:100).

The deficient body is always the primal apparatus; its breakdown is always the machine's first and model function. Speaking machines, for example, were originally modeled after deaf-mutes, who were conceived at the time as already automata. After perpetrating the chess-machine hoax, Wolfgang von Kempelen undertook to ascertain the nature of a deaf-mute's malfunction and so came to conceive of the voice in terms of a functioning machine; he constructed speaking machines at the same time that he developed a theory of the physiology or mechanics of speech. Recognition of the substitutive relation of sense organs which these contraptions apply led one instructor of deaf-mutes, Samuel Heinicke, to advance a theory of "chewing thinking," according to which taste

supplies the place of hearing, and the feel of tones and articulations on the neck the vocal language that cannot be heard.[16] Unlike his French colleagues, who taught only sign language to their
deaf-mute charges, Heinicke sought to resurrect the deaf-mute's
voice. The deaf-mute's chewing thinking already holds the place of
the telephone, but only insofar as one medium always communicates as another medium: as documented by Michael Ranft in his
1728 treatise "Concerning the Chewing and Lip-Smacking of the
Dead in Graves," the dead continue to think out loud by smacking
their lips and gnawing on their own flesh and shroud.

The devices of the technical media, which thus rehearse in
hearses, can always only fill in for some *Mittelglied* they mutilate;
Heinse accordingly charts these contraptions back to the origin of
distinterested pleasure. Inserted into analyses of the beautiful in
place of woman, these automata, which belong to the future only
to the extent that they contain the vestiges and abstractions of past
violence, always reflect the pull of the sublime.

The autonomous creation of Mount Vesuvius evokes, according to Heinse, the sublime or "the sublime and terrible" in sensations of submission and received penetration (7:66). "Sublime . . .
is a higher being which penetrates us with sensations, thoughts,
shape, gesture, action. . . . Everywhere it fills the soul with delight
and wonder, so that time is forgotten, and man is placed among the
gods" (4:177–78). The sublime thus addresses a reverse side of the
beauty of physical form; according to Heinse, beauty always serves
generation, the guiding principle of sexuality. Beauty is always a
"pregnant moment." Heinse can thus conceive of the links and
limits of the arts in terms of the beautiful and the sublime only in
the contraceptive mode: debauchery between partners or between
one individual and a bedpost or a cut of beef is the most that the
visual arts attain (8.1:487–88). Painting is a whore (8.1:502) and
sculpture remains best suited "for love" (4:406); but music, which
manifests *das Nackende* "like a pure harmony to the ear," is not to
be confused with "animal lust" (8.1:527).

From pictorial art to music there appears to be in Heinse's
reflections at once a movement of sublimation and a movement
towards the sublime. Whereas *das Erhabene* (the sublime) has its
source in *Ardinghello and the Blessed Isles* in the *Erhobenheiten*,
the raised parts or tumescences of sculpture,[17] when it finds musi-

cal expression in *Hildegard von Hohenthal*—in the novel Heinse conceived as "exemplar of chastity"—the sublime is sensuous, though only in a physiological sense divested of sexual inflection. This radical reversal of sense does not transpire over time—the very succession of novels presents only the fiction of a development, since each work is culled from the same material collected during Heinse's Italian journey. Rather, both meanings of *Sinn* are always copresent in Heinse. This sublime simultaneity of conflicting senses of *Sinn* attests to the circumvention of that threshold or barrier of repression which would otherwise prohibit their co-occurrence. The sublime in sublimation thus conveys a literal meaning, "under the threshhold," alongside the loftiness its German equivalent preserves.

The doubling of *Sinn* in Heinse's reflections also accomplishes a reversal of background and foreground: music, painting, words are pushed back to the point of displacing forward sheer noise. Heinse leaves behind that part of *das Nackende* which covers the beauty of the naked body. When he goes into the ear instead to determine the manner in which control over the body has been most effectively exercised, he discovers the audio portion of *das Nackende*—pure vibration and onrush of sound. Immediately following his celebration of the castrato voice as supreme embodiment of *das Nackende,* Heinse evokes the deafening noise of waterfalls which, he stresses, surpasses the eloquence of sounds; the castrato voice—that "instrument playing itself"—is thus superseded by noise, whether the crash of thunder—which, says Heinse, surpasses all music—or the silent blackout of night, which obscures the "mechanical character of time."[18] What thus emerges or returns occupies interchangeable places with silence. It is the death drive, according to Freud, that remains mute only to the extent that it resounds in the background of what Freud also calls the "all-powerful melody of the drives."[19]

According to Anton Ehrenzweig, this noise is held in place inside the unconscious by the consciously received articulations which hold its place; in the recognizable articulations of music and speech, tone-color, for example, is the sheer effect of repression of the high overtones which pipe up in the unconscious. This unconscious level of sound reception can in turn be simulated for conscious audition only be playing a record in reverse.[20] The technical media tap into the unconscious at one end and, at the other, re-place missing death cults which were originally and always con-structed, with respect to the realm of the living, around an axis of mirror reversal. According to Freud, every cult of the dead emerges in the trail of death wishes which, like noise, must be kept in some other place. Death wishes thus animate the dead, whose return, however, is only projected.

Cargo Cult refers to itself by the Neo-Melanesian term "noise": "noise" covers the active phase of the cult, governed by excited belief that the second coming of cargo is coming up. In anticipation of the return of the dead only good thoughts are to be entertained—this is called "think think"—and no food is to be gathered, since, though they thus cannot help but fast, they will not go hungry. All possessions must be thrown into the sea or burned; true believers must reduce themselves, in short, to what is called "rubbish." During intensive and protracted "think think," at which point messages from the dead begin to be received, the body begins to tremble, often to the point of uncontrolled convulsions. This trembling is called "noise," which designates in turn the super-natural force inherent in Cargo Cult itself. When it comes time to await the cargo-bearing dead at the cemetery on the appointed day of their arrival, everyone hears the noise of cargo—the clank of metal, ships approaching, anchors being dropped, the static of a broadcast. When cargo nevertheless fails to arrive, belief in cargo is not altered: either the "think think" and destruction of property had been imperfect and feigned or the white man—the phantom at the controls of Cargo Cult—had changed the addresses on the cargo crates to push back, once again, the return of the mourned dead.

LOOKING FOR A MATE

Heinse closes *Ardinghello*, characterized throughout by atten-tiveness to semiotic distinctions and limitations governing the vari-ous art forms, with a final evocation of the sublime, a celebration of warfare within a utopian community organized around the training of the naked body. Life is warfare, Heinse proclaims. And yet warfare, identified with the preservation and transgression of boundaries, resembles nothing so much as that ongoing semiotic differentiation which keeps the arts apart: "Besides, every art has its borders, which no other can cross to make conquest. Painting, sculpture, and music mock in their unique beauties every translation; even poetry, the most powerful of all, must remain at home" (9:282). The limitations within which the arts, much like the pieces of a chess game, must work, are clarified in terms of the way in which they push back the encroachment of one figure or form onto the domain of another.

To close off his entire oeuvre, Heinse accordingly turns to the game of chess, which, in his *Anastasia or the Game of Chess,* advances to the primal place of the arts where it assisted warriors in recalling and recounting the ecstasies of battle (6:193–94). At the same time, because there exist an infinite number of strategies which can be deployed in chess, deception is at play in this game more so than in any other: but deception remains the chief virtue of those living in a state of warfare (6:213–16). Owing to its special figural status, chess is thus a game especially commended to poets (6:205). At this stage of the delineation of the arts, however, mathematics has overtaken the place of premier conveyor of tone; chess in turn attains supremacy by recycling the essential movement—the algebra—of warfare: "All that has been retained from war is the movement, that is three types of directed movement . . . and two types of strength, namely close-range and long-range. . . . The game becomes in this way so simple yet manifold . . . like a basic tone which contains all the other tones. In short, chess is, as it were, the algebra of war" (6:194–95). "The figures in chess are nothing more than elements, hieroglyphs, letters, out of which everyone can at will fashion sense and image. A Lavoisier could even imagine while contemplating them the actual elements, and while contemplating checkmate the resulting products, human beings, animals and plants, all life" (6:205).

Once again Heinse demonstrates his adherence to a view of all phenomena as inextricably controlled within an economy of forces such that he is able to speak about art and warfare as though they were of a kind, differing only in the way energy is directed and expended. Wherever we look in Heinse's reflections there appears to be—or to have been—a war that has been displaced in terms of its territorial claims, and it is this warring displacement which holds together while dispersing all objects of inquiry to which Heinse directs his attention. In Heinse's final contest with himself we find once again a redirection of libidinal energy, here within the context of a game renowned in the chronicle of sports and games for its spirituality. Heinse lays out an ideal of chess, according to which the game would be played between two absolutely equally capable players—between, for example, an accomplished player and a pro-grammed automaton—such that the overall balancing of moves would amount at any given moment to a process of ongoing *Oscilla-tion*. Close up, this sublime scenario revolves about a contest as though between two forces or beings, always verging on, by dou-bling as, suicide. In long shot, *Oscillation* serves the organization of the diffuse energies of entire peoples. Whenever a people seeks to organize the "chaos of forces" it possesses by submitting these forces to its creative spirit, the result is the transformation of that people into a "double power"—into, Heinse concludes, a chess game (6:233).

In his essay on the chess champion Paul Morphy, Ernest Jones analyzes chess in terms of a double scenario of sublimation and the sublime which applies in equal measure to music and warfare. At the level of decision-making chess is, Jones argues, comparable to, to the point of being more ruthless than, warfare, while in terms of their range of memory and store of sensorial imagery, chess players and musicians are interchangeable. Mor-phy's ability to play for days without interruption or fatigue reflects "a very exceptional level of sublimation, for a psychological situa-tion of such a degree of freedom can only mean that there is no risk of its stimulating any unconscious conflict or guilt."[21] But this sublimation is anchored in the proximity of chess to patricide. The object of the game is to paralyze, maim, and mate the king or father. Chess in turn prohibits touching, which Reuben Fine inter-prets as the paternal interdiction against masturbation and homo-sexuality.[22] And yet this prohibition also puts the father in isola-tion: according to Heinse, the goal of chess is the "imprisonment" (*Gefangenschaft*) of the father (9:365). Whereas the king is the only token in the game that is irreplaceable to the extent that it will have been imprisoned, swallowed, and lost, the figure of the queen

114

is the most potent figure on the board. Her power was increased to its current range in exchange for a sex change: she was originally a vizier or counselor who, during the middle ages, changed his sex or dress, owing in part to the proximity in sound of vizier and *vierge*. It is thus the lost token of paternity which organizes the Queen's movements toward its imprisonment. Or as Jones puts it: chess enacts the scenario in which the mother is the most powerful ally of the son against the father.[23]

Prerequisite to Morphy's mastery of chess, therefore, was the binding of patricidal impulses by a homosexual cathexis, which was in turn sublimated; every goal of civilization can be attained only through the "transformation of the Oedipus complex into sublimated homosexuality (i.e., herd instinct) without which no social community can exist."[24] The son must be engendered anew by the father if, beyond penetration, he is to become more closely bound to him. Sublimated homosexuality, the essence of all sublimation, allows the murderous impulses directed against the father to find outlet as creative and restitutive urges with a nonsexual aim. Thus Freud passes over the uncanny to nominate sublimation the conceptual equivalent of the sublime. In his case study of Schreber, for example, Freud calls on a patient whose search to rediscover his father, who had died when the son was very young, always leads him to "what was grand and sublime in nature." Thus, Freud concludes, the sun, as celebrated by Schreber and Nietzsche, is yet another "sublimated symbol for the father."[25] Already in the prepsychoanalytic register, the sublime corresponds to the anticipatory mournfulness of male-to-male transmissions. The reciprocity of bestowal of life between father and son, as when the son protects the aged father,[26] is matched in sublimity only, says Kant, by the ultimate protection of father which the Bible, by disallowing commemoration in name or image of the father-god, legislates.

Eighteenth-century preoccupation with sublimity thus doubled as "an episode in melancholy."[27] The melancholic, who attracted comparison now with the "moral deaf-mute," now with automaton or animal, now with werewolf and vampire, received from Kant the further distinction of possessing a keen sense for the sublime.[28] What was already in place can be found again in Freud, where there is, as Stuart Ende has argued, a close connection between sublimation and the melancholic response to loss: "When an object is lost—that is, when a loved person or thing is no longer available to the mind—it may respond in any of several ways: The mind may choose another object; it may withdraw the energy expended on the other into itself in some unspecified way; or it may 'establish an *identification* of the ego with the abandoned object.' " Ende must double back to come to the end of Freud's thought: in *The Ego and the Id* Freud also called the "transformation of object-libido into narcissistic libido" "a kind of sublimation."[29] This mournful internalization always of the father spans two conflicting demands; on the one hand the demand that the lost object return, on the other that the idealized father, a psychic agency that grows especially powerful and harsh following loss, be satisfied. The dead father must stay—away.

In 1972 Siemens provided a late arrival of the idealized father in the course of realizing Heinse's pursuit of *das Nackende:* the *Kunstkopf,* an artificial head, complete with a representation of the nose, was erected by Siemens to model a newly perfected recording process for the ultimate replication of tone which, conveyed through any headset, gives the listener the sensation that the very breath of the recorded voice can be felt at the back of the neck (*Nacken*). In Heinse's case, a father's organ music installed in his son a veritable *Kunstkopf* which records the barely audible, yet somehow sensible, oscillation of tone, breath, and chess; this pulsating space, which every performing organ player occupies, commences and subtends Heinse's reflections on *Kunst*. The "ideas moulded on that of breath (wind, fire, speech, thought, music, the soul)" lend themselves, according to Jones, "to the most refined forms of sublimation, a quality which is psychologically to be interpreted as a measure of the intensity of the repression" to which the underlying idea symbolized has been subjected.[30]

In Heinse's corpus, repression, in the form of abnegation of the sexual organ, builds a sublimated (distilled and purified) body in the vibratory space another body once occupied. The sensory unit and unity of tone (for which Heinse held in reserve, for example in an aside in *Hildegard von Hohenthal,* comparison with the bond between father and son)[31] is secured through castration. But who occupies the position of castrato-instrument? The son identifies through this instrument with the missing father and organ. The conduit of this mournful identification, the unsexed *Kunstkopf,* is the resurrected body of the father in the son, which like every resurrected body is no longer genitally organized.[32] According to Heinse, chess and the organ are both instruments for improvisation and fantasizing; in each case the player resembles a "god" in his ability to transform a piece of "dead" elephant into a "living rapacious eagle" (9:368–70).

This reanimation project can be detected already in Heinse's *Letters from the Düsseldorf Art Gallery,* written in anticipation of the trip to Italy. By its absence the sublime is brought into focus as that which exceeds Heinse's conception of beauty. Beauty is, according to the *Letters,* largely the attribute of women, since fewer complexities must converge in a feminine unity. Beauty can be grasped even with a limited sensory ability since it is ultimately the list of those attributes which commend a woman for sexual enjoyment. Beauty cannot be made more beautiful, Heinse argues, but only more integrated (*zusammengesetzter*). Painting is accordingly granted priority among the arts. Music penetrates only briefly into beauty's native habitat; nevertheless, it already wields the power to place men "among the gods."[33] The sublime is already exerting a pressure or attraction that yet awaits assignment of a name and proper place. One place holder is the deaf-mute painter who, at the beginning of the *Letters,* accompanies Heinse on a journey.[34] The painter, who was rendered deaf through a cannon blast, can neither spell nor read but communicates through signs of mimicry. This means of communication which war has installed in the painter is preferable to any exchange of words; in it thunder or a maiden's sigh can be conveyed with such precision that in foreign countries he has no need of a translator. He is a veritable "savage," having been spared exposure to the unnatural voice of prejudice which resounds within the educational institution. Within these early reflections inspired by the "beauty of the savage—the beauty of his little woman," Heinse takes his premier excursion ultimately toward the sublime in the company of his double. Celebrated for his brilliant wit and playfulness, his accomplished learnedness, as well as for his consummate skills at playing chess—a game he often discussed as being an analogue of warfare, whereupon he would look up from the chess board, his eyes agleam—Heinse, a misanthrope and mysogynist alone in the archives, was at the end of this excursion still that deaf-mute, savage, or automaton, that com-

117

pletely developed castrato whose naked essence found a final refuge in chess.[35]

In the *Letters* Heinse also already addressed the horrible pleasure which he held in store for his corpse. As with the beautiful body, painting must not contain "spots" "of dead substance." For the artist, substance is the mechanical aspect of creation, and meaning, its essence (*Wesen*). Paints and colors, which are to the painter as words are to the poet, as the tones to the virtuoso, comprise the substance of pictorial art. Essence is literally that which *west* (lives) and *verwest* (decays); it is the germ of life according to Heinse: "Substance without essence in art is death without decay; the most horrible thing imaginable."[36] Death without decay: mummification and encryptment, or the dedication of one's body to science, or, as is now possible, the bestowal of one's most prized organs to new bodies. "Death without decay" is a concept invested with dread fascination in Heinse's corpus; it is kept there secretly, not to reemerge until the end of his life in his desperate bid for a death without death.

Heinse willed his body to science and, specifically, his skull to Sömmering as tribute to their close association as researchers in the area of sound physiology. In exchange, Sömmering had searched for the causes of Heinse's lack of voice. According to Sömmering's son, Heinse, though as a youth a member of the choir, later had "no voice," a condition which after careful examination of his vocal organs Sömmering attributed to ossification of the larynx and to the effect of lopsided posture assumed in consequence of some physical defect. While the testamentary gift fits the topic of their joint labors—under Sömmering's direction Heinse had even written a treatise on the brain—the bestowal of the skull also has a more ancient pedigree in mourning rituals where the skull serves as transmitter for communication with the spirit realm. From the beyond also of castration, the severed skull is always a propitiatory offering that reconciles the dead and the living.

But Heinse died a bachelor; hence according to certain superstitions, the traffic which his remains invited was not restricted to friendly ghosts. The corpse of the bachelor was always especially feared, since no close family survivors would be around to mourn him properly and thus keep him from returning as vengeful spirit. Indeed, the dead bachelor always also represents the actual death of the dead father, whose phantom is thus no longer contained within the superego of some descendant. In certain cultures the unthinkable consequences of this double death could only be averted by burying alongside the bachelor a sacrificial bride. Or the corpse was, at the very least, carried out of the house feet first or through the roof so that it might never find its way back home. The primal practice of double burial meets, by repeating at the other end, the menace of double death. Following the first burial the bereaved remained in quarantine, since they were yet carriers of contamination by the corpse, while the widow could still, between burials, become impregnated by her dead husband. The second burial, the exhumation of the bones after a period of about two years, at which point the deceased had crossed over into the spirit realm, even released the widow for remarriage, though first she and her second suitor had to be whipped until they bled before the grave.

In *Hildegard von Hohenthal* the voice finds its first analogue in the organ, that instrument Heinse had mastered under his father's tutelage. Again in *Hildegard von Hohenthal,* we learn that the harmonies an organ produces embody the relation between father and son. The castrato singer, in whom one organ grows supreme through the loss of another, is an instrument playing itself in ghostly performance. Heinse found another organ specialist to assist him in his researches into the amplification of the oral/aural system, a true father, who would both recognize Heinse's organs and put them to rest. Like a father, Sömmering cannot grant Heinse's request and give him a death without decay: following its dissection, Sömmering had Heinse's corpse properly buried, and only after two years' time—the full extent of a mourning period—had the skull disinterred, gilded, and placed prominently on display.

119

CHAPTER FOUR
NECROFILIATION
(Antonin Artaud)

That night he had a dream in which he was present at the post-mortem on his late wife. The dream was divided into two contrasting scenes. In the one, the separate parts of the body grew together again, the dead woman began to show signs of life, and he embraced her with feelings of the liveliest joy. In the other scene the dissecting-room altered its appearance, and the dreamer was reminded of slaughtered animals in a butcher's shop.

The scene of the dissection, twice presented in the dream, was associated with his wife's operation (*sectio Caesaris*). In the one part it turned into the reanimation of the dead body; in the other it was connected with cannibalistic ideas. The dreamer's association to the dream in analysis brought out the remarkable fact that the sight of the dissected body reminded him of his meal of the evening before, and especially of a meat dish he had eaten.

Karl Abraham, "A Short Study of the Development
of the Libido, Viewed in the Light of Mental Disorders"

THE MUMMY

Post-psychoanalytic readings of the Schreber case have resituated madness, otherwise located beyond the outposts of communication, at the very switches of communication systems.[1] With the emergence of the modern technical media, madness—Schreber's paranoia, for instance—increasingly amounts to direct, unveiled awareness of the amplifications, extensions—the new organs—the media append to our new, organless bodies. The primal scene of mental breakdown always opens onto some machine, which breaks down. According to McLuhan, every modern medium is provided with a "cloak of invisibility"; though a medium ostensibly communicates with intimate directness, it in fact works subliminally or magically to instill in us certain primitive collective responses. "All technological extensions of ourselves must be numb and subliminal, else we could not endure the leverage exerted upon us by such extension."[2] When this veil of subliminal influence, when the work of sublimation, which is Freud's concern in his case study of Schreber, is cast aside, we, too, find that we have in fact always been within the torture-reading-writing-copulating-eating-machine described in Kafka's *In the Penal Colony*.

By the end of his career, Antonin Artaud's sensory shield was so dispersed that he had become the burial site for all toxic waste, including the military emissions of America's sperm banks,[3] just as his body, which, like every body, had been mapped out by the displacements of states of bodily tension from zone to zone, and from orifice to orifice, itself was made to conduct the products and byproducts of technology. His bodily apertures were connected, according to Artaud, by *canalisations nerveuses* (1 supp.: 111) to vaster battle zones of erotic impulse and discharge, to the masturbation rituals of Tibetan monks, for example, indeed to every expulsion or excretion of matter such that, in order to save his "soul" from the drain and pull of this worldwide conspiracy to deposit all loss within him, he would send, for example to Tibet, an as always invisible commando unit to wipe out the offending orifice.[4]

While hieroglyphic writing was being studied with the aim of deciphering rather than interpreting or elaborating its emblematic significance,[5] and while the then nascent discipline of archaeology was engaged in the robbing of tombs, the media had commenced encryptment of bodily organs within new organs, machines of sensory amplification. In his "La Fantasmagorie" spectacles, E. G. Robertson was the first to use the laterna magica in dramatic performances, where it served as a means of casting ghosts and skeletons onto the screen. By placing the magic lantern onto a wheeled cart he was able to project phantasmic images which alternately increased and decreased in size as though now rushing towards the audience, now collapsing and vanishing. To enter Robertson's movie house, located in a cloister, the audience was led down labyrinthine corridors to a windowless room decorated as a mausoleum. This first rehearsal of filmmaking thus transpired alongside a scene of grave desecration; a century later the first motion pictures would carry the exploration of the crypt to the point of awakening the entombed mummies.

In 1932 Karl Freund's *The Mummy* seeks its reflection in a magic pool through which the mummy not only inflicts heart attacks upon his distant pursuers but also superintends every scene in the movie. It is only fitting that film should thus find, in the place of its reflection, another film of some ancient Egyptian improper burial or "nameless death" which lies in the reanimated mummy's— and its own—past. The mummy shows this movie of his and a certain princess's Egyptian burial to Helen, the young woman whose maternal Egyptian blood picked up the telepathic side effects of the mummy's incantation of resurrection rites addressed to the corpse of his beloved princess. The mummy is startled to discover that he has attracted a living woman, who, according to the specular logic of films within films, is the virtual double of the princess precisely to the extent that she must double for her. But this is Hollywood, where even a mummy prefers a hypnotized surrogate to the original mummy bride.

During one of her subsequent hypnotic visits to the mummy's lair, Helen admires the Egyptian look of his habitat which, she claims, lacks anything "modern." And yet 1930s architecture and design, in California, for example, was mock Egyptian, art deco, while the burial and embalming practices of 1930s Hollywood— practices which in the twentieth century only the United States has retained—were late arrivals of the Egyptian cult of the dead. In Forest Lawn, American undertaking, which remains to this day centered on the viewing—the spectacle—of the perfumed and embalmed corpse, rivals ancient Egypt. The avatar of the California death cult is the amusement part, which distinguishes its communities of flimsy, miniaturized reconstructions from the identical communities everywhere else by emptying out its precincts such that, as in cities of the dead, everyday life is mimicked in the absence of living inhabitants. These Disney lands of death were inspired by Hollywood film sets, which hold the place, with respect to film, of the photograph of the mummy taken right after his exhumation which the reanimated mummy holds in his hands. Thus Sir Arthur Evans's reconstruction of Minoan palaces—which, though Evans believed they offered evidence of some proto-Californian bungalow-

and-pool culture, were in fact ancient mortuary palaces—in turn found comparison at the time to the Hollywood movie set which served as its model.

Archaeological excavation is Freud's frequent analogue to the uncovering in psychoanalysis of what has been repressed or "entombed." As Freud explains in "Jensen's *Gradiva*": "There is, in fact, no better analogy for repression, by which something in the mind is at once made inaccessible and preserved, than burial of the sort to which Pompeii fell a victim and from which it could emerge once more through the work of spades."[6] By way of illustrating his remarks on the difference between the conscious and unconscious, where the former is being incessantly worn away while the latter remains relatively unchangeable, Freud, in his case study of Rat-man, points to the antiques in his study, commenting to his patient that they were all "only objects found in a tomb, and their burial had been their preservation: the destruction of Pompeii was only beginning now that it had been dug up"—though Freud rushes to reassure his patient that every effort was being made to preserve Pompeii.[7] When archaeologist or analyst raises unconscious memories out of their ancient crypts, these memorials disintegrate, like the perfectly preserved mummies of ancient Trojans which Schliemann saw—vanish. While Freud invariably shifts corpses onto the Oedipal track occupied by the father's death, where they can be displayed—and lost—among the effects of repression, Schliemann searched now in California, now in Asia Minor, for a missing brother whose phantom signals he followed out and deciphered with stop watch, shovel, and *The Iliad*.

Excavation yields, at the bottom of Jensen's *Gradiva*, a dead beloved who, in the manner of Hitchcock's *Vertigo*, achieved multiply simulated comebacks.[8] Jensen and Freud thus lead each other away from the unmourned woman into a parable of repression ready-made for psychoanalysis. Freud was right: every work of fantasy—all literature—is trivial to the extent that in it wounds are always dressed in the next chapter.[9] In *Gradiva* a young archaeologist travels to Pompeii searching for the phantom of one who, in A.D. 79, had been buried alive; in the course of his search he encounters the woman he loved in his youth, who thus returns from his own repressed past: "his phantasy transported her to Pompeii . . . because no other or better analogy could be found in his science for his remarkable state, in which he became aware of his memories of his childhood friendship through obscure channels of information."[10] In a context in which death and repression occupy interchangeable places such that the dead do return—from the repressed—the archaeologist's friend from childhood can pose the question a phantom back from the ancient past of Pompeii might ask: Did one always have to die first in order to live in his eyes? Under cover of belief in ghosts, the repressed returns without obstacle or distortion. The sublime feat of autoanalysis, which in turn frees the archaeologist from the living death of repression, is the effect of analogies between childhood and the classical past, repression and the burial of Pompeii, about which the archaeologist possessed knowledge through what Freud, at the time psychoanalysis, archaeology, and film were traversing a common ground, describes as endopsychic perceptions, delusional projections which confirm by also projecting psychoanalytic theories.

The Mummy is introduced by two archaelogical expeditions, one led in 1922 by the father, the second led by the son ten years later. Whereas the father prefers the serious scholarship of pottery shards to the "sensationalist" discovery he made by accident of the mummy of a high priest, in 1932 the son seeks out only such sensationalist mummy discoveries. The mummy who, inadvertently brought back to life, escapes the father's expedition, returns to lead the son, whose guilty degenerescence is reflected in his utter ignorance of the ancient Egyptian language, to the tomb of the mummy's beloved princess. Only in league with the sensation-seeking son can the reconstitution of mummy be completed. Yet before they can proceed, the son must first "cable father."

The cabled father who disapproves of the son's sensationalist bond to mummy is, as psychoanalysis has shown, a phantom of current pedigree, though the cable also links up to a far more ancient province. *The Mummy* refers to Isis, who raised Osiris from the dead, though in the myth this reanimation proceeds only to the point of Isis receiving her husband's yet effective semen, whereby she can give birth to his avenger Horus. As Róheim, for example, argues, the murdered yet posthumously engendering father serves, both in ancient Egyptian funerary rites and in the psychoanalytic conception of mourning, as model for all dead persons; upon dying, every Egyptian becomes another Osiris. What

124

Isis accomplishes over Osiris's dead body is also always the case. To secure his seed, she replaces with an imitation or phallus Osiris's missing penis, the only mutilated piece of his corpse which she has been unable to retrieve.

Róheim accordingly situates this phantom insemination of sister by brother within Oedipal zones of ambivalence. The son engendered by his dead father's seed was—according to the ambiguous clash of versions and doubles of the legend and its players—also already full grown at the time Osiris was killed and, in some contexts, even the same person as Set, Osiris's official killer. Set stumbles on Osiris locked-up in a casket from which Isis neglected to release him; Isis rescued her husband from one murder plot—he had been tossed, inside the casket, into the sea—only to leave him behind while she searched for her son. From the cult of Isis to psychoanalysis: every corpse is that of the overthrown, murdered, and devoured primal father. Rituals of mourning expiate the guilt while reenacting the crime. Even the mother is covered in her absence. According to Róheim, the shaman and physician alike represent the "sublimation" of that which is more openly reenacted by the wizard: the sons' murder and consumption of the primal father. But the sons found that, in the course of the meal, they had libidinized and thus animated the father's corpse; they discovered, already secretly attached to the paternal legacy, their original libidinal investment in mother. By eating the murdered father they had at once maternalized his corpse, which suckled them, and—since the act of consumption also holds the place of sexual consummation—adopted a feminine attitude toward his ghost. Hence, through identification, the son is born again through the father, who has taken the mother's place. "The consumption of the father was an act of identification, of ego ideal formation, which blocked further access to mother." At the same time the devoured dead father revives the image of the nourishing mother to which the primal corpse owes its consumerist appeal. Through the bond with the mother inadvertantly reestablished in the course of devouring the father, the shaman henceforward reserves his sadism for the aggressivity of healing practices applied to the ill or nearly dead, whose swollen bodies again evoke the image of the nourishing mother.[11]

In *The Mummy*, as in all monster fiction, the mother is missing, though it is maternal blood which, in terms of telepathic tuning, matches the reanimated mummy's stare and cinematic pool. Not until the mummy has brought about the father's death—the supernatural, death-wish cause of which the son refuses to contemplate—can the junior archaeologist pursue his attraction to Helen. From the very first, he confides to her, she reminded him of the ancient Egyptian princess he had unwrapped only to fall in love with her corpse. Did the archaeologist always have to open graves to fall in love with a woman, Helen wants to know. From this point onward Helen is pursued on two fronts by an archaeologist's and a mummy's wish to lock her up, emtomb her. She, however, does not want to be someone she "hates."

Helen makes the choice recommended by Hollywood and psychoanalysis: better to be playing dead, playing the archaeologist's missing mummy, than to be buried alive and resurrected as the mummy's own undead companion. In this way *The Mummy* swerves from the fantasy of incorporation to which it owes its projection, and reduces the effects of interminable mourning to reducible effects of sexual fear and guilt. In *Frankenstein, Dracula,* and *The Mummy,* the wedding night always promises a problem-free exit for film and film audience out of the mock phantom realm of sexual repression.

MODERN HIEROGLYPHICS

For Artaud, the point of departure of the whole magical and philosophical system of ancient Egypt, on which he bases his conception of a new, hieroglyphic theater of cruelty, was that niche in which the pharaoh's corpse rested, just as the very condition for this entire system was the corpse itself (4:127). In his "Correspondence de la momie," one of a number of pieces he addressed to mummies, Artaud identifies with the corpse maintained through preservation: "Neither is my life complete nor is my death absolutely aborted" (1:241). The global circulatory system of waste products to which Artaud succumbed was for him a vast hieroglyphic system in which he was the cornerstone corpse whose ante-chamber was the asylum:

Those who are alive are living off the dead.
So death must live
and there is nothing like a lunatic asylum for hatching death gently
and keeping corpses in an incubator.
(12:57)

Diderot's "Letter on the Deaf and the Dumb" offered the first juxtaposition of a new organless body with a reinscribed hieroglyphics within which, like the mummy, it occupied the cornerstone. His study of the deaf-mute had exposed him to an original, gestural language of abbreviated images which poetry ever seeks to reinstate within the very sound-shapes of words. Like Freud in the note on the "Mystic Writing Pad," Diderot observes in the scene of writing two hands, one transparently transmitting laws and amassing information into an archive, the other lifting from the wax tablets the celluloid screen which, cleared, veils the permanent inscriptions stored beneath. This double manipulation of writing has always invited delineation as the amalgam of what must be construed somewhere else as divergent lines of writing's reception, indeed as the history of this divergence. From pictogram to hieroglyph to ideogram to phonetic alphabet, Warburton, in his *The Divine Legation of Moses Demonstrated*, charted the steady miniaturization and abridgment of notational systems aimed at holding meaning in the narrowest space possible so as to make the archive more efficient. Though writing had not been invented in order to conceal divine mysteries, the priestly caste, Warburton argued, always veiled writing by appending to it secret inscriptions each time the written code became too public. To safeguard their power as keepers of a reserve of knowledge which, however, became more accessible the more concentrated it became, the priests accompanied the abbreviation and acceleration of written communication with a profusion of superfluous and ambiguous signs.[12]

In the note on the "Mystic Writing Pad" Freud argues that memory, in contrast to those senses extended and intensified through various types of auxiliary apparatus—"for instance, spectacles, photographic cameras, ear-trumpets"—has been equipped with no means of amplification precisely to the extent that memory outstrips all media technology in terms not only of storage capacity of recorded impressions but even of unlimited receptivity to new impressions. And yet philosophical language, Diderot clarifies, can proceed only by keeping in some other place the archive or memory, which occludes while requiring a certain brevity and transparency of writing. Diderot declares French to be superior in ratiocinative clarity, and hence better suited to philosophical exposition, than Latin, Greek, or English, since, unlike these languages, French does not permit free interpretation of word order and thus does not require the back-up support of a good memory, which must be left behind. And yet while circumventing the crowded precincts of a good memory, where only the inventory would have relevance if the most useful items were not already buried amid the sheer accumulation of indifferent goods, French also accelerates beyond the source of poetic language.

Because French is not the outgrowth of its memorials, it remains free of all "vestiges of primitive stammerings." But it thus also lacks the poetic spirit of language, which manifests itself only as a "tissue of hieroglyphs," where the constituent hieroglyphs or mental images can be conveyed only to the extent that they are reanimated through reading guided by certain rhythmical patterns. Poetry must reanimate "the vestiges of primitive stammerings" which its "tissue of hieroglyphs" blots up. Sounds and rhythms thus empower the hieroglyphs of poetry to produce a physiological effect upon the reader. The very gesture which had inspired and inscribed the poet's language is induced in the reader. The poet's rapport to language, insofar as it, too, is ultimately based on gesture, is similar to that of the deaf-mute; to the extent that the reader of the poet's language otherwise remains impervious to sounds and rhythms, he, like the deaf-mute, must make his whole body receptive to the sound-gestures in words—to those most primitive, magical explosions.[13] But, Diderot cautions—only to juxtapose again stammering to the original hieroglyphic language of gesture—if cognizance were taken exclusively of language in its original essence, unqualified by acts of reflective judgment, then stammering alone would remain.[14] The "artful hieroglyph" that "holds hidden sway over an entire description" and that derives its power from the distribution of long and short syllables, of vowels and consonants, thus remains untranslatable from language to language. This hieroglyphic Morse code is always and already hidden, as is the stammering muteness which, Warburton believed, had been summoned only to be kept in some other place when Moses adapted hieroglyphics to Hebrew, where God's name remains doubly protected by the absence of vowel signs.

Every communication in hieroglyphics exceeds itself by doubling as its antithesis. The antithesis, however, remains displaced with respect to the supplementary mute sign in hieroglyphics, the determinative, which disambiguates—like some gesture that might accompany speech—the hieroglyph's double sense. In both the interpretation of dreams and the decipherment of hieroglyphics, there are, writes Freud, "certain elements which are not intended to be interpreted (or read, as the case may be) but are only designed to serve as 'determinatives,' that is to establish the meaning of some other element. The ambiguity of various elements of dreams finds a parallel in these ancient systems of writing."[15] As the interpretation of dreams attests, every hieroglyph is the "twin" of its opposite to the point that there remains otherwise no special indication for the negative.

The pressure exerted by opposing meanings which share one sound shape causes stutters of syllables or single letters to explode at and accrue to each end of the root word.[16] Ultimately, however, a shift in sound irrupted within the primal word whereby its antithetical meanings came be to linked and separated as two words, each the stammered variant of the other. An occasional word was left untouched by the enigmatic force of babble: *sacer,* which never stopped embracing two conflicting meanings, attests, given its proper precincts, to the ambivalence which the primal father, the condition of all proper meaning, could not help but command. Just as the crime that consumes the primal father remains displaced with regard to the law it creates, so the murderous cohabitation of contesting meanings, which stammering slips of the tongue yet manifest, must otherwise, like a ghost, keep to some other place with regard to that which it nevertheless continues to control.

Freud accordingly draws the line between two kinds of symbols, both operative in the language of dreams. Over and against those symbols based on obvious similarities there are also symbols which, based on complex chains of analogies now obscure, embrace a much greater conceptual and linguistic antiquity. These ancient symbols, which always and originally represent sexual organs and sexual activities, thus anchor every "dialect" of the unconscious in a primal scene of language origin.[17] While highlighting his new sexual translations of symbols, Freud yet retains their ancient reference to death: every doubling of sexual symbols, for example, shifts their meaning into the zone of castration and death. Freud thus always shifts his conception of symbolicity down to its most ancient contexts, though through the note he drops to Hans Sperber we enter not the underworld but the vibratory space of the primal mating call and grunt of pleasure.

By focusing on those Germanic roots and stems which attach, ultimately, to the meanings of coïre and vulva—the penis, we discover in a footnote, does not undergo comparable tampering—Sperber is able to follow out the "semological expansion power of sexual words." This pulsation, which takes off from the sense of sexual intercourse, begins with expressions for working poorly, cutting poorly, or unsure movement, and always culminates in such figures of broken speech as stuttering. Repression—which, as Freud notes in "Fetishism," remains "the oldest word in our psychoanalytical terminology"—covers, in a word, Sperber's view of language development, whereby increasing semantic refinement and reach were attained the further articulation of thought became displaced from the original mating call and cry of jouissance that first announced the possibility of speech and language.[18]

Not only does the tail end of these semological trajectories always end up meaning stuttering, but the first sexual words were in fact stammering elaborations and displacements of the mating call. Since the sexual connotations of early methods of work—tilling the soil, for example—called for a repeat of the sexually inspired grunt in technically nonsexual contexts, the words that resulted from the destabilized grunt of pleasure had double meanings, at once significative of sex and of the chore to be accomplished.

Freud ascribes to primal speech not so much an original mating call as that call for a lost person which gives rise to the child's stammer *fort/da*. But Sperber rejects the influence of the "language of children," since the infant's every sound was installed, after all, by the parents. Whereas for Sperber the mating call becomes the call of the name, the last vestige of the original magic of language, according to Freud the management of loss issues in the call of a name which stammers or incorporates an affect aroused by trauma. When Freud investigates the source of the anxiety which accompanies acts of repression, he discovers that repression does not create anxiety anew but reproduces affect modeled after an already available "memory image." Beginning with birth, the affects aroused by traumas are "incorporated" into the psyche, where they can, in certain situations, be reanimated, as is the case, in similar contexts, with "memory symbols."[19] Freud compares these memory symbols, which continue to affect hysterical patients, to a city's monuments and memorials which the typical passerby overlooks.

> If you take a walk through the streets of London, you will find, in front of one of the great railway termini, a richly carved Gothic column—Charing Cross. One of the old Plantagenet kings of the thirteenth century ordered the body of his beloved Queen Eleanor to be carried to Westminster; and at every stage at which the coffin rested he erected a Gothic cross. Charing Cross is the last of the monuments that commemorate the funeral cortège. . . . But what should we think of a Londoner who paused today in deep melancholy before the memorial of Queen Eleanor's funeral instead of going about his business in the hurry that modern working conditions demand or instead of feeling joy over the youthful queen of his own heart?[20]

Much as the hysteric retains the initial trauma or loss commemorated by tomb or name, so the schizophrenic reenacts an original rapport with language which Sperber, by concentrating only on that boundary drawn by the displacement of language with regard to the repressed, could not help but overlook. The schizophrenic projects verbal memorials and monuments as a means of circumventing repression. To this end the schizophrenic has cathected word-representations to the point of projecting them outward as delusional systems which always represent not symptoms engendered by repression but restitution attempts whereby the patient tries to retrieve his lost objects, though he must finally content himself with words in place of things.[21] Like these restitution attempts of funerary memorialization, dreams and animal phobias are also hieroglyphic constructions to the extent that they meet on the common ground of projection: "A dream is, therefore, among other things, a *projection:* an externalization of an internal process. We may recall that we have already met with projection elsewhere among the means adopted for defence. The mechanism of a hysterical phobia, too, culminates in the fact that the subject is able, by attempts at flight, to protect himself against an external danger which has taken the place of an internal instinctual claim."[22]

Determinatives held the place of the slight modification in sound, the stammer, which doubled and divided the primal word into two sound shapes. As the double—now ghost, now stammer—which must be simultaneously evoked, though always in some other register, the determinative thus remains the hinge of hieroglyphic projections. Freud can thus introduce projection into the hieroglyphics of the unconscious only in the place where, in the form of oneirocriticism and animal totemism, they were already in place as the premier points of application of ancient Egyptian hieroglyphics. The determinative accordingly served as the originary identifying mark in that visual demarcation of proper names which brought about the complete phoneticization and conventionalization of Egyptian hieroglyphs. The hieroglyph that meant "harpoon," for instance, conveyed a certain sound, w-, which was required for the sounding out of the place name, "the country w———." The sound had thus to be released from its strict relation to its depicted sense so that it might, in the manner of a rebus, double as name, its separation from the literal meaning of the glyph having been effected by the addition of a determinative, in this example the sign for land lying by water.

In Freud's essay on *Gradiva*, we learn that to put an end to someone's dreaming we need only call out the dreamer's name. The pronunciation of the name—and its phonetic representation in borrowed symbols—disenchanted Egyptian oneiro-hieroglyphs, though always only to the point of their renewed encryptment. Because the hieroglyph bears an affinity to the stammer, itself an explosive, broken utterance which withholds at the same time that it conveys, reanimation of the stammering which incorporated proper names into hieroglyphic and cuneiform texts always and already opened up these ancient writing systems to translation.

Multiply sealed and protected, like a mummy, the royal proper name was at the same time the vulnerable cornerstone or niche of Egyptian hieroglyphics. Within the protective ring, those hieroglyphs which resembled threatening animals or plants were distorted to protect the name bearer. Even those hieroglyphs which functioned not as pictograms or logograms but rather as phonetic signs were, when used in royal proper names, vulnerable to the potential danger of the referents of their visible shapes. When two human shapes were suggested by the hieroglyphs composing a pharaoh's name, the cartouche would not suffer that the one face the rear view of the other, an exception to hieroglyphic writing in general, where the sense in which the text was to be read was indicated by the direction in which all such figures were facing.

Any system that operates with determinatives is haunted. In the case of the Sumerian-Akkadian language, a hybrid which resulted from the application by the Akkadians of their phonetic values to the Sumerian writing system they appropriated when they conquered Sumer, the determinatives, which were not mute as in Egyptian hieroglyphics, retained exclusively Sumerian phonetic values. In conjunction with the syllabic signs of Sumerian, these determinative logograms were actually superfluous, and yet when the Akkadians adopted the Sumerian script they were retained, the vestiges of an encrypted dead yet voiced language within Akkadian. So strange indeed was the exhumation of the phantom language within Akkadian that certain scholars, succumbing to the logic of projection they unwittingly described, proposed that the Sumerian language had never existed as a real language but was a mere cryptographic contrivance of the priests.

Taking the plague as inspiration and model for the new—hieroglyphic—theater of cruelty he would establish, Artaud first recast the plague as a psychic entity which, through a sort of telepathic communication, announced itself in dreams (4:20). As evidenced by Sophocles' *Oedipus Rex,* the plague was, according to Artaud, the physical incarnation of unspecified powers at large which, like incest, have the appearance of destiny (4:90). What Artaud finds most striking about the plague is that those internal organs whose function is regulated involuntarily manifest no lesions, even though they are clearly the site of the worst disorders during the course of the affliction. While these yet intact organs appear to have been mummified, engorged with a black substance which has brought about petrification, those two organs most subject to voluntary intervention, the brain and the lungs, have es-

133

caped mummification and yet, covered with lesions, are the most severely injured organs (4:25–26). While preserving the entrails as its memorial, the plague annihilates the organs that separated man from the anus of the other: the lungs withdrew man from the sea, whereupon the development of the brain came to stand in direct relation to the move to upright posture.

The communication of the plague, a communication which traverses the seas and is forecast in dream visions, emanates from corpses. The source of the plague lies in Egypt where, Artaud maintains, it rises from the cemeteries when the Nile recedes (4:22). The new theater of cruelty, which would take as its model the Egyptian plague, reflects the ancient Egyptian doctrine of Kah, the belief that a shadow soul or breath accompanies the deceased into the afterlife. The actor in this new theater "has to see the human being as a Double, like the Kah of the Egyptian mummies, like a perpetual specter from which the affective powers radiate" (4:156). The new theater must, like the plague, grow, through mummification, new organs no longer genitally organized around the upright body: "We must insist upon the idea of culture-in-action, of culture growing within us like a new organ, a sort of second breath" (4:12). Among organless bodies language remains restricted to "something of the importance it has in dreams" (4:112) where it exercises a certain "magnetic fascination" (2:30). The largely gestural language of the theater of cruelty would project "animated hieroglyphs" (4:65), as when actors use their bodies as screens (4:160) or when, as is the case in Balinese theater, ghosts and phantoms enter onto the stage, effecting an "exorcism to make our demons FLOW," which results in turn in an "intense liberation of signs, restrained at first and then suddenly thrown into the air" (4:73–74).

Artaud hoped to bring back into the theater a cruel, that is, as Derrida has clarified, a necessary and determined application of the "elementary magic idea, taken up by modern psychoanalysis" (4:96), the idea of the hieroglyphic arrangement of dreams.[23] With these dream hieroglyphs, which comprise a "language of space"—a "language of sounds, cries, lights, onomatopoeia"—Artaud imagined he would control thought, and even be able to link up his theater hieroglyphically to all organs (4:107). While admitting to having been inspired by psychoanalysis, Artaud describes the concrete language he would release on stage as a language of gestures, arbitrary attitudes, pounding sounds which would in turn be doubled by reflections "of the gestures and attitudes consisting of the mass of all the impulsive gestures, all the abortive attitudes, all the lapses of mind and tongue, by which are revealed what might be called the impotence of speech" (4:113). To dislodge the stage from the dictation-dictatorship of phonic linearity, the theater of cruelty would thus recycle the refuse of language, those remainders which for the psychoanalyst are of the greatest significance, including the lapsus, the stutter, and, as Ferenczi discovered, even the rumbling of the stomach and other bodily sounds.[24] In his new theater, Artaud elucidates, "words will be construed in an incantational . . . magical sense—for their shape and their sensuous emanations, not only for their meaning," just as the theater space itself "will be used not only in its dimensions and volume but, so to speak, *in its undersides*" (4:149).

THE TWO ORIFICES OF FILM

The theater of cruelty and psychoanalysis are the two twentieth-century programs put forth for the analysis of hieroglyphic projections as found in dreams, much as in that analogue to or mechanism of dreaming, the cinema, which, though ultimately rejected by both Artaud and Freud, had offered these cryptographers a seductive shortcut to realization and circulation of their aims.[25] Shortly after having declined Goldwyn's proposal that Freud, for one hundred thousand dollars, serve as adviser in the production of a movie about the famous love affairs of history, beginning with Antony and Cleopatra, Freud found himself faced with having to decide whether to endorse two other film projects, both of which were aimed at illustrating discoveries and techniques of psychoanalysis. Though Freud withheld his endorsement, he did not discourage Abraham from supporting and supervising the UFA film entitled *The Mystery of the Soul.* Cinema, Freud continues in his letter to Abraham dated June 9, 1925, can present the abstract theoretical constructs of psychoanalysis only in the cartoon hieroglyphs proper to its medium.

Paralyzed by the urge to knife his wife, the patient in *The Mystery of the Soul* is led by his psychoanalyst to confront some traumatic scene from his past; the reanimation of a photograph taken in the patient's childhood opens onto the scene he is repeating and now can remember—to forget. Thus both film and psychoanalysis turn to photography to represent the development of unconscious into conscious thought. And yet photograph and film cannot be kept apart to the point of permitting one to represent the unconscious in place of the other; thus the dream, that frequently applied analogue to film which Freud seems to vouchsafe by never referring to it, finds representation in film not in the photographic and cinematic register but only as some alien representation or foreign body: painting, laterna magica, and kaleidoscope conjoin in the dream sequences.

The Mystery of the Soul was the butt of derisive press releases, which prompted Bernfeld and Storfer to conceive another, improved film on psychoanalysis, though Abraham was quick to warn them that the International Press could not extend its authorization to a second film for several years yet, while at the same time he wrote Freud that he doubted their trustworthiness. In the meantime Abraham was dying: the letter that opens the film dispute also describes the onset of what Abraham took to be a bronchial disorder, though what took him in was the infection spreading from internal wounds inflicted by a swallowed fish bone. The course of blood poisoning emanating from this wound remains parallel to the exchange of letters on *The Mystery of the Soul*. In his last letter to Freud, Abraham tried to push his film project through, and Storfer and Bernfeld to one side, by reminding Freud that in every other warning he had conveyed to Freud, specifically regarding the trustworthiness of Jung and Rank, he had been proven correct, though in each case Freud had at first disputed his advice. This, as it turned out, testamentary reminder provoked Freud's consternation: "We ought not to grant the repetition compulsion too much sway," Freud admonished Abraham. The unpleasant exchange regarding film concluded their correspondence, in the course of which theories of incorporation were first rehearsed and, at the end, mimicked in the alternation of cinema and a disease that shifted back and forth between nadirs of exhaustion and euphoric heights.

In his treatments of melancholia as a mourning disorder and of Ikhnaton as the earliest case study of psychoanalytic theory, Abraham had anticipated, though only to the point of announcing, Freud's corresponding investigations. By his own account Abraham was initially exposed to ancient Egypt when he first visited Freud in Vienna in 1907; Freud even secretly slipped into Abraham's suitcase a few Egyptian artifacts following this first meeting to seal, as Abraham acknowledged, the onset of their association (December 21, 1907). The letter in which Freud praises and emends Abraham's reading of Ikhnaton as the mummy of the modern neurotic with all the Oedipal elements already in place and intact also includes the advice to "dig deeper" into melancholia and mania (June 3, 1912).

The deeper Abraham did dig into melancholia the more problematic became its demarcation from obsessional neurosis which, via Freud's case study of Ratman, had first inspired Abraham to compare and contrast melancholic depression with mourning along the trajectory of sadism: awareness of the incapacity for love that must follow this trajectory summons severe depression (March 31, 1915). Abraham remained convinced that, because obsessional neurosis and melancholia were so closely related, the isolation of their differences would articulate most precisely the contours of each ailment.

The broader envelope of their initial exchange on melancholia and obsessional neurosis—World War I—had introduced a new cluster of relations which Freud and Abraham would map onto a difference which had not yet been drawn. While melancholia was the most readily recognizable element in traumatic neurosis—which Abraham, for example, linked to a breakdown of sublimated homosexuality prior to any shell blast—Freud observed that now that war was underway his obsessional patients were better adjusted: "we have sunk to their level" (October 31, 1914). In contrast to Abraham's, Ferenczi's, and Jones's early studies of World War I traumatic neurotics—in which they defend Freud's theories by coming down hard on these would-be victims who cover up with shell shock the earlier sexual problems which had

137

detonated the blast—Freud pushed the analysis of the blasted beyond charges of personal fear of death or castration toward melancholic management of the other's death. Whereas the obsessional neurotic, whose sublimations are still functional, is a killer, the melancholic and the traumatic neurotic alike are murderers in the sense that they cannot acknowledge without taking full credit for the death of the other. According to Freud, so-called fear of death is secondary to the guilty death-wish economy thrown up between ego and superego which governs identification with lost objects. Like fear of castration, this fear of death does not correspond to any conception one might have about oneself. In the case of castration anxiety, excretion and withdrawal of the nursing breast furnish analogues ultimately only for loss of the other. And yet these signposts of departure, which point the way to "annihilation of life," are converted by the superego—which is always on the watch for melancholic identifications it works to abort—into tokens of dread of one's own death or castration.[26]

Coraggio Casimiro, the slogan that Freud and Abraham exchanged throughout their correspondence, even inserting it on occasion in abbreviated form, originates in the cry of encouragement Abraham received when, during some mountain-climbing expedition, it came time for him to follow the example of his guides and eat rotten raw meat. In the context of their correspondence, Coraggio Casimiro opens onto a primal scene which, with regard to the practices or archaic mourning, Abraham was ever trying to reconstruct.

Hard pressed to keep distinct melancholia and obsessional neurosis at one end, and melancholia and paranoia at the other, Abraham, already in his 1911 essay on melancholia, had to choose between the two main ingredients of obsessional neurosis, sadism and anal eroticism. To that day, Abraham states in his letter to Freud dated March 31, 1915, he cannot do without sadism in every reconstruction of a melancholic's history; his melancholics show too much suppressed hostility in their self-reproaches for this not to be the case. Indeed, certain criminal tendencies abound in these patients, even to the extent that melancholia becomes, for Abraham, interchangeable with kleptomania, which represents the biting off of penis or breast (March 13, 1922). Anal eroticism, however, must be left behind so that Abraham can reserve it as the determinative dividing mark between the otherwise so closely related states of melancholia and obsessional neurosis (March 31, 1915). In the course of analysis Abraham even witnessed a melancholic patient turn into an obsessional neurotic, shifting from sadistic fantasies featuring cannibalism to the obsessional notion that he must strangle bride or mother, a sadistic fantasy which remains manual, and thus anal, in reach (October 7, 1923).

Abraham's main contribution to "Mourning and Melancholia," an early draft of which he read in 1915, was, accordingly, the recommendation that cannibalism be considered as the model for melancholic identification (March 31, 1915). In contemplating melancholia, Abraham thus consults lycanthropy, the classical form of depressive delusion centered on the werewolf that devours human beings. In melancholia the ego nevertheless ends up "impoverished" because it does not eat that which it would like to bite into: "It has lost its content (that is, that which it wanted to incorporate)."

Freud gratefully acknowledged Abraham's reference to the oral phase of libido to which melancholia returns, a reference which, as also needs to be acknowledged, first opened up communications between the theory of ghosts in *Totem and Taboo* and the province of mourning and melancholia. But Freud goes on to caution Abraham not to foreground sadism and anal eroticism in explaining melancholia, but to focus instead on the dynamic, topological, and economic dimensions which alone illuminate the mechanism that engenders and explains the affection: "Anal eroticism, the castration complex, etc. are ubiquitous sources of excitation, which play a role in every case of illness" (May 4, 1915). By thus addressing a focus on anal eroticism Abraham thought he had supplanted, Freud sees through—all the way to its main office or orifice, the anus—Abraham's close-range separation of oral and anal zones which would culminate, in 1924, in his six-stage hierarchy of libidinal development.

Abraham hailed Freud's discovery of anal eroticism as delivering a "bomb" (February 23, 1908), the explosive doubling, in effect, of mouth onto anus, life onto death. Thus, though melancholia is in the main oral, the love object devoured is first embodied by the excrement Abraham's patients encounter with dread as they walk the streets of Berlin with lowered gaze. Abraham's first close-range encounter with "the riddle of the sphincter"[27] emerged

139

at the other end of his request for Freud's counsel with regard to an anxious patient unable to eat or even speak in public. The anxious patient was the casualty of early homosexual rapport with an older brother whose suicide precipitated an uncontrollable transfer of painful symptoms between patient and sister (January 31, 1909). According to Freud, anal eroticism is the key to this lock-up of loss; the patient's own symptomatology openly acknowledged eating and speaking to be private, sexual activities. But sexualization of a higher zone or function always reflects, as with stammering, a displacement upward, "that which receives emphasis as oral activity can be converted back into anal activity (speaking, too, of course)" (February 2, 1909).

At the other end of mourning and melancholia, fantasies and rituals of excreting onto the grave and of devouring excrement reflect "an archaic form of mourning retained by the unconscious,"[28] Abraham writes in studies of melancholia he conducted in the 1920s all the way to his encounter with film. Abraham summarizes: "Here we find literal confirmation of our assumption that the unconscious conceives and evaluates object loss in anal terms, and introjection in terms of an oral process."[29]

In 1915, then, Abraham and Freud thus agreed not to follow up the connection between anal-eroticism and cannibalism which Freud first drew by attributing it to Abraham, who pursued only this connection in his subsequent reflections on melancholia, though always under the cover of inscrutable zoning practices. In the 1920s Abraham followed the connection all the way down to an anal underworld where he encountered, already secretly etched and projected, the primal preview of film.

Freud kept this connection in some other place where its open exhibition left it doubly isolated or veiled. And yet the consequences of the link within Freud's reflections would have set a limit to Oedipal interpretation in cases where disposal of dead siblings was at issue; the Ratman, Schreber, and Wolfman cases would have required recasting. Though a crypt carrier, as Nicolas Abraham and Maria Torok have argued, Wolfman nevertheless attested to the truth of those psychoanalytic theories which find their point of articulation outside the rapport with the living dead. He named himself within scenarios of castration, a word he himself would supply at all the proper junctures; he thus supplied testimony and counter-testimony that rescued psychoanalysis from Jung's assault and then from Rank's. In the case of Wolfman, therefore, we find psychoanalysis serving sanctuary for the haunted. Though psychoanalysis never strayed far from hypnotism, telepathy, or oneirocriticism, it nevertheless furnished interpretations and cures which, by never overlooking but also never penetrating the haunted body to the point of linking up its orifices, its secret metabolism, to the overriding economy of this body's derangement, often helped obscure a crypt as its outermost wall or frame.

Abraham pursued this linking up of filmy orifices at the same time that the cinematic end of projection beckoned. As primal and archaic disorder—or *Urverstimmung*—melancholia is an oral fantasy only to the extent that it is centered on the primal mouth—*Urmund*—out of which the anus directly develops.[30] The original depressive disorder or *Urverstimmung* is thus situated on a stage of the anal-sadistic developmental phase which is deeper and earlier than that occupied by the origin of obsessional neurosis. The "complete rending of object relations," Abraham clarifies, characterizes the origin to which the melancholic returns. The melancholic has, accordingly, shifted down to the biting stage, the primal form—*Urform*—of the sadistic impulse.[31] This form is molded by the chewing muscles, which are the most powerful muscles of the developing body, matched only by the hardness of the teeth. And yet, Abraham adds, the close second and frequent substitute for or agent of the chewing muscles are the muscles of the sphincter.[32] The *Urmund,* essentially the anus with teeth, opens onto the anal/oral recycling system of archaic mourning which, veiled by resistance to chewing or biting, is lodged, according to a logic of double projection, inside paranoia. The aperture of paranoid projection is thus the anus: whereas the melancholic's introjection of the lost object is oral and, hence, total, addressing the entire corpse which must be swallowed whole, intact and undisclosed, the paranoid incorporates anally only body parts, either breast, penis, finger, foot, hair, buttocks, or, and in each case, excrement.[33] Just as the incorporated body rules the melancholic absolutely, so the incorporated excremental part tyrannizes and persecutes the paranoid. Such "partial introjection" in turn projects, Abraham concludes, the spatial dislocations so characteristic, shot by shot, of cinema.[34]

Abraham admitted that he had been unable to follow—had

resisted—Freud's application of introjection in "Mourning and Melancholia," even though Abraham himself had introduced cannibalism into this essay. Was it proprietor's frenzy that prompted this blockage in understanding his own idea, Abraham asks; indeed, no, he quickly continues: the temporary greying of his hair following his father's death kept him from recognizing in theory what he at the time was practicing.[35] Freud in turn responded to Abraham's death by falling ill and by thus mimicking the effects of Abraham's ingestion of a fish bone which, like the hair Abraham had introjected upon his father's death, doubles as excrement: Corragio Casimiro. To his colleagues, however, Freud announced, following Abraham's death, that although the personal loss would be irreplaceable, as regards the work of safeguarding the newly founded institution of psychoanalysis, no one could remain without substitute.[36] In addition, as though there were some connection, Freud decided, publicly, to continue keeping the film medium, which often afforded his colleagues analogies to psychic processes, out of the psychoanalytic research he himself conducted and advertised.

According to Rank, only psychoanalysis can pursue the meaning of the double by first looking at a film. By virtue of its method psychoanalysis lets roll wider and deeper-reaching psychological problems only after starting out from some topical psychic surface.[37] But film represents the double by being the double of the dreamwork. According to Freud, the dreamwork raises doubles or shadows only in order to dispose of them: it guards sleep by displaying and eliminating disturbing "remains" of the concluded day.[38] The remainder that acquires a double life in dreams before it is made to fade away is, in every case of doubling of a loved one, animated—like cartoons—by death wishes. Freud and Abraham thus keep this dream screen under parental guidance—as when they stress that the parent whose death or afterlife the dreamer summons invariably shares and threatens the dreamer's gender.

Dream begins and ends as hallucinatory projection, either of the maternal body—the infant's first, hallucinated, dream screen— or of the dreamer's body, a projection construed, in either case, as the projector's double or sibling. The double, Rank advises, is often originally a younger brother with whom his older brother always enters into the self-relation of masturbation; the paranoid

142

is, accordingly, pursued by the menacing doublings and divisions of this autoerotic rapport.[39] Even Narcissus, in Pausanias's version, takes the image in the water to be that of his dead beloved twin.

Whether shadow or photograph, the double actually cast by the body is always an excremental vestige born alongside the body to which it refers. The primitive conviction that the placenta represents the newborn infant's twin sibling, which must even be cared for until corruption takes over, served, Freud concluded, as origin of belief in the dead double. The punishment of coprophagy, which, according to their tomb inscriptions, dead Egyptians pleaded to be spared,[40] always afflicts, in fables of monster making, the excremental twin granted a continued existence.

Mary Shelley's son William died after the novel that recorded William's murder had been completed. William was also the name of Mary Shelley's father, a name already held by her half brother at the time she claimed it not only for her son, but also for the first victim of Victor Frankenstein's monster. Her first child, an infant daughter, was already lost when Mary Shelley conceived *Frankenstein:* Dr. Frankenstein's animation of the monster repeats Mary Shelley's dream of her dead baby's coming to life again when she rubbed it warm before the fire. William was Mary Shelley's secret moniker: so convinced had her parents been that their next child would be a son that, in their correspondence, they referred to their unborn infant as William.[41] Mary Shelley would ever seek to make good her father's disappointment redoubled by the death her birth had brought about. Upon giving birth to Mary Shelley, her mother died of a retained placenta, that twin already named William, whose murder in *Frankenstein* in a sense animates the monster or fiend within Victor Frankenstein's creation. The monstrous living on of the mother is in William's power; the mother (represented both by the monster and by the medallion around William's neck which attracts the monster) strangles and retains William. William always empowered Mary Shelley to write telepathically: not only in *Frankenstein* did she forecast while repeating some loved one's death, but also in *Valperga* she erected "a monument of what now is": "it seems to me that in what I have written hitherto I have done nothing but prophecy."

The double in *The Student of Prague* who ends up sitting on

143

the student's tomb occupies the place of excrement which mourners in certain cultures drop onto the burial site of the departed; but this excremental double doubles as the name also found above the student's grave. The student draws up a contract with a sorcerer who offers, in exchange for the student's mirror image, opportunity and means to marry into an aristocratic family. But the doubling fantasies at the center of *The Student of Prague* are always matched or exceeded by those emanating from the story's margins: the student will never marry the countess because her family aims to retain wealth and surname through her marriage to a cousin, the last transmitter of a name which is the double of her own. The student's deal with the sorcerer, like every contractual relation with the devil—who remains, etymologically, the "double"—was negotiated with death. This contract is the primal form of relation to the other, negotiated first with the mother in the course of toilet training.

In his contract with death's delegate, the student of Prague in effect insures his life, thereby creating a double of his life: Death is thus pushed back and included in insured form. The insured life or double will outlast Death which, like the devil who is always bound to the terms of his contracts, will also have to pay. As *Despair,* both novel and film, demonstrates, only by in fact surviving oneself can this insurance fantasy begin to be put into effect. Thus Hermann, the protagonist of *Despair,* must, like the student of Prague, murder and merge with his double who was always and already the double only of his corpse.[42] The fantasy of doubling "sends" Hermann, as when he approximates, by writing letters to himself, being at once sender and receiver of that which has been posted.[43] The "yellow signpost" he would erect in the post office as "memorial" on the occasion of his first receipt of letters he has sent to, and as, his double recalls the "yellow post" which already marked the property site on which Hermann planned to murder his double; the yellow post reminded him to execute the fiction of the double as that of the long-lost brother.[44] Although it appears that Hermann would circumvent a certain post by contracting someone else to be his own corpse, he has also incorporated by doubling his long-lost brother, whose corpse has always been interchangeable with his own. Hermann accepts his brother's gift of death, transforming it into a gift of life: when Hermann becomes his double or brother by murdering him, he gives himself, now his reconstituted brother, those returns on insurance—on doubling—which only the double can collect. Hermann always summons film as example of how the effect of the double can be produced and protected.[45] Film, where the insurance scam of the double or understudy is played out, simulates only the desire for the double by covering the loss it projects.

Doubling, a mode at once of projection and of introjection or identification, moves back and forth between a theory of ghosts and that of the work of mourning. The tormenting doubt or obsessive self-reproach which overwhelms the modern-day survivor who has lost a loved one is dealt with differently, Freud argues in *Totem and Taboo*, by so-called primitive peoples, though their animistic beliefs, which remain those of the modern-day survivor's childhood, are retained by the unconscious. Savage, child, and the unconscious deal with unacknowledged though distressingly felt hostility reserved even for the deceased by projecting this portion of their ambivalence onto the dead person, who is thus not at rest but vengeful, seeking to invade the bodies of the living or to drag the living into the undead realm. Originally, Freud argues, all the dead were vampires, and the corpse supplied the concept of the evil spirit; originally there was no concept of a natural death, such that every deceased was a murder victim who could not receive proper interment and mourning. The only antidote to this rebound of phantom projections remains, in accordance with the logic of magic, another brand of doubling, identification.

Those who join in the totem meal imitate in sound, dress, and movement the totem animal they slaughter and eat raw; their group identification with the animal cancels responsibility for the death or murder, which is not only celebrated but also mourned. "The mourning is obligatory, imposed by dread of a threatened retribution." The totem animal represents the dead or murdered primal father who, like Osiris, serves in turn as model for every dead person. The mourning ritual which this totem meal reenacts dislodges the survivor's identification with the deceased by reenacting this bond to the point of its being eaten and digested. "When this has been achieved, the pain grows less and with it the remorse and self-reproaches and consequently the fear of the demon as well." The demon double thus becomes an idealized double, the ancestor spirit which is always a friendly ghost.[46]

Dreyer describes the effect he sought to produce with his film *Vampyr* as being that of a report that some corpse lies outside in front of the door: "At that moment the room in which we are sitting has been completely transformed; every object in the room suddenly looks completely different; the light and the atmosphere have changed, although in reality everything remains as before. We are the ones who have changed, and the objects are as we see them."[47] As soon as the corpse of a loved one has been announced, we start projecting a film, which is also always a vampire film. David Bordwell has underscored the significance of the painting which David Gray, the protagonist of *Vampyr*, peruses at the start of the film: it holds the place of a coherent mode of pictorial representation against which Dreyer's film defines itself. This particular painting represents and contains a scene of dying in which everything is already in place for the commencement of proper burial and mourning. But when film animates this dead image and image of death—as already happens in the course of Gray's perusal—picture and motion picture diverge as the film pulls every image into its own indeterminate zone of doubling.

The frame of that coherent model of representation and interment which the painting first refers to becomes superimposable onto the window frame of a coffin which, in his dream, Gray looks not only into but also out through. The immobile viewer—the vampire who sleeps with eyes open—lies at the limit of a model of representation which would stabilize space around the single perspective a camera embodies by forgoing context to the point of lacking even peripheral vision. In his dream Gray attends his own funeral. But one's own funeral can be represented only to an other; only as an other can one attend one's own funeral. One must have, already and always, identified with the corpse.

Our surroundings are transformed by the report that a corpse lies in front of the door. Opening the door we look through a frame to see the corpse. To frame this corpse is already to begin to bury it. Though we can watch the movies we project in our darkened vaults, death itself cannot be represented. The closest approximation remains that double identification with the dead person whereby we bury the corpse together with that part of ourselves which had always identified with the departed. When Gray wakes up from his dream he goes ahead and puts the vampire to rest, whereupon the film, together with its phantom projections, closes with the image of projector-like machinery grinding to a halt. Superegoical identification with a murdered father has brought corpse disposal to this proper conclusion. Gray's busting of the vampire—who occupies in the film the place of a missing mother—has been aided by a father who exhibits phantom qualities even before he is murdered, though once murdered his phantom powers, represented in the main by the book on vampirism he leaves behind, indeed increase. When Gray helps drive the stake into the vampire, the father's phantom appears to the vampire's minions just before they, too, are annihilated.

Film was the phantom projection that endangered Freud's mourning for Abraham. In *Totem and Taboo* Freud saw the origin of phantoms and ghosts as lying in projection; he thus also expressed satisfaction that psychoanalysis had seen through those ghosts and demons flickering on the defensive "screens."[48] The very first projection of ghosts was conceived, then, as disposal of the dead without proper burial. As Lou Andreas-Salomé reminisces, in 1912 Freud's disciples, with Viktor Tausk at the lead, spent the time they could no longer focus on psychoanalysis at the movies. Film technique, Andreas-Salomé reflects, alone approximates, through its rapid alternation of images, our own powers of imagination, right down to the salient disconnectedness common to both. Film repeats and unwinds the "mental treadmill" of both intellectual and manual laborers: "this consideration for our psychic constitution signifies the future of film."

And yet she and a few fellow analysts were once led by Tausk to replace a visit to a slide show on the most recent Roman excavations (*Ausgrabungen*) with one to the movie theater where "a somewhat similar pleasure" could be secured.[49] Freud's analogies to unconscious processes and psychoanalytic technique always shift between the technical media and the domain of archaeology. But Freud also always borrows these two sets of analogy from his patients, whose delusional formations in turn already double as what Freud calls endopsychic perceptions, which always anticipate by reproducing his own theories of the psychic apparatus. In the course of describing the mechanism of projection in *Totem and Taboo*, Freud was reminded of Schreber, who had found reflected in the destinies of the "rays of God" the links and limits of his libido.[50]

Freud had in fact been so startled upon recognizing in Schreber's "rays of God" his own theory of the libido that he gave evidence in his case study that he had developed his theory of paranoia before reading Schreber's memoirs. Via the mechanism of projection Freud had in a sense witnessed his first film on psychoanalytic theory, and it had made him wonder whether there might not be delusion in his theory or truth in Schreber's delusions.[51]

In the course of elaborating and substantiating the Schreber case study through an analysis of a typical paranoid delusion, that of the influencing machine, Viktor Tausk addressed but exceeded the metaphorical association between the mechanism of projection and the cinematic apparatus. Like Kafka's Odradek, the influencing machine is, in the main, a mythic cluster of allusions:

It consists of boxes, cables, levers, wheels, push buttons, wires, batteries and the like. Educated patients attempt to divine the make-up of the apparatus with the help of technical knowledge and it turns out that with the increasing popularity of the technical sciences gradually all the natural forces in the service of technology are summoned to explain the functioning of the machine, though all human inventions do not suffice to explain the remarkable accomplishments of this machine by which the patients feel persecuted.[52]

And yet the schizophrenic's delusions cannot be readily detached from the technical media borrowed by the schizophrenic to define these aberrations to himself. The main function of the influencing machine is to make the patient see pictures which, unlike more typical visual hallucinations, are seen only in the surface, without third dimension, on walls or window panes. This compels comparison of the influencing machine to the laterna magica and cinematograph which, however, correspond too well, Tausk points out before dropping this analogy, to the delusional effects attributed to them; since the only conceptual error in the analogy is that these projectors are not in fact involved, the comparison illuminates schizophrenia only to the extent that Tausk's analysis of the influencing machine applies in equal measure to the cinematic apparatus.[53]

According to Tausk's analysis of the norm which the influencing machine repeats and skews, the sense organs are organized by something that is always akin to hallucination. Our sense of reality—of the difference, for example, between inner and outer states—relies on projection, as does delusional symptom formation. At the time Tausk treats Natalija A., a thirty-one-year-old philosophy student, who for many years has been writing everything down in lieu of her absent hearing, she is in her seventh year of involuntary servitude to an electrical apparatus which, in the course of analysis, assumes the two-dimensional shape of a cinematic hieroglyph. Telepathy and the technical media project her intact sensorium, which includes effects of seeing and hearing produced by the shifts in libido position which regression and projection record and play back. Helene Deutsch offered her blind schizophrenic patient, who nevertheless witnessed, via projection, only visual hallucinations, as confirmation of Tausk's thesis that we all see only movies.[54]

The delusional formation of influencing machines always begins as the sensation that some metamorphosis is already underway. These hypochondriacal feelings are produced when narcissistic libido ends up backed up and blocked by certain organ functions which thus enter consciousness as states of alteration. The ego always turns away, alienated, from the erect organ cathected to the point of overload. Via projection, then, these organs become alien bodies, though when even this strategy fails, that which was alien becomes inimical.[55] Much as in the case of a certain paranoid patient who could describe sensations corresponding to the movement of the contents of his bowels from beginning to end, and who in time learned to ascribe each peristaltic movement to a separate demon, so the patient at the movies combines a sense of alteration with outward projection of an inner process, initially without recourse to belief in an inimical agent.[56] In no time, however, enemy agents, often physicians and university professors, crowd the projection booth.

Suitors, physicians, and professors appear at the controls of the torture machine precisely to the extent that they always demand, and usually obtain, transfer of libido to themselves. Tausk instructs that narcissistic libido and object libido are opposed in the battle zones of Natalija's delusional system which thus regresses beyond the paranoid's delusional management of sexual preference and identity. The victims of Natalija's influencing machine—once again in contradistinction to paranoid delusions—are linked in passive conspiracy. Natalija's covictims, notably her mother, are, like her persecutors, close to her, demanding of libido, and in charge of her body. But, as Tausk astutely adds, they are close also to the extent that they are nearby, while the persecutors inhabit a certain distance with regard to Natalija, a distance occupied by the telecommunications apparatus from which such objects of identification as her mother are excluded to the point of sharing Natalija's dejected, victimized state. Natalija is bound to dispense with her objects much in the way she acquired them: the proximate ones she identifies with, the distant and, consequently, more demanding ones she can divorce only through the paranoid mechanism of projection.[57]

The out-of-phase alternation between projection and identification builds around its motion in place an influencing machine, which always reflects the deadlock of identification it would bypass. Projection, however, dominates the regular exchange between projection and identification to the extent that it supplies object choice: the newborn's libido is not able to reach beyond his own little body until those stimuli first ascribed to this body have been projected onto some separate entity, thereby linking and separating inner and outer processes. In the beginning, Tausk continues, object discovery is conducted on one's own body, which the infant discovers piecemeal as external reality, reaching out even for his hands and feet, which are alien objects. The infant's psyche is the object of stimuli imposed by the body as though by another body; everything, including bodily functions and movements, happens to the infant, is done to and for him. Whereas object discovery can be performed on one's own person only via projection, it is through identification with the body that these *disjecta membra* are joined together to form an ego or body image.

Not only after but also before the morcellating projection of body parts there remains the newborn's inborn narcissism, his self-identity, according to Tausk, prior to projection and identification. At this point the infant is entirely a sexual being—indeed a genital—for whom eating also fulfills the sexual function just as, Tausk adds, the cell nourishes itself to the point of splitting into two beings. The organs and their functions retain this inborn narcissism, which battles the progressive development of the ego, a battlefield which covers the excremental functions and the autoerotogenic zones since these are brought into relation with the outside world only with the greatest difficulty.[58] By succumbing to an influencing machine, the schizophrenic casts out an emergency projection of his own body to circumvent regression to the innate narcissism of the newborn. The most fervent wish of one under the machine's influence is to remain anchored in that alternation between modes of alteration which, like filmmaking, fragments and sutures a body only to animate its total image. But the influencing machine or projected body always fades away to display the newborn infant's unprotected sensorium.

In "A Metapsychological Supplement to the Theory of Dreams," Freud describes sleep as a return to the womb which the dream work protects and superintends by projecting inner disturbances or demands as no longer troubling external experiences. The sensurround of oneiric projections holds the place of the technical media to the extent that, before sleeping and dreaming, we take off every prosthetic device: ". . . every night human beings lay aside the wrappings in which they have enveloped their skin, as well as anything which they may use as a supplement to their bodily organs (so far as they have succeeded in making good those organs' deficiencies by substitutes), for instance, their spectacles, their false hair and teeth, and so on."[59] Film and dream secure through projection a safe and temporary return to the newborn state in order to prevent the full-fledged return of an untenable libido position, which Tausk's delusional projection patient attempts to flee, though it is too late. Each aberrant projection erodes to reveal the regression it in fact carries out: the psychotic can only take steps or stages back into projection.

The "loss of ego boundaries"—the schizophrenic's conviction that his thoughts are not contained within his head but circulate openly and boundlessly, accessible to everyone, just as they are, to begin with, already in everyone else's head—is a late arrival, mediated by a series of emergency projections, of that early identification which lays the channels of an all-pervasive telepathy which the schizophrenic, by projecting it outside, can no longer keep from noticing.[60] The delusional patient starts out by identifying with a persecutor such that everything this enemy wants and does happens to the victim. Through identification, feelings of alteration are thus projected into the outside world: the patient now feels that he is not shifting uncontrollably among altered states but is in fact under someone's influence.[61] Natalija's double remains connected to her "somehow telepathically" such that every manipulation of the machine produces effects in her body. Her enemies thus manipulate this voodoo double either in order to insert slime and terrible smells into her nose or to give her dreams, thoughts, and feelings which are largely sexual in nature.[62] When they occur in dreams, Freud instructs, machines always represent genitals, to which Tausk adds that the dreamer's own genitals serve as model. The dream machine substitutes, Tausk reports from his end, for the discharge of sperm it inhibits by attracting, with each complication in its construction, the dreamer's intellectual attention in place of his libidinal interest.[63]

The influencing machine, Tausk argues, however, is the projected double not of the patient's genitals alone but of the entire body. But Natalija's machine, like Natalija herself, Tausk concludes, no longer has genitals—a deletion which, according to the logic of exhibitionistic camouflage, recasts the machine, after all, as the very simulacrum of her genitals.[64] Even as Tausk writes down this case study, Natalija's machine continues to shrink and flatten out. According to Tausk, Natalija's double is turning into a hieroglyph; her machine no longer represents a body with appended limbs but rather a two-dimensional stick-figure with "inscribed" appendages.[65] At the same time, however, she is returning to her first description of the machine as resembling in its posterior or rump a velvet-covered coffin lid. Tausk circumvents this coffin by associating velvet with autoeroticism and the lid shape with the pregnant womb.[66] Yet Freud seems to take Tausk to task by emphasizing, during the discussion following a presentation of this paper, that Natalija in effect projects a mummy's coffin which was always a two-dimensional representation of the body.[67]

To see only hieroglyphs or film projections is to have returned to earliest infancy: the patient who senses that his own thoughts and feelings are part of a public broadcast system which also transmits the thoughts of everyone else has in effect announced that his libido remains locked into early identification with the outside world. Hallucinations thus emanate from some stage prior to identification, before an open circulation of thought can be remembered and articulated, while two-dimensional hieroglyphic vision reflects a stage in the development of the sense of sight which is even earlier than the hallucinatory stage, which keeps to the third dimension.[68]

Removal of the genitals and replacement of the limbs by their two-dimensional projections or inscriptions describes a conversion of genitally centered libido back into pregenital libido which rendered the whole body a libidinal zone or genital. To be without genitals, to be the battery or extension of some machine, amounts to being sheer genital, a fantasy which in turn belongs to the womb or mummy complex: Natalija's identification with her mother is such that she remains the unborn infant or battery within her mother's womb, rump, or coffin.[69] The mummy, Freud remarks, again in discussing a tentative version of Tausk's essay, returns through physical death to the maternal body, the schizophrenic through spiritual death—a death which, in each case, serves corporeal resurrection.[70] The mummified body, which, like every resurrected body, is not genitally organized, is thus conjugated with the unborn fetus or "egg"—a term which also always designates the mummy's casket.

In the discussion following Tausk's first presentation on influencing machines and their film-like projections, Freud brought up one particular aspect of such paranoid delusions which Tausk did not then address, and which had served Freud, in "On Narcissism: An Introduction," to qualify much of what, in his Schreber case study, seemed to belong in the movies. In the discussion Freud focused on the role of thought control in paranoid delusional systems, specifically as it related to the belief commonly held by the infant that others know its thoughts, a belief justified, Freud suggested, to the extent that, in receiving language from others, the infant has also received their thoughts.[71]

Tausk included this observation in the final version of his essay, relegating what he calls the "loss of ego boundaries" to a stage beyond which delusional projections regress and rebound. He thus does not take into account Freud's elaboration of ego ideal and its adjunct, the "court" of conscience, the trajectory along which narcissism, according to Freud, is always projected. The unborn or undead state, which Tausk saw as that destiny of the schizophrenic which emerges in the effort to escape it, is, according to Freud, already contained in everyone's ego ideal: "That which he projects ahead of him as his ideal is merely his substitute for the lost narcissism of his childhood—the time when he was his own ideal." The "court" of conscience, the ego ideal's support system, insures, by constantly superintending the ego and assessing it according to the ego ideal, that narcissistic gratification is obtained from this ideal. The paranoid, who believes he is being observed and watched, thus has a heightened awareness of what is the case with everyone else.

The institution of conscience, which knows our thoughts and which watches us—and even invents and announces the time—finds its analogue not so much in film as in radio: the paranoid is made aware of this observation post by voices, voices which broadcast not only ancient parental criticisms but even public opinion. In this alliance of ego-ideal and the institution of broadcasting Freud recognized the censor who, in dreams, often reports and comments on the obvious: "Now he is too sleepy to think . . . now he is waking up."[72] Following Schreber's insight that delusional projections were *hingewundert,* the miracular effects of a wound, Freud, in his exploration of narcissistic disorders, pursued a trajectory of incorporation alternating with projection which was less visual than it was auditory (and, hence, according to a logic that remains to be heard, anal as well). When worn by the ego, the "hieroglyph cap" which Freud cites in his essay on "Femininity" is, as Freud makes clear in *The Ego and the Id,* an acoustic cap which collects and turns into words the remnants of overheard words.[73]

Unable to disengage cinema from the linearity of its printing press pedigree, Artaud turned to yet another media outlet—the radio—when it came time to turn on his new theater of cruelty. According to McLuhan, radio represents the first step away from the entire direction and meaning of literate culture, of which film had been the last projection, in that the radio reinstated those gestural qualities which the printed page effaces. Radio first irrupted in the midst of literate society as a kind of tribal drum. According to McLuhan, the drummer summoned by radio's broadcast out of the primal past was, in the case of Germany, Hitler: "The subliminal depths of radio are charged with the resonating echoes of tribal horns and antique drums. This is inherent in the very nature of this medium, with its power to turn the psyche and society into a single echo chamber."[74]

Artaud's conception of the way in which poetry is to be read always called forth the sputtering of radio broadcasts: ". . . it is only outside the printed or written page that an authentic line of poetry can take on meaning and there it requires the space of the breath between the flight of all the words" (11:187). To reanimate the words of the poet, the syllables of his lines would, Artaud emphasizes, have to be *"expectorated*—For, it is in this way that their hieroglyphs become clear" (11:187). Though "the printed page puts them to sleep," "pronounced between lips of blood," Artaud again intones, "their hieroglyphs awaken" (11:198). Indeed, Artaud's own late poetry is inscribed within a syllabic sign system he identifies as hieroglyphic. Artaud pushed this dissolution through novel syllabification of words or names to the point of introducing a language of sheer stammer, a language of invented words, which, though he thought it would be intelligible to all, was actually recognizable only as the product of glossolalia. In his "Revolt against Poetry," Artaud declared that he would separate this language of his own creation from the words belonging to "some astral libido, quite conscious of the formations of desire" inside him (9:144).

Of those poems Artaud wrote and recorded for a radio broadcast which was, however, never aired, "The Search for Fecality" presents the necrospective of that career or corpus which came to an end a few weeks after the aborted broadcast:

> There where it smells of shit
> it smells of being.
> Man could very well have avoided shitting
> and kept his anal pocket closed,
> but he chose to shit
> as he had chosen to live
> instead of consenting to live dead.
>
> The fact is that in order not to make caca
> he would have had to consent
> not to be,
> but he could not resolve to lose being,
> in other words to die alive.
>
> There is in being
> something particularly tempting for man
> and that something is precisely
> CACA
> (*Roarings here.*)
> . . . .
> Two roads were open to him:
> that of the infinite outside,
> that of the infinitesimal inside.

155

And he chose the infinitesimal inside.
Where it is only a question of squeezing
the rat,
the tongue,
the anus
or the glans.
(13:83,85)

LOCATING THE CRYPT

Shortly after the death of his three-day-old brother Robert, Artaud was afflicted with what was diagnosed as meningitis, a diagnosis, however, left open to question. Artaud retained this inflammation of the brain in the form of symptoms that kept him henceforth a heavily sedated patient. His first symptoms, headaches and vomiting, coincided with the death of Robert, the first of six infant mortalities conceived after Artaud, one of three children to survive the Papa-Mama copulating machine which came, in turn, to be subsumed by warfare.[75]

The only one of the dead siblings to survive long enough to establish her place in the family, such that her death at seven months left a place unoccupied, was Germaine. Artaud dates his first speculations on origins—specifically the issue of his own existence—to his age at the time of her departure. Germaine serves, then, as the name for all the infant mortalities whose un-mourned remains received secret burial when their mother deposited them in Artaud. Such a secret transmission has far graver consequences than the scenario acted out, for example, by Rilke and his mother in which Rilke had to play the role, for a limited period of time, of his deceased sister and be a little girl for his mother. To be a little girl or boy, a little anything for mother and to her delight is the fantasy of a perfect childhood.

With Robert's death Artaud's mother first entrusted Artaud, and not her daughter Marie-Ange, with the task of keeping to himself the unmarked graves of her dead children. One consequence of her secret action destined Marie-Ange to be one of those uncomprehending sisters later found tampering with her brother's legacy. At

156

the time of Robert's death, Artaud was given a new name by his mother, Nanaqui or Naki, allegedly to keep his name apart from that of his father, Antoine Roi. She changed her son from name bearer to crypt bearer also by giving him her own mother's name, Neneka, and thus investing him with the powers of life and death she relinquished.

The attacks of stuttering which would afflict Artaud throughout his life first invaded Artaud's vocal apparatus as the baby talk Robert, as a two-year-old, would have been babbling. Artaud's overriding interest in incest, which, from age nineteen on, ruled his every effort as writer, actor, and philosopher, commemorates the continuing existence of Germaine's seven-month-old corpse. Not until Artaud turned nineteen was Germaine old enough to serve as object of incestuous fantasies. As though his own identity were at stake, Artaud begged Gance to assist him in obtaining the role of Roderick Usher in the film version of *The Fall of the House of Usher*. At the end of Poe's tale, Roderick witnesses his dead sister, who had been his incestuous partner in life, break out of the crypt.

In his 1946 "Preamble" composed for the edition of his collected works, Artaud pledged that out of the "black pocket" (*poche noire*) would emerge those he called his daughters, including Germaine, his maternal and paternal grandmothers, as well as, in this case, a certain Yvonne Allendy, who, according to Artaud, was found to have drowned under mysterious circumstances. At the time Artaud writes this preamble all his daughters were deceased, though they had subsequently been preserved by Artaud, who confined them to the black pouch along with his magic dagger and cane, which he had also lost yet retained.

Of these daughters the first had always been Germaine, who had been observing him from her grave in Marseille, though in 1931, Artaud reports in the "Preamble," she suddenly began to watch him in close-up. Germaine served as the name bearer for Artaud's heritage, which, like that of an ancient Egyptian royal house, was thoroughly incestuous. Germaine was, accordingly, the sole or original occupant of the crypt; her usual companions within this pouch—and at the time he wrote the "Preamble" Artaud was obsessively compiling lists of the pouch's contents—her paternal and maternal grandmothers, must be viewed as close-range reincarnations of Germaine. Since their two grandmothers were in fact sisters, and their mother and father first cousins, they and their siblings were all literally german cousins (*cousins germains*)—where german (*germain*) means, etymologically, "of the same parents" and is related to germ (*germe*), which bears a root meaning of "fetus." Thus Artaud's obsessive themes—incest, the German destiny, and the organless body—are among Germaine's effects.

Artaud sounds out, in cosmogenic scale, the secret location of the black pocket by turning to and tuning in the ancient Mexican deities who, "like holes of shadows" "where life growls," controlled human consciousness from its four corners—sound, gesture, the word, and the life-engendering breath (8:204). Artaud's rethinking of what he names with the child's stutter caca is accordingly broadcast through the growling holes found at both ends of divinization and doubling. Thus the Kah—or Kah Kah—which accompanies the deceased down the corridors of the underworld remains at once excremental double and "second breath." Indeed, as Artaud makes explicit: "caca is the matter of the soul" (9:192), while, to express what he means by the soul itself, Artaud makes use of the verb "rémaner," which he defines as follows: "to remain in order to re-emanate, to emanate while keeping all of its remainder, to be the remainder which will reascend" (11:194). The dark growling holes of the Mexican cosmogony, like the black pocket itself, would, then, appear superimposable onto what Artaud calls, in "The Search for Fecality," the "anal pocket," which, for Artaud, is further superimposable onto stuttering "lips of blood."

In discussing Lewis Carroll's constipated nondelivery or stillbirth of fecality in "Jabberwocky," which Artaud was deciphering at the time as part of his translation of the Humpty Dumpty chapter of *Through the Looking Glass,* Artaud speaks of the anus as site of terror. The anus is a site of loss, certainly, the site/sight of the body dropping away from itself, but also of production and reproduction and even of articulation along what Artaud called the "anal larynx of putrefaction" (11:200). Addressing "the corpse of Madame Death, madame uterine fecal, madame anus," Artaud writes: "The breath of the dead bones has a center and this center is the abyss Kah-Kah, Kah the corporeal breath of shit, which is the opium of eternal afterlife" (9:191, 192). Even Coleridge's treason against poetry consists, according to Artaud, in a misreading of the anus: "Coleridge is not one of the poètes maudits, reprobates capable of oozing through at a given moment, of ejecting this little black mucus, this waxy fart of frightful pain at the end of a tourniquet of blood, released at the ultimate extreme of their horror by Baudelaire or his real ghost, by Edgar Allan Poe, Gérard de Nerval, Villon perhaps."[76] If the anus is a locus of horror it yet commends itself for the theater of cruelty, which would have been realized at last, Artaud was convinced, in that held-back radio blast of fecality.

As amplified by Artaud's translation, "Jabberwocky" already approximates the stuttering, farting incantation which would characterize Artaud's final poetry, just as it characterized the way he read poetry so as to make the hieroglyphs audible once again. In "Jabberwocky," the spurting articulation or "hieroglyph of a breath" emanating from two interchangeable orifices always announces Humpty Dumpty, at once sheer head and egg or fetus (*germe*). Though according to the nursery rhyme he cannot be put back together again, Humpty Dumpty discusses with Alice only the guarantees that he will be reconstituted. The dissolution of Humpty Dumpty's organless body is in fact never confirmed.

Already in Artaud's first film, *The Sea Shell and the Clergyman*, we witness the strangling of an invisible woman—Germaine, Artaud claimed in his preamble, was strangled—followed by her decapitation; this severed head is placed into a fish bowl where the water seems to preserve or pickle it while at the same time it surrounds but does not drown, as if cushioning, a suspended fetal head. For Artaud, who could not accept the idea of a natural death—when defining what he meant by cruelty, for example, he pointed out that every life was another's death (4:121)—those who died had either been drowned or strangled, while those who had been born, as he knew from the circumstances of his own birth, had in fact been invaded and kidnapped by a thieving god and placed inside the "shiny membrane" where, splashing about, they had endured, for nine months, masturbation by the membrane which "devours without teeth" (9:64–65). Immersed in water, deep inside the womb, one is drowned, strangled, devoured, though once the waters recede, the corpse, which the water has embalmed, releases hieroglyphic messages and emanations. From that Book of the Dead he had found inscribed within the membranous shell of the womb and of his own intestines, Artaud had drawn his knowledge that life consisted of an eternal recycling of corpses aimed at creation of the organless body. The ring of this recurrence was the anus.[77]

Hieroglyphic ventriloquism always dominated—to the point of surviving—Artaud's rapport with cinema. The identifying mark *germain* (German), yet another mute double of Germaine, resonates at this end of Artaud's screen memories. Artaud participated, in Berlin, in French language versions of German films, performing, for example, in the French double of Pabst's *Three Penny Opera*. This practice of producing a film in two versions in different languages was eventually superseded by the American innovation of dubbing, a procedure Artaud addressed in his brief essay "Les souffrances du 'dubbing.' " Though Artaud expresses concern for the actors displaced by dubbing—dubbing replaces the souls of genuine actors with artificial personalities—he makes clear that dubbing is not an isolated or new event in talking cinema, which had always reached completion through the delayed synchronization of sound and picture.

Doubling and dubbing, being in doubles and speaking another's voice, characterized Artaud's efforts for "germanic" cinema in Berlin, where even the shop-window dummies behind their glittering membranes held a certain erotic fascination for Artaud. And Germaine teleguided Artaud from her own traveling observation post not only to Berlin, that site of dubbing and doubling, but also, through the cane of St. Patrick, to Dublin. This cane, like its partner, the toledo sword, which had earlier been bestowed on him by a black sorcerer, was received by Artaud as magical instrument, the significance of which he sought by consulting Tarot cards. This turn to Tarot inaugurated Artaud's career as prophet and bringer of salvation through destruction—it was the Tarot card of the Tortured Man which had given Artaud his instructions—just as this reading of the ancient Egyptian cards or pages of the book of Thoth marked the beginning of the destabilization of his name. From this point onward he would declare only anonymous publication to be suited for his works, since soon he would either die or be in a situation where he would no longer need his name.

For a period of about one year he would adopt his mother's maiden name Nalpas, declaring "Artaud" to have perished. Indeed, the destruction of "Artaud" turned out to be the catastrophe which, scheduled for 1937, was prophesied with the aid of Tarot, itself the anagram, phonetically seen, of Artaud. This catastrophe, which commenced in Dublin, was fulfilled when, upon his return to France, Artaud was interred in an asylum. Artaud fulfilled his prophecy of destruction with his own name, and at the same time identified that part of himself which did not sign with the patronymic with a certain "German" destiny, as when he dedicated his own copy of his book of Tarot prophecies of doom, *The New Revelation of Being,* to Adolf Hitler.[78]

THE FINAL DESTINATION

That Artaud destined his haunted writing in this way touches on a secret that needs to be deciphered. Hitler was the unspeakable final destination of so many phantom transmissions. Hitler was conceived in the wake of a triple loss: all three of his mother's young children, who had been born in close succession, died within a few weeks of the third child's birth. Having commenced conceiving her brood with her employer, whom she called her uncle though he was her legal cousin, while his wife lay dying in bed, Hitler's mother Klara received this triple loss as testimony to the guilt of her near-incestuous, if not murderous, relation. The birth of Hitler, by contrast, seemed a counter to this testimony.[79] To secure this testimony she gave Hitler her breast and retained one of his testicles, thus establishing that they would in effect share one body and one crypt (cryptorchism).

Klara remained infertile for the four years she kept Hitler feeding at her breast. At once still nursing the offspring she had lost, Klara in effect protected Hitler from the sort of contagion that had deprived her of her first three children by killing off the three children who might have been born in the interim. Following Hitler's departure Klara's breast was accordingly removed; it was surgically removed by a certain Dr. Bloch, though too late to arrest the cancer that afflicted it. Hitler returned to the scene of his departure to press Dr. Bloch to apply painful, costly, yet pointless iodoform treatments to the open wound, treatments so toxic that

161

Klara died in seven weeks time. Dr. Bloch, who was Jewish, was so revered by Hitler that even as late as 1940 Bloch's emigration to the United States was not part of the problem. Only his preservation could protect against the threat his continued existence provoked: the treatments which saved Hitler's mother from cancerous contagion only by killing her were so costly that Bloch remained the recipient of all *Schuld*. Here we find the master plan that Hitler would carry out within an ever-expanding Germany.

Once Germany comes to carry his mother's unmourned corpse,[80] Hitler again urges the expedient excision of the now Jewish cancer which threatens her well-being, no matter what such radical intervention and extended treatments might cost. And this systematic cure through poisoning once again achieved the murder of the mother, while again billing the Jews. In the final recess of his bunker or crypt, Hitler, cornered, railed against the Germans whom he condemned to death, and thereby, perhaps, began to undertake the work of mourning, though indeed he was too late.

BREAKING INTO THE CRYPT

In the wake of the destruction of his patronymic, Artaud commences profusely stammering messages about and from the crypt, messages which conceal or mislead at the same time that they indicate that there is inside "Artaud" a recess to be exhumed. The remains of the patronymic were inscribed within that syllabic sign system, that hieroglyphic expectoration of sounds which culminated in the radio broadcast. But this concealment and dispersal of the name could not repair the already existing cracks in the crypt. Alongside the stammering of the name, itself a desperate attempt to create a diversion, the crypt continues to crack open.

As early as in Artaud's play "The Spurt of Blood," the crypt shows fissures, knicks in Germaine's protective pocket which, however, permit Artaud to spurt out sounds, as Artaud always did when reading aloud his poetry. The crack permits the hieroglyphic reading, just as it makes the word spurt and stutter. "The Spurt of Blood" was, then, the first stutter of what Artaud called an inner language, a language he equated with hieroglyphics. Having conceived of the hieroglyphic origin of language out of writing as having been first rehearsed as engraving on flesh, whether tattoo or acupuncture, the stammerer Artaud turned to the hieroglyphics of his intestines to read his entrails, just as he picked up and transmitted a literal ventriloquism. "The Spurt of Blood" is the first opening of the protective surround, of the black pocket. And yet what is eaten away by the cancer that kills Artaud is the inner writing, the writing on the outer crypt walls, eaten away towards the anal pocket, thus marking the beginning of a decrypting that never made it, the opening of the vault that allows mourning to begin, though too late.

To the corpse of Yvonne, Artaud ascribed the mysterious symptoms of drowning, though, according to Artaud, at the time of her death she was nowhere near water; before Yvonne could be included within his crypt she first had to be embalmed through drowning. And Yvonne's corpse was offered no other refuge; upon her death she had been replaced as Mrs. Allendy by her sister Colette, who even sought to replace Yvonne as Artaud's close friend. By introducing the embalmed Yvonne into his black pocket, he for the first time consummated a relation with the other woman, one of many other women who competed with Germaine, who, before Yvonne, alone had penetrated Artaud. Yvonne is, then, the illegitimate intruder; Artaud's endless list-taking of the daughters within this black pocket no doubt attests to his sense that something was not quite right. And indeed the incorporation of Yvonne is followed by the introduction into the membranous pocket of the sharp sword and cane.

Did the rats Artaud claimed were devouring his anus[81]—the cancer and its attendant pains were approaching from a different direction—in fact come to the rescue of the pocket? Artaud himself was something of a rat, having been kept underground for over eight years, just as there is an hommage to the rat within the remains of his name. And to read this hieroglyph, one might consult the Egyptian *Book of the Dead* where we find that it is Rā who is entreated by the soul of the deceased to give it a place in the "bark of millions of years." Certainly rats are always found scurrying about whenever tombs are opened, the tombs of mummies or of vampires, and in the case of Dracula rats come to the count's rescue. But well-meaning friends guarded Artaud's corpse for three days to keep the rats from penetrating, and Germaine had to perish with her brother.

Anal penetration by rats represents, according to Freud's case study of Ratman, not only penetration by the penis but even child-birth, since coming out of the rectum can always be represented by the opposite motion. On Easter Island rats are used as currency.[82] In Ratman's hieroglyphic language, *Ratten* (rats) and *Raten* (pay-ments) are each the stammering translation of the other, such that prostitutes, for example, are doubly represented by the rat which, by dint of its excremental associations, represents both penis and money. Freud tries to anchor these rat payments with which his patient can never catch up in a *Schuld* relation to the dead father.[83]

In *Totem and Taboo* Freud cites Ratman as exemplary totem bearer. The totem is, like the hieroglyph, a "written sign" which is adopted as name; by succumbing—as children, for example, must—to the power of the name, the bearer identifies himself with the totem animal, which always represents the dead father. Rat is Ratman's totem only to the extent that the rat he glimpses coming out of his father's grave—where it had, he surmises, chewed on the corpse—is his own double from childhood.

The hieroglyphics of rat and rate first emerges by infiltrating the postal circulation of packages sent per *Nachnahme:* COD, of course, but also per surname or *Nachname.* This scenario of the somehow unpayable COD and patronymic, which reduces the fa-ther to *Spielratte,* inveterate gambler and whoremonger who gam-bled with the name he risked loosening and losing, is a reversal of charges which in turn reverses the circumstances of the first emer-gence of the rat totem. As a young child Ratman, in the course of being punished by his father for having bitten someone, calls his father a series of indiscriminately selected names which, by thus gnawing loose the proper name, keeps Ratman henceforward in a safety zone with regard to paternal punishment and intervention, a zone shaped and safeguarded by the magical power of his words and wishes.[84]

During the two-year period alotted to healthy mourning, Ratman always awaited his father's ghost at midnight. Ratman would then let out another rat belonging to his hieroglyphic system by pulling out his penis, which he showed to his father's ghost at the same time he reflected it in the mirror. These initial meetings of dead father and rat within a specular realm—which is also always, according to the logic of the reverse or backside, an anal province[85]—do not cause the son the anguish of perpetual miscalculation until, two years after the father's death, Ratman enters his uncle's "house of mourning" only to discover that his living dead are slaves to his wishes.[86] Ratman now realizes that his dead father must continue to pay for the son's evil thoughts and wishes, while yet living persons must, in consequence of these wishes, join the father in the crypt which the anecdote that sends Ratman to Freud has disturbed. Ratman reports to Freud only with great difficulty the tale he heard of a torture in which the criminal sits down on a pot containing rats which—Ratman concludes just as Freud breaks through his resistance—bore their way into the anus.[87]

Like Freud, who, in this case, finishes Ratman's anecdote for him, the father has always known Ratman's thoughts: from age six on, from the time he first suffered erections (rat visitations), he has been convinced that his parents know his thoughts as though he had uttered them without himself having heard them. Such reasoning, Freud reflects, "sounds like a projection into the external world of our own hypothesis that he had thoughts without knowing anything about them; it sounds like an endopsychic perception of what has been repressed."[88] Just as he here delivers endopsychic perceptions which project psychoanalytic theories, so Ratman first names for Freud that "omnipotence of thoughts" which, as Freud argues in *Totem and Taboo,* created the original ghost when the first survivor of a dead loved one shared this omnipotence with the deceased. The jamming of broadcasts that only superintend Ratman's thoughts—which are known without his knowing it—can only appear on the endopsychic scanner, and thus precisely at the intersection or threshold between the technical media and their underworld.

"Mourning for the father," Freud concludes, is the main source of the intensity of Ratman's illness.[89] Obsessional neurotics are burdened by the guilt of a mass murderer, as Freud puts it, to the extent that they still subscribe to the childhood or totemistic belief in the telepathic power which enables their thoughts and wishes to bring about even a person's death. The omnipotent death wish gives impulse to ghosts and to the technical media. But the father is banished to the realm occupied by the dead in the Cargo Cult: the dead father must engage in a kind of slave labor in exchange for Ratman's omnipotent thoughts. The dead father in effect sustains the rat economy much as his corpse nourishes the rat in the cemetery. This rat which the dead father slaves to animate is not, however, Ratman, who must, as always, share the omnipotence of his thoughts with a dead person, in this case not the father. Ratman's real name, it turns out, is *Leichenvogel* (carrion bird), a nickname he earned among his siblings by demonstrating devotion to funerals he cannot stop attending even to the point of imagining his commiseration with survivors of yet living persons.[90] Whenever Ratman catches himself thus counting on someone's death he throws himself onto the floor to show contrition—though at the same time he in effect performs his underlying identification with a corpse.[91]

Before Freud makes it back to the relation to father, a relation which also always covers the next world, by pointing out that Ratman entertained thoughts of his father's death at an early age, he notes that some slightly older sister had died when Ratman was between three and four years old. In a footnote Freud concedes that the death of the sister figures in certain "epic" fantasies which he and his patient had been unable to pursue according to the terms and conditions of the analysis. But Freud does establish that the sister's death gave rise to a frenzy of misbehavior on Ratman's part culminating in that biting incident which first marked his straying away from the patronymic into the rat clan.[92]

Freud points to the belief that, owing to their rapid movements, such animals as rats bear association with the soul's departure from the body at death. Also in *Totem and Taboo*, Freud cites a colleague who would rather leave rat phobias out of the psychoanalytic explanation of animal phobias as displacements of fear of father onto such animals as horses.[93] In a footnote to the Ratman case Freud allows that rats, which are not so much disgusting as they are uncanny, chthonic animals, represent the souls, specifically of dead children.[94]

Ghostbusters take Ratman at his word and call him carrion bird; the part of rat goes to his dead sister. When the sister died, her brother, now carrion bird, consumed the rat he henceforward carried inside. In *Totem and Taboo* Freud refers to a certain Indian tribe in California which preserves the skin and feathers of the buzzard it murders and mourns.[95] Birds do not die; their skin and feathers are stuffed by that which they animate and cover over. The rat under cover of the carrion bird's skin and feathers is at the controls of Ratman's cargo cult. Those pulled into the crypt—pot or anus—by the rat that penetrates them must slave to pay for the rat's every wish, which is their command. In exchange the rat does not convey the messages of the dead to her brother, whose thoughts are known only without his knowing it.

When that rat tried to get out to vampirize someone other than her brother, the carrion bird could protect her only by creating a diversion that lasted the rest of their life. Freud comes close to—only to stop short of—letting the rat out of the bag. Like Wolfman in Abraham and Torok's reading, Ratman was yet another corpse carrier who found shelter within Freudian analysis.

In a footnote to his observation that we all share with Ratman belief in memory, even though there is not the slightest guarantee of its trustworthiness, Freud celebrates this shared uncertainty as reflecting the great advance made in civilization when matriarchy was exchanged for patriarchy, and the testimony of the senses was dropped in favor of inference and speculation. Freud closes this note on testimony by referring to the hieroglyph for "witness," always a representation of the male genitals. Only thus, Freud concludes, can the connection in German between *Zeuge* (witness) and *zeugen* (to engender) be conceived.[96] In Latin or English, too, the testes are included in testimony, testify, and testament.

Since another witness is always required, the witness is always double; testimony always doubles as counter-testimony. The consequent prolongation of the trial, which Ratman's obsessional thought also always puts into effect, summons "the old German courts of justice, in which the suits were usually brought to an end, before judgment had been given, by the death of the parties to the dispute."[97] Into the construction of every crypt enters doubled testimony: both Artaud and Hitler, for example, bore testimony that their mothers were not murderesses, while literally they bore within them the counter-testimony, in each case, of six siblings. Artaud, for example, claimed he knew himself because he was "a witness of Antonin Artaud" (1:89). And the consequences of Hitler's mission, which his mother had lactically infused in him, to make a testicle of himself, remain final, and unspeakable.

In hieroglyphics, then, as Freud reports from the footnote underworld of the Ratman case, the meaning of witness and testimony is conveyed by a representation of the male genitalia, which thus suffer, within this testamentary zone, the uncanniest of doublings. In *The Interpretation of Dreams,* as also in "The Uncanny," where testicular and ocular anxieties become, as on Roman *phalloi,* interchangeable, we find that doubling in hieroglyphics provides, in the absence of any special indication for the negative, either the plural form of a hieroglyph or the abnegation of its literal—its double or determinative—meaning. The doubling of the hieroglyph "witness" always also means castration, the catastrophic destiny of doubled testimony.

At his end of transference and counter-testimony, Freud was ever encountering resistance to psychoanalysis, resistance which, as in the case of Wolfman, would ultimately manifest itself as constipation. These transfers are conducted and blocked along the anal channel which, originally and always, opens onto the first production, testimony—and sacrifice. In multiple contrast to Girard, Freud drops the term sacrifice into a current context only when contemplating every child's submission to toilet training, the greatest sacrifice a child can offer, and which can be made finally only for love of mother.[98]

The anal bond between mother and child includes, in the zone of its sacrificial displacement, an audio portion as well. Stammering, Freud remarked in a letter to Ferenczi, towered over a displacement upwards of some traumatizing turn taken in the course of sphincteral training.[99] According to Ernest Jones, the mouth and the anus are the only two bodily orifices which, through the controlled release of air, produce sounds. The idea of breath and respiration belongs to consciousness, not to the unconscious since the child first takes cognizance of and interest in an expelled air other than breath. The gaseous inflation of the body thus gives the child a first conception of the mechanism of birth.[100] And yet, at the same time, as Jones argues in some other place, the inevitable equation, among savages and children, of corpse and excrement, has always led to the belief that babies come from some dead person.[101]

A line of distinction and necrofiliation thus begins to be

drawn between excrement and flatus. Jones thus summons Praga-
pati, the Lord of Existence, who created mankind with the "downward breathings that escape from the back part"; of the five sacred
breaths in the Vedas, downward breathing is accordingly associated with speech. The fart not only marks a beginning, of life and
of language, but also possesses the power to regenerate beyond
death as when, in the guise of thunder or of trumpet blast, it wakes
the dead and summons them to eternal life.[102] The view of flatus
as the primal model and ghost of speech finds final confirmation,
Jones concludes, in the expressions flatus inflates: "hot air," "flatu-
lent speech," "poetic afflatus."

In the determinative mode, the gastrointestinal channel transmits by doubling and dubbing, through a literal kind of ventriloquism, the audio portion of cinematic projection. *Fort/da* issues
from this track as that long-distance call for someone close, whose
departure or loss was also, from the survivor's perspective, a close-
call. Thus, Abraham argues, omnipotence of thoughts is always first
rehearsed as the omnipotence the young child attributes to bladder
and intestinal functions.[103] Freud agrees: "the omnipotence of excretions." Excretions are indeed, Freud continues in his letter to
Abraham dated December 15, 1919, "productions like thoughts and
wishes."

One of Abraham's patients, paralyzed by resistance to analysis, had only one defensive measure left: cursing. Rather than
concentrate on the work of analysis he would brood on the destiny
of his curses, wondering whether they reached God or the devil,
and on the destiny of sound waves in general. This brooding ques-
tioning, which pursued not only sound but also smell, originated in
the neurotic's primal reception of flatus, which can be tuned in to
the extent that it, like stuttering, keeps something in, leaves something inside, is the advance emanation of what is yet retained.[104]
Shitting (*Scheissen*), by contrast, embraces conceptions of cutting,
division, and loss. Flatus permits, at the other end, a fart/*da* game
of its own.

The double which the body drops is always a corpse born
alongside the body to which it refers. The primitive conviction,
Freud writes to Jung, that the placenta represents the newborn
infant's twin sibling, which must even be cared for until corruption

takes over, serves—as that loss which can only be projected—as origin of the belief in doubles and ghosts. The excremental vestige or determinative which the body thus casts leaves conceptions of natural birth or death in some other place. Every dead person thus remains, in the unconscious, a murder victim whose remains cannot be flushed but only made to sputter and flicker in anticipation of their viewing, which remains pushed back. This sensurround of projection is thus always and already the primal rehearsal or repetition of our own media-technical sensorium, which is also predicated on the unrepresentability, to the unconscious, of death and castration.

The final point of articulation of this primal endopsychic triad can be found already in a letter to Fliess, where Freud lists those epigraphs to which he hopes to append written works.[105] For a study of resistance Freud has already borrowed as motto the following lines from Goethe:

Mach es kurz!
Am Jüngsten Tag ist's nur ein Furz!
(Cut it short!
On Judgment Day its's just a fart!)

In "On the History of the Psychoanalytic Movement," the history he had already telegrammatically written or anticipated in his letter to Fliess, Freud uses these lines as an epigraph to the chapter on resistance on the part of former colleagues who, like Jung and Adler, had left the movement as though leaving it behind. The motto is curious in many respects. It serves as one of Freud's few graphic references to castration ("Cut it short!"); that which is cut short is pushed out the back, out the anus. Here, however, the anus covers a site of explosive loss, loss not of excrement but of flatus. But is the fart really a loss? Does not the short cut in fact retain while projecting loss?

Like any notational system, the fart makes a long-winded message short, it has the explosive temporality of the hieroglyphic stutter and spurt. Summoned before the forum of the living dead, it issues from the Book of the Dead inscribed within the entrails. On Judgment Day, before the highest tribunal, after years of compressing a lifetime of negotiations into the shorthand taken by the court stenographer, or by the listening analyst, the rapid fire of a fart, it seems, will signal the end of all resistance, for example at the end of an analysis. Freud closes this chapter on counter-testimony and resistance by turning his backside to all those who had not felt at home reading the hieroglyphs "in der Unterwelt der Psychoanalyse," "in the underworld of psychoanalysis."

CHAPTER FIVE
REGULATIONS FOR THE LIVING DEAD

(Gottfried Keller)

I was sitting around in my room, sad and put out, and surveyed my hitherto unruly (*regelloses*) and often poorly applied life. . . . then I thought, how vain is your brooding and complaining. You must get out and celebrate your birthday with splendor (*Glanz*) and joy. And I jumped up and seized cap and stick, but as I reached into my pocket and . . . discovered there only a rusty penny, all splendor and glimmer (*Glanz und Schimmer*) faded away into futile smelly smoke. . . .

Gottfried Keller to Johann Müller, July 20, 1839

On a visit to Zürich Kafka made a point of visiting the "Keller-Rooms" but found them locked (*versperrt*).[1] This "Versperrung," which had earlier kept Nietzsche from penetrating to Keller—though in Nietzsche's case it was Keller's sister Regula who intercepted the philosopher's approach—designates the crypt effect of a corpus that was always and already—to borrow the title of one of Keller's earliest cycle of poems—"Buried Alive."

Nietzsche, who singled out Keller's *Seldwyla Folks* as one of the very few German books which could be affirmed to the point of relentless rereading,[2] remained convinced that, at least in terms of its formal accomplishment, his own work on "sphinxlike problems born mute" could be dedicated to Keller.[3] When Walter Benjamin joined the select crew of Keller rereaders he focused on what Keller himself had referred to as the "quiet underlying mournfulness" without which he could not live.[4] By charting this sorrow back to mythic cult contexts, Benjamin swerves from the Oedipal reading of Keller only to complement it. Benjamin's insight that Keller's humor resounds within the "grotto and cave marvel" of "his melancholic-choleric being"[5] can in turn find support only in contexts which Benjamin keeps out of sight: Freud defines humor as the sole fringe benefit which a nonnegotiable, that is, melancholic, contract with the superego—with the swallowed and preserved dead father—permits.[6]

According to his autobiographical novel *Green Heinrich*, Keller's own profound mournfulness, like that of the novel's eponymous hero Heinrich Lee, commenced in early childhood in the wake of his father's departure. Rather than swerve from Oedipal structures which, as always with the *Bildungsroman*, are themselves the first applications, *avant la lettre*, of psychoanalytic theory, it proves necessary to read the "Versperrung" effect of Keller's corpus literally as improper burial conducted through and under the cover of the bond between mother and son, and the haunting of this bond by the dead father. Keller's father had not been the only one to go; Keller's melancholia conceals and preserves a two-year span of multiple deaths which, by the end of his early childhood, left him alone with his mother and his sister Regula. Keller sustained his own (and his mother's) inability to put the dead to rest through and within his relation to Regula, whose birth, which coincided with the deaths of Keller's sisters Regina and Anna, marked the onset of the two-year period of unmournable deaths. Although Keller lived with his sister for most of his life, not even in his autobiographical writings did he represent the place Regula occupied in the household they shared. And yet this place which could not be represented but only kept, hidden and preserved, in some other place, was the motive force shaping Keller's writing and painting.

DRAMATIC NEUROSIS

After Heinrich has witnessed his first theatrical performance, he compares the dark auditorium (*Zuschauerraum*) of the empty theater to a "blind eye,"[7] and the raised curtain, in turn, to an eyelid

173

which had earlier distinguished the luminous, present world of the performance on stage from the vague void behind the fallen curtain (16:192–93). The *Zuschauerraum* encircles a certain *Schauer,* that dread thrill which Heinrich experiences whenever his mother tells him her dreams about the return of his dead father (3:23). The scene rehearsed by mother and son is Oedipal ("blind eye") but also Oresteian to the extent that it centers on the urge to retrieve a lost father. The scene of the presumed-dead father's return was, moreover, the sole subject of Keller's first literary productions, namely, his early dramas, texts addressed to an audience. Heinrich later compares the trembling shut eyes of his father's mother to a curtained stage on which, on the other side, some former life which included his father is granted, illuminated by some former light, a repeat performance (3:212).

According to Heinrich's parodistic double, the atheist Peter Gilgus, all the world is not so much a stage as an ocular orb: The anatomical model of the human eye, which he carries with him at all times and which he calls "the true eye of God," represents, for him, the physical limits of any knowledge to be had by him in the world contained within his field of vision (6:227). And yet this model replicates the dead, gouged-out organ of sight, just as it parallels Heinrich's own prop, the human skull he takes along on his journeys. In his explorations of the nature of vision and light, Heinrich projects and reconstitutes some enormous organ of sight capable of meeting the gaze of the dead. He distinguishes, for example, between the vision of the animal or "unconscious" being and that of the "conscious" being; with each opening of the unconscious eye the world appears for the first time again, and each time it closes, another world is erased (19:40–41).

The dead eye—which can, however, be carried and kept—opened onto a theater stage, where Heinrich was at once among the enchanted and one of the enchanters. The scene in which Heinrich participated on stage was the witch's laboratory, and the role he played, that of *Meerkatze* or green monkey—literally, "sea cat." As Winfried Menninghaus has pointed out, Heinrich thus found himself repeating an earlier encounter with a "cat," though, in the meantime, they had exchanged roles.[8] The scene of the first encounter was Heinrich's own laboratory, where he kept a collection of embryos he constructed out of wax and embalmed in water-filled jars. As complement to this collection Heinrich drew up a series of maps of the moral and physical universe, including the eye of God which doubled as portal through which Heinrich's father could observe him and his mother. But when Heinrich commenced animating the fetuses by pounding the table and examining the charts, a scared cat emerged suddenly to disturb this spectacular reconstitution of a dead eye's visual field or world (3:113).

In a sense the cat was the apparition Heinrich's ceremony had summoned—at least that is how the neighborhood "witch," who had instructed him in the necromantic arts, interpreted the encounter. Age-old symbol of mother deities, the cat which leaps out of the corner of a resurrection attempt outside normal reproductive channels is the witch's constant companion and double. Thus the seductive witch-child Meretlein—whose story, essentially the chronicle of her slow murder and premature burial, Heinrich feels compelled to "incorporate" and "preserve" within the opening pages of his autobiography—is granted not nine lives but a stay of burial alive: she springs back to life and out of the grave "like a cat" (3:55). Does Keller's autobiographical novel in fact develop some primal scene of resurrection inside the vast eye on stage behind the curtain or eyelid?

Though Keller always hoped above all to make a name for himself as dramatist, even when, as an adolescent, he was largely preoccupied with painting, success ever eluded him. Alongside his successful production of lyric poetry and epic narrative, Keller pursued and kept in some other place the for him unattainable artistic goals of painting and drama.

Drama, it can be argued, is always Oedipal to the extent that it knows only symbolic positions occupied by actors and rehearsed discourse. But by the same token, if it is true, as Gerhard Kaiser, among others, has argued, that the scene that Keller was ever striving to dramatize rendered itself inaccessible according to some necessity, then the unseen and unheard interdiction on which "Therese," for example, founders need not be part of its Oedipal scenario. *Oedipus* is always a possible drama; "Therese," according to Kaiser, is "impossible."[9]

Keller wrote "Therese" alongside his composition of *Green Heinrich*, and then rewrote the play at the same time that he revised his autobiographical novel. "Therese" was based on events in the life of Keller's cousin Heinrich, who, upon losing his young wife to mortal illness, was, as Keller learned from his own mother, beset by his mother-in-law's advances. In the first version of "Therese," a young missionary, who has just returned from Africa, proposes marriage to Therese's daughter, though he in fact desires only the social advancement their union would guarantee. But, like her daughter, Therese has fallen in love with the young schemer. "In this way the entire social circle artificially erected by these refined people collapses and buries the sweet star of this girl beneath its dusty ruins."[10] In the final, though similarly abandoned version, the cynical missionary has been replaced by Richard, who not only is loved both by Röschen and her mother Therese, but sincerely loves Röschen, and even loves Therese as he would his own mother. For Therese, however, the "mother" that comes between her and Richard is a "hated word." Desire for Richard has denatured her. And yet she warns her daughter and her daughter's betrothed that their union can only amount to matricide. Unable to make Röschen renounce Richard and make Richard love her instead, Therese prepares to commit suicide while Richard, in listless panic, leaves the collapsed social circle Keller designated as a place of burial.

For Kaiser and Eduard Hitschmann the dilemma at the bottom of "Therese" is plain enough. Indeed, the drama commences with this search for the misplaced keys to the cellar: *Kellerschlüssel*. And yet the play does not hold its focus on the choice the son (in-law) is asked to make between his fiancée and his mother (in-law). Therese's love for Richard, for example, is, she claims, the "brother" of her love for God; the former triumphs in her heart as must any persecuted child on the verge of being banished from his father's house (20:134–35). While within this extended metaphor Therese occupies the position either of mother or of sister, there is a clear-cut reversal of generation in Therese's proposal to her daughter that, in exchange for the latter's renunciation of Richard, Therese will carry her daughter and revere her as she would her own mother (20:150).

Another fable to which Keller returned every ten years or so with yet another plan for its dramatization had as strong a hold on him as "Therese." In his letter to Emil Kuh, dated December 6, 1874, Keller summarized the fable which so fascinated him:

A man buries his good wife, whom he mistreated. She was, however, only seemingly dead, and, when the grave digger opens the crypt that night to rob the corpse, climbs out of the tomb, takes the fleeing grave digger's lantern, and goes home and rings the bell. Her husband wakes up and, first filled with terror of the presumed spirit, then filled with hatred for his returned wife, does not admit her into the house but instead casts her out into the inclement weather in her shroud so that she might die, and locks the house. Then she falls into the hands of the one who loves and rescues her etc.

According to Keller's sketch for "The Provençal Woman," one of his planned dramatizations of this fable, the presumed-dead woman is also an actress who, upon returning from the grave, attempts in her theater garb to win back her husband. He nevertheless rejects her, not out of brutality but because he takes her to be a phantom. Here, as in "Therese," a woman, shadowed by death, proposes the impossible, namely, as "The Provençal Woman" makes clear, that the survivor choose not some other living person but the phantom instead.

The return or reanimation of the missing father was the main concern of Keller's early dramas, written between the ages of thirteen and sixteen. In "The Witches' Covenant," for example, a certain Urbino has been kidnapped by Satan, who would make the boy his heir. But Urbino refuses to acknowledge this stepfather. Just as Urbino is about to be punished by Satan's minions, his father comes to his rescue. The father's declaration to his son that nothing will ever again separate them closes this "Episode for Small Theaters." Though "Fridolin or the Walk to the Iron-Works" is, in the main, the dramatization of Schiller's ballad, Keller added to Fridolin's escape from the furnace tomb the return of the boy's presumed-dead father. Only by chance did victim and persecutor exchange places, and Robert burn alive in Fridolin's stead. Nothing short of such miraculous coincidence could convince Fridolin's master and surrogate father Count Saverne that the boy's devotion to the Countess remains innocent. Not only are good fathers returned when needed, and ambivalent father figures reconciled, but even bad fathers return from the grave, as is the case in "The Death of Albrecht, Holy Roman Emperor."

While in these early works the father thus appears phantomized along Oedipal lines, along, that is, the double track of ambivalence, the loss that shapes and shatters from within "Therese" and "The Provençal Woman" has a different pedigree. When at age

177

sixteen Keller wrote "The Friend," he left behind his overwhelming preoccupation in his earlier drama fragments with fathers returning from presumed death to rescue a son from menacing father figures. "The Friend," which Keller composed upon having read *Emilia Galotti,* focuses instead on a daughter threatened with loss. A loss in this register would seem to have guided Keller's pen already in "Fernando and Bertha or Sibling Loyalty," one of his first attempts at dramatic writing. The fragment breaks off before disclosing the nature of the catastrophe which has transformed into a place of "deepest mourning" the "spectacle" which formerly united father, mother, courageous son, and beautiful daughter "as though they were off to a wedding." Yet when next the grieving family members are named, the daughter is no longer mentioned.

This lack of mention may well have been Keller's closest approximation to the drama of the missing daughter and sister, the drama he ever fell short of attaining. As Keller wrote in his letter to Hermann Hettner dated September 16, 1850, even "Therese" was his "nameless drama." In "Fridolin or the Walk to the Iron-Works," by contrast, the force of nomination was such that Keller could even sign a letter to Ferdinand Freilingrath on April 30, 1857, "Gotfridolin Keller or in Waddling Commemoration of the Walk to the Iron-Works." Keller thus signed with this caricature of his own dwarfishness, thereby situating the dwarf's journey within the return of the dead. The dwarf openly bore another, though secret, identifying mark. Fridolin was also a saint who brought back to life a dead witness to help decide a judicial dispute. In depictions of Fridolin, this witness, Ursus, is represented as a small boy or as a skeleton placed at the saint's feet.

When the dwarf or perpetual boy Keller was granted a stipend to study the theater in Berlin in preparation for the plays he planned to write, he spent his first months on loan not making any of the connections that were readily available to him. He did not visit Varnhagen, for example; instead, as he wrote Hettner on May 29, 1850, he quite stubbornly decided to keep still and remain unknown for the time being, like, one might add, a corpse or secret star witness. Indeed, certain cultures still hold that the corpse is that witness that can be summoned even from the grave to bear conclusive testimony. The boy or dwarf at Fridolin's feet could bear testimony only by attending his own funeral. Live burial is the

178

poet's destiny in Keller's early lyrics: the poet is the "lie" which the liars have buried alive and which death now vampirizes (1:153). The prematurely buried poet can only hope that at midnight he, like the actress from Provence, will be liberated by a thieving grave digger (1:162).

In a letter to Rudolf Leemann dated September 16, 1845, Keller assured his painter friend that he had conceived "dramatic and other spooky apparitions." The hovering phantom actress, the undead poet, and the resurrected dwarf at the magistrate's feet: these are the spooks of the spectacle Keller pursued but kept in some other place. To describe this other place one might summon Bram Stoker, just as one would cite Sophocles in another context. For Stoker left legibly etched on his corpus the premier non-Oedipal and unrealizable drama.

Stoker alleged that he first conceived the Dracula story in a dream brought on by an overly generous helping of dressed crab. All Stoker tells us of this dream, however, is that in it the vampire king rose from his grave. One must look to another dream and to Stoker's convulsions consequent to its recitation to animate this obscure dream image. The actor Henry Irving commemorated his first meeting with Stoker by reciting "The Dream of Eugene Aram," in which murder and the victim's refusal to die are placed alongside references to Cain and Abel and the Wandering Jew. Recollecting his hysterical reaction to Irving's rendition of the poem, Stoker reflects that only once before, in his childhood, had he known such weakness, namely, when he, born so weak that he was several times declared dead, remained bedridden for some seven years before he first "stood upright." Like the vampire, Stoker, lying in bed, had cast no shadow; according to the superstitions Stoker would recompose as *Dracula,* his own continued existence was, right from the start, posthumous.

Sealed by Irving's bestowal on Stoker of a freshly inscribed photograph of himself, the life-long bond silently forged between the two men on that occasion also conveys some secret shared between the two, between one who refused to die and a great actor. Stoker wrote an account of the great impostors of history, which included Mesmer but centered on a legend of Queen Elizabeth: Elizabeth allegedly died in her youth, whereupon the governess, fearful of the king's most certainly violent reaction, disguised a young boy to take Elizabeth's place. When Stoker uncovered proof that Queen Elizabeth had in fact shared a secret with her governess, he became inspired by the prospect that this legendary transvestism just might be true.

In *The Lady of the Shroud* Stoker brought vampirism into proximity with an impostor's deception. Here the female vampire who traverses the seas in her upright coffin turns out to be a princess who must assume this imposture. This imposture of standing upright, ever conferred on such undead beings as mummies by putting their coffins in an upright position, is part of the crypt effect of Stoker's legend later transferred to—as—film. In an attempt to assuage the leg pains he retained from his performance of Dracula, Bela Lugosi became a drug addict as first station of identification with a role which typecast his entire career. The one apparent exception—which, however, also taps into Stoker's crypt-transmission—was his role as narrator in a film about sex-change operations. At the other end of identification, Lugosi requested that he be buried in his Dracula suit. In this way the proscenium arch of theater, film screen, or coffin once again proffered refuge to one who could not stand upright.

Unable to stand or even exist except through the imposture of theater, the phantom would appear to be maimed in that part of the corpus that has ever borne association with property and possession (*pedis sessio*). The wound inflicted on Oedipus's foot, by contrast, was not disabling; recuperated within his proper name "Swollen Foot," this wound empowered him to translate the riddle of human existence into one of standing upright. Mourning, as the etymology of *Trauer* confirms, is always a fall. In ancient Babylon, for example, the bereaved prostrated themselves, just as the Jewish mourners described in the Old Testament rolled about on the ground in ashes and dust. The prostrate corpse was the emblem of human frailty (*Hinfälligkeit*); it proved that before God, to whom everything is owed, man is wholly nothing. Hence, like the Roman and the Blackfoot, the Jew went barefoot when in mourning since he could only appear before God like the corpse he must put to rest, that is, without possessions, without a name—that is, barefoot.

The baring of the feet may have been a remnant of the ancient mourning practice of ritual nudism or, by the same token,

part of the general tendency discernible in mourning rites to assume a theatrical costume, whether the dark vestments of proper
bereavment, for example, or the tattoos and wounds which the
grief-stricken natives of Australia carve onto their mourning bodies. In like manner, the strewing of ashes over one's head during
mourning can be seen as a vestige of the once-widespread practice
of writhing in the dust. And yet this ash mask, as with other
practices of upright mourning, including change of attire and
change of name, may in fact represent the survivor's most fervent
wish that he not be recognized by the phantom of the deceased.
While in many cultures the period of mourning reaches its proper
conclusion in step with the healing of self-inflicted wounds or the
growing back of cropped hair, the shortest period belongs to the
culture in which, right after interment of the deceased, a race is
conducted among the mourners, who, taking many detours, rush
home in the hope that the phantom will be left behind in confusion. Thus in certain West African cultures a shackle for the feet is
tied around a child's neck to keep the spirit locked inside so that
the child will neither die nor, falling short of that aim, return.

DAD ON ARRIVAL

For Keller and his mentor Feuerbach, reconciliation—
Versöhnung—remains the implicit aim of both sign and son: to
become the son (*Ver-söhn-ung*) means to become the acknowledged second person, sign, likeness—and, ultimately, the original
image—of the father. As Feuerbach clarifies in *The Essence of
Christianity*, we cannot form an image of God, since He is, in
essence, imageless. Yet the son of God, described as God's likeness, is essentially image, that which alone is accessible to "sensual and comfortable man."[11]

Every "speculating subject," Feuerbach argues in his "Critique of Christian or 'Positive' Philosophy," mirrors himself in
himself. Against the "dark ground of the phantasm," a "concept-
less" backdrop which "representation" (*Vorstellung*) supplies the
otherwise "transparent" "phantasm" of thought, thought (*der*

Gedanke) becomes a "mirror" in which the subject finds his reflection, a reflection so greatly magnified, however, that he takes the iconic image (*Ebenbild*) to be at once another being and the originary image (*Urbild*).[12] "The subject dreams with open eyes. Speculation is philosophy in the state of somnambulism."[13] Or, better yet, "Speculation is inebriated philosophy."[14] The speculating subject, which thus sees double, "hates" "sober" philosophy, philosophy "proper," which is able to unite within the identity of self-consciousness the doubling and division of the self. The speculating subject views his own being as that of another: by thus deceiving and exchanging himself, the speculator "always says the same thing, only he says it twice."[15]

The phantasmic difference between divine and human consciousness, which results from the speculative belief in double or nothing and which thus obeys the logic of inversion, God being but the reverse image of man, is not the only concept which mirror images, according to Feuerbach, project and disperse. In *The Essence of Christianity,* for example, Feuerbach declares the image to be the Beyond, much as in *Reflections on Death and Immortality* he deems the image, as that which always and ultimately survives the corpse, to deliver the concept of immortality. This concept is the "conscious," "mirror" reflection and reversal of "unconscious" acknowledgement of irrevocable loss. Through such mirroring, Feuerbach argues at length, the dead are animated, though in such a way that they are comparable only to stars or, perhaps, to the name itself.[16] Alongside or underneath this projection of the dead onto the night sky, he continues, we bear another relation to the departed which is not remote and brilliantly focused but illegibly close-range, parasitical, indeed vampiristic. "Originally," Feuerbach points out, mankind viewed every death as unnatural or murderous, and to this day the only thing the dead leave behind is their pain and anger over being dead. The dead demand blood not so much to sustain their nonlife as to exact compensation and retribution for their violent, unnatural deaths.[17] The deceased loved one, according to Feuerbach, haunts the survivor's circulatory system, a system of blood and of money.

Keller on occasion felt compelled to repay publishers with interest for long-forgotten debts even or especially when, the creditor having died in the meantime, the son would now receive the reimbursement. When Heinrich succumbs to the "passion . . . of unbridled spending, of squandering as such," he considers himself not so much a thief—he is, after all, stealing from himself, he reasons—as the prodigal son who departs with his patrimony in order to squander it (3:151, 162). As with any instance of infinite indebtedness to a father or father-god, of a debt which never can be completely alleviated by restitution or reversal, so Heinrich's relation to his own dead father must be negotiated with credit-signs—signs which Heinrich characteristically takes two ways, where the one is always the morbid, secondary consequence of failure to take the other.

The gleaming appearance of coins prompts Heinrich to spend excessively and illicitly. His very first box of paints and brushes, with which he inaugurates his art as rendition of gleaming appearance, in fact stems from this time of excessive spending and borrowing. And yet, now that the money is gone and the frenzied compulsion to spend banished, Heinrich sees his very paints as the "ruins" of this time of free spending. During the period of "mourning" which he feels the "need" to observe after he has completely depleted his casket of coins (3:171–72), Heinrich paints his first landscape. Heinrich's failed attempts as painter, specifically his inability to capture light in his paintings, can thus be seen, according to Norbert Haas, as already inscribed within his sole recollection of his father:[18]

> Curiously, my clearest memory of him reaches back an entire year before his death to a single beautiful moment when on a Sunday evening he carried me through the field in his arms, pulled a potato plant out of the ground, and showed me the tumescent buds, already endeavoring to awaken in me recognition of and gratitude to the creator. I still see the green vestment and the shining metal buttons next to my cheeks and his shiny eyes into which, looking away from the green plant which he held high in the air, I stared with astonishment. (3:21)

So absorbed was Heinrich with his father's glimmering raiment that he took no cognizance of the lesson his father would have imparted to him, namely, that no person, indeed, no living thing, is created out of itself. The paternal voice having thus been displaced, there remains but the glimmer of his father's glance. And while Heinrich's inner image of his deceased father's actual appearance is but an obscured intimation, his inner image of his father's essence is the coalescence of those disconnected bright points which already punctuated his childhood recollection of his father: "The darker the intimation is which I carry in me of his outer appearance, the brighter and clearer an image of his inner essence has established itself before me, and this noble image became for me a part of the Infinite" (3:24).

Upon his death bed Keller would dream that two knights in golden armor stared at him all night long while standing in front of the little cabinet. When he related the dream to Wilhelm Petersen, he could not let up elaborating on the glitter of the armor, the helmets having cast the faces in shadow: "Over and again he came back to this apparition and could not go far enough in the description of the marvelous gleam."[19] The doubled father—death's delegate in a conserving can—attends his son's departure, though his gleaming appearance in this case obscures the little cabinet in the Keller household.

Keller draws the equation (22:322), and etymology has always confirmed it: Green Heinrich's extra name, that green (*grün*) which refers to those vestigial remnants of his father's vestments which Heinrich wears, is tied to a certain notion of becoming (*Werden*)—a connection more accessible in the French "Henri vert," as Keller referred to his novel in letters to friends. And yet, that "old green path of remembrance," as the narrator characterizes the novel in its second version, covers over what in the first version had been Heinrich's grass-covered tomb, while in both versions we learn that the greenest green grows above the grave. Even "his green name, evocative of the fresh forest" (17:139) pales away as the referent erodes in his artworks, in which "the technical means and the truths of nature . . . could not produce a whole truth and hung about the outline of the drawing like bits of gay tinsel about a skeleton" (18:54–55).

In his first attempt at depicting things in nature, Heinrich sees natural objects as doubling or picturing themselves by "drawing themselves;" he observes, for instance, a tree "whose leaves, arranged in regular rows, were each one distinct, and like the trunk drew themselves simply, clearly, and gracefully against the clear gold of the evening sky" (17:35). Yet Heinrich cannot duplicate the process whereby a tree is seen to outline itself in advance of the artist's own linear approach, because in focusing on each linear segment he renders parts that exceed their original relation to the whole (17:33). Heinrich nevertheless captures a recognizable image: the billowing outlines he always ends up with can, he discovers, be drawn together to net the object, to haul or draw it in (17:35–36). Thus only his uncle, an ardent hunter, immediately appreciates this first sketch and, in effect, congratulates Heinrich on his catch: "enthusiastic hunters have always been inclined to approve of art, inasmuch as it glorifies the scenes of their joys and exploits" (17:37).

Heinrich henceforward conceives his attempt to draw from nature as a "hunt" after "appearances" (17:128); but once he binds these natural images "into the clumsy formulae" of his "virtuosity" their "life and glory are lost" (17:127). The nonmimetic elements of Heinrich's drawing, the lines on the paper and their formulaic arrangement, comprise a kind of net with which appearance can be ensnared. Heinrich later characterizes his sketches from nature as "a small treasure," "since they exhibited only real things" (6:78), a treasure on which Heinrich's "conceptual art" feeds, just as the very brush of the conceptual artist sucks up through the handle the "fresh life of nature" (18:55): "Having passed the better part of his youth in the outdoors, he had preserved in his memory, supported by a lively imagination and his old sketches, a considerable knowledge of green nature, and this treasure of his youth was of great use to him now; for he lived on it all these years" (18:140). Once "this reserve finally paled completely" (18:140), Heinrich constructed "out of nothing" a pictorial art described as being "but a whitewashed grave . . . which enclosed a world which never was, is not, and never will be" (18:145).

Heinrich's miscarried quest as painter to retain the fresh indices the hunter tracks down in nature (17:37) was first rehearsed in that frenzied childhood drama of collecting which, Adolf Muschg argues, doubles as Heinrich's early and primitive rite of mourning for his father.[20] In addition to wax embryos and the assortment of maps of his dead father's field of vision, Heinrich—fascinated, as always, by their "external appearance alone" (3:108)—collects rocks, butterflies, and a veritable menagerie of small animals. Though motivated by Heinrich's then characteristic inability to look on "that which had died or been discarded," each collection ends up recollecting the vestigial remains of what was once alive and which now, though lapsed into lifelessness, speaks to Heinrich in some ancient idiom of mourning that cannot be silenced: "Each one of the miserable remnants made me that much more melancholy, since it was the memorial of a day's adventure in the open air. From the time of their imprisonment to their death in torment, I suffered with them, and the dumb remains spoke to me in a language of reproach" (3:110).

Once even the living creatures he has collected are shadowed by decrepit mournfulness, Heinrich is compelled to kill them off with flaming spear. Stopped short in the midst of the "blood bath" by the "convulsions of the ruined organism," Heinrich quickly buries the dead, half-dead, and yet living, leaving behind a site of murder and premature burial which remained for him a place of dread: ". . . I never dared satisfy that childish curiosity which ever prompts one to dig up and examine that which was buried" (3:112). Heinrich thus ends up collecting the unmourned remains of that which he has at best repressed, that is, buried without looking.

The artistic endeavor that falls short of the hunt it models itself after is also a miscarried mourning ritual. Happy hunting grounds were always and originally grounds for haunting to be conceived. Amulets worn to ward off menacing phantoms and attract friendly ghosts represent the dying glance of the haunted animal which, like the human sacrifice, could destroy pursuers with a now evil eye.[21] The head of the hunter's spear was the original shorthand cipher for death, while on cave walls the speared steer that yet emitted a cartoon caption of breath represented rebirth.[22] The hunt is the preamble to and model for that primal drama which emerges as commemorative ritual always in place of mummification and monumentalization of the deceased. Following the funeral hunt in which the deceased is avenged and redeemed, the dead person's reception into the society of souls is enacted and danced before an audience, which in turn represents the living.[23]

The net Heinrich casts out finally comes back empty, and his art, which had always taken possession of what it depicted, accordingly culminates in an empty, endless, and abstract net-work, described now as "vast, grey spider web," now as "unending web of pen strokes" (19:17–18). Like the abstract work constructed and interpreted within Balzac's "The Unknown Masterpiece," Heinrich's painting has become virtually invisible since, in the course of representing every detail of the model one after the other, the reconstitution of details, which never closes or comes into focus, reveals that each detail exceeds, according to the logic of the remainder, the relation of part to whole. Whereas Balzac's painter joins Dr. Frankenstein in reanimating an amalgam of once-living parts which ends up larger than life, Heinrich concentrates on perfecting his canvas-net in the absence of any quarry. What proves, then, to be his main representational means, and the very end of his art, was first cast out by his mother who weaves unceasingly, in Heinrich's absence, an expanse of linen or canvas into a kind of net: "She sits at the window the whole day, spinning. . . . It looks as if she thought, by this store of white cloth . . . to snare good luck for Heinrich as if in a spread net . . . just as learned men and writers might be tempted by a book of white paper to write a good work upon it, or painters by a stretched canvas to paint a picture" (19:156).

Before Heinrich reaches the conclusion of his art, the only subject he paints masterfully are white clouds, a subject for which, during his first visit to an art exhibit, for example, he felt he had "an inner sympathy." As a child he had spontaneously contrived the name "white cloud" to refer to a young girl, the first person other than his mother who had attracted his affection (16:97). "White cloud" names, then, a sister's empty place, the missing place of each of Heinrich's doomed attachments: Dortchen, Anna, and even Meretlein. "Mountain" (Berg) is another "empty sound" the child Heinrich assigns as he sees fit, and often interchangeably with "white cloud." As he gazes out the window, the mountains and clouds on the horizon so cover up (bergen) and displace each other's boundaries that they appear to form one fluctuating mass.[24]

Heinrich's "free invention" of "allegorical landscapes" (5:177; 18:144) is but a late arrival of this childhood assignment of empty echoes which first culminates in the compelling lies or fictions he narrates at school and attributes to the power of his "creative word" (3:92–94). As Tausk, for example, argues, the lie is the child's first respite from total thought control by his parents.[25] Through the lie the child for the first time keeps something to himself, keeps a secret (*verhehlen*) and receives stolen goods (*hehlen*) in some secret place, in any one of the etymons of *verhehlen* and *hehlen: Hölle* (hell), *Höhle* (cave), *Keller* (cellar).

While Heinrich's pursuit of cloud cover obscures his subtler quest after some missing person, the hunter's net, which is at once Heinrich's means of representation and the sole subject of his depictions, is compared to the grey web of a spider (19:18) and to the grey network of the nervous system, both of which feed on lifeblood (19:47). Indeed, the linen both mother and son weave and cast out is first associated in the novel with shrouds and winding sheets. And the *Grauen* (dread), which resonates in *das graue Netz* (the grey net) he and his mother are ever casting out and drawing in, hearkens back to that "secret *Grauen*" which overwhelms the young child Heinrich as he tries to imagine his mother missing (3:40). While Heinrich must and yet never can capture the starlike pinpoints of glimmering appearance—without, that is, rendering them, in close-up, lifeless vestiges phosphorescent with decay—the mountains and clouds which Heinrich's art encompasses "like a whitewashed grave" (18:145) are in fact the placeholders for missing persons whose absence neither mother nor son can fathom or penetrate.

In his mock disquisition on the philosophical implications of the abstract painting, Heinrich's friend and colleague Erikson congratulates him on having cast out all referential ballast (19:21). Though Erikson concludes that "the damned net" (5:313) is not empty but rather has ensnared Heinrich himself, when next Erikson destroys this net-work, and departs, it seems to Heinrich that it is Erikson who has in fact escaped: "One minute later it was deathly still in my room, and the white-painted door through which . . . Erikson had vanished glistened before my eyes like a canvas, from which, with one sweep, a picture of warm life had been wiped out" (5:314). Even after Heinrich renounces art, he continues to chase this "picture of warm life" which has eluded his canvas-net: he makes "life the true object of life" (19:210), and becomes "a mirror of his people, which reflects nothing but the people, who in turn are, and should be, but small mirrors of the vast living world" (6:291–92).

Though Heinrich thus tries to reach to the other side of this analogy where his narrating self would mirror—and reverse—the blindness of his experiencing self, the "mirror world" of Keller's works, Benjamin points out, necessarily exceeds and subverts any reversal that merely links and separates opposites.[26] Like a photograph, a mirror image, because it registers an emanation, is a material vestige of the referent it neither merges with nor reflects.[27] Heinrich thus cannot help but collect vestigial pieces of "warm life" which, like the green life Keller celebrates in his early poetry—still surviving because sequestered in a tomb—are neither living nor dead.[28] These vestiges cannot be embodied but only developed into "mere shadowy symbols, ghostly designs" (17:140–41).

Heinrich views light as always indexical of its source, as when he interprets a pinpoint of starlight as beaming the "fate" of some distant star. The star in the night sky, which cannot be glimpsed "simultaneously with its real, momentary existence," as can the nearby tree, emanates from a remote and, perhaps, extinct referent (14:40). The perhaps extinct referent: this is what photography always commemorates, even while the photogenic or "light-producing" body yet lives. In "Do You See the Star" Keller views the light-writing of starlight as comparable in its essence to the commemoration of the dead. As is the case with the photograph, the index starlight holds together in one image what has already happened and what will happen but has not yet occurred.

Perhaps already one thousand years ago
The star burst into dust;
And yet its mild light [*milder Schein*] still shines
Over there, quiet and distant.
The essence [*Wesen*] of such shining [*solchen Scheines*],
Which is and yet is not,
Resembles, Dear, your graceful being,
When you have passed away.

Before Keller goes on to explain, in his letter to Petersen dated April 21, 1881, Green Heinrich's affiliation with the "so-called conceptual painters in landscape art," he refers to the changes he has made in the second, "retouched" (*retuschierten*) version of *Green Heinrich*, defending, in particular, the new conclusion on account of its "serious tone [*Stimmungston*] . . . which does not hurt the mother in her grave." Keller's choice of the term *Retusche* from the lexicon of photography to characterize his new *Green Heinrich* suggests that unwanted or unflattering details had been suppressed. Heinrich's dream of a bridge on which persons appear now as living, now as depicted, and time itself appears as "one thing," includes, as part of the bridge, its own retouching mechanism which, in the second version, is in turn retouched. For as the first version alone makes clear, this bridge—which, in its retouched form, has served many interpreters as symbolic embodiment of the view of time central to Keller's works[29]—guarantees the "identity" of persons and their depictions by discarding, during their interchange, all that is dissimilar and different: "There were various holes with fitted granite covers in the polished granite floor of the hall, and whatever appeared mysterious or strange in the commerce and traffic was swept down into these holes with a big broom into the river flowing below, which quickly took it far away" (19:175).

It would appear, then, that with Heinrich's dreams of homecoming, the time scheme of safe return can be represented only as the suppression of indexical relations: time emerges in these dreams as "one thing," as spatial continuity and ever-present movement without intervals, only to the extent that the sequential relation of effect to cause can be rendered a simultaneous one. Thus when Heinrich dreams that William Tell and the arrow Tell launched are both perpetually present, the arrow, the premier indexical or pointing sign, has been rendered nonfunctional, and time itself "wide" (19:162–63).

Photography converts time into "one thing," although, owing to the rule of inversion it must observe, this single thing is never superimposable onto itself; time develops as image lapses into image, negative into positive. The photographic copy, at once indexical and perfectly reproducible, embodies both Heinrich's indexical art and his dream of a bridge on which images and objects are identical only to the extent that each image is itself its object again, and all strangeness appearing between the two is retouched. The photograph captures the image of an object; it ensnares a part or remnant of that object. Like the lock of hair next to it in the album, the photo is always commemorative. Every photograph applies *Retusche* or makeup to a corpse which is yet vulnerable, like Heinrich's mother in her grave. And yet, as is the case when photographs cite and consist of other photographs, any work on the photographic copy itself, including retouching, summons the specter of photographic self-reference, a specter which haunts an endless Piranesi-like spatiality of rooms and frames. Like Heinrich's dream representations, every photograph verges on doubling which is, in effect, internal to it. The implicit and explicit serial proliferation of the photographic copy along an axis of inversion—both inside and outside the frame, for example—confers on photography its phantasmic, occult, and dreamlike aspect.

In his dreams Heinrich develops a circulatory system, one of linen, gold, and blood, in which life and death, proximity and distance, here and there are exchanged like steps in a dance. A dance which at once covers and preserves distance: this, according to McLuhan, is the essence of photography.[30] "We're here and yet we're there," Heinrich's loved ones, both the still living and the already dead, chant in chorus as they sway back and forth (6:121–22). But as with the gold coins which, in Heinrich's dreams, do not connect, but double on contact, the otherwise indexical or deictic points of reference "here" and "there" cannot link together in sequence but only accumulate in place. Although everything in these dreams, even the most remote—Heinrich's mother weaving at the bottom of the gorge, for example—is seen close up, that is, in miniature rather than far away, nothing is ever brought closer. Neither Heinrich's mother nor his dancing, swaying relatives can break out of their holding patterns; they grow pale and vanish, etiolated or occluded by their motion and proliferation in place.

Heinrich compares the circulation of images and persons on the bridge to the "cycling of blood in transparent arteries" (19:175), blood being for him "the general stream of organic life" (19:47), and its cycling and recycling "essence" itself. Though all the images and objects on the bridge are related in their essence, those persons who have most recently turned into their depictions within this circling exchange of objects and pictures "then shone in colors all the brighter since they had emerged in every fiber from the essence of the whole" (19:174). The "essence . . . of things" (18:8) is deemed in the novel the ultimate goal of perception

(18:10), of cognition (19:46), and, here, of representation, and yet in each case this essence is seen as the doubled appearance (*Schein*) of the things themselves. Heinrich, who witnesses natural objects withdraw from his sequential drawings by drawing themselves, can only "draw the essential to the surface by shaking the things themselves" (19:50). The essential, Heinrich discovers, cannot be represented, but only ensnared or shot.

In his dreams Heinrich in effect stands before the interior of the natural symbol, the law of his art. But as Heinrich passes from room to room within this specular and utterly artificial realm, he finds at the far end of every scene of doubling a framed vestige of green life. The irreducible interior of these dreams is always a room which, displaced with regard to Heinrich, holds the now sharply focused, now fading phantoms of his loved ones. Heinrich cannot enter his mother's house, for example, since it is turned inside out. What appears to be his mother in her youth strolls in the garden inside, while Heinrich clings to the facade which consists of highly polished interior walls, cupboards, and shelves. Though he is inside he remains locked out, since the windows open from the other side. To see but not touch the green interior he must block the mirroring glare of the window with his hand. This room to which Heinrich cannot penetrate is, literally, a *camera*. And the camera is a room with a window and with a small reflex mirror.

This camera belongs to Heinrich's mother; indeed, she was always the one shooting the pictures in this mother-son romance. And it is by the strings of her incessant weaving and spinning that she guides Heinrich. In these dreams her spinning is immediately transferred as though via teletype to Heinrich's growing bundle of shirts (*Hemden*). This growing reserve of shirts is the initial or primal scene of doubling to which every subsequent irruption of doubling refers. This is the case with Heinrich's proliferating store of gold, for instance, which has the power to reanimate "dead magistrates," who climb out of the painted court scene followed by the painted criminal (6:134). Above and beyond this gold, it is the abundance of fresh shirts which gains Heinrich entry into the festival of return.

And yet, owing to the linen's proliferation in place, Heinrich is hard pressed to select and don a new shirt so that he can join his dancing relatives; once he changes his clothes his beloved departed cousin Anna appears at his side. Yet he is unable to get rid of his ragged vestments; even when he finally succeeds in casting them out into the river, the water stands still and the rags refuse to sink. This shame that shadowed his reunion with Anna returns at and as the end of his dreams of successful homecoming. As he seeks entry into his mother's house, a specter from his childhood, specifically from the period of his free spending, exacts restitution by ravaging Heinrich's bundle of shirts. Heinrich is thus again reduced to rags he is ever unable to replace or hide (*bergen*). At the very moment of his father's return, shame over these rags drives him away from his mother's house which now appears decrepit, its windows "blind" (6:138).

Heinrich's dreams cover the precincts of an improper burial, the phantom effects of which can be detected as already secretly woven into the contractual bond between mother and son. *Scham* and *Hemd*, which happen to be etymologically related, are the terms of this contract. *Scham* also designates, in the mother's case, the womb, and indeed she reproduces the shirts her son must carry. Etymology invites us to add to *Scham* and *Hemd* the term of the contract that went without saying, namely, *Leichnam* (corpse), that which the son has been delegated by his mother to carry.

At the end of Heinrich's chase after "warm life," there emerges not only an abstract painting but also, on the other side, that part of the novel itself which corresponds to Keller's reception of it as empty representation: Keller referred to *Green Heinrich* now as a "monstrous, immeasurable knitted stocking form" and a "desolate and inept construction," now as "a formless and curious experiment" of which the style is "arbitrary and the content monotonous and morose."[31] Like Heinrich, Keller worked on nets which caught him in a spider's or vampire's repast. Thus he identified with his mother, who was the spider, weaver, and dreamer teleguiding her son's hunting and haunting. The homecoming dreams attributed to Heinrich, for example, were first written down by Keller's mother, who dreamt now of her son's impoverished return, now of his homeward journey astride some splendid horse.

In addition to the incestuous Keller circle of vampirizations, a veritable corporation was formed in Zürich to protect with grants and prestigious state positions a certain investment in Keller. Corporations today can lie about their names but not about their single invariable name which is kept in a secret file to which auditors, for example, nevertheless have easy access. When we look up the names of the Keller corporation in *Green Heinrich,* we find Heinrich's own testimony that his refusal to mourn his father's departure made him the delegate of doomed missions. But the secret file is kept somewhere else. There is, then, in Keller another place of mourning or not mourning covered over in *Green Heinrich* by clouds. In the dream he jotted down in his *Dreambook* on February 2, 1848, Keller surveyed the ground beneath the clouds and the stars. It is the Keller landscape in nuce, the landscape or groundplan of Keller.

> I strolled through a lovely garden, which was mine to boot. . . . The flowerbeds were irregular [*unregelmässig*] in the rural manner, without borders, having the most arbitrary forms, the paths wound themselves [*schlängelten sich*] throughout, soft and smooth, and disappeared [*verloren sich*] and came together again between the most glorious flowering bushes. The garden gradually merged [*verlor sich*], without partition or hedge, with the shady grounds at the apex of the town square. The grounds showed the most gleaming green, the two rivers shimmered in the sun, blue and green, like frolicsome snakes [*Schlangen*]. . . . White butterflies the size of doves billowed slowly above the blue and red flower fields. I wanted to catch one . . . filled and ignited a pipe in order to kill the bird quickly with tobacco juice, but, after taking a few puffs, I was ashamed . . . the colorful garden vanished; grey [*Grau*] surrounded me, and I now saw nothing other than the mighty silvergrey willow which wrestled with the strongest storm wind. It was a picture of the most profound contrition. As though in a frenzy its branches tossed about and roared and sang in such heartrending tones, that I listened full of fear and yet with voluptuous trembling.

EXCAVATIONS

According to Haas's interpretation of Green Heinrich's sole recollection of his father, it is precisely Heinrich's refusal to acknowledge his father's voice and lesson, a refusal redoubled in Heinrich's inability to acknowledge his father's death, which destines Heinrich to pursue a doomed mission. This mission has, moreover, as Kaiser emphasizes, been delegated to him by his mother, who indeed can be seen as the painter and writer teleguiding Heinrich's artistic endeavors. But has she implanted her husband's corpse in Heinrich or in Keller? It is true that Heinrich's mother dresses him in the recycled green cloth of his father's vestments. Nevertheless, such interventions transpire openly and, despite their grotesque theatricality, betoken more the work of mourning than the refusal to assimilate loss.

Keller appended to his diary entry of August 8, 1843, an incident recollected from childhood which has generally been seen as his sole reference to the period of his mother's remarriage. Shortly after his mother married a certain Mr. Wild, Keller, asked by a schoolmate whether the man in the window were his father, assured him that his father was dead, that the person on display was in fact a stranger. Now this exchange, including the allegation of the father's death, has, arguably, already and always taken place: for Keller the father was ever suspended between absence and wild, savage strangeness. "Irascibility" and a "hard head" were, Keller recalled, his father's salient features. The mother, by contrast, always complied with her son's wishes, discarding Mr. Wild, for example, this time after a delay of eight years, and henceforward living solely for the sake of her son.[32]

Keller composed and kept in some other place the "wild" relation between father and son which his autobiographical novel could not accommodate. When in "The Poor Baroness" the protagonist marries a somewhat older woman—just before he gets around to proposing marriage to her, his father contemplates doing so—he stages for their nuptial feast the humiliation of her brothers and former husband who, following her father's example, had systematically maltreated her. The vengeful sadism of the scene of restitution is so strikingly excessive that Keller's colleague Theodor Storm was compelled to send Keller a letter of protest. In such works as "Mrs. Regula Amrain" or "Pankraz the Pouter" the departure or lack of the father is more deeply desired than it is ever regretted. In "Therese" an "unloved" husband and father had, in some former time, been part of the household, but no more: the women are now free to adore the son. And when in "Mrs. Regula Amrain" the father in fact returns, his son is in a position to put him in second place. But first the mother warns her son that the father who has just returned appears "strange and wild," and acts "as though" he wanted to "devour" them (7:257–58).

Situated in the corner of the commencement of Heinrich's autobiography, enigmatic references to parents shadowed by some calamity already suggest that though there is indeed in Keller an Oedipal plot, it is not superimposable onto the family plot or site of secret burial within Keller's corpus. Following his praise of the child who never forsakes or denies a degenerate father, Heinrich singles out for praise the daughter who stands by her mother even on the scaffold (3:22). And "Pumpernickel," which together with "weisse Wolke" and "Berg" belongs to Heinrich's first, freely invented language, contains "Nickel" which, as gleaming metal, hearkens back, as Haas has shown, to the buttons on the clothes of Heinrich's father. And yet it is not simply the dead father who has thus been conjured up by Pumpernickel, but, inasmuch as Heinrich himself deems this word the most fitting designation for the letter P, this stick figure, the letter P itself, also represents a "pumped" up, pregnant father who bears another death in addition to his own.

Along with stepfather Wild, Keller's sister Regula was denied a place in Keller's autobiography, even though each time he returned to Switzerland he lived together with her and his mother, and, after their mother's death, he lived solely with Regula until the end of their lives. It was not until he witnessed her survive a mortal illness, in 1847, that he came to realize just how much he depended on her continued existence. His vampiristic feeding on the "life of mother and sister" was the self-portrait which he, like a vampire, could never render or find in the mirror of his autobiographical novel:

My sister is recovering physically but her spirit and disposition seem to have been affected by the illness: she is confused without fever. At the same time she evinces wit, and the profundity of a tender soul in need of affection has manifested itself for the first time. Mother has been sitting up with her all alone now for fourteen nights. I am a useless ornamental plant, the odorless tulip which sucks dry all the juices of this small heap of precious soil, the life of mother and sister. If God helps me out of this warning, this trial, then everything will be different. Meanwhile I am proud of our secret suffering and of the strength and vigor of my poor old mother and of my sister's quiet worth. (21:77)

Regula's feat of survival could only confirm reservations made early on: her birth in 1822 coincided with the death of Keller's two sisters Regina and Anna Katharina. Another sister, Anna Elisa-beth, born within a year of this calamity, died in 1824 and, only three weeks after the second Anna's departure, Keller's father perished. The child Keller's mother was carrying at the time of this second installment of double death died the following year.

Regula had been left out of *Green Heinrich* along with all these infant mortalities, just as she was left out of the cluster of dreams her thirty-year-old brother recorded in his *Dreambook*. Though only Keller and his mother are recognizable in these dreams, the displaced references are to infant mortalities as much as they are to the dead father or to the death of the father in Keller. In the first dream Keller entered into the *Dreambook*, two figures point to the deaths of his sisters following Regula's birth: both the "child murderess" who sits upright and motionless (*aufrecht und reglos*) with a dead child on her lap, and the young girl who takes the dreamer away from the scene of justice only to double herself into "sisters," one slightly older than the other.[33] Similarly, the somewhat menacing conclusion to this dream sug-gests a fatal birth: the dreamer, huddled together with his sisters, is snatched by the hair by old women, before whose approach he and his sisters had fallen silent and still.

The importance of determining the stillness of a child re-appears in the next dream of the *Dreambook*, in which the dreamer encounters a snake lying on the threshold formerly occupied by the cat, which has died. His mother informs him that the snake is harm-less, though the walking, talking serpent frightens them by collaps-ing and appearing dead: "I . . . called it . . . by name, a name which I have forgotten. Suddenly, however, the snake hung dead." The sentence ends in German: *die Schlange tot*. What was given a name is that "they are long dead," *die Sch-lange tot, schon lange tot*. The snake springs back, however, deriding their fears, joking that one must apparently die to merit their respect. The snake, which is interchangeable with a cat, seems, like the snake at the end of *The Epigram* and like the cat in "Mirror the Little Cat," human and childlike. And in myth the snake, ancient symbol of secret knowl-edge just as it is often the keeper of secret treasures and tombs, was believed to offer human souls a receptable in which to live on after death.

The "game," as it is called, of the snake's death and resurrection, which is played indefinitely in the dream, is in fact often played by bereaved mothers who, fearing the loss of their remaining children, shake them awake whenever they appear menacingly motionless (*reglos*) in their cribs, only to soothe them back to sleep, though in the process they have installed in them the effect of a crypt. Whether or not Keller was submitted to such rituals of resurrection—whether or not his alcoholism was in fact another, late arrival, in alchemical variation, of such practices—this much is certain: his dead siblings were deposited in Keller and he was buried alive alongside them. In the Glattfelden registry Anna Katherina's death was first entered under the name Gottfried, which stands crossed-out alongside the dead sister's name. This mistake was repeated on the occasion of Anna Elisabeth's death.[34]

Such partial death or "decapitation" was what Keller relived when he, like Green Heinrich, was expelled from school.[35] This multiple expulsion, which, as beheading, evokes still birth—and which had thus been rehearsed in each effacement of his proper name and identity along another departure of Anna—kept Keller a head or several heads short of normal height. As witnessed by Athena's birth and by the story of Humpty Dumpty, the head is also an infant-sized womb or tomb. In *Green Heinrich* a transportable skull is the hinge Heinrich shares with each of his doubles, with Zwiehan, Gilgus, and Meretlein. And Heinrich carries this skull, which can be called his own in the same way that a child is called one's own, to its place of burial, just as the patron saints of Zürich, the martyred siblings Felix and Regula, carried their decapitated heads to their own funeral.

At the time of Regula's almost fatal illness Keller wrote down the dreams chronicled in his *Dreambook,* even though the child-murderess dream, recorded together with the snake dream on September 15, 1847, had been dreamt in August 1846: "the dream is still entirely present to me." On December 3 Keller has another dream: a sick kite with shut wings slowly sinks to the ground, directing its mute appeal to Keller while "the neighbors with their children" throw coins at the hovering creature. Keller rushes into the kitchen to find nourishment for the bird, but it is too late: the bird has died and Keller can only defend its corpse from depluming and desecration by the neighborhood children. A young girl suddenly appears offering red carnations, which were "not really carnations," in exchange for three *Schillinge,* but Keller has only two. She sticks every one of her "burning red" flowers into his vase, and agrees to accept only two coins. Here the bird and the red flowers of the landscape, which, in Keller's dream of February 2, 1848, was eclipsed by the grey branches of a weeping willow, fall into place. Birds transport omens, and Keller's wingless creature, not unlike his snake in appearance, conveys the message of an infant's death. But in phoenix-fashion a young girl stands in place of the bird. The red flowers she carries are, as symbols of death and cremation, juxtaposed in the dream to feathers, which served already the most ancient conceptions of the underworld to clothe the dead or undead. While Keller experiences a thrill of pleasure as he watches the girl insert the flowers into his vase—an indescribable sensation which accompanies a mother's mapping out of her infant's body and all its secret cavities—he is stricken by sorrow and anguish once all the flowers are in place in his receptacle, which has a place for as many flowers as are worth two *Schillinge:* two *Schlangen* or long-dead infants.

It is the mother who, largely through sphincteral training, shapes her child's body into a territory which she alone can read like a treasure map indicating sites of secret burial. To this end the body is organized according to time zones of regularity. According to Abraham and Jones, it is not only cleanliness that is demanded of the young child's relation to his anus but even—most stringent demand—regularity in production whereby, in addition to the prohibition against affection for excrement itself, the child's delight in the very process and movement of excretion is also inhibited.[36] The only way to survive this blow to one's narcissism is to identify with the trainer of the anus by taking pride in the regularity the child thus offers up as his first sacrifice performed for love of mother.

As Freud clarifies in *Totem and Taboo,* the taboo which renders the dead, newborn babies, and menstruating women at once sacred and uncanny guards them and those they tempt in their helplessness from illicit desire. This taboo is the oldest law, Freud notes, which has, moreover, been issued against some ancient surmounted phase of development where the menstrual cycle endowed sex, for example, with a kind of migratory regularity centered on scent rather than vision.[37] In everyone's childhood, Freud continues in *Civilization and its Discontents,* this same law is directed against anal eroticism, the sense of smell being once again the indicted function. Since the shift from regularity based on smell to regularity based on repression of delight taken in smelling is repeated on the niveau of the gods, leaving those of surpassed cultural periods to become the demons of today, Freud can conclude that the ancient order of menstruation—of what is called, in German, the *Regel* or rule—persists to this day in demonic, gorgon form within certain haunted contexts.[38]

Regula's deathbed scene and her endless spinning and weaving have been replaced in *Green Heinrich* by the contrivance of a bond between mother and son, just as it was Regula, herself an accomplished drawer of sketches—and not her mother, who ceaselessly calculated the high cost of frames—who followed her brother's career in Munich so closely that she almost followed him to Munich to launch her own career. In Keller's actual autobiographical fragments, moreover, Regula is completely missing; she is included only in his fourth and final abandoned attempt at an autobiography, which he wrote after Regula's death. And even when Keller appears to pay tribute to Regula in "Pankraz the Pouter," for example, in the form of Pankraz's beautiful sister Estherchen, who, in order to await her brother's return, remains with her mother and grows into a distinguished spinster, Regula has essentially been left out, as her own incomprehension whenever guests would address her as "Estherchen" attests.[39] In "Mrs. Regula Amrain," Regula joins her mother by serving as model for the young mother Regula, who has been abandoned by her husband and is assisted in resisting the marriage proposal of another man by her five-year-old son. Regula is in a sense that mother who did not remarry, but remained loyal to her five-year-old, dwarflike brother. For Keller did interfere in his sister's walks in the moonlight, which, as with the boy's intervention in the story, bound him for life to Regula.

In the story Regula insures that the son will keep his end of the bargain. When he attends a wedding celebration wearing Regula's finest dress, and participates, unrecognizably beautiful, in mythological marriage rites, Regula intervenes, forcing her son to return home with her, and even burning her dress after having retrieved it. Herbert Anton has examined this and other examples of transvestism in Keller in light of the interrelated myths of double sexuality and statue-animation.[40] Such switches of clothing and of gender marks—as Keller's references to the Pygmalion legend in particular make clear—were originally part of marriage and mourning ceremonies which symbolically reenacted or rehearsed the mirror reversal that links and separates life and death. According to these ceremonies, the realm of the dead is the point by point reversal of the world of the living: sun and moon move from west to east; the dead descend stairs not by foot but on their heads; they sleep during the day and wander about at night; their words and ours have opposite meanings. Thus to signal that mourning is in progress some reversal is required: the bereaved wear black instead of lighter colors; in certain cultures clothes are put on inside out for the duration of the mourning period, while in others mourners are stripped naked or, if clothing is not generally worn, covered up.

Since the worlds of the living and the dead are separated topographically, the cemetery, together with the mourning activities it organizes, serves as the premier border zone and crossing where the two overlap. Mirrors represent but also destabilize and overflow this holy and taboo zone which the cemetery holds in place. There were cultures in which it was customary to turn mirrors around when someone died, lest the released soul be stolen and kept in the house. For behind the mirror stood an evil spirit which stole and corrupted even one's youthful appearance unless appeased by sacrifice of human blood. Jones links this demon to the emergence of regularity in childhood. The logic of mirror reversal—which governs, for example, the "inverted world" of Heinrich's dreams (6:135)—is always that of the backside: the various cameras within cameras that project Heinrich's homecoming inhabit the anal underworld of regularity.[41]

The various rites of passage emblematized, for example, by the *venus barbata* are most amiably conjoined in such works as "Eugenia," where a statue is animated and its model made to return from the other side of the gender boundary, and "Little Dance Legend," where Musa decides, as she lies dying, to exchange her sack cloth for a white wedding dress. They billow apart, however, in "Mrs. Regula Amrain." What transgression is represented by the very wearing of the dress, of any of the beautiful dresses Keller bestowed on Regula and which she never wore, though she proudly displayed them to visitors and neighbors only then to lock them up? Out of place in the story itself, this miscarriage of transvestism nevertheless dramatizes, within another context resonant with the enigmatic force of nomination of a proper name, the *Regula* or rules of Keller's art. The main injunction these rules convey is implicit in Keller's emphatic denial that his sister had ever served him as model for one of his fictional characters. Keller acknowledged that his sister's tyranny over him reflected "higher instructions." Art itself, in Keller's view, carries out "higher," systematically interrelated instructions: on the one hand, portrait painting, for example, must never resort to allegory or idealization in depictions of significant persons; on the other, the plastic arts must "ennoble mankind, show it the beautiful, the true, the sublime" (22:334). It is hardly surprising that the instructions that rule Keller's household should also govern the aesthetic economy of his art as well. Simply put, Keller must make Regula the guiding principle of his art, even if this means looking the other way. He must never, in words, paint, or person, represent or impersonate her. The art Regula regulates at once conceals and preserves those unmourned bodies she wore like protrusions on her big body.

Coupled as her birth was with such large-scale death, it is only fitting that Regula would be ugliness incarnate, that death that will not die. Regula was in fact so repulsively ugly that she literally scared away Keller's visitors. And when Nietzsche came calling on Keller, Regula chased him out, prompting him to concede to that other harridan, his own sister Elisabeth, that he was indeed fortunate not to be burdened with such a sister as Regula.

Green Heinrich's legacy from his mother, the poem "Lost Rights, Lost Good Fortune," depicts the son as an ancient mariner who, having lost at sea the right to his good fortune, resembles, in his grey, paralyzed restlessness, the "shield of Medusa." Medusa, the only mortal daughter of Phorkys, was slain by Perseus, who was conceived and born in his mother's grave. Perseus kills Medusa by forcing her, in effect, to glimpse her own ugliness. Her severed snake-adorned head was taken by Athena who mounted it on her shield where it for the first time became visible without risk. The shield of Medusa was even commonly attached by the ancient

Greeks to their graves either to protect the dead from evil spirits or the living from the dead.

Keller's aesthetization of his Gorgo-sister can only leave or reserve an empty place for that which excludes itself. This in nuce is Friedrich Theodor Vischer's analysis of the untenable place the ugly holds within the aesthetic perspective that observes rules which rule out ugliness. Vischer and Keller were colleagues and friends: each published laudatory essays on the other's work, work which, in the course of their correspondence, they had already commented on, recommending emendations and revisions. In his "Pfahldorf Stories" Vischer went so far as to attribute certain of his own poetic efforts to his fictional character Guffrud Kullur, a parodistic amalgam of Keller's poetry and persona.[42] In response to one of the few criticisms of his work Vischer had ventured, Keller protested that he had never imagined that the nose-hair braids he had included among the comic accoutrements of the barbarian knight in "The Virgin as Knight" could bear the associations Vischer had identified and called into question, namely those of "nasal mucous and the like," which, Keller conceded, would indeed be "nauseating."[43] Keller had thus provided another concrete instance of what could not be recuperated within Vischer's dialectical conception of aesthetics, according to which beauty is recycled back to itself via the sublime and the comic.

Vischer had located the "dreadful" wandering Jew and such incarnations of the "uncanny" as vengeful ghosts outside the wide arc of beauty.[44] Nose hair, by contrast, dangles at the physiological and physiognomic edge of Vischer's aesthetics. Though sight and hearing are, according to Vischer, the exclusive instruments of aesthetic pleasure, smell approximates to these spiritual organs, since it is linked up to fantasy, while the tactile sense, albeit veiled and spiritualized, enables visual appreciation of sculptural beauty.[45] Vischer's essentially physiognomic conception of the visual arts, though privileging irregularity of appearance, indeed requiring a certain interruption of regularity so that the composition can become "eloquent" (*sprechend*) and "essential," is nevertheless demarcated in equal measure by Vischer's incessant warnings against excessive pursuit of such microscopically or photographically detailed aberration as description of nose hair might be said to exemplify.[46]

Vischer delineated the opposition between landscape painting and historical painting as one of the cornerstones of his aesthetics, and the destabilization of this opposition, specifically the straying of landscape painting from its proper place, as central to *Green Heinrich*.[47] As Heinrich's "conceptual art" amply demonstrates, "disembodied poetry" or "idea painting" must result, as Vischer cautioned, whenever drawing, which is the moment of invention in pictorial composition and as such represents the concept, dominates a painting. The "purely idealistic" "historical or heroic landscape," in which natural and allegorical details are arranged with such regularity that no physiognomic texture can be discerned, also reflects back the artist's overreliance on drawing, that sculptural aspect of painting which can perform only "direct idealization" and render only that which is simply beautiful, that is, not only harmonious but regular in form.[48] At the other extreme, according to Vischer, indefinite, hovering cloud cover results from the pursuit of the painterly side of pictorial representation to the exclusion of drawing.[49]

If Green Heinrich's art would appear to occupy the two extremes outside the fragile orbit of beauty (as described by Vischer), then it would appear that this art has been emptied out and effaced in the face of an ugly irregularity of features so beastly that it could not be dissolved into the sublime or into the comic, and thus ultimately sublimated, distilled into beauty. For the sublime, according to Vischer, is that "fermentation within the beautiful itself" which allows beauty to swallow ugliness and nevertheless collect itself.[50] The ugliness that would correspond to a fermentation without interruption and recuperation, a distillation into nothingness or facelessness, could even be seen to exceed death itself since, according to Vischer, death is a hallmark of the sublime, while various forms of living death are aberrations too dreadful to be considered either as death or in terms of the sublime.

And yet artistic production, according to Vischer, is a recycling system which could be termed vampiristic if it were not at the same time based on guilt. Vischer thus begins with the genius who is *per definitionem* one who creates a technique which he has newly animated and which consists of rules (*Regeln*) which cannot, however, be formulated: "the genius does not make rules, but is rather the rule personified." The genius transmits to his disciples this innate conception of rules through the study not only of works of genius but also of objects of natural beauty which art always contemplates and transforms through retrospection.[51] This glance backward makes the imagination (*Phantasie*) guilty toward nature. The imagination swallowed (*zurückgeschlungen*) the object which appeared naturally beautiful and which must now succumb to the imagination's own originary image of perfection. But in this way the appearance of the beautiful in its objective existence is digested, destroyed. The subject who thus engenders the inner image is nevertheless compelled to communicate and externalize it, to attach it to and impress it upon some material so that it can be dispatched. The sorrow that inevitably afflicts the subject whose inner images do not correspond to any outer production is nature's "revenge," the guarantor that restitution will be made to nature. The imagination's guilty debt to nature is canceled when the imagination, in order to give a kind of objective existence to the internal image and thus release that objectivity it transformed into merely subjective life, falls back upon and returns to the naturally beautiful object and imitates it. It remains, however, the inner image, which the naturally beautiful object does not possess, that is transmitted in the intersubjective response brought forth by the contemplation of art. The material out of which art is shaped must therefore be "dead"; the inclusion of living substance, actual trees or animals, within artistic representation (including drama) is always revolting and alienating precisely because nature observes its own rules and not those of the artist.[52]

Not unlike Nietzsche, then, Vischer assigned a prominent place within aesthetic reflection and production to the guilty imagination or bad conscience. In Vischer's view, too, it is ugliness which is in a sense the motive force behind "the beautiful arts." In this regard, Vischer turned to Lessing, the first to address the place of ugliness in artistic representation.

Like the beautiful, the ugly is, according to Lessing, composed of parts, albeit unfitting ones, which can be surveyed at once. But in the visual arts ugliness is all too present, and the viewer is compelled to look the other way. In poetry, by contrast, ugliness of form ceases to be repulsive, indeed, ceases to be ugly owing to the change of its coexistent parts into successive ones. Ugliness is not, however, simply locked out of pictorial representation, nor does it immediately billow apart in poetry. Lessing stressed that ugliness and nausea must first be transformed, respectively, into the terrible and fear.[53] According to Vischer, in post-antiquity ugliness plays, even in the visual arts, a larger and more decisive role than Lessing allowed. The art of antiquity required for each trait that fell outside the "pure circle of the genuinely human"—the ugly, the wild, the uncanny—a separate "depot" (*Ablagerungsstelle*) where it could develop a kind of particular ideality. Thus centaurs and sphynxes, for example, the "remains" of symbolic formations in the mythic realm, flourished in the corners of this art.[54] In the meantime, however, ugliness has entered art and toppled this "aristocracy of physical form."[55] Ugliness requires and brings with it a dialectical recasting of the aesthetic process.

In the arts of the modern era, direct idealization has been replaced by indirect idealization, whereby beauty emerges as the total effect of a plurality of forms, each of which need not be beautiful since various degrees of disproportion raise artistic interest. But this inclusion of ugly parts must appear as the consequence of the artist's volition and not as accident.[56] Ugliness and accident occupy interchangeable places inside and outside the aesthetic perspective mapped out by Vischer; the admission of ugliness into art is at the same time the entry of chance. Dialectical sublation (*Aufhebung*) insures that this infiltration by chance or ugliness remains without risk for art.[57] And indeed, when art has been prepared for the confrontation, when all its support systems are on alert, ugliness is not only admitted but even summoned, desired by art. Summoned by art, ugly irregularity appears already in a state of disappearing, since it is immediately sublated into something else.[58]

The very notion of ugly irregularity of course refers to the most purely developed norm of regularity imaginable, just as in the ugly individual who presumes to be beautiful there lies embodied the idea of beauty reversed and preserved.[59] This ugly individual articulates a contradiction which engenders reconciliation. The reversal of the beautiful in the ugly is in turn reversed in the claim of the ugly individual to be in fact beautiful. The beautiful, the idea from which the ugly excludes itself, is that which alone has value, according to the ugly.

Though the ugly individual does not exist for aesthetics, according to Vischer, still aesthetics can distill something of value from ugliness, as when ugliness supplies the transition from beauty to the sublime or to the comic. The turn to the sublime or to the comic divests the ugly of its barb (*Stachel*), so that while the ugly remains ugly it becomes at the same time something else.[60] In this way ugliness is not repressed but sublimated and put to rest: the uncanny impression which distorted, diseased bodies make, for example when parts of the body appear animal-like, must be transformed into a terrible or comic effect if this corpus is to be granted, like the beautiful corpse of Christ in the plastic arts, an aesthetic reception.[61]

Because it represents a stage in the unfolding of the tragic sublime, historical painting is the pictorial art form in the best position to convert large amounts of ugliness.[62] Into all verbal artifacts ugliness, together with phantoms and the very small, has more or less free admittance, the only general condition being that it seek transfer to the sublime or to the comic. The representations of poetry are directed in large measure to the inner eye, and that which poetry conjures is cloaked and always partially dissolved in "uncertain sight."[63] The impact of ugliness is weakened by the shutdown of external sight; when confined to the dark chamber of inner vision the effect of the terrible, by contrast, is in fact heightened. Even that sense impression which renders the ugly disgusting, namely stink (*Gestank*), can be made present in poetry where it is, however, but a lever used by the poet to effect the switch to the terrible; nausea thus becomes dread.[64]

One way, according to Vischer, in which the comic supplies antibodies to ward off the ugly, thereby allowing the beautiful to be restored to itself, is through miniaturization: the idea, which has no objective status within the comic perspective, is transferred for safekeeping to the infinitely small and to the subject shadowed by the infinitely small, the subject that in engendering comic contradiction knows that it alone constitutes every content.[65] This rescue operation whereby the comic leads the ugly, from which it springs, to reconciliation has been attributed by Muschg, for example, (independently of Vischer's aesthetic theory) to Keller's literally diminutive style. The ugliness that art processes is always a death that can be put to rest.

In step with Keller's own comment, in a letter to Hettner

207

dated May 29, 1850, that in great drama, for example, humor always stands in complimentary relation to the "dark backdrop of immense mourning," Muschg deems Keller's humor miniaturist precisely to the extent that it always has reference to death's dominion. Keller's pursuit of the miniature is ruled ultimately by his ability to recognize kinship with the "death of a mosquito," Muschg concludes,[66] or with the premature burial of a fly within a doll's skull, as is the case in "Romeo and Juliet in the Village." What is miniaturized attains a certain perfection of detail and has the sensuousness of that which, like a doll's skull or a photograph, can be held in the hand. In a letter dated November 21, 1880, Keller thanked his friend Marie von Frisch for her photo-portrait: "the delicate photograph of you in your disguise (*Vermummung*) with the most charming little louse cap (*Läusemützchen*)." And yet he could not help but detect in her miniaturization and concealment a certain mummification; he was able to discern or foresee, Keller wrote his friend, in her still youthful visage the death's skull already fully developed.

Among the toys which abound in Keller's works, the premier miniature is the "little death" (*Tödlein*) in "The County Bailiff of Greifen Sea." This photograph-like reduction of a human skeleton with each tiny detail intact, visible, and even audible is a memento of desire (9:218) comparable to Green Heinrich's beloved Anna, his "little gem" (*Kleinod*) shadowed by death. And in "Romeo and Juliet in the Village" the future lovers and joint suicides Sali and Vreni play the children's game of touching and counting the prostrate other's teeth, that part of the skull which is always visible, even prior to death and decay (7:96).

Rather than the diamonds which encrust the underworld inhabited by the dwarf, Heinrich encounters in his at once miniaturizing and serializing dreams of homecoming tiny, intensely perfect women encased in crystal. This miniature dreamworld, in which living and dead, near and far, here and there are copresent, is preceded not only by the news of Heinrich's mother's deranged longing for her son's return—and this has been the focus of most interpretations of Heinrich's dreams—but also by Heinrich's confrontation with the problem of disposal of the dead. His landlady died giving birth to a son, who soon followed her, leaving father and sisters behind, a mother-son romance (*Roman*) which represents, by point-by-point reversal, the catastrophic circumstances attending Keller's own "romance," though here, too, the other woman, Regula, has been kept in some other place. Just as Keller cannot represent, replace, or render diminutive—cannot put to rest—the ugliness Regula bears, so he is himself denied, like the tiny weaver in his poem "In Mourning," the dwarf's customary mourning garb. These two interdictions are interlocked. The precise contours of the mourning unavailable to Keller and his sister can be found tucked inside *Martin Salander* in a fairy tale about a dwarf people (*Geschlecht*) for whom the work of mourning is rule of thumb. When the time has come for the dwarves to die out in a particular region, the tiny folk gather together for a final farewell feast. Following this funeral banquet the youngest single female of the clan stays behind, alone, to collect, clean, and bury the tableware, whereupon she sets out to find another miniature people to whom she can transmit the remembrance of the departed. She even stands a good chance of marrying a member of the new host tribe (12:36–39).

Regula's ugliness presides over Keller's art: his landscape painting, for instance, was devoid of figures, which he was in fact incapable of drawing. This did not of course transpire in the sense of that regularity (*Regelmässigkeit*) which, according to received aesthetic theory, determines the suitability of a face for depiction, but rather as the injunction her physiognomic irregularity imparted to Keller not to read or write the inscriptions on her face that could otherwise not be rejected.

Every resurrection of a dead sister in Keller's works names the aesthetic rule that keeps Regula in some other place. The premise of "Regina," for example, is that "the face is the transparent sign (*Aushängeschild*) of the physical and spiritual person; it cannot deceive in the long run . . ." (11:57–58). Regina's beautiful face typifies the same *Regelmässigkeit* even her handwriting evinces. And yet the regularity her face displays is unreadable, mute, inanimate. She has never been anything other than that corpse her husband tries to bring back to life after her suicide, and which he had animated once before when, in Pygmalion fashion, he recast his "lucky find" through education.

Regula's ugliness—or rather the revulsion it engendered—was the regulator of Keller's faceless art. Regula had to be left out so that, elsewhere, in some little place, her wish that she be found pretty might be granted. This little place in the heart is held in *Green Heinrich* by Dortchen Schönfund, whose surname refers to that serendipity (*Schönfund*) whereby she became the cherished foundling daughter who was found pretty (*schön gefunden*): "all women are gathered together in her," Heinrich reflects, "with the exception of the ugly and bad ones" (19:276). Dortchen, whose given name is the diminutive of place, and who enters *Green Heinrich* alongside her request that Heinrich give her this little place in the continuation of his memoirs, is in fact made to point to an absent place. Though Dortchen believes that life has reference only to presence such that her "distinctive sign" (*Wahrzeichen*) is her refusal to believe in an afterlife, Heinrich acknowledges the noncoincidence and nonsimultaneity of points of reference within his experience of "Dortchen" when, bemoaning her temporary absence, he identified Dortchen with the deictic *dort* embedded within her name: "Dortchen ist nicht Hierchen" ("There-*chen* is not Here-*chen*") (19:302).

The little place that "Dortchen" designates is also held by Anna's coffin window, marvelously veiled by the photographic imprint of the etching of angels the glass had formerly covered. Here the beauty of the dead is preserved as the portrait Heinrich cannot paint. The sole instance of his portrait depiction of a pretty regularity of features is here represented by a coffin window, itself a token of the wish that the corpse remain exquisite, immutable. What at first seems the most transparent symbol imaginable—the image imparted by a picture of angels to the glass that framed it—is an indexical imprint, a photographic negative or mirror image of the picture the glass once covered. And when Heinrich places this imprinted glass into the coffin-window which opens onto his deceased cousin Anna's visage, he in effect buries a portion of his own "life in symbols":

> Then I lifted the pane of glass . . . and when I held up the shining glass, high, against the sun and looked through it, I saw the loveliest marvel that I have ever seen. I saw three boy-angels making music . . . but the vision was so thinly and delicately transparent that I did not know whether it was hovering in the rays of the sun, in the glass, or merely in my imagination. . . . Since then I have been told that copper-plate engravings or drawings which have lain undisturbed for a great many years behind a glass,

communicate themselves to the glass during these years, in the dark nights, and leave behind upon it something like a lasting mirror image.

The last ray of sunlight now illuminated through the pane of glass the pale face beneath it; the sensation which I felt at that moment was so strange, that I can only designate it with the alien, pompous and cold word "objective," which German aesthetics has invented. I believe that the pane of glass cast a spell on me, so that, in lofty and solemn mood but in complete calmness, I watched that which lay behind it being buried, as if it had been a portion of my own experience, thus framed and placed behind glass. (5:87, 90)

Heinrich buries that part of himself that was Anna, and swears that even if everything belonging to and comprising her except the name were to vanish then this alone would be good reason for him to remain faithful to her (5:93). As Anna lies dying she is said to have prophetic dream visions; imagining that her "phantom eye" sees him even when he sleeps, Heinrich assumes an "ideal" pose in bed, and lays himself out like a corpse (5:43). Anna's model and Heinrich's secret namesake was Keller's cousin Henriette over whose early death Keller grieved with greedy eloquence. Here was a crypt on which he could write openly and endlessly; "The Grave on Zürich Sea" (1838) was his first serious work which was recycled in parts throughout his poetry. The death of the first person onto whom he had successfully transferred his love for his mother, Keller reasoned, stunted his love life or confirmed that there was some boundary he could not cross.[67] Like Dr. Frankenstein, Keller imagines that he was and will continue to be the victim of a vengeful fiend—even though it was Henriette who had to go. And of the two women who, after Henriette, were likewise recipients of Keller's "mother love," one committed suicide and the other went mad. The grave on Zürich Sea was the dwarf's open secret and subterfuge. While kneeling at the glass coffin of his Snow White, Keller, like a true dwarf, nevertheless kept to himself knowledge of buried treasure which was in some other place.

Before "Dortchen" or the mirror image and mirror name "Anna" enter Heinrich's chronicle, the beautiful, murdered child Meretlein, whose portrait offers Heinrich his first glimpse of that *Regelmässigkeit* he himself can never represent but only frame and bury, is already in place. For her portrait Meretlein had to carry a child's skull, having refused to hold the adult skull her mother had insisted upon. And this substitution was effected by the painter himself, who had argued that his "Kunst-Regula" reserved little skulls for little hands. Only since the sixteenth century have children been portrayed and dead children commemorated. Children were first represented on the tombs of their parents; included in the parents' deathbed scene were both the living and the already dead children, the latter recognizable as long dead by their relative smallness and by the skulls they carried.

"Kunst-Regula" guard some transportable recess to be exhumed and reserve it for some little place. The skull Heinrich carries on his *Bildungs*-journey, and which only Dortchen can persuade him to inter, is such a recess, as is the cellar Keller bears in and as his name. The cellar is a place of concealment, as even its etymons (*verhehlen,* for example) attest, as well as the site of alchemical or, to borrow another etymon of *Keller,* "occult" activities. Keller, who punningly referred to himself on occasion as "Auerbachs Keller," situated his name not only within a cellar, but specifically in a wine cellar, in Goethe's wine cellar, a place of communion with Goethe.

According to Nietzsche, aesthetics has ever been aesthetization of ugliness, whereby ugliness leaves itself out of the picture: "For, what would be 'beautiful' if the contradiction had not first become conscious of itself, if the ugly had not first said to itself: 'I am ugly.' "[68] The other German invention, according to Nietzsche, aimed at making the ugly disappear, while retaining it as dyspepsia and hangover, was the consumption of alcohol, in which Keller indulged with such regularity that he could not be found when it came time to take leave of his dying mother. According to Nietzsche, the generation of the positive image of beauty out of the self-effacement of a defective face has been rehearsed daily in central Europe, the bottle-field of nations and cultures. The very word alcohol, associated originally with eye makeup, would seem to suggest that this conjunction of aesthetics and alcoholism points to some integral affinity. Eye makeup in particular bears association with ancient Egypt and its funeral practices; alcohol in turn supplies the embalming fluid.

Muschg has underscored the secret *Weinen* (weeping) in Keller's *Wein* (wine) consumption.[69] And indeed wine, owing in large measure to its association with blood, has always been part of death cults. Upon entering the Egyptian underworld, for example, the dead were served wine by Shesmu, god of the winepress. While in his poem "The Wine Year" Keller juxtaposed wine and human skeletal remains, in "Panard and Galet" he gave the farcical account of two poets who deem Rhine and wine the best rhyme and Death itself a vintner, and who "climb out of the wine cellar resurrected." Though wine has always been credited with alchemical powers of purification and rejuvenation, it is the hangover, in German the province of the cat, which, by making possible the alternation of euphoria and recovery, underlies the age-old association of wine with resurrection. In ancient Egypt, for instance, the resurrected deity Osiris was not only divine ruler of the realm of the dead but also god of vegetation and, hence, of wine. Birds, cats, and snakes, the often interchangeable carriers of resurrection, also lurk in the underworld of the *Weinkeller*. The omen that attends Green Heinrich's acceptance of his patrimony, for example, is the momentary juxtaposition of Heinrich, the glass of red wine on the table in front of him, and a snake-eater (*Schlangenfresser*) who suddenly appears beside him, attracted by the wine (5:107).

Asked to account for the genesis and meaning of his early cycle of poems, "Thoughts of One Buried Alive," Keller responded, as his interlocutor reports, with the following anecdote: "The hospital orderly Leonhard Ziegler at 'Zum Egli' had, together with a good tokay, an invincible dread of being buried alive. One day he offered the poet one hundred bottles of his excellent wine in exchange for a generally useful poem on the theme."[70] Thus preserved in spirits, the thoughts of one buried alive indeed course through Keller's early poetry, as Luzius Gessler has demonstrated.

Keller's early allegorization of his writing self in terms of premature burial addressed, as Keller made clear in "Motives," his terrible sense of isolation following his return from Munich, a state of dejection which was itself, the poet declared, ultimately a delayed reaction to his having been unjustly expelled from school:

And now after a long, long time, returning from a foreign land,
Suddenly the long hidden security deposit rolls out of the innermost recess.
And only now is the tear released which had swelled up in the unfortunate child.
I believe my songs originated in that blow.
(13:108)

This double exclusion, which Keller charted back, in *Green Heinrich*, to the death of his father, was a moment of arrest for him. His childhood was henceforth occluded by oblivion, "buried" in his youth, itself a "dream world" which Keller equated, in his "Love Songs," for example, with a "garden of the dead:"

> Vain dream! I have wooed
> A corpse, I have wooed death itself!
> Well then, let my love henceforth also be
> Dead and numb!
> (14:146)

Cut off from the "roots" of childhood, even the poet's physical growth has been cut short, shrunken, such that he appears old and wizened at age twenty-seven. And the field of vision of this proportionally large and yet somehow shrunken head is bound by the walls of a crypt:

> The day sends out a meager, troubled glimmer,
> Like lamplight in a vault.
> (14:57)

Gessler argues that the style Keller develops in his early poems and then wields with great subtlety in *Green Heinrich,* for example, "is the style of one buried alive."[71] Though nature at times offers the "half conscious" poet release from his plight, the poet's crypt, protected and carried by his *Regula,* his "style," invariably asserts itself "like a stone on the path to light:"

> A foreign body, without form and echo,
> Thus, it seemed to me, did I lie in the living universe!

And, the poem concludes, upon impact with the poet's "foreign body," "the tranquil mild lustre" is shattered and dispersed.[72]

EPILOGUE

Like melancholia, alcoholism emerges when sublimation exceeds itself: the discrete sublimations polite society requires break down, leaving only such archaic forms of sublimation as alchemical distillation and embalming practices.[73] Alcoholism springs from, safeguards against, and pickles alive a narcissistic and homosexual disposition, the sublimation of which is thus the bar. At once under and over (sublime, *erhaben*) the "threshold," that is, the bar of repression, communal drinking allows an inhibited desire to achieve acceptable form without having to undergo repression. In this way a sublime simultaneity of sensuousness and chastity, a copresence of both meanings of *Sinn,* can be attained—though not for long.

The premier verbal accompaniment of alcoholic liquidation of debt or guilt is, accordingly, rhyme. Keller's deathbed rhyme, "Ich dulde, Ich schulde," for example, is not a confession but an unreadable source of pleasure. Karl Weiss advises that rhyme is pleasurable to the extent that it repeats and interrupts: we have the sense of finding once again something very familiar. Rhyming under the influence refers to the twin products of the very first sublimation, namely the infant's rhythmical sucking and babbling. Rhyme, the reanimation of baby babble, pushes back the poet's autoerotic libido, his narcissistic disposition, thereby clearing a place for the poem itself. The coupling of rhyme in fact holds the place of mature, non-narcissistic object-choice which, once effected in an individual's development, often replaces the writing of rhymed verse: Many are those who preserve the poems of their youth and know not why, since then, they have been unable to write verse.[74]

The sexual activity at once evoked and annulled by alcohol is represented in the behavior of those under the influence by the delirious execution of redundant tasks which verge on endlessness, such as the folding of linen or aimless travel, even though the tasks themselves have the character of undeferrable urgency. Since, Tausk continues, anxiety increases as the interminable labor progresses, the activity is interrupted, either by replacing it with another chore or by starting over again. Or someone else can interrupt the undertaken task, fix the drunk's attention, and elicit humorous replies, which reflect the relief at being interrupted before anxiety outruns and eclipses the endless task while at the same time dissimulating that the anxiety has been endured. This anxiety can be seen as standing in for fear of impotence, though the loss of the narcissistically chosen other can also give rise to anxiety in need of

215

diversion through spirits. Alcoholism floods the friable ground of melancholia while threatening to spill over into paranoia.[75]

Keller confided to Schleich, whom he loved for his "marvelous ability to hold his liquor" (*wunderherrliche Sauffestigkeit*), that he could not bear to hear a certain poem he himself had once written and which Brahms had set to music; his identification with the little boy in the poem who stands helpless before life was such that he could only weep uncontrollably.[76] In the wine cellar the eternally young boy or dwarf held communion regularly with the men he loved for their drinking prowess. But friends who drink together think together: in the light of sobriety the charge of plagiarism disrupts every friendship.

The fragile status of friendship was, beginning with such early dramas as "Fridolin" and, of course, "The Friend," a recurrent theme branded into Keller's writings by the miscarriage of friendship described in *Green Heinrich* (17:137 ff). Barred from attending school, Heinrich sets up at home a place of study and research which resembles the laboratory of an alchemist. Through his best friend, Heinrich nevertheless remains tapped into the school circulation system of printed or dictated information. Through this friend he also has access for the first time to that other institution which has always occupied interchangeable positions with the institution of academe, namely, the bar. But once the friends throw up a third circuit between them, that of letter writing, Heinrich discovers that the letters he receives were plagiarized from established works, just as he senses that his own letters, though not copied directly from books, are yet amalgams of educated hearsay. No longer thinking and drinking together but each in isolation trying to think in ink, the friends find themselves exchanging charges of plagiarism.

The thoughts of one buried or pickled alive—the thoughts, that is, of one deaf and blind—must, of necessity, be borrowed. When Helen Keller, for example, published her first story within a year of learning to speak, the story turned out to be not her own, and the ensuing social scandal canceled a few friendships. The fear of writing another's words traverses *The Story of My Life:*

> Now, if words and images come to me without effort, it is a pretty sure sign that they are not the offspring of my own mind, but stray waifs that I regretfully dismiss.[77]

I have never played with words again for the mere pleasure of the game. Indeed, I have ever since been tortured by the fear that what I write is not my own. For a long time, when I wrote a letter, even to my mother, I was seized with a sudden feeling of terror, and I would spell the sentences over and over, to make sure that I had not read them in a book. (68)

This habit of assimilating what pleased me and giving it out again as my own appears in much of my early correspondence and my first attempts at writing. (69)

It is certain that I cannot always distinguish my own thoughts from those I read, because what I read becomes the very substance and texture of my mind. (70)

When Helen attended college she found that she was "practically alone" in the lecture hall. Though the lectures were spelled into her hand as rapidly as possible, the lecturer remained "as remote as if he were speaking through a telephone." But in this respect, she reflects, she was not "much worse off than the girls who take notes" (98). Helen and the note-taking girls did not "meet the great and the wise face to face" at college; "one does not even feel their living touch. They are there, it is true; but they seem mummified" (100). This mummification is the result of excessive commentary and interpretation, Helen concludes.

Helen "shrank from touching" the Egyptian mummies displayed in the anthropological department of the Worlds Fair which she attended with Alexander Graham Bell in 1893. In the electrical building they examined the telephones and other inventions through which Bell, as she writes in her dedication to him, "has taught the deaf to speak and enabled the listening ear to hear speech from the Atlantic to the Rockies." If only mummification, that is, "needless interpretation," could be banished, then Helen, even though as if on the phone, could be brought before "literature in all its original freshness and power" (100).

Without interpretation there is only plagiarism or there is no longer plagiarism as we know it. This is the sincere wish of one buried alive, to be free from the dread fear of plagiarism.

CHAPTER SIX
BURN NAME BURN
(Adalbert Stifter)

Whatever can be determined about the nature of the absolute mark
[*Mal*], that is, about the mythic essence of the mark is important for
the entire sphere of the mark in contrast to that of the sign. Now the
first fundamental difference is that the sign is imprinted whereas the
mark emerges. This indicates that the sphere of the mark is that of a
medium. Whereas the absolute sign does not predominantly appear
in the living, but is rather also stamped on lifeless buildings and
trees, the mark appears pre-eminently in the living (Christ's stigmata [*Wundmale*], blushing, perhaps leprosy, and the birthmark
[*Muttermal*]). . . . Most striking is the way the mark, in accordance
with its emergence in the living, is so often connected with guilt
(blushing) or innocence (Christ's stigmata). . . . Insofar as the connection of guilt and atonement is a temporally magical one, this
temporal magic in the mark appears pre-eminently in the sense that
the resistance of the present between past and future is eliminated
and all three, united in a magical fashion, break in upon the sinner.
Yet the medium of the mark has not only this temporal significance
but rather at the same time also a significance in that it dissolves the
personality into certain primordial elements, as blushing, in particular, so strikingly demonstrates. . . . But the actual problem of painting is to be found in the claim that the image [*Bild*] is indeed a
mark. . . . but that, on the other hand, the image, in that it is
named, is related to something which it itself is not, that is to something which is not a mark. This relation to that according to which
the image is named, to that transcendental to the mark is accomplished by the composition. This is the entrance of a higher
power into the medium of the mark. . . . This power is the spoken
word. . . . The sphere of the mark emerges also in spatial patterns. . . . Above all they in fact appear as tombs [*Toten- oder
Grabmale*], but of which, of course, strictly speaking only architec-
tonically and plastically unformed shapes are marks.

Walter Benjamin, "On Painting or Sign and Mark"

Through the telescope which emerges spectacularly in Stifter's "Condor" and "Mountain Forest" as embodiment of the narrative perspective, Rilke found reflected back, in at once magnified and dismantled form, a veritable primal scene: "Some reflective reader of Stifter . . . could be brought to surmise that for this lyric narrative artist his inner vocation had appeared inescapable on that unforgettable day he first sought to summon through the telescope an outermost point of the landscape and then, in utterly dismayed vision, experienced a flight of spaces, clouds, objects, and terror in the face of this abundance, such that in these seconds his open ambushed spirit conceived world, like Danae the discharged stuff."[1] Within this rebound of dislocated vision Rilke draws an analogy to Stifter's "inner vocation," which is at once a line of necrofiliation: as she lies in her tomb, Danae conceives Perseus, slayer of Medusa, upon being showered by Zeus with his golden rain. Covering in long shot Freud's rereading of the Promethean origin of civilization, Rilke focuses close up on telescopic vision as one conduit of Stifter's Danae-like conception of writing. At this end fire and water are interchangeable conveyors of a double insemination.

As Benjamin and Derrida have also brought into focus, the arts of magnification cover the central stations of the mourning process—idealization, dematerialization, and spiritualization—by always investing the otherwise inconspicuous elements they enlarge with a surfeit of meaning. In this regard the psychoanalytic perspective finds its endopsychic analogues; in particular the work of mourning—the work on the remainder—proceeds according to a logic of magnification; it blows up each detail or vestige it memorializes. Thus Derrida reads the French verb "magnifier" in English as instrument of magnification, and overhears in this reading the word fire, "which points to death or to the pyromaniac uses of an optical instrument."[2]

The funerary rite of cremation was first introduced when the time came that no crypt would be safe from desecration by entrepreneurs whose escapades, which have been recorded as heroic rescue missions conducted within the underworld, yielded treasure which, on the other side of legend, served as capital invested in new social orders.[3] The original funeral pyre thus burned—and preserved—the complete contents of a mummy's tomb. The notion

219

of an underworld as an actual place that could be penetrated and plundered gave way to the conception of a realm of shades which were, however, corporeal to the extent that, before they could communicate with the living, they first required drinks of blood. These shadows perpetually developed in baths of blood mark a certain vampiric origin of the visual technical media, a stage in the progressive spiritualization of and beyond the maternal realm of verification occupied by mummy and treasure vault. And yet these insubstantial projections hold the place of the monumentalized embalmed corpse which, only through cremation, attains the concealment that always also preserves.

Thus, in Stifter's "Condor" we find, emanating from the funeral pyre of the magnifier, a "ghostly" contraption of "shrouds"; inside this balloon explorers look back through telescopes at the familiar ground below now rendered a "monster."[4] The first flying machines can be charted back through the mythology of flight to angels, ghosts, griffins, and fire-breathing dragons. To this day the word for dragon in German can also mean kite: the hollow representations of dragons erected at certain festivals in the late middle ages seemed to grow lighter, even to hover, when, to simulate the dragon's legendary breath, a flame had been placed inside. Soon experiments with hot air or smoke balloons were underway; since the uncomprehending populace took flight to be the exclusive province of demons and ghosts, early aviators were invariably buried or burned alive.[5]

Magnified vision belongs to this end of flight: the girl cast in Stifter's "Abdias" as zombie only because she is blind achieves reanimation through the lightning shock which gives her sight. But just as a bolt of lightning grants her vision and life, so another bolt puts her to rest. In between she appends her sense of sight to her original blindness as though it were a telescopic instrument: she can see things that she cannot touch (3:94–95). The electric current of reanimation, which was turned on when the new Prometheus, Dr. Frankenstein, created a monster out of corpse parts, was first conducted, according to Freud, by the *Rohr* or reed through which Prometheus brings fire under control: glasses, *Fernrohr* (telescope), microscope, camera, gramophone, and telephone were modeled after this double *Rohr*.[6] Since urine and not fire is carried concealed in every "Penisrohr," Freud can argue that the Prometheus legend symbolizes an early interdiction against extinguishing fires through aimed micturition.[7] Prometheus thus does not steal fire from the gods; instead he forbids that men follow out their homosexual urge to put out every phallic flame with matching streams of urine. This forbidden desire in turn becomes the divinized attribute of the gods who, as embodiments of instinctual drives, are yet permitted to aim golden showers at their flames.

Through the technical media and their excremental models we, too, become, up to a point, god-like. Omnipotence of thoughts was accordingly first advanced in every childhood as that omnipotence of bladder and intestinal functions which the giant infants conceived by Swift and Rabelais celebrate when they put out flames to the point of flooding whole towns.[8] But omnipotence of thoughts always first emerges alongside the premier run-in with death or castration.[9] Through this omnipotence, which gets pressed into service after the first renunciations of instinct are already in place, the child represents to himself each defeat of his drives as a self-imposed victory that would correspond, however, to no real change or diminution in drive power. Hence in the Prometheus legend the phallic regrowth of liver and the relentless return of the bird represent the indestructibility of the libido, which is extinguished only to rise and flicker again.

Before fire could be ignited by rubbing a stick inside some hollowed groove, fire had to be preserved from homosexual flooding; the initial means of controlling fire was to keep it burning. This eternal flame, which Prometheus's prosthetic device thus contains and conducts, also commemorates the first sublimation of homosexuality; lodged inside the technical media as their primal precondition, this "renunciation of instinct" precedes and overtakes what Freud calls the "progress in spirituality." Hence when media-technical or archaeological analogues crowd the endopsychic scanner, psychotic simulation of this sublimation signals its breakdown.

"My first attempts at writing literature," Stifter recollects, "reach back to the time of my childhood when I incessantly described thunderstorms." Stifter in turn bore a "volcano" inside him; thus he described the love he was capable of offering and accepting.[10] But the lava he would spill would always burn and bury alive that which his cherished archaeological projects—as described, for example, in *Indian Summer*—excavated and reconstituted. This distance which repression introduces but keeps apart is already in place in "Condor"; a painter aims his telescope at the balloon transporting two men and a woman who in turn look through their telescope at the "maternal countenance" of nature and the "paternal house" below (1:19, 21). Ensconced within this maiden voyage of Stifter's magnifier art we find a primal scene in which two men accuse the woman between them of *Schwindel*, which in German designates both faintness and deceit. When she faints dead away, thus putting an end to their flight, the men are nevertheless conjoined in disgust at the prospect of "woman," who "cannot endure the heavens" (1:23). At the other end of male bonding, the penis-reed emerges as part of Stifter's patronymic, as *Stift*, the writing instrument with which the name is signed. At this end of Stifter's telescope we glimpse the fire of magnification, and inside its hollow interior the eternal flame of interminable mourning. *Brandstifter:* arsonist.

BETTER DEAD THAN READ

The repetition of *Nach-* can only amplify a mystery it also names: in Stifter's *Der Nachsommer* (*Indian Summer*) and in his "Nachkommenschaften" ("Progeny") disclosure of the protagonist's *Nachname* (surname) is, in each case, postponed until the closing pages.[11] Whereas in *Indian Summer* mention of the protagonist's patronymic simply emerges within the narrative, in "Progeny" the protagonist Friedrich Roderer deliberately and yet no less enigmatically withholds communication of his surname: "Why didn't I tell him that my name is Roderer?" Friedrich ponders upon listening to his neighbor Peter Roderer expatiate on the Roderer name (13.2:291). Only at the close of the novella when he asks Peter for his daughter Susanna's hand in marriage does Friedrich release his name. He had held onto his patronymic up to this point, Friedrich explains to Peter, since its mention would have diverted him from painting by precipitating involvement in genealogical research (*Verwandtschaftsforschung*) (13.2:293). In exchange for his renunciation of painting for marriage, Friedrich becomes or remains the narrator of "Progeny"—the chronicle thus of his name's emergence—just as Peter Roderer, who had in his youth abandoned poetry in favor of marriage and progeny, tells stories of his family name: *Roderergeschichten* (13.2:293).[12]

Friedrich's suppression of his surname while he is pursuing painting is but one manifestation of an overriding injunction against naming which, according to Stifter, indwells both painting and poetry. That which must be commemorated in painting or poetry without, however, being named is repeatedly referred to by Stifter, for example in his writings on art, as *das Göttliche* (the Divine): "The artist has the thing in his soul, . . . which no one can name. Some call it Beauty, Poetry, Fantasy, Feeling, Depth, etc., etc. . . . but these are all just names which do not signify the thing. 'Call it Jehova, Love, God' says Göthe—I would perhaps like to name it the Divine [*das Göttliche*]" (19:199–200). Stifter's conception of the divine mark in art invokes the Old Testament injunction to commemorate God without, however, directly naming Him. Indeed, even by choosing the expression *das Göttliche*, by choosing, that is, an adjective to stand in place of a noun, Stifter seeks to accommodate this injunction.

Yet how can the artist in fact commemorate the divine mark without translating it into some name, and how can he translate it without transgressing, exchanging, or changing it? Both in Stifter's own artistic pursuits as in those of artists portrayed in his writings, the translation of the divine mark into a proper name is, though necessary, yet condemned. But even attempts to refuse to translate the divine mark, to postpone this translation process within pictorial and verbal art, cannot help but find their culmination in a name. Thus in *Indian Summer*, as in "Progeny," the name which is pushed back till the end rebounds as the signature, that name which always comes after, at the end, say, of a letter, or in the corner of a completed painting.

Stifter invariably began the letters, which he concluded by claiming "never" to write letters, with apologies about "unavoidable delays" that kept him from starting or stopping (17:70). Before they were ready to bear his name as destined publications, Stifter's literary works also dragged on and on before completion, owing to endless corrections and revisions. The efforts to publish and not to publish his name orchestrated his career: Stifter's lifelong friendship with his publisher Heckenast, for example, was established when Heckenast agreed to remove already printed pages from the 1842 issue of *Iris* to make room for early publication of "Mountain Forest." As Stifter wrote Heckenast in requesting his story's early release, the very "thought" that the "publication" or "emergence" (*Erscheinen*) of his "name" could be "displaced" or *verrückt* by one year "persecutes," haunts Stifter (17:79). The derangement of the name which could thus be commemorated in the mournful mode of publication was, however, first rendered in the manic manner of funeral-pyromania. In "Mountain Forest" a telescope looks onto the site of a family's destruction and cremation, while those who had been on the surviving end of the telescope return to remain in the ruins for the rest of their lives in the unmarried state of perpetual mourning.

Stifter's paintings, which were indefinitely prolonged before being signed, seldom survived the process of emendation or translation from version to version. "In a word," Stifter confided to Siegmund von Handel, "I got myself into the laughable predicament of having to rub out the finished picture from top to bottom, inch by inch, and painting on it a new, similar, better one. It is much better, but not finished. . . . It is my personal misfortune, I cannot hold onto one of my pictures for long before I start making improvements, and continue making improvements until I throw the picture away" (17:171–72). Winterstein traces the urethral-anal-erotic origin of Stifter's paintings, which always open onto rock formations alongside or in bodies of water. To render this subject, Stifter would first observe close-range the effects produced by the little rocks he sloshed about in a pan of water. In the letter to von Handel, the painting which Stifter cannot help but forward to the flames of annihilation first attracts Stifter's revision when the boulders he has depicted appear to him to protrude from the water "like excrement."[13] *Brandstifter*, who alternately floods and burns the excremental parts and parameters of his paintings, rarely leaves behind his name, mute and sepulchral in the corners of tableaux; instead he lets the name "appear" in flames which at the same time, however, commemorate that which thus remains without the name.

Enter the grandparent, the trans-parent guardian of the

name. In "Health Village" Stifter portrayed his paternal grandmother as his double to the extent that, as "living chronicle," she
"spins the threads" of her grandchild's "destiny" (1:182). According to Ernest Jones, the grandparent is always an ancestral spirit or
friendly ghost who is also the grandchild's twin. The grandparent
thus gets pressed into service in the "fantasy of the reversal of
generations" which renders the grandchild, because he doubles as
grandparent, the parent of his parents.[14] Only while away from
their parents can Stifter's protagonists accept instruction in the
"science" of their names. Friedrich Roderer's grandmother is, accordingly, a veritable "researcher" in this science (13.2:242, 271).
Although her research uncovers what parents otherwise pronounce, only she can talk about the shriveling and expansion of the
Geschlecht—the family line—without her grandson overhearing
that his own *Geschlecht* or sexual member has been addressed or
threatened. "My grandmother says that our ancestors always had
an abundance of descendants [*Nachkommenschaften*], and that our
family line [*Geschlecht*] had never been so shrunken [*zusammenge-
schmolzen*] as right now, but that it was once again beginning to
spread out [*ausdehnen*]" (13.2:236).

Zusammenschmelzung and *Ausdehnung* emerge, in a series of
adjacent contexts, as contrasting principles which animate at one
end Friedrich's painting and, at the other, his *Geschlecht*. Thus in
rendering in his art "real reality" Friedrich must merge depicted and
picture to the point that "one could no longer distinguish the
painted from the real" (13.2:233, 271). According to Peter's chronicle of the Roderer name, expansion, effected through the displacement of goals, has characterized the development of each member
of the Roderer clan: "for centuries now a family [*Geschlecht*] has
existed which in each case always attained something other than
what had been passionately pursued from the start. And the more
glowing the aspiration, the more certain one could be that nothing
would come of it" (13.2:254–55).

As Freud elaborates in his essay on *Gradiva*, in the absence
of psychoanalysis only the fortuitous doubling of the scenario of
repression can effect, without monstrous issue, a return or recognition of that which has been repressed. Friedrich and Peter are
doubles within a session of auto-analysis. Friedrich is attracted to
painting by the same oceanic sensations of fusion which Peter in his

own youth had sought in poetry (13.2:264). Peter's Roderer story repeats in advance the chronicle of Friedrich's conversion: though Peter's desired aim had been the embodiment in poetry of the "real truth" (13.2:264–65), he was yet able, upon his father's death, to resign this passion and seize upon a surrogate goal: "an expanded business [*ein ausgedehntes Geschäft*] conducted in several languages" (13.2:266). But what Peter takes to be his ultimate goal, the cultivation of fields—that "most original" occupation known to man (13.2:268)—emerges as the absolute command of his patronymic. "Roderer" literally refers to *Roden*, the clearing and making arable of fields. This designation for the primal occupation of the family was thus, at the beginning, the only name: "At that time first names hardly existed" (13.2:257). It is the Roderer name, then, that designates the pattern of expansion through uprooting and displacement of goals which informs each chronicle of yet another Roderer on the way to the literal meaning of his name.

The detour on the way to this name is conducted through literal acts of *Lesen,* from reading in a linear or furrow fashion to the cultivation of fields: the cognates of *Lesen—Auflesen* and *Nachlesen*—describe that gleaning of harvested fields which remains comparable to reading. Peter has adopted alongside the cultivation of fields as its caption his dead father's favorite pastime of reading. In Stifter's remarkably scant recollections of his own father, who died, as did Peter's father, in a wagon accident (though Stifter was only twelve at the time), his father invariably retires to the bedroom to read privately the books he keeps to himself. Stifter remembers stealing books from his father: the book he reads up in a tree describes the abuse of an innocent wife by her enraged, unjust husband. When he drops down from his tearful reading he encounters his father, who assumes that little Stifter has returned from a street fight. Now it is Stifter who is innocent of the crime for which he must pay; his father punishes him for an infraction other than borrowing books that are off-limits to the son.[15] But even Stifter's infraction transgresses against something other than the father's library. As Abraham advises, the theft of a father's books can represent his castration or the "rescue" of the mother from his rule.[16] Though this notion of rescue would keep Stifter in line with the father he thus sought to replace, the scenario of punishment puts him in the mother's place, with which he has identified.

According to Abraham, rescue fantasies open onto a street scene where horse and wagon charge out of control until the son intervenes. The son rescues the father only by interrupting the primal scene. Cart and horse are, in this rescue stunt, symbols of the mother, though the charging horse of course also embodies the phallic power the son would assume and apply as he sees fit. The street where son rescues father—the very street where Oedipus, for example, enacts the meaning of this rescue by killing his own father—represents the female genitals.[17] When glimpsed from inside the womb—a common phantasmatic perspective among neurotics, Abraham alleges—the primal street scene covers the maternal path or channel where the father's wagon blocks the unborn's passage. Oedipus kills his father en route to parents who are still unknown to him: the son thus must, in order to be born to parents who are as yet mere strangers, keep the man who turns out to be his father off the street. When the father hits the street, he is thus struck down by death wishes; nestled beside the mother in the bed he again shares with her, the son wishes and wills that the intruder currently on a trip never return.[18]

Shifting from one meaning of *Lesen* to the next meaning,[19] the son finds the same conflict as in the Oedipal street scene, only on turf doubly charged with maternal associations spanning incest and death. In primal rituals dedicated to the cultivation of fields the couples that dance to represent and thus promote the fertility of fields wear masks of the totem animal sent by the gods to instruct them in agriculture. The dancers thus recast the tilling and sowing of the earth according to a sexual model. But the natives do not restrict their animation of plants to pantomimes of copulation and propagation; since the souls of the dead must also attend the reproduction of plants, the dancers representing ghosts capture and bind to the fields the traveling spirits which had been lost or banished. The exiled ghost which must be bound to the maternal place is that of the son. As Freud clarifies in *Totem and Taboo:*

> The introduction of agriculture increased the son's importance in the patriarchal family. He ventured upon new demonstrations of his incestuous libido, which found symbolic satisfaction in his cultivation of Mother Earth. Divine

figures such as Attis, Adonis and Tammuz emerged, spirits of vegetation and at the same time youthful divinities enjoying the favors of mother goddesses and committing incest with their mother in defiance of their father. But the sense of guilt, which was not allayed by these creations, found expression in myths which granted only short lives to these youthful favorites of the mother-goddesses and decreed their punishment by emasculation or by the wrath of the father in the form of an animal.[20]

As the out-of-phase doubling between Peter and Friedrich begins to summon the withheld name, Peter announces the tax of renunciation that must be paid: "One must frequently remove or renounce what one cherishes the most. . . . through persistence one usually attains the goal; but one changes the goal several times" (13.2:244–45). That most cherished thing which Peter encourages Friedrich to dislocate and devalue refers to the moor which Friedrich attempts to represent and preserve in its "real reality" but which Peter is laboring to drain and make arable.

Peter's own shift from poetry back to *Roden* had originally substituted for the "emptiness"—*Leere*—that his father's death had occasioned (13.2:265). *Leer,* which is cognate with *Lesen,* stems from the Old High German *lari,* which designated a field in a two-fold sense: the same field which, from the owner's standpoint, was completely harvested and, hence, empty—*leer*—was, from the point of view of the laborer, not empty but still suitable for gleaning. Whereas Peter would make the moor arable, turn it into a useful gleanable field, Friedrich would hide and keep for himself this moor which holds the place in its vacancy of the "real reality." In effacing the moor Peter is literally exercising the name Friedrich would refrain from imposing, sensing that the very process of painting is threatened: "but I must paint it, for the rich man is going to destroy it eventually, and then there is nothing to paint" (13.2:237). And yet, already locked through the family name into the famulus or servant dialectic of *Lesen,* Friedrich is destined to lose out to the servant perspective, that of yet gleanable fields, of yet legible, nameable images.[21]

Already through the convergence of his surname with that of his neighbor Peter, Friedrich, now uttering his name and hearing another's, hearing his name and speaking another's, comes to read his name, which is neither empty nor entirely his own: "Mr. Roderer?" Friedrich wonders upon hearing, from his landlady,

Peter's surname, "Why, Roderer is my name too" (13.2:240). But when his landlady goes on to assuage Friedrich's anxiety over this coincidence by suggesting that Roderer is perhaps a common name like Meier or Schmid, Friedrich replies: "So, Meier . . . Schmid . . . these common things; but Roderer?" Try as he will to set his name apart from what he deems more "common" ones, his own name is in fact held in common or shared such that Friedrich can use this name only upon hearing it uttered, as is the case when he converses with his landlady. Thus when at this point in the novella the name Roderer is first made known, it is revealed through doubling.

Before his name has been communicated, however, Friedrich already looks to Peter like a Roderer double. Thus on the basis of doubling alone, Peter predicts that Friedrich will, in Roderer fashion, renounce his most cherished pursuit and, in place of fusion, fasten onto surrogate goals of expansion. On the very morning following Peter's prophecy, Friedrich takes part in the initial laying out of the foundation of a log hut (*Blockhaus*) on the edge of the moor. Designed to hide from view his painting of the moor, this hut is the ultimate frame of Friedrich's art. Not only does Friedrich not design his art for showing, as he at one point admonishes would-be viewers of his work (13.2:248), but, being independently wealthy, he need not exhibit and distribute his paintings in exchange for "money or good words or love of relatives" (13.2:235). Rejecting every form of indebtedness, of exchange or circulation, Friedrich conceals and preserves both the process of painting and the patronymic itself; so as not to lose his name, he holds on to it, withholding it even from his paintings, which he never completes and, hence, never signs.

Though built to isolate his art from any and all relations of exchange, the log hut in fact contains the dissolution of Friedrich's art. For it is within this edifice that Friedrich burns his moor masterpiece together with his paints and brushes, sparing only the frame, the site of caption or name. Thus the sensation of expansion, which struck for the first time when Friedrich framed the nearly completed moorscape, now—as the flames consume his work—overwhelms him (13.2:302, 279).

The terms of some internal pact must, through the destruction of the moorscape, be fulfilled before the marriage contract between

Friedrich and Susanna can be signed—twice—with the Roderer name. And yet this destruction marks but the continuation of a practice he had followed out with each of his paintings: "Whenever I paint a picture, and when every feature comes out just right, I take such pleasure in it that I wouldn't sell it for any price, whether offered money or good words or love of relatives, till by and by I ruin it and burn it up" (13.2:235). It seems, indeed, that *this* process of *Zusammenschmelzen,* of, etymologically, cremation and digestion, has always been the culmination of Friedrich's *Malen* (painting) or *Mahlen* (grinding up, milling). Milling (*Mahlen*), which is carried out on the estate in *Indian Summer,* is, as Benjamin noted with regard to the estate in *Elective Affinities,* "an ancient symbol of the underworld. It may be that this derives from the dissolving and transforming nature of milling [*des Mahlens*]."[22]

Friedrich's art of "fusion" had always guaranteed that his pictures would be burnt secret offerings to an internal *Mal* (mark or moment) or *Denkmal* (monument); indeed, though he comes to renounce painting, Friedrich nevertheless continues to "paint," though "in thoughts"—in, that is, that inner medium which he had always held in reserve (13.2:234). For, as Susanna assures Friedrich, their bond—which has been conceived and contemplated without exchanging words (13.2:290–91)—will continue to serve his internal *Denk-Malen* (thought-painting or monu-mentalization): "Your pictures are extremely beautiful; yet if your thoughts are more exalted, and you feel yourself humbled by your productions, then destroy them. I love you that much more. We shall unite our hearts, they will carry something out, and it will not be small and lowly and insignificant" (13.2:301).

The "fire" which Roland, the painter in *Indian Summer,* bears within him must lead to self-destruction or melancholy if withdrawn from external objects (8:234). But this withdrawal into thought is always the consequence of pursuit in painting of the divine mark since painting is a material medium and not a conveyance, as is the accelerating word of poetry. The fire inside the painter must burn the materiality not only of the objects to be depicted but even that of the picture itself in order to convey thought that remains, however, inside in all its flickering purity. In *Indian Summer, Dichtkunst,* a term applicable in the novel to the highest achievements of poetry and painting (7:178), comes close to conceiving *das Göttliche:* "And even if all the arts achieve this divine quality [*dieses Göttliche*] in a gracious form, nevertheless they are tied to a material which must mediate this form: . . . painting to lines and color . . . ; poetry alone has practically no material vestiges, its material is thought in its widest sense, the word is not the material, it is only the conveyor of thought, just as air conducts sound to our ears" (7:35).

Stifter on occasion felt that he was a *Dichter*, as when he conceived the aim of his own art to be the redemption of language from its Babylonian confusion. The inflation and decay of contemporary language, as he saw it, must be restored to the simplicity which characterized the divine gifts of speech and writing: primal language—consisting, according to the Old Testament account, of only a "few words" or the "same words"—conveyed thought perfectly, transparently. These few or same words, however, served as the very foundation for the highrise tower of Babel with which man, motivated by fear of dispersion and translation, had sought to scrape his signature across the heavens, a transgression God punished by *condemning* man to translate; for translation would henceforward be at once necessary and against the law (16:156, 100–102).[23]

Though in "Progeny" Friedrich plans to restore art to the simplicity of "real reality"—the simplicity, that is, of God's own creation (13.2:272)—his plan nevertheless culminates in the building of a block house within which his attempt to commemorate divine creation gives way to acknowledgment of his surname. That this inevitable translation into the surname be held in check is in fact the underlying fantasy of "Progeny." Though here, as elsewhere in Stifter's works, matrimony amounts to the ultimate commitment to the surname, in the marriage of Friedrich and Susanna, Friedrich's patronym is yet restrained from exercising its power to change the wife's name and exchange it for his own. This union commemorates without naming or translating that "real reality" which, pursued by Friedrich in painting and by Peter in poetry, has not been lost through acknowledgment of the surname. Indeed, the ultimate embodiment of this doubled reality turns out to be Friedrich's marriage to his patronymic in which the wife's—the mother's—name will not have been lost, a union hailed by the Roderer clan as "the doublerodererblessing for endless time" (13.2:302).

In one of Stifter's very first, though never completed, literary ventures, the fragment "Julius," the orphan painter Julius, whose sole recollection centers on the abuse and humiliation of a young woman, rescues a woman he then adores. It turns out that he has fallen in love with a near relation whose father predicts Julius's renunciation of painting in favor of marriage. The story, which commences in necrospective, after the characters have all died, and breaks off as the two men depart for dueling practice, would appear to be the omen of the possibility of miscarriage of the very aspirations allowed to triumph in "Progeny."

"Progeny" does not break off ominously—indeed, its humor (*Humor*) is unique in Stifter's oeuvre—but culminates in two feasts (*Mahle*) attended by the entire Roderer clan to commemorate the union of Friedrich and Susanna, a union which has at once reunited and expanded the Roderer line (13.2:299). The Roderers, who have repeatedly demonstrated their capacity for taking names literally, particularly their own, are, at these *Mahle*, commemorating— literally taking in—this moment or *Mal* of union.[24] Though in his painting Friedrich had sought in vain to commemorate the *Mal* without, however, translating it into his signature, in his union with Susanna Roderer a commemoration without translation appears to have been attained.

This fantasy of incorporation, of literalization and doubling of the name, governs not only Stifter's works—specifically those works devoted to marriages between relatives—but even the extra-literary chronicle of his own name, a name which possesses enviable literal power: *Stiften,* to institute and establish, is the constitutive act of *Bildung,* of a concept which became Stifter's life work; *Stift* is not only a place of *Bildung,* but also, most importantly, the very metonym of writing, drawing, signing one's name.

Conceived out of wedlock, Stifter was almost illegitimate— virtually without, that is, his potent patronymic—a circumstance which prompted him to falsify the date of his birth as well as the age he was when his father died. Threatened by near illegitimacy at one end, and childlessness at the other, Stifter, obsessed with the itinerary of his patronymic, was compelled to "marry" this name over and again. It would even appear that Stifter was rescued by his surname when, for example, upon his father's death, he escaped having to become a mere farm hand by being sent, by his maternal grandfather, to an academy, a *Stift*. Inside the *Stift* he received his first instruction in drawing and painting, though his first *Bundstifte* (crayons) had been given him, the firstborn, by his father. Stifter departs upon his father's departure and seeks sanctuary in the name, his alma mater. While he was away at school his mother also remarried, only six months before giving birth to another nearly illegitimate son. For the greater part of Stifter's life his mother's name was, then, Magdalena Mayer. Magdalena humbled at the feet of the bearded man who must make her an honest woman is the icon of Stifter's burning shame; Mayer remains among the common surnames Friedrich Roderer declines to compare with his own name.

Though in his letters to Amalia, Stifter rarely commented on his works above and beyond mentioning the commission he had earned, he wrote to his wife with regard to "Progeny" that he himself was another Roderer (20:147). Like Friedrich Roderer, Stifter conceived a double loyalty not only for his literal name but also for the unnameable mark or *Mal* of the mother. For a long time Stifter professed to be primarily a painter, even during the early part of his literary career, at a time when the heroes of his first literary works were invariably painters. Stifter was ever engaged in determining the proper balance in his allegiance to both *Stiften* and *Malen*. After he had repeatedly failed—not without his own complicity—in securing an academic position, he finally succeeded in entering the institution of academe at a time when he acknowledged writing—an activity which became increasingly synonymous for Stifter with *Stiften* (18:204)—to be his primary concern. Alongside his administrative activities in the school system of Linz, which involved him right from the start in the founding of institutions, he was, as conservator for upper Austria—a position he had expressly sought—furthermore engaged in preserving historical monuments (*Baudenkmale*) and monuments of art (*Kunstdenkmale*), including excavations or exhumations (*Ausgrabungen*) of Roman structures and other "remains of ancient culture."[25] In the long run, however, these arrangements did not succeed in offsetting Stifter's increasing despair over the time spent fulfilling his duties as school administrator.

If with each "remarriage" to the patronymic, with each return, that is, to the literal meaning of his name, Stifter could not help but push aside his mother, he nevertheless appeared able, for a time, to compensate for this imbalance by adjoining his name to that of his wife: Amalia ("O Mali!" Stifter often addressed her), evokes the chain of name equivalents binding Stifter to *Malen* (an activity to which her name indeed exhorts him: *Mal ja!* Go ahead and paint!), thereby making his *Stiften* possible. Indeed, it has been argued that Amalia's replacement of Stifter's renounced first beloved, Fanny Greipl, in fact furthered his career as author. Though Stifter did pen several poems in Fanny's honor, he published them under the pseudonym or *Deckname* Ostade, the name of a painter. The married name Amalia Stifter, which effectively marries the quests for *Mal* and for *Stift,* is, ultimately, Stifter's full name; both in fact signed themselves on occasion A. Stifter.

Yet writing in this name would not always prove effortless. Stifter was afflicted by two severe writing blocks, one in 1854 when he was trying to see ten to fifteen works through to completion at the same time, and the other in 1862 when simultaneously engaged in three major projects. In each case he overcame the blockage by expanding and completing one particular piece of writing: the closing pages of *Indian Summer,* completed shortly before his mother's death, and his "Progeny," upon the completion of which, in nine months, he found himself severely depressed. In each case the pages written in overcoming his writing block contained revelation of the protagonist's surname.

MY LIFE

One year before his suicide, Stifter visited his place of birth, Oberplan, to have a tombstone erected on his mother's grave. Once again able to write, as had become more and more the case during his later years, only in Amalia's absence, Stifter was compelled during his stay in the house in which he was born to record his autobiographical fragment "My Life." "My Life" is a triptych of eidetic memories commemorating scenes from Stifter's early childhood. On one side we find Stifter's earliest recollection, which reaches back into infancy; on the other a memorial to his accession to language. Little Stifter starts naming various objects after over-heard words, thereby granting the words literal meanings. But when he weaves together pine shavings in order to "make" or represent Schwarzbach, a sheer name he has only overheard, he evokes, literally, an excremental analogue which is also the river Styx: "black creek."

The intervening memory commences with mention of a change in the mother's name from *Mam,* which in German is also a young child's word for food, to *Mutter,* a moniker the introduction of "father" always assigns. In this central panel Stifter wounds himself by shattering a window but cannot break his mother's silence. The only incident from Goethe's early childhood recorded in *From My Life: Poetry and Truth* also opens onto the little boy at the window; as elucidated by Freud, Goethe's casting of pottery out the window conveys death wishes directed against rival siblings, who in fact had to go.[26] Goethe thus committed murder to defend his exclusive rights to the cherished mother, a crime which—through *Werther,* for example—continued to count casualties: Goethe found *Werther* comparable to the vengeful phantom of a dead brother. Though, according to "My Life," Stifter would leave behind a rather more abbreviated legacy of suicide, his self-mutilation in a window accident, which Stifter's fatal "shaving accident" only repeats, nevertheless enacts his own double-edged bond with mother.

Far back in empty nothingness there is something like bliss and enchantment, which penetrated, powerfully grasping, almost annihilating my being, and which nothing else in my future life equalled. The features [*Merkmale*] that were retained are: there was shining, there was tumult, it was underneath. . . . Then there was something else, which went through my innermost being softly and soothingly. The feature [*Merkmal*] is: there were sounds. Then I swam in something that had a gentle, fan-like movement, I swam back and forth, I kept feeling softer and softer, then it was as if I were intoxicated, then there was nothing anymore. . . . More and more I felt the eyes that watched me, the voice which spoke to me, and the arms which soothed everything. I remember that I called it *Mam.* . . . (25.3:177–78)

Mam, which I now called mother [*Mutter*], now stood out before me as a shape, and I distinguished her movements, then father, grandfather, grandmother, aunt. I called them these names. . . . I must have already been able to name other things. . . . I found myself once again in the state of dread, of being destroyed. . . . Then there was ringing [*Klingen*], confusion, pain in my hands and blood on them, mother dressed my wounds [*verband mich*], and then there was a picture, which is now so clear to me, as if it were painted in pure colors on porcelain. I stood in the garden. . . . mother was there, then the other grandmother. . . . in me there was relief, which always [*alle Male*] followed the mitigation of the terrible and ruinous, and I said: "Mother, a stalk of grain is growing over there." Grandmother then answered: "One doesn't talk to a boy who has broken windows." I didn't of course understand the connection, but that extraordinary thing which had just left me, came right back, mother actually spoke not a word, and I recall that something quite monstrous settled on my soul; that may be the reason why that incident yet lives inside me." (25.3:178–79)

Then the room is distinctly and lastingly delineated [*zeichnet sich*]. . . . The table . . . had in the middle a red Easter lamb. . . . Every double wedge was reddish like the Easter lamb. . . . Since, in addition, the word "Conscription" was uttered very often, I thought these red figures might be the Conscription. . . . the windows in the room had very wide ledges, and on the ledge of this window I very often sat . . . whenever I began to read. . . . I also lined up pine shavings on this window sill, one after the other, and probably also connected them across with other shavings, and said: "I'm making Schwarzbach." (25.3:180–81)

"My Life" opens with mention of a *Fernrohr,* and focuses on that near synonym of *Rohr* which in English can be translated as blade. Right at the outset of "My Life" Stifter expresses his wonder (*Verwunderung*) over the close connection between his life and a blade or stalk (*Halm*) of grain: "I am often overcome with wonder [*Verwunderung*] in comtemplating my life, which was simple, the way a stalk [*Halm*] grows" (25.3:177). One might hear resonating in Stifter's *Verwunderung* over this stalk the wound (*Wunde*) of his mother's silence as he points out to her the growing stalk of grain. Even as Stifter writes down that the wound associated with his mother's silence continues to live on inside him, he sees the stalk: "I see the tall slender stalk of grain so clearly, as though it stood next to my desk" (25.3:179). Thus attached to writing as to Stifter's life, the stalk seems a *Stift*-like writing instrument and, by extension, an image of his patronym as *Halm* and perhaps also, anagrammatically seen, as *Mahl.*

Along with the stalk of grain, which Stifter can yet see beside his writing table, is the image which his mother's binding, his bond

236

with her, engenders: "a picture, which is now so clear to me, as if it were painted in pure colors on porcelain." And within this image, as Stifter continues to assure his mother—as well as his "other grandmother," his other mother or father—a stalk of grain yet grows. But the other grandmother warns Stifter that the mother will fall silent, will die, and the stalk will go unacknowledged, if Stifter persists in breaking windows.

The bond between Stifter and his mother, together with the other grandmother's warning that this very bond may lead to the mother's silence—to her death—and to the nonrecognition and illegitimacy of the stalk or *Stift*, all this, according to Stifter, constitutes a "process" which continues to live on inside him, the process of *Malen*. For Stifter will ever seek "relief" from "the terrible" by demanding through destruction and self-mutilation the binding of his mother, the bond of their *Malen*. But as soon as it comes time to sign his name to their picture—and this time must come, for this is his other desire, that the Stifter name be acknowledged—he is brought face to face with his mother's silence, and "the terrible" returns.

As indicated in his diaries, those in which he kept a strict accounting of every hour and minute spent on painting, for example—he also devoted separate diaries and timetables to his cigar smoking and to his general health, including sleep, appetite, mood, and bowel movements—Stifter's loyalty to his mother through *Malen* amounts to an unending *Mahlzeit*, indeed, *Gericht* (at once "course of a meal" and "tribunal"). Following virtually every meal time (*Mahlzeit*) so scrupulously observed, and which, together with his interest in cactus (*Kaktus*) plants, increasingly afforded him his only comfort in his closing years, he found himself susceptible to psychosomatic disorders of the gastrointestinal system and of the throat, the first such disorder being, perhaps, his refusal of food upon his father's death. Stifter's works—including "Turmalin," which indeed centers on a *Mal,* and "A Walk [*Gang*] through the Catacombs"—testify to the existence within this corpus of an indigestible *Mal, Denkmal,* or *Grabmal,* the repository of a moment that had to be kept secret.

Whatever this secret may be, it no doubt involves Stifter's knowledge, which he kept to himself, of his being nearly illegitimate, conceived, that is, out of wedlock when his mother was twenty, forcing (*zwingen*) his parents to marry, a compulsion which dictates his near obsession with the number twenty (*zwanzig*). To name just two examples related to "Progeny": while Friedrich jocularly predicts that at his death there will be twenty wagon loads of paintings if not one perfect painting (234), Stifter exhorts his wife to bet on the number twenty in the lottery, basing his intuition on a dream he has on the night following submission of his "Progeny" manuscript to the publisher, a dream in which he measures a canvas that is twenty inches in length (20:149).

During his twentieth year, Stifter was afflicted with smallpox, the scars of which he partially concealed by growing a beard. The beard, an age-old emblem of patriarchal authority, which as such is frequently used interchangeably with a related emblem, the blade, covers up, in Stifter's case, a *Muttermal* of sorts. Arriving at that border where the patronymic must be signed—or even grown— Stifter discovers at that very place the *Muttermal* already secretly etched, forcing him to waver perpetually between resigning and re-signing his patronym. Abdias, who grows up in a "cave" beneath the ruins of a Roman town "lost from history"—a "city of the dead" over which "hovered silently the dark secret" (3:7)— wears Stifter's sole selfportrait, the pockmarked face which, in Abdias's case, is Jehova's *Merkmal* (3:19).

In "Progeny," what first gives away to Peter the secret of Friedrich's surname is the other distinguishing trait, alongside the surname, of the Roderer clan, namely a short beard, the very style of beard which Stifter himself wore. Indeed, the diminutive form of *Bart* (beard) is homophonous with Stifter's childhood name—in every sense, his first name—Bertl, the name Stifter moreover lost when, following his father's death, he entered the *Stift*, whereupon he was first dubbed Adalbertus or Adalbert in place of his original Christian name Albert. When Peter remarks to Friedrich that his short beard resembles that worn by the men of the Roderer clan, Friedrich, however, replies: "That is a coincidence, . . . now it is the custom with many men to wear a short full beard. I like the custom, and I feel more comfortable grooming my beard with scissors and comb rather than with a razor" (13.2:262). Though designed to avoid the razor blade, this short beard in fact conceals while tracing an incision, that of Stifter's "shaving accident."

While reading one of his father's books—an infraction for

which his father would punish him—little Bertl felt that only he could "rescue" the "innocent" woman depicted therein who had been humiliated and, then, executed by her jealous husband (1:42). And again:

> He retained but a single image from his early childhood, which was far removed and cast a dull shimmer up into the present like a distant light through the fog. He saw himself in a wide hall with very many columns among which there were pictures of great bearded men. A beautiful pale woman kneeled in this hall and sobbed. In front of her stood an old man in a black coat around which he had a gold chain. This man had his arms folded and stood there with such a frightful look that it indelibly impressed itself on the boy's brain. Regardless of how much he tortured his memory, it afforded him nothing more than the recollection that he had ridden for a long, long time with a man in a wagon, and that he was very hungry. (25.3:129)

What could Bertl have done or said to clear the beautiful woman's name? Whatever it may have been that Bertl had to say, Bertl's will to utter it on the one hand, and—on the other—Stifter's will to silence it, ultimately meet along the blade of a knife, another *Stift*-like instrument.

While countless readers had sought, in vain, the key to his works, his mother, Stifter confided to his publisher shortly after her death, immediately comprehended the meaning of his writing, not needing interpretation or translation (19:113). One year after his mother's death, Stifter was forced to witness the rapid and seemingly unending dissolution of his family line (*Geschlecht*), which he had founded and expanded through adoption. In February 1859 Josefa, one of the Stifters' several substitute offspring on loan from Amalia's family, died, while her sister, Juliana, ran away from the Stifter household and, having left behind the note, "I am going to join my mother in the great service" (her mother was long dead), drowned herself.[27]

Yet another of his foster daughters, Josefine Stifter, died of consumption, as had earlier her sister Louise. Shortly before Louise withdrew into mortal illness, she and Josefine, upon reading Stifter's name in the newspaper, signed theirs in a letter of inquiry to the celebrated author inquiring whether they might all be related. As there was no doubt in Stifter's mind that the Stifter sisters were in fact his most cherished relations, he opted for their adoption. The demise of his family of foster daughters could only have confirmed the foreboding circumstances surrounding Stifter's initial commitment to progeny. Amalia, it seems, gave birth before their marriage to Stifter's sole heir, an illegitimate child that died in infancy.[28] That settled the future; but even in the past his *Geschlecht* collected corpses. Former fiancée Fanny died giving birth to her husband Fleischanderl's legitimate but dead heir.

Stifter and Schreber meet within the excavation project(ion) of a *Geschlecht* threatened by extinction. According to Freud, Schreber was haunted by the prospect of dying childless: Schreber's delusion that in exchange for his emasculation he would fill the world with a new race of men born from his spirit cuts off the cutting off of his *Geschlecht*.[29] In the suicide's estate we find, left behind, a. letter without address or date in which, thus, Stifter alone appears: "Esteemed friend! Yesterday, on the way home, I solved the riddle. The solution is 'castrato.' How, I wonder, will girls go about finding this solution" (22:254).

In search of a legacy, Stifter repeatedly turns to Goethe. Goethe (Göthe), Stifter frequently notes, is the unique artist capable of naming that which otherwise cannot be named in genuine art, that is, *das Göttliche*. Goethe—who like God or a masterpiece painter always signed himself, simply, Goethe—could indeed name *das Göthe-liche;* it was his proper name.

Stifter sought to translate his epigonal relation to Goethe— his temporal predicament of coming after (epi-gone)—into a new poetics of "coming after" (*Nachkommen*). This process of "translating" successivity into a new poetics underlies the writing of *Indian Summer* (*Der Nachsommer*); while the first version mourned missed chances, the published version celebrates belatedness—"an indian summer without preceding summer" (6:35)—as constitutive of true *Bildung*. No longer an epigonal poet, Stifter would become, instead, as he put it, "no Goethe, to be sure, but one of his kinfolk" (28:225); the founder (*Stifter*), that is, of another poetry, one devoted to the "gentle law" of kinship and progeny (5:6).

Though he thus believed that in fulfilling the duties of office and marriage he had sacrificed his potential to compose masterpieces of art comparable to Goethe's (28:193, 224), thereby necessarily limiting himself to the telling of Stifter chronicles devoted to "coming after," Stifter nevertheless allowed, as he confided to his publisher, that some future reader of his own works might well be inspired to write works even greater than Goethe's (28:225).[30] Yet Adalbert Stifter—or was it Bertl—does not in fact end on this affirmative note. Four days before his suicide, in his last letter, Stifter once again entreats his publisher to rescue him: "Do not abandon me in the misery of my home [*lass mich in dem Elend meines Hauses nicht im Stiche*]. I'm sure everything will be settled again. You will set yourself and me a monument [*Denkmal*]" (22:182).

In the corner of every commemorative monument which Stifter erected, he paid tribute to his mother. Thus Goethe's main attraction for Stifter is that he always lets the mother sign and countersign; in *Indian Summer,* for example, the markings of a mother's *Stift* have been preserved between and alongside the lines of Goethe's collected works (6:271).

Stifter carves his tribute to *das Göthe-liche* onto the marble sculpture he had otherwise reserved for comparison with "true male friendship" (27:33) which in turn always pays tribute to the mother's stylus. In his review of Kaulbach's *Göthe's Female Figures,* Stifter recommends that the sole pictorial medium capable of embodying Goethe's unique "magic" is marble (*Marmor*) (14:172–73), the very material out of which the central symbol in *Indian Summer,* a sculpture of Nausikae holding a stylus, is carved. The sound-shape *Marmor* orchestrates maternal associations also via *Moor* and *Meer,* the sea which overwhelmed Stifter when he saw it for the first time late in life during his Italian journey. Following the trip to Italy Stifter believed he could realize his own *Nausikaa* project, the drama Goethe never quite got around to completing. Though Stifter assured his publisher that he had found "the edge [*der Rand*] of Italy very favorable for *Nausikaa*" (19:40), he could not retain the edge and remained, alongside Goethe, short of ever finishing. The edge or corner where Stifter thought he might rush to sign his name before Goethe could sign his turns out to be the very place of commemoration and lateness he would never, when it came time to overtake Goethe, leave behind.

The edge of Italy is of course the strand, the sort of locale Stifter, a passionate swimmer in his younger days, had regularly attended also to display and see exhibited male nakedness.[31] Nausikae always faces toward the main attraction to which her name discreetly refers, that of Odysseus stripped naked on the

241

beach. Above and beyond the childhood pleasure of showing off, exhibitionism—which the Nausikae episode covers by rendering Odysseus's exhibitionism his plight—protects the parts of the body which might otherwise be destroyed or found missing. A cover-up worn to ward off castration, nudity also veils and deceives death. Mourners, who, as a rule, do not want to be taken alive, and yet must express their deep identification with the corpse, can tear off their clothes to commemorate the loved one's final initiation into the afterlife. Only the corpse, Rank paraphrases Flaubert, can be truly, openly naked.[32]

In "A Walk through the Catacombs" Stifter imagines with dread anticipation that the well-preserved female corpse he admires could easily be stripped naked, illumined, turned around, and stared at by some intruder. Only he could rescue the corpse from the intruder Stifter imagines looking at the dead woman's backside. Stifter rearranges the shroud patches to cover her shame. The diversion of a certain river or its damming up, Stifter continues to muse on his stroll through the crypt, would one day expose to grave robbers the secret site of Attila the Hun's burial in multiple caskets within caskets beneath the river bed. The draining of the moor in *Progeny* excavates, in the corner of the moor, the naked corpse of a mother's name—*Malen*—which Friedrich cremates and preserves.

CHAPTER SEVEN
WARM BROTHERS

(Franz Kafka)

Where I come from parents tend to say that children mirror their parents' age. Those without children must seek the reflection of their age in their ghosts, where it is all the more visible. I know, when I was young, I attracted these ghosts more forcefully, I was bored without them, they did not come and I already thought they would never come. For this reason I nearly cursed my existence. Later they came after all, only once in a while, it was always a special visit, one had to bow even though they were quite small, often they were not at all small, in fact it only appeared so or sounded as though this were the case. When they really did come they were seldom wild, one could not be very proud of them, at the most they jumped onto you the way the small lion mounts the bitch, they bit, but you noticed this only when you located and pressed the bite mark with your finger nail. Later, however, they grew larger, came and stayed as they chose, fragile bird backs became the backs of monument-giants, they entered through every door, locked doors they broke down, they were big bony ghosts, nameless in the crowd, you could handle one of them, but not all those hovering about. When one wrote they were all friendly ghosts, when one did not write, they were devils and you could only lift a hand above the pressing crowd to show where you stood. The way in which one twisted one's hand up in the air was indubitably not one's own doing.

Kafka to Grete Bloch, June 8, 1914

Telephones all over the country are somehow mysteriously coming to life. Their owners unaware, the phones start dribbling out electronic digits. Occasionally, the devilish dialers come up with 9-1-1, and a light on the local emergency switchboard glows. The operator responds, but no one's there. Has the caller passed out? Frantic attempts are made to trace the number and ring it back or else dispatch the police to the scene. Surprised residents, sometimes roused from deep sleep, deny ever having made the call. The common denominator: A cordless telephone that dialed by itself.

Consumer Reports, November 1986

THE AERO-TRACE

On Kafka's side of the Tower of Babel, the heavens, the imperial palace, and the highest court still transmit the Old Testament double injunction whereby "the Law" invites entry or transgression and then renders itself inaccessible, as, by law, it must. Kafka's response, however, as Deleuze has argued, was to marshal a "nomadic war machine," a "battering ram directed against itself," and not to construct another "ivory tower."[1] As demonstrated by "The Great Wall of China," any attempt to erect a "new Tower of Babel" yields a potentially endless series of isometric segments linked and separated by gaps such that the entire construction finds a kind of cohesion only through the delayed messages conveyed by persons traveling along its expanse. In turn, any attempt to reattain the "true name of things" would, as the following passage from Kafka's "Description of a Struggle" instructs, meet with endless tautology—would, as in the following case, amount to calling a poplar a poplar, thereby setting forth the first two terms of a series that can be extended indefinitely:

> I have experience, and I do not mean it jokingly when I say that it is a sea sickness on terra firma. The essence of this sickness is such that you have forgotten the true name of things, and so in haste you overwhelm them with arbitrary names. Now quickly, quickly. But scarcely have you run away from them, and already you have once again forgotten their names. The poplar in the fields which you have named "the Tower of Babel"—for you did not want to know that it was a poplar—sways again namelessly, and you have to name it "Noah in his cups."[2]

In the place of the missing true name—the place of death— sea sickness or, literally, nausea emerges at one end of the work of mourning or metaphor. At the other end Kafka encounters, as he writes in his diary entry of January 21, 1922, the "dreariness of the replacement." What Kafka calls metaphor belongs to this end of proper burial. Language in pursuit of analogies can only survey and demarcate the property relations of the phenomenal world: "For everything outside the phenomenal world, language can only be used in the manner of allusion" (*KGW* 3:92). Allusion hovers over this world on the side of mourning that remains reductive and interminable: "the incomprehensible is incomprehensible" (*GS*

244

5:95). According to Barthes, Kafka's antimetaphorical conception of allusion harbors, like the corresponding notion of repetition in *Beyond the Pleasure Principle,* a "defective force" that signifies by undoing "analogy as soon as it has posited it."[3] Stanley Corngold can thus conclude that allusion—the metamorphosis of metaphor—ultimately and always creates monsters.[4]

Also emerging from this melancholic's laboratory, however, we can yet discern, as recorded in "Investigation of a Dog," an allusive "separation" which is also the takeoff of some new skywriting: "Actually I thought I recognized that the dog was already singing without yet knowing it, and indeed that the melody separated from him and hovered above him through the air according to its own law, as though it did not belong to him, directed only towards me, towards me" (*GS* 5:276). At the target end of this autonomous emission we find, closing in on Josef K., or on the officer of the penal colony, a certain p-unitive fantasy. When Kafka decided to share the fantasy, he nevertheless allowed, in his diary entry of December 8, 1911, that it was "no artistic desire" that thus compelled him to imagine merging with his writing at the instant that it emerged from him. The nonartistic urge to retain the deep inscription or underside of one's own writing in ecstatic acceptance of penance or shrift lies on the other—though always reversible—side of the phantasm of writing as autonomous flight. By ceaselessly testing the links and limits which tie his writing to metaphor, Kafka secretly commences count down.

On December 6, 1921, Kafka records in his diary two radically separate entries which, thus taken together, nevertheless span the introjective and projective reach of Kafka's anti-metaphorical rapport with writing. At one end Kafka includes a report of premature burial: "Two children, alone at home, climbed into a large trunk, the lid shut tight, they couldn't open it and suffocated." Above the closeted remains of two children Kafka opened the entry with reflection on a metaphor he had received through the post. Kafka sees reflected back the constraints metaphor puts on his own writing. And yet he cannot help but evoke, by revoking it from the start, the possibility of writing's independence and autonomy. "Metaphors are among the many things which lead me to despair over writing. Writing's lack of independence, its dependence on the maid who heats the stove, on the cat warming itself by the stove, even on the poor old person who warms himself. All these are independent activities ruled by their own laws; only writing is helpless, does not dwell in itself, is a joke and a despair."

In Kafka's works we see something of the "joke and despair" of writing that should "dwell in itself"—of a procedure or process, in the case of *The Trial,* that turns out, as Kafka assured Max Brod, to be capable of being "prolonged into infinity," whereby it attains a kind of autonomy, though it never actually attains resolution, never actually reaches "the highest Court" (*GS* 3:283). Indeed, the parable in *The Trial*—in which the Law, mediated by a potentially endless series of doorkeepers, is seen as unattainable, as a distant glimmer—may be extended to include the impasse of writing that *should* be autonomous, ruled by its own laws. "Admittance to the Law" is not an option for writing, since the Law is always mediated and supplemented by the Court, a helpless joke and despair forever dependent on maids, cats, and doorkeepers.

Though writing cannot enter the Law, cannot be literally autonomous, this perpetual falling short of a goal, this infinite delay within the Court, yet provides allusive analogues to the hope that failed. Thus we find in *The Trial,* in the place of writing's autonomy, a circulation system of bureaucratic writing—called "Court-organism"—in which "everything is, after all, connected" only to the extent that "everything"—including the connection between trial and verdict—must "eternally remain hovering in a state of abeyance" (*GS* 3:131). In turn, the Court painter Titorelli's depiction of justice, in which the bearer of the scales is portrayed with winged feet, is based on a "connection" with the goddess of victory which can be maintained only as hovering in place (*GS* 3:156). But this motion in place is not restricted to the background of the portrait where justice is depicted on the backrest of a throne; even the magistrate portrayed, who seems ever verging on getting up from his chair to deliver the verdict, embodies, in K.'s eyes, the hovering connectedness of the Court:

> He was particularly struck by a large picture . . . and bent forward to see it more clearly. . . . The strange thing was that the judge did not seem to be sitting in dignified composure . . . it was as if in a moment he must spring up with a violent and probably wrathful gesture to make some decisive observation or even to pronounce the verdict. The accused might be imagined as

standing on the lowest step leading up to the chair of justice. . . . "Perhaps
that is my judge," said K., pointing to the picture with his finger. (118–19)

K. always tunes in the station of identification which broadcasts
the invitation to his own funeral: he sees the hybrid figure of
justice and victory fuse into the goddess of the hunt—who, in turn,
advances towards him (157)—and the magistrate rise to pronounce
K.'s own verdict. But identification always repeats repetition; the
introversion of libido, whereby the ego offers itself up as yet another object or target, is matched, on the outside, by Titorelli's
serial art. Thus K.'s identifications, which put him at the target end
of the points of cohesion he discovers in a single magistrate portrait, hold the place of the many "strikingly similar" portraits that
he subsequently finds crowding the Court (156). Titorelli thus exhibits his heathscape paintings to K. one after another like a projection also because he is convinced that K. already harbors an affinity to the pictures. K. projects the "same old heathscape" (174) in
the place of what remains a series of images, in which no image can
be called the original exemplar repeated and referred to in turn by
the others. Each "same old heathscape" supplements its own deficient sameness through images of itself.

According to Henry Sussman, this towering accumulation of
signs in *The Trial* even constricts the air flow in the Court precincts.[5]
In this airless mummy's vault only photographs remain: the photographs disturbed during K.'s opening scene of arrest, since they
could not be set in order again, alone record the "disturbance"
introduced by the Court. Paradoxically, then, Kafka viewed the
photograph as an act of forgetting.[6] On this side of paradox, the
heathscapes find their hallmark in "the gloomy" (*das Düstere*)
(175), the dark concealedness which seriality ever confers on that
which it renders immediately accessible and infinitely reproducible.
What emerges from that serial amalgam of copy machines, porno-
graphic literature, and sado-masochistic sessions coextensive with
K.'s encounter with the Court is the refuse of refusal to mourn—to
kill and remember—already in place in K.'s morning arrest: mourning arrest.

"Pop Art" thus weighs down K.'s name: whereas prior to his
arrest he had been able to give his name "openly," at his own

discretion, afterwards even his name circulated so openly—K. no longer needed to introduce, to represent himself, for example— that it became a "burden" to him (221). Already at his first hearing, the Court records K.'s occupation as painter, though K. protests that, just as he is in fact a *Prokurist*, someone who represents and stands in for others, so his trial is comparable not to some appeal before a lineup of painted magistrates, as Titorelli suggests (160), but to the sign it embodies, a sign that represents by proxy an absent meaning: "What has happened to me is only a single instance and as such is of no great importance, especially as I do not take it very seriously, but it is the sign of a procedure which is being directed against many other people as well. It is for these that I take up my stand here, not for myself" (52). But in Kafka the relation to the signature—the relation of identification—is always also with machines in place of fathers such that the conscience, for example, is carried alongside its "translation," the super ego, and human folly alongside machine projections in place of vision or voice.[7] Oedipalization, which already in Freud is conducted along channels of the technical media, is thus followed to the letter in Kafka only to be reversed point by point.

Kafka's instruments and organisms of writing allow for and insure against the possible disturbance (*Störung*) of their sign functions, though in fact disturbance is integral to these functions to the extent that the sign always manifests itself as *Verkehrsstörung* from which it is inseparable. *Verkehr:* traffic, transport, correspondence, sexual intercourse. Arrested while still in bed, K. must get up and search for identity papers while the guards rifle through his underwear. The only document he can find to bring forward, his bicycle permit, attempts to cover for his *Verkehr*-identity, the "disturbance" of which thus marks the onset of his trial, the irruption of the Court-organism within his bedroom. Like the father according to Freud, the Court, which can introduce disturbance into every private space, can in turn substitute for any disturbance which challenges its functioning. As lawyer Huld counsels K.:

> Try to accept that this vast Court-organism remains in a sense eternally hovering in a state of abeyance, and if, on one's own, one introduces change into the immediate surroundings, one in fact takes the ground away from under one's feet and plummets, while the vast organism itself effortlessly

provides compensation elsewhere for the small disturbance—everything is, after all, connected—and remains unchanged. (131)

The "Letter to His Father" has always invited Oedipal interpretation to the extent that Kafka already delivered it when he delivered the letter to his mother knowing full well she would never forward it. In the letter, Kafka addressed his father as the highest court of appeal; as *The Trial* confirms, however, this evocation nevertheless remains an allusion, a metaphor posited only to be demolished and outdistanced. The father's place in *The Trial* is displaced with respect to a Court-organism which encircles K. only because it is already inside him, and resembles, on either side, machines. When the hovering organism casts out or punishes one of its disturbing agents—in this case Kafka's own namesake, the guard Franz—the victim's shriek "did not seem to come from a human being but from a tortured apparatus" (96). The coherence and continuity which Kafka's other namesake, K., claims to recognize in Titorelli's Court paintings he must first supply within a context or apparatus of seeing that animates that which it takes in, always to the point of its serial division. Like the cinematic apparatus which, according to Kafka, imposes onto the observed object, in place of the viewer's steady gaze, its own restlessly repeated motion,[8] K. projects an isolated instance as a series of identical stills.[9] On one occasion K.'s blinking eyes render the stationary figure depicted in the periphery of a painting the film of this figure's motion in place:

> He illuminated the altar painting with the flashlight. The eternal light hovered disturbingly before it. The first thing K. saw and in part divined was a large knight in armor who was represented at the extreme edge of the painting. . . . He appeared to be observing attentively an occurrence transpiring before him. It was amazing that he remained standing like that and did not move closer. . . . K., who for a long time now had not seen any paintings, contemplated the knight for some time, even though he had to blink his eyes constantly, since he could not endure the green light of the lamp. (216–17)

When K. tries to get the picture and yet remain out of it, he always offers, true to his name, the abbreviation and vestige of what Politzer has called the "metaphysical frame of reference," the "absence" of which in Kafka's writing delivers "fundamentally end-less narrations."[10] There are no sons or signs (in the *Prokurist*-like sense) within the infinite *Prozess* inasmuch as the highest Court, as Titorelli instructs, remains beyond everyone's reach. A defendant can therefore never obtain authentic acquittal (*wirkliche Frei-sprechung*), which accordingly exists only in legend and hearsay (165, 169). Hence there is no conflict in *The Trial* that could be Oedipally organized. As Adorno puts it, the nonidentity between terms in Kafka is always the "complement of their copy-like iden-tity."[11] Even when Titorelli advises K. to block, through repeti-tion of its advance signs, the emergence of the verdict, the painter can only confirm what K. has been repeating all along. K. cannot set out to repeat: repetition, at least in his case, is a structure, not an intention.

Without access to any highest Court, all activity within the Court takes the form of an interminable production and circulation of bureaucratic texts, a writing project to which the Court is so committed that it can never "speak freely" (*freisprechen*), but rather can only systematically "misinterpret speech" (*verhören*). The defendant, in turn, can only pursue, in place of authentic acquittal, the counterfeit alternatives of "ostensible acquittal" and "postponement." Unlike genuine acquittal, which brings with it the absolute destruction of all documents, both ostensible acquittal and indefinite postponement entail the ongoing supplementation of the original dossier with additional documents and petitions. Since, Titorelli clarifies, a defendant must perpetually petition for further acquittals and postponements, his only alternative is, in effect, re-petition:

> In true acquittal the documents relating to the case are said to be completely annulled, they simply vanish from sight, not only the charge but also the records of the case and even the acquittal are destroyed, everything is de-stroyed. In ostensible acquittal, by contrast, the documents remain as they were, except the affidavit is added to them and a record of the acquittal and the grounds for granting it. The whole dossier continues to circulate, con-ducted along, as demanded by the uninterrupted intercourse of the Court chancelleries, to the higher courts, being referred to the lower ones again, and thus swinging backwards and forwards with greater or smaller oscilla-tions, longer or shorter delays. . . . The second acquittal is followed by the third arrest, the third acquittal by the fourth arrest, and so on. This is implied in the very conception of ostensible acquittal. (169–70)

The authentic acquittal must be abandoned, Titorelli advises K., since it would eradicate all writing, all re-petition—indeed, "everything"—so that the verdict can be spoken freely. Both methods of seeking acquittal within the Court are thus counterfeit alternatives, counter-fictions which, by working both against and with the larger trial-fiction within which they are constructed, keep the trial and its writing process from ending. Authentic acquittal remains an extra-textual alternative to *The Trial* itself: " 'Both these methods have this in common' "—Titorelli sums up—" 'that they prevent the accused from coming up for sentencing.' 'But they also prevent the authentic acquittal,' K. said softly, as if ashamed at having recognized that" (173). At the end of the novel this shameful recognition returns to survive K.'s ultimate union with his verdict along the rotating blades of a knife: " 'Like a dog.' he said; it was as if the shame of it must outlive him."

As his verdict begins to emerge from out of the proceedings, K. finds himself taking a great many business trips. He arrives at the cathedral—where the Court will again call out his name—as just another tourist who, in his case, must act as tour guide for a visiting Italian businessman. To this end he carries with him an album of tourist attractions he himself has compiled. He holds neither the prayer book the Court chaplain would have expected nor that other prayer book, the German-Italian dictionary featuring *Prokurist*-like connections between signs and meanings which he has left at home. The chaplain censures K. for having based his judgment of the Court solely on his own experiences, his *Erfahrungen*. And yet the tour book of replicas and recurrences which K., on the chaplain's command, lets fly across the cathedral floor also traces a certain space of survival in Kafka.

As Kurz has reminded us with reference to the travel suit worn by one of the guards who arrested K., the border zone between life and death has always been explored and emblematized as a journey which K.'s arrest thus signals.[12] The other guard in attendance at the trip's onset guarantees that K. will feel or experience with his own body the law he claims not to know (16). The officer who supports but falls victim to the torture-writing machine at the center of "In the Penal Colony" literalizes this metaphor of an experience felt in advance of its comprehension.[13] But another meaning of experience associated with travel parachutes out of the metaphor or fantasy of fusion. *Erfahrung*, which designates, etymologically, "exploration while traveling," thus finds its literal agent in the traveling explorer who survives the torture machine's autodestruction by entering a supplemental text which Kafka attached to and severed from the rest of the story by a wide margin. Just as, in K.'s case, the textual appendage contains the shame that survives, so the traveler's survival is shameful: he at once resists and admires, in equally glib measure, the death sentence within designs he simply cannot read.

Travel, the trail of mortality, which, like every writing process in Kafka, is always endless, commences alongside an experience harbored by the body. Following each exposure to the serial repetition of the Court, K. responds—as though to the other meaning of *Gericht* which lies indigestible inside him—with dizziness and queasiness. One of the side effects of travel has always been nausea, which first emerged as the "sea sickness" it literally designates. After he has passed through one of the countless Court tracts found in the attic of every tenement, K., overcome with nausea, fears that the *Prozess* directed against him is, after all, but the outermost projection of an internal *Prozess* in which his own body prosecutes him (83). The *Prozess* that will be survived only by K.'s "shame" is also carried inside K., bracketed by his nausea, the sensation, specifically, of sea sickness on terra firma.

The verging effect which K. resists to the extent that he produces it reflects, according to Adorno, the dread, pushed-back impulse to vomit which the reader is in turn invited to share.[14] Vomiting, Freud discovered, can take the place of the act of utterance such that, in the course of a session, the analyst may be required to induce free-flowing speech in his patient before the pent-up urge to vomit becomes unbearable: "and if we cannot force him to speak he actually begins to vomit."[15] That which cannot be comprehended and verbalized but only swallowed and thrown up inhabits scenarios of doubling and death. Nausea commences as vertigo in the face of doubling only to culminate in doubling, on the face, of anus onto mouth. Once peristalsis puts the gullet into reverse, the *Urmund* returns to dispose of some indigestible remainder. For certain hysterics doubled over with nausea everything that goes down must come up since it remains a "foreign body"[16] which, according to the melancholic, always also doubles as unmournable corpse.[17] Thus when Freud goes into the symptom formation of hysterical vomiting he comes up with examples in which a train trip or a piece of rotten fruit, though they appear to be the immediate causes of vomiting attacks, cover for the chance sighting of a corpse. And yet, Freud continues, this example is poorly conceived: only early sexual trauma can lock this corpse into a return circuit.[18] Corpse or sexual trauma: a line of necrofiliation begins to be drawn.

In Adorno's reading, the vertiginous impulse to regurgitate corresponds to that experience of déjà vu which populates Kafka's works with undead doubles: "Perhaps the secret aim of his writing in general was to make déjà vu available, technical, and collective."[19] Like telepathy, déjà vu was an area of inquiry in which psychoanalysis rivaled the occult. When Freud refers to interpretations of déjà vu which precede his own he always takes cognizance of the "mystical" and "vague" conviction that this double take refers to experiences from another life. Freud converts haunted two-timing back into the currency of repression: in déjà vu an unconscious impression has been reactivated, brought into consciousness by another impression related to the former but not at the level one thinks. Freud twice gives the example of a young girl who was overwhelmed, while visiting friends whose brother was mortally ill, by the sense that she had been there before. But it was the event that was repeating itself: her own brother had recently recovered from the same malady, though not in time to dodge the death wishes his sister had addressed to him. This scenario, which she had repressed, thus returned veiled as déjà vu, displaced from event to locality.[20] When, in a dream, the locale appears particularly familiar, that which has returned is the womb, the place we have all been to before.[21] The doubling of the brother doubled by death wishes is displaced, here as always, onto the return of the womb.

The death-wish bond which psychoanalysis detects lodged between siblings opens onto the phantasmic scenario of shame which, on its German etymological track, covers both womb and corpse. We swallow our shame, even though we cannot hold it down. Throwing up belongs to the human body's innate means of reversing gravity and taking off. Through serial repetition all one-way movement takes hovering flight: flight, in turn—like vomiting—always goes the way of return. The unburied undead have, ever since the mythological beginnings of flight, booked passage on what is always return flight: the first beings known to fly were, besides birds, spirits or ghosts.[22]

The nausea Kafka writes down in his diary on October 18, 1916 embraces the sensation of being perpetually unborn:

> The sight of my parents' bed . . . can provoke me to the point of vomiting, can turn me inside out; it is as if I had not been definitively born, were continually born anew into the world out of the stale life in that stale room, had constantly to seek confirmation of myself there, were indissolubly joined with all that loathsomeness . . . my feet . . . are still stuck fast in the original shapeless pulp.

For Kafka this nauseating unborn state could yet be exchanged for an undead condition in a blinding flash of takeoff. In his diary entry of August 6, 1914, for example, Kafka likened his frequent sensation of being dead while yet alive, his eternal dying, to a taking off over and again into high regions. Kafka especially enjoyed executing death scenes since, as he clarified in his diary entry of December 13, 1914, he was thus able to play, in his writing, the "game" with death he otherwise always played spontaneously and incessantly with his mother. This game, Kafka acknowledged in a letter to Brod dated July 5, 1922, permitted him to hover over both his own death and the mourning over this death; Kafka thus attended his own funeral, a funeral to which are also always invited, as Nicolas Abraham and Torok have argued, the beloved dead whose return is thus the secret purpose of this game or fantasy.[23]

Incorporation—a kind of internal vomiting, as Derrida puts it[24]—can seal off loss by opening onto the endless serial division everywhere in evidence in the *Prozess* also inside K. The "hovering connectedness" of serial division thus follows the internal feeding and grinding schedule of *Malen*. On another side of *The Trial*, Kafka could be found chewing his vegetarian fare or fear—horror of meat always embraces and replaces the cannibalistic rituals of archaic mourning—over forty times, such that he was left chewing even when there was nothing left to chew.[25] Cereal art.

AIR MALE

The traveling explorer's superficial mode of reading circumvents the penal colony's torture-writing machine, though only to the extent that this traveling shot crosses to that other side of shrift—shameful fleeing—where it must remain. But Kafka could be found defending and participating in such itinerant activity which, in the case of reading, amounted to "flying over" a text (*überfliegen*), and in the case of travel could be a "flight outwards" (*Ausflug*). Mapping out this flight trajectory we find the coordinates and props of Kafka's Californian preoccupation with health. Kafka claimed that if he were wrong about the various "nature cures" he pursued—including travel, nudism, vegetarianism, and the agrarian praxis of Zionism—he would also be wrong about everything else. Turning away from conventional medicine to seek out nature cures, Kafka gave as his reason the deaths of his younger brothers Georg and Heinrich at the hands of incompetent physicians. His brothers had not, therefore, died of natural causes; as murder victims they retained the right to haunt. Thus as Freud stipulates in *Totem and Taboo,* only the animistic analogue or model of modern medicine—homeopathy—could apply in Kafka's phantasmic reading of bodies. Homeopathic ritual, which is based, as in weather changing ceremonies, on the similarity between the acts performed and the results expected, thus remains prior to and separate from the Oedipal structures of communication with some deity.[26]

For the young child the first encounters with the necessity of divine intervention in reading and interpreting correctly a body or text are the doctor's visits. Like a god the doctor arrives to interpret the child's pain and prescribe that it have a meaning and end. As a young boy Kafka witnessed these visitations issue in the unnatural deaths of his two younger brothers. This evidence of fatal misreading or malpractice—or, put differently, the unmournable deaths of his brothers—thus shifted Kafka away from the medical interpretation of symptoms and signs to the more primal method of treatment Hahnemann advanced in the eighteenth century.

Homeopathic medicine countered the modern medical reading of symptoms as transparent signs of causes which can be treated only through the abnegation of symptoms. Close range, then, Hahnemann sought an alternative to such radical pseudo-remedies as bloodletting and trepanning. By diagnosing and treating them as symptoms, modern medical science or "allopathy" suppresses such external disorders as itching and scratching; insanity and asthma emerge then as the effects only of the causal reading itself. According to Hahnemann, disease can not be ascribed to some offending agency working against a specific organ; illness is an overall derangement of the "immaterial vital principle" which pervades and animates the body. Since this vital principle remains invisible, its effects could only be diagnosed in terms of symptoms which, however, must never be taken for the disease.

Though the vital principle is otherwise able to deflect the disturbing effects of offending agents, in the deranged state this restorative potential is temporarily suspended and paralyzed. In this case the body's life principle must be shocked into response through administration of manageable doses of the insulting agent. The dose prescribed on the basis of this animistic law of *similia*—that like be cured by like—creates in the body an artificial and miniature form of the illness, one which, for all its intensity, the body could nevertheless combat. Without this summons for assistance to which "auxiliary troops" could thus respond, the "vital powers" of the body are helpless in their struggle against the "enemy."

The homeopathics of textual survival which Titorelli prescribes to K. emerges from a maternal transmission. Medicine and insurance comprised the dual legacy of his mother which Kafka came into at both ends: one of her brothers, who was head of the Spanish railway system, obtained for Kafka his first insurance position; another brother was the country doctor who served Kafka as model for the frenzied drama of reading bodies he found himself rehearsing and then repeating. The country doctor's voice was "inhumanly thin . . . bird-like . . . piping out of his constricted throat."[27] Thus, in delivering his reservations regarding the allopathic aspect of psychoanalysis, Kafka sides with "maternal ground." In turn Kafka rejects "the therapeutic side of psychoanalysis as a helpless error. All these alleged illnesses, as sad as they might appear, are facts of faith, anchorings of the person in need in some maternal ground . . . Such anchorings though, which are fixed in real ground, are not a singular, substitutable possession of man but are rather performed in his being and, after the fact, continue to form his being in the given direction."[28]

Kafka thus finds and dreads even in psychoanalysis the suppressive applications of allopathic medicine borrowed from and modeled after exorcist technique. Yet as Wolfman and Ratman could testify, psychoanalysis is also homeopathic to the extent that it allows for the rapport with ghosts which are never busted: the mournable death of the father emerges in the Freudian reading of bodies only to the extent that attention has thus been diverted from the dead sibling—in the patient's and Freud's own crypt. In a dream Kafka recorded in his diary on October 2, 1911, we find the maternal transmission of burial ground emerge in the merger of mother and dead child:

> A terrible apparition in the night: a blind child, apparently the daughter of an aunt who, however, has no daughters but only sons, one of whom once broke his foot. . . . This blind or nearly blind child wore glasses over both eyes, the left one beneath the fairly distant glass was milky grey and protruding, the other receded and was covered by a close-fitting lens. So this eyeglass could be optically properly affixed, it was necessary, instead of the standard clamp around the ear, to append a lever, one end of which could be attached to the head only through the cheek bone so that a little rod went from the eyeglass down to the cheek, disappeared there through the pierced flesh and ended up in the bone while a new rod emerged and went back behind the ear. . . . I was so weak today I even told my boss the story about the child. Now I remember that the glasses in the dream belong to my mother who sits next to me evenings while I play cards and looks out at me, not too pleasantly, from under her pince nez. Indeed, the right lens of her pince nez—something I do not remember noticing before—is closer to the eye than the left.

The ocular apparatus worn by the apparition also covers the mother's aspect at one end of this transmission of ground. In a letter to Freud dated March 15, 1916, Lou Andreas-Salomé thus clarifies with regard to the maternal place of the camera in a certain paranoid delusion analyzed by Freud: "Also in the case of the supposed camera, I am reminded of the mother's *eye*, which like God's eye 'sees everything,' which has always seen the child all alone naked and stripped."

In Kafka's works the mother always introduces or holds the place of mourning. In *The Trial* Josef K.'s father is already dead— it is his uncle, "the ghost from the country," who reminds K. of his

Schuld to family and name. But K. is survived by his mother, who thus inhabits the shameful survival of name remnant or change of name. What is always and ultimately a maternal mark has been appended to a full first name, that name in isolation from the patronymic which remained the only name Kafka's brothers, dead in infancy, had in fact possessed.

Kafka's mother's "beautiful" son Georg,[29] who died at about the age of two, was engendered anew in "The Judgment," which Kafka described both as a "birth"[30] and as "the ghost of a single night."[31] In "The Judgment" the mother, who has been dead for two years, appears never to have been properly mourned. This incapacity for proper mourning is ascribed to Georg's Russian friend whose written condolence seemed to reflect nothing so much as the inability to grasp the magnitude of this grievous loss.

The "birth" Kafka achieves with the writing of "The Judgment" is conveyed within the story as Georg's creation of a phantom friend also to the extent that both deliveries circumvent while holding the mother's missing place. The phantom friend embodies "the connection between father and son," Kafka writes in his own exegesis of the story.[32] This embodied connection is shadowed by the post—the friend is phantom precisely to the extent that he is exclusively a letter-writing friend—just as it embodies the loss between father and son, the two-year-old loss of the mother.

The power a father exercises over his son takes the specific form, in "The Judgment," of his intercepting and derailing the son's rapport with a phantom. The father calls into question the existence of the letter-writing friend only to claim that he has all along been corresponding with this phantom who obeys only the father's commands. This interception of the phantom transmission which drives the son over the edge corresponds to Kafka's own shifting rapport with the ghosts that always attended his writing. By the end of his career the phantoms had turned sinister, even turning off Kafka's diary with a menacing gesture that betrays the superegoical source from which all phantom communications in Kafka by now emanated. "More and more fearful as I write," Kafka records in his final diary entry; "It is understandable. Every word, twisted in the hands of the spirits [*Gespenster*]—this twist of the hand is their characteristic gesture—becomes a spear turned against the speaker." The phantom call of incorporation in Kafka always switches between rescue or flight signals and the command to jump.

The double command can be overheard in "Eleven Sons," in which each son, as Kafka informed Brod, alludes to one of the eleven stories he was composing at the time.[33] The eleventh son is "The Dream," in which Josef K. glimpses his name shard at the instant it commences surviving him on his tombstone over the grave into which he falls. Through a show of weakness, which is in truth a secret capacity for flight, this last son circumvents by refusing to survive his father:

> My eleventh son is fragile, probably the weakest of my sons; but deceptive in his weakness. . . . It is not, however, a shameful weakness but rather something which only on this earth of ours appears to be weakness. Is not readiness for flight [*Flugbereitschaft*] for example, weakness too, since it is a teetering and indecisiveness and fluttering? Something like this is what my son conveys. The father is of course not pleased by such qualities; they clearly aim at the destruction of the family. At times he looks at me as if to say: "I will take you with me, father." . . . And his glance seems once again to say: "May I then at least be the last."

"A Fratricide" corresponds to the second son, whose physical beauty and ability to perform high dives into the water are marred by what the father views as a flaw—which could only refer to the ineradicable remains of the murder victim in "A Fratricide," the *Reste* which continue to speak to the murderer in "a mute language."

Writing ever represented Kafka's attempted flight from his father, he claimed in his letter to his father, and on January 27, 1922, he reaffirmed that writing is a flight and a taking off away from "murderers' row," from complicity in the murder covered by "A Fratricide," the second of eleven sons, or in that death by diving to which, in "The Judgment," the namesake of another second son was condemned by his father.

> The strange, mysterious, perhaps dangerous, perhaps saving comfort that there is in writing: it is a leap out of murderers' row; it is a seeing of what is really taking place. This occurs by a higher type of observation, a higher, not a keener type, and the higher it is and the less within reach of the "row," the

more independent it becomes, the more obediant to its own laws of motion, the more incalculable, the more joyful, the more ascendant its course.

But this evocation of an autonomous writing in flight collides, in the same diary entry, with the hotel manager's insistence that Kafka's name is "Josef K."—the name that outflies the eleventh son's fall into the grave. On the one hand, as Kafka writes in his diary entry of January 29, 1922, his own "world," though "forsaken," continues to attract and pull him upwards: "in happy moments I enjoy on some other level the freedom of movement completely lacking to me here." On the other hand, as Kafka recorded the day before in his diary, his family, which thrusts forward just as it disposes of every remainder, cannot help but eject him.

Kafka admits to having attempted to inject "disturbance" into the family "peace" and so to upset its balance; but he "could not allow a person to be born elsewhere" while he was "making every effort to bury him here." The new person born elsewhere, whom Kafka was striving to bury, is heir to the paternal "weapon" mentioned at the beginning of the entry. This missile continues to ascend while the pilot son, together with the paternal transmitter inside him, must bail out. As Kafka puts it in the fragment " 'You,' I said . . .": "This dissolution takes place as an apotheosis, in which everything that holds us to life flies away, but even in flying away illumines us for the last time with its human light."

On the rebound and in reverse, the dream Kafka enters into his diary on October 20, 1921, covers the precincts of an improper burial which double as landing strip on which the cargo cultist Kafka awaits the return of the dead whose advance signs fly overhead:

My brother has committed a crime, a murder, I think, I and other people are involved in the crime; punishment, solution, and salvation approach from afar, loom up powerfully, many signs indicate their ineluctable approach; my sister, I think, keeps calling out these signs as they appear and I keep greeting them with insane exclamations, the derangement grows with their approach. My individual exclamations, short sentences merely, I thought, since they were so succinct, that I would never forget them, and now I cannot clearly remember a single one. They could only have been exclamations because of the great effort it cost me to speak; I had to puff out my cheeks and at the same time contort my mouth as if I had a toothache before I could bring out a single word. My feeling of happiness lay in the fact that I welcomed so freely, with such conviction and such joy, the punishment that came, a sight that must have moved the gods, and I felt the gods' emotion almost to the point of tears.

This flight trajectory could be projected at one end only by taking out insurance at the other. Before Kafka could assume his first insurance position he was obliged, in applying to the police for a certificate of good conduct, to supply all information relating to himself, all of which the police wrote down, even registering his dead brothers. Every bureaucracy in Kafka's works is an institution of writing which, as Titorelli emphasizes, retains while concealing "everything" (170). These bureaucracies embrace what Adorno calls Kafka's "brotherhood with death,"[34] a resurrected brotherhood which is always also a warm one. Mecke accordingly argues that Kafka's bureaucracies are coteries of conspirators in homosexuality who put the K.s on trial for desertion.[35] The fluttering of arms and wrists "like short wings," which signals to Benjamin that a metamorphosis is underway,[36] helps Mecke identify the denizens of the Court as homosexuals who, for purposes of identifying themselves to each other, rely on such secret codes and signs as lip reading and silver buttons.

In a letter to Felix Weltsch, dated September 22, 1917, Kafka interrupts his analysis of his double bond to his fiancée to ask a favor—"By the way, a further request, which fits well here"—namely that Weltsch send him Wilhelm Stekel's reference in his *Masturbation and Homosexuality* to "The Metamorphosis." Though in his letter to Weltsch Kafka derides Stekel as one of Freud's popularizers, he nevertheless must have been struck by the place into which Stekel stuck reference to "The Metamorphosis." In his work on homosexuality, which puts forward the thesis that the homosexual has taken refuge in inversion in order to escape his otherwise uncontrollable urge to commit crimes of passion against women, Stekel cites, in a footnote, "The Metamorphosis" as a clear example of a sado-vampiric fantasy featuring the bedbug, which sucks blood. This footnote is appended to clarify the dream of one of Stekel's patients: "He was pursued in bed by a great mass of bedbugs and finally himself turned into a bedbug" (this is where the note to Kafka is indicated). "Like all homosexuals he had for a time the fear of infection and especially of tuberculosis. He was almost convinced that he would die prematurely of tuberculosis. We are also familiar with tuberculosis (as well as syphillis) as the representative of what is evil, of incest and homosexuality."

The bedbug, which, like every small animal, represents, according to Freud, a younger sibling,[37] inflicts a vampiric wound which, as Kafka stressed in the criticism of psychoanalytic therapy he conveyed to Milena, remained, in its various guises, the constitutive possibility of his "being a writer,"[38] at once his dissolution and flight. The autonomous buglike hovering which Raban, in "Wedding Preparations in the Country," imagines attaining while he sends his body out to arrange his marriage is, as in the case of Schreber's "wondered" projections, the effect of a wound which covers homosexual incest only to the extent that "intercourse with ghosts"[39] has also been covered. The skeleton in Kafka's closet is, according to Mecke, his homosexuality; but the ghostly pedigree of this sexual predilection cannot be overlooked. Whereas Mecke attributes Kafka's inability to go ahead and marry to homosexuality, Kafka remained convinced that, if ever realized, his marriage plans would, "like worms," "finish off the corpse."[40]

To the extent that aberrant mourning was always involved, homosexuality would present itself to Freud along channels of the technical media. Paranoid projection animates and puts on fast forward the photographic process which Freud and Ferenczi originally reserved for analogy with the relation between the psychoneuroses and the perversions, where the former provided the "negative" for the latter. But slipping from one side to the other of media-technical analogues, which always and ultimately illustrated a breakdown of sublimation, the one-sided homosexual perversion would always be displaced, in its psychoanalytic reflection, with regard to vaster stereo structures.

Thus, according to Ferenczi, inversion or "homosexuality of the subject" belongs to the perversions since it remains the vestige of an early stage of development, while active "object homosexuality" is a form of obsessional neurosis which is, in fact, intensely heterosexual. The most typical brand of heterosexuality among modern men is also obsessional, Ferenczi concludes; coupled with characteristic rejection of all forms of intimacy among men, this obsessional heterosexuality is the very measure of a deeply homosexual disposition.[41] This paradoxical unlocatability of one sexual

identity in isolation from its alleged other dominates the psychoanalytic exploration of bisexual difference and preference, though always in such a way as to leave heterosexuality aggrandized and
homosexuality nowhere to be found.

Bisexuality holds the place of an original disposition only to
the extent that it can never be applied as such but only as one
disposition at a time. Since social organization cannot tolerate the
stereo broadcast of bisexuality, one sexuality must always go under
cover; the management of this imposed subterfuge continues to
distinguish the normal from the neurotic just as sublimation is to
be distinguished from repression. Psychoanalytic theories of social
development can never accommodate the notion of original bisexuality in any way that would make a difference: while the family, by
and large, keeps to the heterosexual zone, every institution outside
the family, even those institutions which are but extensions of the
family in which they also thus inhere, are not only masculinist in
origin but specifically homosexual.

This view, which reflects in part Freud's reconstructions of
the primal horde and its destiny, was advanced in full by Hans
Blüher whose work *The Role of Eroticism in Masculine Society*
Kafka had read by the middle of November 1917. Blüher concludes that, to this day, homosexual congress remains the highest
aspiration and ultimate transgression within all-male institutions
ranging from the university to scout organizations and including
even the state. Psychoanalytic discovery of mainsprings of homosexuality in the places where refugees from that urge had tradition-
ally conceived their safety zone "unsettled" Kafka, as he wrote
Brod upon reading Blüher. Though he was at first unsettled by the
work, however, afterwards, as always happened to him when reading psychoanalytic studies, he was strangely dissatisfied, a shift in
affect he nevertheless accounts for from within the Freudian system: "Psychoanalytically 'of course' very easy to explain: express
repression. The royal train is the one most rapidly dispatched."

As he wrote down "The Judgment," Kafka was, he claimed
in his diary entry of February 11, 1913, thinking of Freud, "of
course." The *Gespenst* is always the carrier of an "attraction" it
etymologically conveys; the psychoanalytic theory of ghosts first
arose to account for Leonardo da Vinci's homoerotic disposition,
and then returned within the study of Schreber's paranoia once

again to address the technical media in terms of sublimation break-down. In both cases it is the common fate of repressed homosexuality and attachment to the dead to project and pursue fantasies of technologized, mechanized conveyance and writing.

Leonardo's unwed mother gave him, in the absence of father, every undivided attention he asked for until, having gone too far, she gave him, too soon, the "highest erotic bliss." This double charge of child abuse and castration—Leonardo's mother "robbed him of a part of his masculinity"—succumbs to the contest between sublimation and repression it would describe. Thus to chart Leonardo's trajectory across the masculinist province of sublimation, Freud cannot help but summon from the footnote underworld of Leonardo scholarlship a certain Muther. Psychoanalysis cannot, Freud concedes, penetrate the mystery of the contest between repression and sublimation in Leonardo precisely to the extent that the father was never its referee. Leonardo's first five years saw only one divinity, the vulture-headed goddess Mut, whose homonymy with *Mutter,* Freud notes, need not be accidental.[42]

Analyzing Leonardo's sole recollection from infancy in which a bird's tail passed between his lips, Freud concludes that the inventor-artist had enjoyed, unchecked by paternal censorship of his sexual researches, a bird-bond with his mother and then, as his mother, with stand-ins for himself as a boy, a bond which gave impulse to his pursuit and prophecy of mechanical flight. Leonardo's sustained rapport with his phallic mother shaped his affinity with birds which suckle him as he sucks their more penislike than breastlike tails. Mythological accounts, Freud reminds us, always imagined birds in isolation from sexual differentiation; certain birds and bird-divinities, including the vulture Freud claims stuck its tail into little Leonardo's mouth, were believed to share only one gender, which conceived through the wind. To this day bird flight accordingly carries association with erection, impregnation, and giving birth.[43]

In order that the child reach the finish line as researcher or artist, sublimation must outfly repression, which, however, always has a head start. Owing to his bird bond with his mother, Leonardo could immediately take off into zones of sublimation once the one repression that no one can outmaneuver, that of love of mother, struck. From this point onward sexual repression fueled his flight with a "surplus of sublimated libido." Though the libido invested in his sexual researches could be transferred instantly to research conducted in a more sublime register, the undistilled sexuality that always remains behind had little or no sexual outlet or exhaust; the ultimate sublimation Leonardo attained in his art eventually backfired, shifting him back down to scientific study, that close approximation of sexual research which, having first propelled his art, now consumed it.[44]

Every young sexual researcher conceives of his childhood, at the time, as a prison in which he does time; the fantasy of flight is accordingly the phallic focus this research commonly assumes. Mut, for example, was represented as having not only a vulture's head but also an erect male member. But vultures eat corpses. The improper burial which birds grant the dead has always issued in an airborne, undead state both acknowledged and feared. In Hitchcock's *The Birds* avian frenzy has been summoned by "incomplete mourning."[45] Mut's son Chons was represented in the form of a young mummified man wearing the Ibis head of Thoth.

Freud recommends what psychoanalysis, however, cannot carry out: biological exploration of the specific bisexual constitution which supports Leonardo's "alchemical" and "occult" capacity for sublimation which even sublimates the supplementary sublimations it calls for. As Sadger first pointed out, the homosexual was not to be conceived as having been continuously or inherently so inclined, but as having been anchored originally, in a way more intensely heterosexual than would regularly be required, in Oedipal hatred of the father and passion for mother. The homosexual son salvages his maternal bond by adoring, to the exclusion of the father in himself, simulacra of himself as the boy his mother had loved. As Freud clarified, in Sadger's scenario the son has in effect identified with the mother, thus adopting, as well, her desires.

In this case homosexuality would embrace a testamentary structure which, even if only in anticipation, commemorates the mother's love, which can never vary, in the mode of mummification. Leonardo's retentively meticulous accounting of the expenses of his mother's funeral—comparable only to accounts he kept on expenses incurred for his pretty boy pupils—tallies the safe deposit inside him of his own early bond with mother, whose separation from him, even though effected at a very early age, could not stop asserting itself as he passed through a relay of stepmothers shadowed by infertility and early death. The homosexually disposed always retains the bundle of desires called mother or, as Freud also allows, brother as a foreign body inside him transmitting commands and wishes not proper to the host body, which must, however, mimic them. When the brother has been lodged inside, homosexuality reflects surmounted rivalry (*überwundene Rivalität*).[46]

Ferenczi discovered that the homosexual patient is, accordingly, particularly susceptible to hypnosis and telepathic rapport; indeed, one of Ferenczi's homosexual patients, who repeated during analytic sessions Ferenczi's every thought from the day before, was the source of Ferenczi's and Freud's intense interest in the possibility of telepathic communication whereby Ferenczi's experience of déjà vu would refer not to the collision of unconscious and conscious impressions but to telecommunication with another life. As Jones writes of Freud's reaction to the record forwarded by Ferenczi of the homosexual's telepathic powers: "Freud, however, was deeply impressed by the data and said emphatically that they put an end to any possible remaining doubt about the reality of thought transference. Henceforward the new knowledge was to be taken for granted."[47]

An older brother, who died before Van Gogh was born, had borne, as displayed by the tombstone Van Gogh passed each day on the way to school, the same name, "Vincent," whose stereo ears framed the point of impact of the artist's self-destruction and self-portraiture. Telepathic telecommunications and the homosexual bond with the dead converge in the case study of Schreber, where Freud argues that the paranoid's delusional system was not part of the pathology but represented instead an attempt at recovery and reconstruction in the wake of loss. Precipitated by the repression it culminates in, this catastrophic loss takes the form of Schreber's complete withdrawal of all libido from the world. His delusional formations are thus the very measure, measured in reverse, of the "wealth of sublimations" which "the catastrophe of the general libido withdrawal has brought to ruin."[48] Disappointment in love, erotic amplification of feelings not allowed to emerge as such—or the death of a loved one—can clog the psychosexual exhaust system, giving repression the lead over sublimation. The corpse that dislodges sublimation cannot be found beneath "the familiar turf of the father complex" to which Freud believes his analysis of Schreber can safely return: sublimated homosexuality, that is, sublimation proper, organizes cultural institutions to the extent that it always remains among the effects of proper mourning for a dead father.[49]

Talking birds and eagles are part of the paranoid system which culminates in Schreber's belief that God—who, however, takes cognizance only of corpses—had chosen him as transsexual consort to conceive with divine rays a new race of men. Birds thus hover over the machines which conduct this Frankensteinian corpse construction. Complex machinery in delusional formations project the patient's genitalia. In Schreber's case, both terms of this translation are represented side by side: so that he may conceive a new race in the wake of the one he lost, Schreber acquiesces in his "emasculation" by divine rays regulated by complex celestial machinery, writing machines which, in rendering him God's consort, also make him the locus of countless inscriptions. Schreber's desire to be transformed into what he calls woman—a sexless resurrected body—is at once the desire of a writer, a *Schreiber,* to be transformed—in the absence of any verbal expression, since Schreber's organs of speech and respiration have been shut down—into a body of writing conducted and amplified by machines which take down every detail of Schreber's existence so that the rays can later read what they have, in effect, written.[50]

This process of taking off and taking down will, however, never be completed but remains the protracted consummation of pleasurable attachment to his every organ of machines which are new machine-organs. Only through the process of taking off, whereby the genitally organized body is discarded, can corpses be imitated, can one's own body serve as the resurrection of another; in keeping with his sacrificial mission Schreber must become the repository for "the poison of corpses": "There arose the almost monstrous demand that I should behave continually as if I myself were a corpse."[51]

It has been pointed out that Freud, in rushing to represent a young son's relation to a father who is also a famous physician as being of necessity one of worship, overlooked the unbalanced rigor of Schreber's father's interest in the physical well-being of children.[52] The various machines of Schreber's delusions can indeed be seen as corresponding to the makeshift harnasses and contraptions with which the father shaped his son's bearing, often through the painful consequences, built into the devices, of lax or uneven posture. But in correcting Freud, these intellectual historians neglect to reevaluate, according to the shift of emphasis they introduce, the impact of the suicide of Schreber's older brother, a loss which Freud takes into full account, though only to isolate it, ultimately, over and against "yearning for the father." Though Freud meticulously uncovers the fantasy of sibling incest around which Schreber's citational system circulates, he nevertheless assigns the brother in Schreber's system the position of divine double of the father god. And yet Freud's own example of deification of the dead is that of the Caesars who, beginning with Julius, became gods upon dying.[53]

The healthy regimen the father imposed on life counted among its graduates one suicidal and one delusional son. That Schreber goes delusional is the good news: his paranoid system safeguards against the quiet evacuation of libido which led to his brother's self-effacement. But the older brother was always on a suicide mission, intercepting the full force of paternal designs he deflected from Schreber. The brother continues to fulfill his mission in the phantom form every suicide leaves behind. Schreber's delusional system rescues two brothers from their father, whose death is secured through Schreber's castration, which, like his brother's suicide, is directed against the father inside them.

HEIR MAIL

Before the advent of Cargo Cult the Melanesians had engaged in ancestor worship which centered on legends of voyage and homecoming. The first cargo monuments erected in place of these ancestral trips were flag poles and telegraph poles, in each case analogues or citational props of the media-technical range of the white man's sensorium. But these extended senses also belong to their dead; according to the funerary logic of reversal, the Melanesians had originally and always conceived of the ancestors as white men.

The telegraph introduces a short circuit into the trip that once circulated the post: direct communication with the dead emerges in the place of initiation rites and journeys linking life and death. The postal structure of the trip is accordingly altered: tribalized. Melanesian witchcraft and cannibalism, which the white guests and ghosts came to encounter and record, had attained prevalence, according to the testimony of certain Melanesian grandfathers, only with the first arrival of white men.[54] The primal medium of rumor thus emerges alongside the new technical media:[55] "wireless" is a neo-Melanesian term covering both the medium who communicates with the spirit of some dead person and the local gossip. The spread of rumor, which preceded the arrival in each village of the prosthesis god—and which carved out what would henceforward remain the god's primal habitat—struck pregnant women first, who, in order to survive their demise rumored to arrive with the white man, aborted their unborn offspring. This frenzy of abortion emerged in the absence of any model or ritual; abortion had scarcely been practiced prior to the rumored arrival of white men.

These gods or resurrected dead men had returned in place of worship of the distant mourned dead: this close-range encounter with living dead in the absence of any exchange of communication or cargo produced collective seizures when the cold wind called zona, believed to be caused by the spirits of the dead, began to blow. To protect against the zona on one side and their own shivering on the other, the Melanesians built large houses in which, contrary to tradition, men and women were together assembled. By the time the media-technical death cult had taken shape around the trembling or, as the Melanesians called it, "noise," the houses came to be regarded as the emptied-out place-holders for the expected cargo they would in future store. The traveled distance of their legendary past thus came to be centered for the Melanesians, as was already the case for white men, around terminals in which noise is kept in the background of waiting around.

Thus readdressed by the advent of telegraph and telephone—whereby it accelerates beyond the place it had once shared with travel—the post served Kafka, as Deleuze and Guattari have emphasized, as the overriding mode of all his writing.[56] Rather than simply take the train to Berlin, Kafka pursued in his courtship of

Felice Bauer a strategy of long-range missives. He timed with great precision his letters to Felice, sending some three letters a day, calculated, in each case, to reach her in specific contexts at home or at work which would guarantee his messages the reception they anticipated. To effect this surveillance Kafka would even alternate a barrage of letters with sudden recourse to telegraph or telephone.[57]

By having dedicated either explicitly or implicitly each of his published works, Kafka, in effect, gave each a postal address, just as he distributed his unpublished manuscripts among various coordinates of his correspondence. Kafka's correspondence, which proliferated to an ever-increasing number of destinations, not all of which could be reached, itself amounted to a network of correspondences in which resolution is left in a state of suspension, though the network itself was capable of indefinite expansion, in fact expanded on contact. Grete Bloch, for example, having once intervened by letter to mediate a dispute between Kafka and his fiancée Felice, soon found herself receiving and responding to numerous letters from Kafka in which he addressed her as passionately as he did Felice. During his travels Kafka engaged every available female correspondent within his reach. In Weimar Kafka even proposed a correspondence with the daughter of the Goethe house custodian (*Beschliesser*). Not only for Kafka is the connector to the post always woman, whose equal rights emerge—though always shadowed by repression—alongside the advent of cargo. Felice was a typist who worked with parlograph and telephone.

Kafka's writing might well have remained a literally itinerant activity, one destined never to arrive once and for all as the fiction of a collected corpus, had it not been for Brod. Even before Kafka had written anything with the express intention of publishing it, Brod had, in one of his literary reviews, celebrated Kafka along with Blei, Heinrich Mann, Meyrink, and Wedekind as being a major living German author. Though Kafka deemed this maneuver an inappropriate and threatening prank—as witnessed by his having promptly requested that Brod stipulate in some future review that the name Kafka "will have to be forgotten"—he may thus have been challenged by Brod's misplaced praise to go ahead and publish. Inasmuch as Brod was ultimately to transmit both Kafka's collected works and Kafka's wish that they be destroyed, he was destined to carry out the first institution of a name which was coupled with the bearer's injunction that the name be forgotten.[58]

Despite Kafka's wish that his name be forgotten—indeed, that his works all be burned upon his death—at one point Kafka himself felt a sense of urgency to get his work into print, as he confided to Brod with regard to the publication of his *Country Doctor* with the publisher Wolf:

> Thanks for your intercession with Wolf. Ever since I decided to dedicate this book to my father it is very important to me that it appear soon. It is not as if I could become reconciled with my father in this way; the roots of this animosity cannot in this case be eradicated but yet I would have accomplished something. For even though I had not emigrated to Palestine, I would yet have traveled there by moving my finger across the map.[59]

Yet how could this double publication of his patronymic in any way move him—if only in the sense of motion in place—as though towards Palestine?

The name Kafka was originally adopted in consequence of Emperor Joseph II's decree that all Jews adopt non-Hebrew and etymologically transparent names; the name means, in Czech, jackdaw, a crow-like bird. Kafka on one occasion elaborated to Janouch his dual identification with this bird name: "I am a completely unusual bird. . . . I am a jackdaw—a kavka. . . . I hop about among men in a state of confusion. They view me with suspicion. For I am a dangerous bird, a thief, a jackdaw. But that is only an illusion. In reality I have no sense for shiny things. . . . A jackdaw, which yearns to disappear between the stones."[60]

What Kafka translates into Czech, Gracchus translates into Greek: "The Hunter Gracchus" suspends the jackdaw-name between the life and death borders of an endless trip. In an aphorism, Kafka delivers this injunction he thus bore within his own name, to fly and yet be unable to fly: "Crows maintain that a single crow could storm the heavens. This is doubtless the case, but proves nothing against the heavens, for the heavens signify, after all, the impossibility of crows."[61] And yet these carriers of the Kafka name also join the ranks of an uncodifiable nomadic force. Screeching "like jackdaws," unreachable by language or sign language, the nomads in Kafka's "The Old Page," though ever suspended between embarkation and arrival, nevertheless are, as Deleuze advises, en route: "But the nomad is not necessarily one who moves: some voyages take place *in situ,* are trips in intensity."[62]

While attending a Zionist convention in Vienna in 1913, though he had in fact traveled there originally to take part only in the "International Congress on Rescue Procedures and Accident Prevention," Kafka had himself photographed with three Zionists inside a picture of an airplane in flight. Kafka can be found at the helm: ecstatic. Among the countless "paralyzed pictures"[63] circulating in Kafka's writings, this is the only one in which a machine achieves juxtaposition with Kafka, the author celebrated for introducing or depicting the technologization of writing to the point of conceiving his own self-rapport with literature—"I am nothing but literature"—as "being the placing of script" (*Schriftstellersein*).[64]

Josef K., who is not granted the freely spoken verdict, is, however, granted, in "The Dream," a glimpse of his full name as it chases across the tombstone above him. It was granted to Kafka actually to enter the mechanized version of his own name, of that bird-name which, even in the form of its first initial, the K shape, suggesting as it does the imprint of a crow's foot, irritated him; he was forced to conclude that these K's were indeed characteristic of him.[65] While beneath his father's letterhead there was a picture of a jackdaw perched on a branch, over Kafka's writing we thus find hovering a stationary airplane, somehow associated with Zionism, though in 1913 Kafka claimed to be unable to find the "right connection" to Zionism.[66] It would be up to Brod to find and use all the right connecting flights between Prague and Palestine, taking with him and rescuing what would become Kafka's collected works. By 1922 Kafka sensed, as he wrote down in his diary on January 16, that Zionism and the possibilities of flight it held open would keep his literature—itself an "onslaught against the limits"—from becoming a secret doctrine.

It was in fact Kafka who was the first author of German letters to write about airplanes. His piece "The Airplanes in Brescia," written in 1909, was the product of the first of many writing competitions Brod instigated to keep Kafka writing. As was always to be the case with this writing team, each alongside the other undertook his own pursuit of a common subject, only the finished products of which they later exchanged and compared. In the case of the impressions they recorded of the Italian airshow which they visited on their first trip together, Brod took it upon himself to submit Kafka's piece for publication without first seeking Kafka's consent. In this airplane piece, Kafka in fact sees the aviator Rougier's airplane in flight as itself a kind of writing machine: "Rougier sits at the controls like a writer at his desk. . . . He ascends in small circles . . . and never ceases to ascend."[67]

From the quill pen to airmail, from the Ibis to the Kafka, writing has always stood in close relation to natural and mechanical flight. Not only have flying and writing alike been viewed as modes of conveyance, but each, moreover, has been seen as conveyed upon the medium of air. The development of aviation technology demonstrated, however, that the very currents which had given rise to the notion of flight were in fact inimical to the process of flight as such. Indeed, the blowing currents of air—what Kafka called the "invisible danger" confronting the pilot-writer[68]—must be battled to obtain flight control. Both writing and mechanical flying amount to supplemental expedients through which it becomes possible to extend beyond those limitations which otherwise govern the dynamics of transfer over air (voice and wind), while both auxiliary mechanisms aim for and yet push back the utterly free articulation of air.

At the end of Kafka's airplane piece we find Max suggesting that they engage the Wright brothers to demonstrate their skills in Prague. Yet in a sense the Write brothers, who met in 1902 and commenced bringing out works in 1906, were never jointly to leave Prague's orbit. In 1909 the Wright brothers formed their own company; they also filed suit, that same year, for infringement of their patent, which, though applied for in 1902, had not been granted until 1906. The patent protected their inventions of an airplane rudder and of a technique, modeled after the flight of buzzards, to give the proper torsion to the plane's wings. It was not until these inventions were coupled with a propeller, however, that "free flight" was achieved in 1903 in Kitty Hawk. Indeed it was only with the invention of the propeller plane that man actually came to understand just how birds accomplish flight. Rather than the airplane modeling a bird, the bird, in the manner of a Kafkan metamorphosis, can be said to have been transformed into a living airplane.

In his letter, dated May 13, 1900, to the renowned aviator Octave Chanute, Wilbur Wright, while seeking Chanute's advice on wing torsion, had proposed that, in order to simulate protracted flight through a sort of flying in place, a tower 150 feet tall be constructed which would serve to stabilize the aircraft at that height. Since this tower-apparatus served to counterbalance the effect of wind drift, it actually served, as Wright emphasized, "in place of a motor." Not until 1904, however, did the first controlled flight take place when, after four trials, the Wright plane succeeded in completing a circular flight path which brought them back to and beyond their starting point above the first airport in history.

The Wright brothers imagined that with the advent of aircraft would come the abolition of war. Called on to advise the military during World War I regarding tactical applications of flying machines, Orville Wright stressed that flight was an extension of the sense of vision: by gaining control of the bird's-eye perspective, "the enemy's eyes can be put out." This the allies accordingly aspired to accomplish with their new "stretched skin" monocoque plane. By the close of World War II, Orville Wright no longer believed that with airplanes warfare, at least in the traditional sense, would become absolete: "I once thought the aeroplane would end wars. I now wonder whether the aeroplane and the atomic bomb can do it."[69] In the interim a new mechanism or agency for the regulation of flight patterns had emerged: warfare would therefore remain, though on some other plane, determined by the coordinates of destination, mission, and missile.

In the beginning the usefulness of air warfare had been compromised by the inability to monitor flight trajectories such that pilots in nomad fashion were subject to arriving at random destinations, at times finding that they had landed not at home base but behind enemy lines. Owing to the all-important function of eyesight in guiding the first aircraft, early pilots experimented with cocaine as a means of amplifying vision. At the same time Freud could be found experimenting with cocaine, which bestowed on him the "most gorgeous excitement."[70] Freud's cocaine research ushered in and advanced the use of local anesthesia in eye surgery. What ended up as introduction of euphoria into the painful operations evoked by the vulnerability of the eyes also began in the zone of the uncanny. As Freud instructs, cocaine had already always conferred zombie numbness on the resurrected bodies of ancient Peru: "The leaves were sacrificed to the gods, masticated during worship and thrust into the mouth of the dead, in order to secure a favorable welcome yonder."[71]

Cocaine gave rise to the dream of "Irma's injection," the dream which revealed to Freud, when he submitted it to the first complete psychoanalytic dream analysis in history, that fulfillment of a secret wish is the essence of every dream. The dream of Irma's injection, framed by a restaurant with a view, opens onto a mouth scarred over with infection. Ronell has discerned in the *Urmund* out of which psychoanalysis was born Freud's cancerous wound already in place, embraced both by the prosthesis Freud at first believes Irma bears and wishes to keep hidden inside her mouth and by the beard found missing from a certain Dr. M.'s face.[72] Behind the infection in Irma's mouth lies the nausea Freud's patient in fact suffered from, and the injection which, in the dream, returned to Irma's mouth that which was nauseatingly unclean.

The oldest and most reliable use of coca, Freud acknowledges, has always been, alongside its aphrodisiac qualities, the reversal of nausea.[73] Freud's Irma dream analysis demarcates in terms of the recycling of nausea "the familiar turf" of Freud's avuncular complex: Fliess, whose area of medical specialization covers the coordinates of queasiness, appears in the corner of this analysis as covictim—rather than the culprit he in fact was—of the specter of infection. Freud has identified with Fliess to the point of claiming as his own the unclean syringe which emerges as the source of infection; Freud had in fact recommended cocaine to a certain von Marxow who promptly started injecting the drug to the point of self-destruction. The syringe is thus the conduit of death-wish charges in a funerary setting where each omen of malpractice focuses on the outside chance that some actual disorder be discovered in place of symptoms believed to be of psychogenic origin.

Off on the horizon of the interpretation of the dream of Irma's injection lies Egypt, from where a patient's postcard has recently arrived: the patient had been sent by Freud, in place of and outside analysis, on a cruise, as though to counteract hysterical gastrointestinal symptoms according to the law of *similia*. But the hysteric has been held back in Egypt owing to a renewed outbreak of what was diagnosed this time around as dysentery. In Irma's case a contesting diagnosis would release psychoanalysis and Freud from the phantasmic reach of her mouth. Irma and her double in Freud's dream are, outside the dream, widows, a condition of want which, if found to be the cause of Irma's persistent pain, would clear Freud's—and Fliess's—blame for shortcomings of the treatment already accorded her. But widowhood, a cause of pain thus interchangeable with the scarring infection of mouth and throat, belongs to a certain Egyptoid past or exterior of psychoanalysis which nevertheless returns. Psychoanalysis commences as the Bellevue which, in the precise terms of wish fulfillment, cocaine first afforded. But within this view we can also discern as already invisibly in place that double of wish fulfillment—the death wish—which keeps the embodiment of the wish in mummified concealedness while tuning in a central control of either superegoical or telepathic provenance.

In this regard psychoanalysis parallels a certain development of aviation technology, which in turn finds its parallel in the invention of the typewriter. In all three cases, then, an element of blind mediation was introduced into processes hitherto dependent upon direct visual superintendence. This element of blindness made flying—rather like writing, according to Kittler's analysis of the advent of the typewriter[74]—automatic, that is, virtually unconscious, indeed resembling more instinctive migration than conscious, visually monitored navigation. Much in the way art, according to Kafka, is locked into a holding pattern around truth, so, in place of direct control of flight, aircraft obey signals emanating from some central control:[75] "Our art is a being-blinded-by-truth. The light on the fleeing grimace is true; but nothing else" (*KGW* 3:46). "Art flies around truth, but with the explicit aim of not burning itself."[76]

To put, in his lecture on *Weltanschauungen*, the demonstration of his argument on fast forward (*beschleunigen*), Freud creates, in lieu of some adequate representation of the history of the religious view, "a Phantom."[77] To the extent that religion centers on central divine authority, it always retains the young child's worship of the father. Before assuming the shape of actual religions, however, the religious impulse, in its earliest phase, gave rise to animism, whereby the world was crowded with "demons" which, though feared, were not entirely outside man's control: to obtain rain from the weather spirit, for example, man performed a similar act such that his first "weapon" in the struggle with his environment was "magic, the first precursor of our current technology."[78]

Before Oedipalization of the religious impulse there was, then, the zone of omnipotence of thoughts. At one end of what Freud has designated a principle of acceleration, both phantoms and the technical media project intense sibling rivalry. At the other end, this rivalry underlies, to this day, the wars among nations. World War I, for example, together with the ensuing economic crisis, had only one direct cause, according to Freud: "the conquest of the air. That does not sound very illuminating, but the first links at least in the chain are clearly recognizable. English politics were based on the security which was guaranteed by the seas that washed her coasts. In the moment at which Blériot flew across the Channel in his aeroplane this protective isolation was breached; and in the night during which (in peace-time and on an exercise) a German Zeppelin cruised over London the war against Germany was no doubt a foregone conclusion."[79]

As Freud clarifies already in *The Interpretation of Dreams* the airship symbolizes the male genitalia also to the extent that, like insects, it refers to the brother, another nickname for the penis.[80] The dream of flight is, like dreams of falling, losing teeth, and finding oneself naked, one of the "typical" dreams.[81] As such it is often entertained alongside spitting in dreams, and in place of ejaculation. In the dream of a homosexual patient, hovering flight traverses certain scenarios of being cast out and of ejaculating in turn.[82] But the fantasy of flight injects or introjects that which has been thrown up: flight does not come to arrive but only to return.

Thus, as Freud clarifies on the margin of one of his own typical dreams of being undressed—a dream which borders on his Julius complex—*Spucken* and *Spuken,* spitting and haunting, together stammer out the return trajectory.[83] The primal scene monitoring flight dreams features the uncle—that guest or ghost—who once threw the dreamer into the air to the point of pleasurable or distressing dizziness.[84] While the uncle throws one child, the other looks on. A dream of flight that leaves the dreamer behind opens Freud's premier publication of the wish which is the rule, the wish, as displayed in the dream, that one's siblings, like angels, grow wings and fly away.[85] The death wish takes flight.

The fantasy of flight remains interchangeable with the phantasm of imprisonment or encryptment which is its launching pad; according to McLuhan, at the very point of takeoff, airplane flight in turn incorporates its disposable contexts in a series of metamorphoses: "The road disappears into the plane at take-off, and the plane becomes a missile, a self-contained transportation system. At this point the wheel is reabsorbed into the form of a bird or fish that the plane becomes as it takes to the air."[86] The metamorphosis Kafka describes grants Gregor not only a bug body—the body of a sibling, according to Freud—but, as Nabokov discovered, even wings.[87] But before Gregor and his bug body can spread their wings the father condemns the metamorphosed son to death.

Despite their initial euphoric acceleration into the skies, the first write brothers soon found themselves following the commands of heir-power. Once radio instrumentation replaced blindness and eyesight with controlled flight patterns, the religious impulse, and with it the structure of warfare, was reorganized around the new Control Tower of Babel. Though Kafka first suggested that the advent of aviation would ultimately make "order and casualties alike impossible,"[88] he later expressed his doubts about air power in a letter to Milena:

> Mankind has invented the train, the car, the airplane in order to exclude to the extent possible that which is phantom-like among people, and in order to attain natural intercourse, the peace of souls, but it will not help anymore, these are inventions which are made in the course of plummeting, the opposing side is so much calmer and stronger, it invented after the postal service, the telegraph, the telephone, the radiotelegraph. The phantoms will not starve, but we will be destroyed.[89]

This condemnation of the phantom control exercised by telecommunications over even the post, hitherto Kafka's chief support system, follows Kafka's outright disapprobation of letter writing, indeed of "the very possibility of letter writing" as cause of all his life's misfortunes:

For it is intercourse with ghosts and moreover not only with the ghost of the addressee, but also with one's own ghost which develops secretly in the letter one is writing. To write letters, however, means to reveal oneself to the ghosts who await them. Written kisses never arrive, but are rather sucked dry en route by the ghosts. Through such nourishment they proliferate so outrageously.

Yet how does it happen that Kafka is replaced at the very switches of postal *Verkehr* by the menacing "ghosts" and "false hands" of telecommunications?

GAG ME WITH A PHONE

In a letter to Grete Bloch dated April 5, 1914, Kafka described the telephone as an invention which for him was "new and almost impossible to handle" to such a degree that he was constantly stopped from saying anything, for example by the slowness of the exchange. In his phone calls to Felice, Kafka could scarcely discern her words and could only convey or comprehend such announcements as, for instance, that he would be going to Berlin, an announcement that, in his state of disorientation, he would repeatedly shout into the receiver.[90]

The first torture-reading-and-writing machine elaborated by Kafka is actually not that of the penal colony but rather the telephone switchboard of Hotel Occidental:

Over there for example were six bellboys at six telephones. The arrangement, as one immediately recognized, required that one boy only receive calls, while his neighbor transmitted by phone the orders the first had written down and passed on to him. These telephones were of the newest variety, the kind not requiring booths since the ring was not louder than a chirp, one could speak into the phone in a whisper and still the words arrived at their destination in a thunderous voice owing to special electrical amplification. That is why one scarcely heard the three speakers at their telephones and could have believed they were mumbling to themselves and observing some process unfold within the receiver, while the three others, as though benumbed by the noise penetrating to them, though inaudible to bystanders, dropped their heads onto the paper which it was their duty to write on. And here again there was next to each speaker a boy standing by to help out;

these three boys did nothing but alternately lean their heads and listen to the operators, and then quickly as though stung looked up the telephone numbers in huge yellow books—the turning masses of pages were by far louder than the sounds of the phones. (*GS* 2:197)

Even the victim of the penal colony's torture-writing machine who "purses his lips as though listening" and who, rather than speak, must suck on a felt gag, is on the phone. For either machine to work the one who receives the messages must, in lieu of throwing up, insert the gag into his throat.

The telephone, as McLuhan has pointed out, so engages one's entire person that one cannot visualize while telephoning, its overall effect being that everyone is rendered a normally operating functionary devoid for the duration of the call of all neurotic symptoms. When McLuhan remarks that the phone extends ear and voice to embrace "a kind of extra-sensory perception" only to cross over into the psychiatry of criminal and normal behavior where the captivating effect of the phone call can be observed,[91] he has attended to while spanning the double register of telephone communication—at once telepathic and Oedipal—which Freud had already addressed. Even Alexander Graham Bell, who invented the phone to realize his father's dream of making speech visible, inserted his invention into séances to which all the ghosts were invited.

The advent of the telephone coincides with the institution of psychoanalysis also to the extent that both new organs were installed in Freud's apartment in time for Freud's father's death in 1896. In 1899 the convergence of the publication of *The Interpretation of Dreams*—at once Freud's testament, he claimed, and his *Trauerarbeit* over his father's death—with the assignment of a new telephone number (14362) foretold Freud the date of his own death. Freud had to "dial" with the same word with which one "chooses" the casket that chooses you. In Freud's interpretation, King Lear, who wants to "hear" how much he is loved, ends up succumbing to, as though choosing or dialing, the death he had at first refused to answer.[92]

Psychoanalysis would always accommodate the occult to the extent that the ancient link between dreams and telepathy could be pursued through a connection of media-technical provenance, the connection between telepathy and the telephone, which, even in conversation, as Jones reports, Freud was ever ready to draw.[93] Freud never claims exemption for psychoanalysis from these analogies. In his every excursus on telepathy Freud demonstrates that his analysis of an allegedly telepathic dream, rather than the dream itself, first renders the dream truly telepathic: "We must admit that it is only the *interpretation* of the dream that has shown us that it was a telepathic one: psychoanalysis has revealed a telepathic event which we should not otherwise have discovered." Or again: "do not forget that it was only analysis that created the occult fact—uncovered it when it lay distorted to the point of being unrecognizable."[94] Occult evidence is thus not recognizable as such, not until psychoanalysis uncovers the telepathic text of the dream that corresponds to the dreamer's secret wish. This is evident in prophecies which, though never fulfilled, struck and stuck to the dreamer with an enigmatic force so compelling as to outlast every proof that the forecast had not come to pass.

This strong unconscious wish always, Freud concludes, "made itself manifest to the fortune-teller or medium by being directly transferred to him while his attention was being distracted by the performances he was going through."[95] But not only wishes are thus transferred. What is more frequently conveyed along the telepathic channel, according to the examples Freud gives in his essays on occultism, is communication with dead siblings. In one example, a mother's recollection is telepathically transferred to and lodged within her son, where, since without its proper context, it remains what Freud is compelled to call a "foreign body."

This occult transfer blocks the therapeutic conversion of a patient's souvenir into associations. Hence the patient must be kept from writing down his first recollection of his dream, since this record would insert between patient and his dream—in lieu of associations—a resistance as complete as the total forgetting of the dream. "For even if the text of a dream is in this way laboriously rescued from oblivion, it is easy enough to convince oneself that nothing has been achieved for the patient. Associations will not come to the text, and the result is the same as if the dream had not been preserved."[96]

In "Should Patients Write Down their Dreams?" Karl Abraham extends the question to include technical recording devices.

In every case of a patient recording dreams instantly upon awakening—in writing and on dictaphone—the patient produces only unintelligible screed, gibberish, or static. One patient turns to a technical medium to rescue from repression his most important dreams, only to find repression match repression: "He owned a dictaphone and spoke his dream into the machine. Characteristically he ignored the fact that it had not been working properly for some days. The record was therefore not clear, and had to be largely supplemented from the dreamer's memory. The analysis of the dream was accompanied without very much resistance, so it can be assumed that it would have been preserved equally well without being recorded." But when the handwriting can be deciphered or its audio portion made out, either the content is so confused that it becomes superfluous in the course of supplementation from memory, or the stamp of repression's passport control at the border of transferential precincts alone remains: "As in Case 1 it was somewhat difficult to decipher the few words she had scribbled, owing to the indistinct writing. The words were these: 'Write down dream despite agreement.' Her resistance had won. The patient had written down, not the dream, but only her intention of doing so."[97] What is thus recorded is every dream's purpose: the disposal of unwelcome thoughts through their display or projection.

Thus transference triumphs over recording at this end; at the other end, the same lines of communication which have been tapped into by telepathic transfer of corpses also yield transference, which guarantees that every transfer will have been, after all, Oedipal: that is, plugged back into the father's death. But transference had always—and at the same time—been cause for Freud's greatest concern regarding the efficacy and effects of psychoanalysis. Thus, even though the psychic apparatus, like the torture apparatus of the penal colony, can, as *Apparat,* simply be translated as "telephone," Freud always opens up the telephone analogue and exchange within psychoanalytic precincts by forgetting to *use* the phone. Thus Freud forbids—and thus dares—the analyst to adopt the position of the patient's ego ideal and issue dictation or the dictator's call. But Freud also applies this interdiction at closer range: "It is quite an everyday experience that the generation of affect inhibits the normal passage of thought, and in various ways.

This happens, firstly, in that many paths of thought are forgotten which would ordinarily come into account—similarly, that is, to what occurs in dreams. Thus, for instance, it happened to me during the agitation caused by a great anxiety that I forgot to make use of the telephone, which had been introduced into my house a short time before."[98]

The nondelivery of the so-called lectures in which Freud addressed the relation of psychoanalysis to the occult indeed doubles, as Derrida points out, the telephone exchange between speech and writing which the lectures put through.[99] The telephone is conceived in these lectures as telepathic medium to the extent that both media await hookup to psychoanalysis, which alone can elucidate by forgetting to use them.

> What we call "telepathy" is, as you know, the alleged fact that an event which occurs at a particular time comes at about the same moment to the consciousness of someone distant in space, without the paths of communication that are familiar to us coming into question. . . . For instance, Person A may be the victim of an accident or may die, and Person B, someone closely attached to him—his mother or daughter or fiancée—learns the fact at about the same time through a visual or auditory perception. In this latter case, then, it is as if she had been informed by telephone, though such was not the case; it is a kind of psychical counterpart to wireless telegraphy. . . . The telepathic process is supposed to consist in a mental act in one person instigating the same mental act in another person. What lies between these two mental acts may easily be a physical process into which the mental one is transformed at one end and which is transformed back once more into the same mental one at the other end. The analogy with other transformations, such as occur in speaking and hearing by telephone, would then be unmistakable. And only think if one could get hold of this physical equivalent of the psychical act! It would seem to me that psychoanalysis, by inserting the unconscious between what is physical and what was previously called psychical, has paved the way for the assumption of such processes as telepathy.[100]

The telephone, then, occupies the place of the unconscious: whatever the unconscious may be, as regards its role in psychoanalysis it might as well be the phone or on the phone. Free association allows the unconscious to emerge until a strong transference is established within which the patient finds that his freely made connections were, after all, always on the same Oedipal wave length. Like a telephone receptionist, the analyst puts through, within the system of transference, the ultimate transfer, the transfer of the call, of that direct line to the first five years of the patient's life. This reception of the call disconnects telepathic lines: what commences, even in Freud's case, as the call placed to one's own death, that is, to some dead person, switches to the father's collect call which calls the caller.

In his "Recommendations to Physicians Practicing Psychoanalysis," Freud points out that since the resolution of transference "—one of the main tasks of the treatment—is made more difficult by an intimate attitude on the doctor's part," the doctor should remain to his patient "opaque," "like a mirror," and yet, at the same time—as Freud stresses in summing up in a single precept the technical rules he has been recommending—like a telephone:

> Just as the patient must relate everything that his self-observation can detect, and keep back all the logical and affective objections that seek to induce him to make a selection from among them, so the doctor must put himself in a position to make use of everything he is told for the purposes of interpretation and of recognizing the concealed unconscious material without substituting a censorship of his own for the selection that the patient has foregone. To put it in a formula: he must turn his own unconscious like a receptive organ towards the transmitting unconscious of the patient. He must adjust himself to the patient as a telephone receiver is adjusted to the transmitting microphone. Just as the receiver converts back into sound waves the electric oscillations in the telephone line which were set up by sound waves, so the doctor's unconscious is able, from the derivatives of the unconscious which are communicated to him, to reconstruct that unconscious, which has determined the patient's free associations.[101]

The superego is derived by Freud from a certain acoustic sensitivity worn like a "cap"—or receiver—by the psychic apparatus.[102] The superego's broadcasts remain, for Freud as for Adorno, less comparable, however, to the phone than to the radio, since they are one-way also to the extent that they address public opinion only by mimicking it. Psychotic breakdown is, accordingly, represented always as a telephone that asserts itself as some public address system that cannot be turned off. Schreber, for example, believes the telephone to offer "a satisfactory explanation" for his service to talking rays.[103]

In his "On the Psychology of Dementia Praecox," Jung investigates the neologistic "word salad" of his patient, who has retained, alongside her cryptic discourse, a coherently critical agency she calls the telephone, by himself picking up the phone, or taking up its place for the patient, and issuing her "buzzwords" to which she must respond.[104] That the telephone's "speech tubes," which are plugged right up into her anus, mock and block even her attempts to breathe freely constitutes for the patient her "hieroglyphic suffering."[105] For Jung, his patient's schizophrenia has eroded the "covering of consciousness" "so that one now could see from all sides the automatic machinery of the unconscious complexes."[106] By thus reading the hieroglyphs of his patient's delusional system through the telephone, which protests the "nothingness" of delusional projections it has installed, Jung focuses on that apocalypse of sublimation which, as was the case with Schreber, can only reveal technical media growing into and out of everyone's orifices and sense organs.[107]

The ring of the phone, Benjamin recalls, came out of that night which always precedes "true new birth"; in the case of the telephone, this gave birth anew to the voice slumbering inside machines. Benjamin immediately recognized the newborn as his twin, though he soon found that his double's "alarm signal" attracted and conveyed the father's "threats and thunder words." When he now answered the phone to hear himself speak he "was surrendered, without mercy, to the voice that spoke there": "There was nothing that could soften the uncanny power with which it penetrated me."[108] Benjamin's inability to swerve from recommendations and commands ordered by phone describes a scene of telephoning discernible also in Kafka's *The Castle:*

> It seemed as though out of the humming of countless childlike voices—but it was not even humming but rather the song of distant, extremely distant voices—as though out of this humming and in a virtually impossible manner a single high yet strong voice were developing, which struck the ear as though demanding to penetrate more deeply than only into the mere ear. . . . K. hesitated to name himself, he was defenseless in the face of the telephone. (*GS* 4:32)

The advent of the telephone installs in everyone an indestructible umbilical cord whereby the family is rendered all-pervasive: there can be no *Verkehr* without that with parents into which the phone call inserts us like the condemned man of the penal colony between the copulating halves of his machine. Together with psychoanalysis the telephone projects the cohesion of the family over large distances, even introducing this binding distance or *tele* into the home, the unity of which was thus shattered at the moment it was amplified. The double invention of telephone and psychoanalysis introduces the nuclear family as we know it, forever disbanded and bonded through the phone, forever keeping in *tele*-touch. Before the telephone the family was an institution only after the fact; that is, only once the child departed for the university, for example, could the child be seen as a product and the family as the institution which had produced it. In the age of the phone there are no eccentric pathways of flight and travel that would transpire outside any particular institution, since all circuits are held together within the earpiece, and all are *besetzt* ("occupied," that is, "busy," or, in Strachey's translation, "cathected"). As Freud clarifies, the increasing accessibility and endlessness of travel called for that which it cannot outdistance: "If there had been no railway to conquer distances, my child would never have left his native town and I should need no telephone to hear his voice."[109]

In *The Castle*, the song that one hears on the phone orchestrates ceaseless telephoning within the Castle bureaucracy: another "brotherhood with death." But the voices of singing children give way to the central conduit of command. In a letter to Felice dated January 22/23, 1913, Kafka discovers at the bridge of endless *Verkehr* which closed "The Judgment" a telephone in the place of the rescue ring. Kafka dreams of the music K. hears while waiting on the phone. He picks up the phone lying on the balustrade of the bridge: "I . . . did not hear anything through the phone except a sad, powerful wordless song [*Gesang*] and the roar of the sea [*Rauschen des Meeres*]. I well understood that it was not possible for human voices to penetrate through these tones, but I did not give up and go away." In the dream Kafka concludes that no human voice can penetrate the song at the other end of the line. But in "The Judgment"—conceived alongside thoughts of Freud "of course"—the son's attempt to tune the father out of telecommunications with the phantom Russian friend only turns up full blast the superegoical broadcast.

Nietzsche in *On the Future of Our Educational Institutions* saw the voice of instruction attached umbilically to the hands and ears of the students taking dictation. In *Genealogy of Morals* this educational apparatus comprised of isolated prosthetized bodily parts—reading mouth, listening ears, transcribing hands—assumes, by directly converting will to power into will to nothingness, a more compact shape. The over-and-out call that renders man over while summoning overman, who is put on hold, is issued by the phone that the modern musician has, under Wagner's direction, tuned and turned into: "he became an oracle, a priest, indeed more than a priest, a kind of mouthpiece of the 'in itself' of things, a telephone from the beyond—henceforth he uttered not only music, this ventriloquist of God—he uttered metaphysics: no wonder he one day finally uttered *ascetic ideals*."[110] But the inward turn of ascetic broadcasts can only be conceived with respect to some corpse to be interred.

The Freudian consumerist perspective on the technical media has been exceeded within the genealogy of media; and yet with regard to the corpse this perspective must yet be retained. The development of technical media has turned away from corporeal analogues or prostheses and pursued instead a logic of sheer acceleration or escalation. The functioning of the newest media thus surpasses any *sensorium* of warfare it nevertheless serves and simulates. And yet at the end of this escalation even the computer retains as its constitutive moment the possibility of total loss of that which has been entrusted to it. The destinal logic of its invention and first application notwithstanding, every technical medium achieves its ultimately only prosthetic range and portrait in the course of disposing of the dead. Thus work on the remainder refastens each new medium to a sensorium which, as Schreber realized, takes cognizance only of corpses. The genealogy of media always returns to life's internalization and definition as excrement of death.

But the phone does not register a vestigial part—the corporeal death—of that which it must develop. And yet, to achieve its first direct conversion, only the membrane of a human ear would suffice. Bell accordingly built into the first functioning receiver the ear of a corpse attached to a stylus which inscribed onto a plate the sounds whispered into the dead ear. Nietzsche's analysis of the university as merger of father and mother, of death and life, thus fits into this primal phone: "a telephone of the beyond" to which the divine cadaver has lent an ear.

The voice originally fills the mouth void of breast; the phone allows this *phonē* to assume, like the *fort/da* bobbin on a string, the corresponding suckable mouth-size shape. But the telephone ultimately serves as bond and bondage of identification with the Oedipalized past or repast. Through the telephone the commands of the parental monolith are amplified and carried out. Since the phone conversation is entirely nonvisual, mourning and proper burial cannot be conducted while on the phone; and yet, for Kafka, phantom communication with siblings becomes equally impossible. The call from the Oedipalized past taps into and outblasts telepathic lines of communication with dead siblings; it intercepts, in Kafka's case, the flight pattern and issues the command to crash.

In the lecture on dreams and occultism, Freud argues that telepathy, which holds the place of the more expedient interchange of physical signals that replaced it, was the original, archaic form of communication yet observable in the brotherhood of insects. Vestiges of such a telepathic mode of communication can, Freud maintains, yet be detected both in the anxiety of children who fear their parents know their every thought and in a passionately agitated crowd which in effect operates as a single body, the telepathic call or command being transmitted in this case as the virtually imperceptible rumor, imperceptible not so much because it is but a murmur but rather because it is a loud outcry.[111]

In the course of developing a veritable rumorology, Ronell picked up this phone: we can only anticipate, then, in the mode of augury and hearsay, the connection that can be drawn between phone and rumor. *Gerücht* (rumor) is linked etymologically to *Ruf* (call) and even in the sixteenth century, for example, was virtually synonymous with *Geschrey* (scream). That is, *Ruf,* which means not only call but also name and reputation, is related to *Gerücht* which, as a collective noun, signifies a great many, if not too many, calls.

Before Freud picked up the phone, Schreber's "rays of God" had appeared to him the best illustration of certain psychoanalytic insights. The rays do not only take down and take off; they, like the birds, also speak, specifically in the manner of chatter or rumor. According to Schreber, rumor and gossip, possessed of ever accelerating speed, participate in the emptying out of individuals who are replaced by "cursory contraptions."[112]

Except for a brief reference to the gossipy chatter of Schreber's birds, Freud pushes the issue of rumor into the periphery of his exegesis, namely, into a footnote to Jung's "A Contribution to the Psychology of Rumor."[113] Here Jung recounts the case of a rumor which circulated to the effect that a teacher had molested one of his charges. The rumor began as a schoolgirl's dream, which she related to a classmate who in turn told it to others until, having circulated no longer as dream but as rumor, it assumed the charge of child abuse, a charge which corresponded to certain latent wishes in the original dream. "So far as the interpretation of the dream is concerned," Jung concludes, "there is nothing for me to add; the children themselves have done all that is necessary leaving practically nothing over for psychoanalytic interpretation. The rumor has analyzed and interpreted the dream."[114] The buzzing rumor, charged with telepathic powers also of acceleration, runs the course of the analysis of a dream, producing punishable effects indistinguishable from the decision making of a court of law.

According to Freud, surveillance by plane is a late arrival of oneirocriticism: "For the Greeks and other Oriental nations, there may have been times when a campaign without dream interpreters seemed as impossible as one without air reconnaissance seems today."[115] Jung interprets rumor along this double trajectory charted by telepathic prediction and advance surveillance. The ultimate application of "the psychology of rumor" reaches all the way to the flying saucer, which Jung interprets as visionary rumor: "The unconscious, in order to portray its contents, makes use of certain fantasy elements which can be compared with the UFO phenomenon."[116] And yet Jung always affirms the occult and the technological only by leaving out that part of the interpretation he himself, as interpreter, embodies. Thus Jung praises as intimation of his own vaster notion of collective unconscious Freud's discovery of the superego, which can thus be left behind (42). The rumor now both places and answers the call; rumor is "a spontaneous answer of the unconscious to the present conscious situation" (131).

According to Jung, the modern pilot continues to practice an occult science to the extent that he cannot help but bear witness to the UFO rumor:

Today, as never before, men pay an extraordinary amount of attention to the skies, for technological reasons. This is especially true of the airman, whose field of vision is occupied on the one hand by the complicated control apparatus before him, and on the other by the empty vastness of cosmic space. His consciousness is concentrated one-sidedly on details requiring the most careful observation, while at his back, so to speak, his unconscious strives to fill the illimitable emptiness of space. His training and his common sense both preclude him from observing all the things that might rise up from within and become visible in order to compensate for the emptiness and solitude of flight high above the earth. Such a situation provides the ideal conditions for spontaneous psychic phenomena. (34–35)

A certain UFO dream reported to Jung accordingly reveals its own projective character by focusing on cinematographic operations conducted by two rival film producers (67).

The flying saucer is, then, an apparition or rumor that assumes and anticipates a technological interpretation, just as in the sixteenth century, Jung points out, visionary rumors conformed to military conceptions (96). The blaring noise of the past has given way to the subliminal buzz of the background music that accompanies a psychotic prophet on each of his flights to another encounter with extraterrestrials (117). In this context the anticipated Jungian reading has been jammed by its borrowed instruments. The flying saucer fantasy of course heralds rebirth. As such the fantasy is also literally hysterical, inasmuch as it features a wandering uterus (27). The flying saucer is also a "ship of death" (66). The saucer which thus carries the souls of the dead resembles an insect now hovering, now darting along telepathically transmitted beams. The flying saucer is accordingly comprised of prosthetic devices and "manned" by representatives of afterlife. This can be confirmed through a reversal: in one vision cited by Jung, man is enslaved by outmoded technologies to the extent that he embodies the afterlife of superior extraterrestrial beings who keep this underworld of shades under constant surveillance (115). Thus California is, Jung concludes, "the classic saucer country" (66).

In *The Trial* authentic acquittal, like the highest Court which hands it down, must, as Titorelli counseled, ever have the status of legend, which is to say, it circulates throughout the Court-organism merely as superstition, opinion, or rumor. This is how the law is disseminated among the defendants, for example, and, according to lawyer Huld, the very decision-making process of the Court (*Gericht*) operates "by rumor" (*gerüchtweise*) (124).

Arrest, awakening, and rumor coincide in the opening sentence of *The Trial:* "Someone must have spread a libelous rumor about Josef K., for although he had done nothing evil he was arrested one morning." Since Josef K., like Gregor Samsa, awakens to find that his life has been metamorphosed, in K.'s case by the Court's *Ruf* of his name, his ensuing trial can be seen as the unfolding of a dream which the Court- or rumor-organism interprets.

Josef K. is summoned to his first Court hearing, which, in German, is also literally a mishearing (*Verhör*), by a deficient phone call that K. supplements by asking, in lieu of the address that was not delivered, the whereabouts of a certain carpenter Lanz, the name K. freely selects to designate the Court. But K. has not invented this phallic name; it belongs to a neighbor who knocked on the wall to protest when K., in the course of seducing Miss Bürstner, reenacted for her his arrest to the point of shouting out his own name and arresting himself. By introducing a disturbance from without, Lanz takes up the position of the Court, which, in turn, answers to the name "carpenter Lanz." The *Ruf* continues to circulate on automatic, eliciting the Court's designation of K. as "housepainter."

Rumor in Jung's case study—like the phone according to McLuhan—detonates crowded precincts and makes room. The amplified *Ruf* clears the way in the wake of death. Around the deceased, the tribe gathers to yell and call out so that their collective noise might frighten off spirits intent on stealing the dead person's soul. The relatives of the deceased, or even, in certain cultures, all surviving members of the tribe, must adopt, as part of the mourning costume and makeup they also assume, a new or changed name, since the dead person has taken along a list of names with which to come back calling. Gongs must be struck during interment to keep back these spirits or even to chase away the spirit of the deceased. In this way, the ringing of bells, which in our own culture signals and attends funerals, is a late arrival of the funerary gong as of the metallic clapper with which the Egyptians armed their dead to scare off with its noise any demons even the dead encounter. The competing mourning broadcast—utter stillness—not only affords identification with the corpse but also deceives the spirits which, traveling overhead, pass over the place they take to be uninhabited. In dreams the stillness of a person represents that person's death. Under waking conditions the ring of the church bell resounds as harbinger of death. Alexander Graham Bell.

In his work for the Prague post office, Brod was in charge of the telephone department.[117] The year Brod published Kafka's name—and set its *Ruf* circulating precisely according to the logic of opinion and hearsay—Kafka entered the insurance business. As with the relation between the Court-organism and the authentic acquittal, insurance is predicated on there being some intrinsically uninsurable catastrophe—the forgetting of Kafka's name—which can only be talked about. Thus in *The Trial* the proliferation of the *Ruf* simulates only to safeguard against that unvisualizable, illegible blast of the *phonē,* which, if put through, would eradicate "everything." Without some fabulous catastrophe such as nuclear war—"the total destruction of the archive"—insurance itself would be inconceivable.[118] To the extent that this catastrophe cannot mark a beginning, since it is without remainder, it is the end of a process that has already begun, the process whereby insurance always anticipates catastrophe.

Only once did Kafka let his various insurance policies lapse, only once, that is, did he attempt to break off relations with his ghosts, though this move toward an authentic acquittal proved as impossible as had been the case with Josef K. Having entered the heterosexual triad consisting of himself, Robert Klopstock, and Dora Dymant—heterosexual in the sense that the passion that ends up in the woman in fact lies unconsummated between the two men—Kafka was confronted with the fiercest attack of phantoms he had ever withstood, and this at a time when his body was carrying out the literalization of those fantasies and fictions of incorporation he had hoped, apparently, to abandon. Now that use of his voice and normal intake of food were so severely compromised by the tubercular constriction of his throat, Kafka found that the formation of his bodily symptoms and the unfolding of his writing, specifically his composition of *The Hunger Artist* and *Josephine the Singer,* proceeded together as if connected via teletype. In desperation Kafka considered burning all his writings, and in fact did burn several manuscripts, hoping to escape the ghosts or, perhaps, put them to rest. His fear of this phantom onslaught was by now inseparable from his fear of being reinstated in his parents' apartment. Brod, who had been locked out of Kafka's newfound heterosexuality, in fact returned Kafka to his parents. And although Kafka died in the midst of Klopstock and Dora, one of Brod's frequent phone calls to the hospital almost reached him even on that final day.

The long-deferred work of mourning—of edition—thus emerged in the place of the phone: in 1924 Brod ceased working in the telephone department of the Prague post office. In his poem "Telephone" Brod had already supplied the terms for this switch from radiotelegraphic and telephonic control to the visualizations of mourning. The phone booth is a grave in which the one buried alive is reanimated by a woman's long distance breathing: the grave opens. The poet finds that he, too, is on the phone. As he looks into the receiver at his end of the end of the call, he visualizes—alongside the distance he thus traverses—the woman with whom he has conversed. In her place he accepts the charges of mourning.

CHAPTER EIGHT
ARISTOCRITICISM

(Karl Kraus)

The libertinism of the entertainment industry, the quotation marks
with which the court reporter frames the word lady when he wants to
feel out her private life, and the official expression of indignation are
all of the same blood.

Theodor Adorno, "*Morality and Criminality*"

FEEDBACK

Walter Benjamin draws the analogy between visual media of
magnification and psychoanalysis, which, in their separate takes,
bring into focus that which otherwise remains outside a normal
range of the senses. What film, for example, projects is in fact
projected in psychoses, hallucinations, and dreams. These states of
isolation, however, are granted the common or communal currency of the waking state in films featuring "figures of the collective dream such as Mickey Mouse orbiting the globe."

If one takes into account the dangerous tensions which technical mediatization and its consequences have engendered in the vast masses—tensions
which, at the critical stage, take on a psychotic character—then one cannot
help but recognize that this same technical mediatization has created as
protection against mass psychoses psychic inoculations via those films in
which a forced development of sadistic fantasies or masochistic delusions can
prevent their natural and dangerous ripening in the masses. . . . The monstrous mass of grotesque events which is now being consumed in film is a
drastic indication of the dangers threatening mankind from the repressions
which civilization brings with it. American grotesque films and Disney films
effect a therapeutic detonation of the unconscious.[1]

On the other side of this debate—at least at this point of injection—we find Adorno and Horkheimer warning against this administration of immunization or, as they prefer to address it, sublimation: "The accomplishments of civilization are the product of sublimation, that acquired love/hate relationship with body and earth." By the eighteenth century, Adorno and Horkheimer continue in that appendage within *Dialectic of Enlightenment* entitled "Interest in the Body," the natural conditions and rationale for the development and improvement of the body and its functional properties have disappeared. The body became the corpus constructed in one laboratory setting—the university—and reconstructed out of its maimed remainder in that always adjacent setting, the fitness lab. "The body cannot be remade into a noble object: it remains the corpse however vigorously it is trained and kept fit." Those who today nevertheless go ahead and build their bodies "use the body and its parts as though they were already separated from it." "They measure others, without realizing it, with the gaze of a coffin maker." "They are interested in illness and at mealtimes already watch for the death of those who eat with them." Adorno and Horkheimer argue that the segregation of the races duplicates the split carried within an individual between his evil, exploited body and the spiritual occupations which are asserted to be the greatest good. "The love/hate relationship with the body colors all more recent culture."[2] Phantasms of segregation and corpse concealment, the double legacy of a maimed body, conjoin most amiably in the university, where every individual, student and professor alike, awaits his turn to receive equal but separate news coverage, while in the process countless theories and theorists are kept artificially alive. Even when interdisciplinary exchange overflows the close-range boundaries between departments, the beyond of institutional segregation remains displaced with regard to a certain standard reception of newsworthy texts and theories.

In *Dialectic of Enlightenment* Adorno and Horkheimer argue that the university, like the rest of the culture industry and like the radio in particular, is democratic: it turns all participants into auditors subjected to broadcast programs which are all exactly the same.[3] Television takes this one step further: the norm of killing time in front of the TV set is the institutionalization of Freud's discovery of the mechanism of repression. Constant, addicted viewing corresponds to the unceasing expenditure of unconscious psychic energy accompanying the effort to keep that which must not enter consciousness in the unconscious, the unconscious being, on the other side of the analogy, the TV medium itself, indeed, the all-pervasive public sphere (*Öffentlichkeit*). For, with the advent of television, Adorno continues in his essay "Prologue to Television," private existence and the culture industry have come to occupy interchangeable places. Television realizes the culture industry's goal, that dreamless dream in which the entire sensual world is held again in duplicate, an improved copy which can penetrate to every organ. On television we watch ourselves trying to conform. And repeated viewing cloaks this otherwise unbearable pressure to conform, a pressure which is constantly exerted on our organs by their media extensions. This pressure must be rendered subliminal (McLuhan)—must be sublimated (Freud)—if paranoia is to be averted. Or, as Adorno puts it, television shows the audience how to behave by calling up images resembling those which "lie buried in the viewer."[4]

Like the funnies, to which, according to Adorno, television is most closely related, television broadcasts are miniaturist and hieroglyphic to the extent that words have been reduced, on television as in all mass media culture, to inscrutable labels or trademarks. Words have become rigid formulas both through their endless repetition and through their rapid appropriation of the things to which they, in themselves meaningless signs, are affixed. What had once been restricted to the advertisement columns of newspapers, a certain coldness, now inhabits all of language, which has thus been brought closer to its opposite, incantation. Names, too, are "undergoing a chemical change" on their way back to their archaic past. Both the Californian predilection for first-name basis and the interchangeability of given name and surname in the concocted monikers of movie stars render names vestiges of a tribal past, archaic remnants worn by members of a team.[5]

As Adorno and Horkheimer argue in the section of *Dialectic of Enlightenment* entitled "On the Theory of Ghosts," the replacement by "petrified alien terms" of "concepts like sorrow (*Wehmut*) and history, even life"—which, formerly, "were recognized in the word, which separated them out and preserved them"[6]—reflects, ultimately, a "disturbed relationship with the dead—the forgotten and embalmed." The petrification of language defines life only by its inconceivable opposite, destruction, such that the past, a suspect source of anger, can be forgotten. What is thus forgotten once history, mournfulness, and even life have been eliminated is the degeneration of existence—which, however, continues. That which disappears: that's history. More than anything else in society, mourning must be diluted and distilled: the corpse is beautiful and the "hardened survivors" odor free.[7]

Alongside this disturbed relationship to the dead, mass media culture conducts that endless work of mourning Freud called melancholia. The cult of the dead in any given culture is coextensive with the media extension of the senses current in that culture. Psychoanalysis, our culture's institution of mourning, keeps open lines of communication with the deceased which are precisely lines of telecommunication. Freud's disinterment of the phantom voices of the superego, for example, coincides with the advent of phonographic or radio recording whereby the voice become reproducible and, hence, posthumized,[8] just as photography and film project and animate those phantoms which, in *Totem and Taboo,* haunt those who are unable to grant the dead proper burial. Each new media extension of the body replaces the sense organ amplified with a new organ born, however, posthumously. Or, as Adorno and Horkheimer put it, the culture industry first reproduces the lives of the people it does not immediately do away with, such that to go to the movies is to attend one's own funeral.[9]

Films are always about the double to the extent that viewers witness what, from the point of view of those who control them, they have already become. Film accordingly serves as instructions manual to operation of and acclimatization to all the other media. In the twenties and thirties countless films featured and advertised the use of the phone. In *Bride of Frankenstein,* for example, Dr. Frankenstein must listen for the beat of his new creature's heart through a headset attached to the reanimation apparatus. He hears the heart respond to the electric shock: "She's alive! She's alive!" But once again he falters before bringing his work on the monstrous bride to completion; he demands some guarantee that his beloved Elisabeth, kept in some other place as ransom for the other bride, is still alive. Dr. Pretorius assuages his colleague's anxiety by introducing him to a new technical device through

which one can talk to Elisabeth even in her absence. Dr. Frankenstein picks up what is plainly a telephone and hears the life signs of
his bride: "She's alive! She's alive!" The telephone is thus inserted
on the side of horror which will achieve domestication. The bride
resurrected within the underworld laboratory of endless mourning
is exchanged, as analogue, for the other bride: Elisabeth shadowed
by her citizenship in the underworld of Dr. Frankenstein's sexual
repression. By doubling to the point of exceeding and replacing the
reanimation machinery, the phone call has etched the route of
rescue: what thus escapes to the outside as the outside of the
crowded precincts of corpse disposal is the consummation of wedding banns banning repression.

The story of Simonides' invention of mnemnotechnics thus
covers the mythic origin of every medium: photographic recall of
scenes of crime or catastrophe in the service of proper corpse
disposal. As sole survivor of a catastrophe that killed and pinned in
place dinner party guests to whom he had recited verse just prior to
the collapse of the ceiling which buried them alive, Simonides was
able to identify for proper burial the mangled corpses of the guests
by recalling the places they had occupied at dinner. He inferred
from this that in order to train the faculty of memory one must
select places in which to store mental images of the things that
needed to be remembered. To extend the visual sense in this way,
mental images had to be selected that were especially memorable,
and to this end ancient handbooks recommended that the figures
placed in the niches of one's memorial vault be exceptionally beautiful or singularly ugly, bloodstained, or, on the lighter side,
smeared with mud or paint.[10]

Cartoons, according to Adorno and Horkheimer, accustom
our senses to the tempo of the media, to the constant friction
whereby our resistance is broken down. Originally, cartoons at
once electrified creatures and objects and then gave the maimed
specimens a second life. Mourning had become electric. But in
the meantime this second life is our own. In the improved copy of
our life which taps into and seals shut all our sense organs, we,
too, do not die, do not come to any end, but collapse out of
exhaustion only to spring back for further battering.[11] As the
cartoons make clear, occult and technical media are indeed, as

Kittler has stated, one and the same: "their truth is fatality, their field the unconscious."[12]

The either gigantic or dwarflike spooks of the visual technical media always verge on seeming comical or cartoonlike, Adorno argues in "Prologue to Television." And yet, he continues, dwarves are the mythic inhabitants of chthonic underworlds. If television is not watched in darkened rooms, then, as Adorno suspects, it is indeed because the little people delivered right into our homes are uncanny; yet they are both dwarflike and uncanny, Adorno adds, precisely in contrast to the normal-sized voices emanating from them. Because the reproduced voice is always the same size, it is the most uncanny of all media doubles. McLuhan has also observed that whereas we tolerate our images in mirror or photo, since the "photo and visual worlds are secure areas of anesthesia," we are made uncomfortable by, we flee, the recorded sound of our own voices.[13] The radio, Adorno and Horkheimer argue, is a sublimated printing press.[14] Or, as McLuhan puts it, "radio is really a subliminal echo chamber of magical power to touch remote and forgotten chords." And radio is haunted by "archaic tribal ghosts"[15] because its vibratory space has been animated by sublimation.

In *The Ego and the Id* Freud expands his conception of sublimation to cover certain effects of improper burial. Sublimation is here doubly expanded: on the one hand, Freud allows that identification with lost objects is the general method of all sublimation; on the other, he stresses that the process of setting up a lost object inside the ego is by no means limited to melancholia but is in fact rehearsed unceasingly in the formation of the ego—and of the superego, itself the residuum of the ego's earliest identifications. Because it converts object libido into narcissistic libido, identification always amounts to sublimation. But at the other end, standing behind the ego ideal, is the earliest or primary identification, which is always with the father and is always brought about in the act of devouring him. The superego which sublimation thus erects covers this improper burial. And yet when in melancholia the ego seeks to incorporate an object which, unlike the devoured father, has been lost to the extent that it was once alive, the superego strikes close range; the superego takes over the controls of consciousness; it rises from its grave, like a vampire, threatening lethal bites of conscience (*Gewissensbisse*). In melancholia the ego, like the son in Kafka's "The Judgment," cannot swerve from the superego's condemnation since the object of the superego's scorn is already inside the ego.[16] But these transmitter-tombs are not suddenly thrown up during melancholia. According to the paranoid's testimony, they are always and already in place.

Paranoia is, like melancholia, essentially a sublimation disorder. According to Freud, Schreber's delusional system holds the place of the "wealth of sublimations" which has been lost: rays emanating from a god who takes cognizance only of corpses transform Schreber into a body of writing conducted and amplified by notational machinery. The paranoid scanner, which lacks a subliminal veil, can only protect the paranoid by projecting once again the unbearable pressure exerted on his sense organs by the alternation between their amplification and amputation.

In his revolt against the institution of conscience, which knows our thoughts and watches us, the paranoid encounters this main support system of the superego not in some interior place but as a hostile influence that reaches him from without. And the paranoid's heightened awareness of what is the case with all of us renders the censorial institution of conscience a radio. The voices which make the paranoid aware of this mental institution and observation post report back to him his every action, word, and thought in the third person—"('Now she is thinking of that again' . . . 'now he is going out')"—such that he experiences his life simultaneously with its transformation into or out of the news. The voices broadcast not only ancient parental criticisms, for example, but even, Freud adds, public opinion.[18]

According to McLuhan, the radio—just like the superego according to Freud—taps into prehistory and awakens tribal ghosts. And like the alliance between the superego and the institution of broadcasting in paranoia and in melancholia, the radio "is that extension of the central nervous system that is matched only by human speech itself."[19] In McLuhan's view radio can render the leverage it exerts on its audience subliminal and numb but cannot safeguard auditors against its tribal magic, which merges psyche and society in a single echo chamber.

In lining up the advent of radio with Hitler's rise to power,

McLuhan joins Adorno and Horkheimer, who hear every recommendation made on the radio turn into an order: "The inherent tendency of radio is to make the speaker's word, the false commandment, absolute." Or again: "The gigantic fact that the speech penetrates everywhere replaces its content."[20] Only long-term exposure to the printing press, McLuhan argues, can push back the instant tribalization which radio commands. And yet McLuhan views radio, to borrow Adorno and Horkheimer's phrase, as the sublimation of the printing press. Sublimation, Freud argues at the close of *The Ego and the Id,* veils thought control but cannot prevent the superego's destructive cruelty. Indeed, by weakening those erotic components which might otherwise have bound that destructiveness not intrinsic to the superego but added on (*hinzugesetzt*), sublimation cannot help but build a monster.[21]

The radio shares with the printing press a certain monstrous physiognomy. Adorno makes this clear in his essays "Radio Physiognomy" and "Punctuation Marks." Though punctuation marks are traffic signals they are not, Adorno argues, signs of communication but of delivery, a delivery which transpires not between language and reader, but within the interior of language (*im Sprachinnern*). No text can discard these marks, Adorno concludes. "Every text . . . cites them on its own, friendly spirits from whose incorporeal presence the corpus derives sustenance." Colons and, in particular, quotation marks remind Adorno, as they did Karl Kraus, Adorno adds, of hungry mouths.[22] And in Kraus's view quotation marks both render subliminal our attachment to public opinion and hold the place of hungry mouths bearing the citation-marking fangs of the vampire. Like Adorno, Kraus sees citationality as evident even in the absence of quotation marks. The existential *es*—as in *es werde Licht* (Let there be light)—can assume citational status; this *es* is, Kraus maintains, the "mental substitute for quotation marks" and enhances the "fluid nature [*Fluidum*] attached to citation." And the enigmatic fluid content of citation is juxtaposed to what Kraus refers to as the "immunizing effect" of citation.[23]

In attacking professors of literature for being nothing but failed journalists and, hence, failed prostitutes, Kraus notes, however, that the "institution covers the journalist" such that anything Kraus might write against this institution would, by being partially assimilated by it, be rendered innocuous.[24] Roland Barthes desig-

301

nated this process "the inoculation": dominant institutions prevail over opposition by assimilating small doses of the contesting discourse, which is thus replaced, at every point of impact, by decontextualized but internalized surrogates.[25] Kraus calls the discourse of the professor of literature, which resounds with mixed metaphors and jargons, that of a "blood sucker" who feeds on a circulation system, for example on the circulation of library books. Yet Kraus emphasizes that this "blood sucker" does not so much cycle or recycle as drain lifeblood from literary texts—does not, that is, via citation so much commemorate or incorporate literature as inoculate his discourse against literature. All professors and professionals occupy with journalists a closed economy which embraces the judicial system, an economy in which professionals and other witnesses inform reporters about a certain crime or issue and then quote these journalists to tell other professionals and themselves just what the issue is. This self-contained informational relay system of self-quotation and opinion is nowhere obliged to encounter a single thought or word.

Kraus claims that "belief is always stronger than knowledge";[26] since the advent of the feuilleton, belief or opinion (*doxa*) has grown stronger than the word. Thus by the time Hitler triumphs, the inoculating influence of the press enables one to disbelieve and hence not know what is manifestly visible. Opinion is always public opinion; *doxa* circulates openly—in fact, Kraus protests, it is impossible not to come into contact with it—and its utter openness makes it inscrutable, blinding, unknowable, and yet somehow invincible.

Knowledge is thus doubly modulated so that *doxa* can prevail. The same control that censors knowledge of the external world is also internalized as a control which prohibits belief in any knowledge which might nevertheless be obtained. To superintend these controlling agencies, Kraus must make conscious both the knowledge censored and the control that censored that knowledge, which, internalized again as censor, prevents belief when the knowledge is given. Kraus's cultural rereading of censorial institutions emerges, with respect to Freud's conception and casting of the psychic apparatus, as veritable endopsychic projection. Kraus thus attacks the press in the same move that pushes back Freud's theory of repression. Kraus's famous dictum that psychoanalysis is the illness it seeks to cure resonates within this contest, which is in fact the out-of-phase contrast between moments and analogues in a united reading with and against thought control.

But how can the satirist successfully call attention to those unsettling events otherwise neutralized by the information gathering and transmitting institutions with which the perceptual systems of individuals would thus be coextensive? Instead of the exaggerated caricatures the audience is presumed to expect from the satiric artist, Kraus delivers, without warning, direct citations from nonfictive reports whereby, after the fact, certain assimilatory effects of citation are reversed and blocked. At first led to respond to the cited material as though it were satiric art, namely with greater attentiveness and appetitiveness than would have been the case in the face of real events or, interchangeably, the news, the auditors, who have thus been lured outside their customary defenses, are doubly shocked by the subsequent admission that what has just been admitted and consumed under the aegis of art was in fact the direct hit of a quotation dropped from a nonfictive report. "Since," as Manfred Schneider clarifies, "that bit of truth which has been brought close to the audience in artistic confidence threatens to stick in their throats, their defensive reaction immediately sets in." According to Schneider, this bit of reality is taken in by each member of Kraus's audience, whose digestive or apperceptive habits are thus momentarily disrupted.[27] Kraus's anxiety about reference—his anxiety, for example, about the aesthetic/anesthetic effect which the phrases and opinions of the feuilleton have on the reception of real events— leads him to introduce, between the lines, reference from behind the lines, that is, in the throat. And he attains this referentiality, indeed a sort of double referentiality, not so much by citing as by plagiarizing newspaper reports.

Kraus finds the decline and corruption of language among the effects of the feuilleton, that incursion of journalism into literature and philosophy which, in the case of German letters, he attributes to Heinrich Heine. From this point on, words fueled a newspaper's circulation; but another circulation system internal to the word—that of rhyming and naming—could only end up depleted. Within the open circulation of phrase and opinion, words lose their status as name and, at the same time, the rhymes of which they were a part.[28]

Kraus declares that "Origin is the goal" toward which his

"avenging" of language is directed; the context of this point of return is restored through rhyme.[29] As generative and regenerative process of language, rhyme can be called—and this is Kraus's call—"the motherhood of language."[30] Beyond mere "acoustic amplification of memory," rhyme bears the word back to an origin where it is born again as name: as that which remains "adapted to the rhyme and as seal of deeper understanding calls for this resounding, which must result from the metaphysical necessity of representations which keep their word."[31] Or again: "The rhyme is only then such, when the verse calls for it, and calls it forth, so that it resounds as the echo of this call."[32]

According to Kraus, then, rhyme, the hallmark of language, is an erotic coupling in which various differences, for example of syllabic length, as opposed to perfect symmetry, guide the selection of words to be rhymed. Hence Kraus protests that the standard notion of masculine and feminine rhyme must be discarded: taken literally, it guarantees that each coupling of rhyme-words would, since homosexual, rhyme to the point of never engendering the "true" rhyme, which is always internal to, and yet between, the two words it exceeds.[33] Thus Kraus projects the complete scenario, doubled at each end by the possible breakdown of its sublimation, of return to a maternal origin. But if these standard notions or options describe for Kraus a deadlock, the rhyme that carries its coupling to fruition, according to Kraus, will have engendered a phantom, indeed Death itself. In various essays on rhyme, including "A Quotation from *Faust*," Kraus sees the union of Faust and Helena as the allegorization of his own conception of rhyming. Sealed through Helena's tutored facility with rhyme, this union begets the child Euphorion. But not only is the product of this union soon given over to death—indeed, it introduces death into Arcadia—but Death itself appears to Faust as a rhyme-word: "Four I saw come, but only three go hence, / And of their speech I could not catch the sense. / The echo suggested Distress [*Not*], / A gloomy rhyme-word followed—Death [*Tod*]" (11398–11401). The rhyme-word follows the testamentary, commemorative logic of the proper name to the extent that it calls Death forth and is the echo of this call. And yet, like citation, the rhyme-word is itself without a proper name; just the same, it, like citation, calls by name, that is, "sets in motion" and "summons forth" (*citāre*).

304

Kraus's every effort as writer—from exposing injustice per-
petrated against individuals, often sexual offenders, to taking in-
correct punctuation to task, the latter case being no less pressing
for Kraus than the former—is played out within the precincts of
justice. In this sense, to cite the journalistic phrase is to summon
it before that court over which Kraus, speaking in the name of
language, presides. And Kraus even equates rhyme with a court
(*Gericht*) before which marital squabbles are muted into tone,
thought, and poetry.[34] Yet these courts presided over by Kraus
belong to that final forum, the Day of Judgment, *das letzte
Gericht* or *Weltgericht,* indeed, the Apocalypse, *The Last Days of
Mankind.* As, etymologically, a process of unveiling or making
visible, apocalypse inhabits citationality to the extent that quotation marks drop between them the veil of citation they also lift by
setting words off from adjacent words. And just as the apostle
John's apocalyptic visions include the judgment of the great
whore Babel, so Kraus's apocalyptic writing exposes that of the
one-time whore language: "With hot heart and brain / I ap-
proached her night after night. / She was an impudent whore, /
Whom I made into a virgin."[35]

Kraus imagines himself the savior or Christ who, by restoring
the mother tongue to virginity, guarantees that the hymen will
remain intact. The mother tongue cannot be without this cover or
hymen precisely because there is nothing there to cover up, no
truth, for example, to which, according to Kraus, the actual prostitute is closest.[36] It is against the pornography—literally the "prostitute writing"—that Heine had made of the German language, that
Kraus champions what Benjamin calls "Platonic love of language:"
in this conception, citation language indwells as the guarantor that
the erotic relations between proximity and distance—between
rhyming and naming—will remain always only simultaneously invoked. Close up, this double relation reflects back love of the
name, according to which possession of the other's name keeps its
bearer—at a distance. Or, as Kraus puts it: "The closer one looks
at a word / the farther it looks back." This is Kraus's experience of
love, according to Benjamin, the experience of "the way in which
the beloved becomes distant and blinking, and all her smallness
and gleam is drawn into the name."[37]

In *The Origin of the German Sorrow Play* Benjamin finds

mourning, in which a tendency to silence is ever present, as already inherent in naming: "To be named—even if the name-giver is god-like and saintly—perhaps always brings with it a presentiment of mourning."[38] But the shift from naming to mourning undergoes acceleration into empty, manic frenzy when the allegorist must read the name in its absence. This nameless shard emerges in the context of Benjamin's essay on Kraus as the journalistic phrase: the portable placeholder of a missing name which unceasingly consumes just as it is consumed without consummation. In "On Language as Such and on the Language of Man," Benjamin argues that what is "more melancholy" than being named by a godlike namer is the multiple naming that issues "from the hundred languages of man, in which name has already withered." This babble in the wake of Babel—which in the case of the German language is linked and limited by Kraus to the advent of the feuilleton—takes the form, Benjamin clarifies, of "over-naming": "over-naming as the deepest linguistic reason for all melancholia and (from the point of view of the thing) of all deliberate muteness."[39]

The empty circulation which Heine thus installed in language takes the form of "contagion": "opinion" always requires "direct infection" in order to be adopted and spread. Thus the journalistic phrase, which effaces the maternal word, achieves consumerist appeal and subliminal packaging as "envelope of opinion."[40] On the way to its mass consumption, the phrase becomes libidinized. Through his loose use of rhyme and word play, Heine accordingly rendered the German language a widely accessible collection of "ornaments" and "paper frills"—*Papierkrausen*.[41] Kraus's analysis can only begin—again—with the dropping of the name in passing. Having thus doubly inscribed his patronymic—his father having been the owner of a paper factory—within the immediate consequences of Heine's debasement of the mother tongue, Kraus yields to the scenario of degenerescence he analyzes: the demise of language could never have commenced without a certain insertion of the patronymic into a maternal place.

Kraus's essay "On Plagiarism" opens, accordingly, with this slippage and spread of the proper name: "The aggressive intellect who has called me 'St. Crausiscus' and who uses humor, satire, irony without any deeper significance and is consequently an inexhaustible maker of puns without conceptual content, in other words a genuine fool, has demonstrated that I have taken the basic elements of my poem 'Apocalypse' from the Revelation of John."[42] Maintaining that one would have to copy the entire work of a true poet, one in the service of the word, to do any part of it justice, Kraus declares that it is accordingly impossible to imitate or plagiarize in part, that is, to cite a true poet; by the same token, inferior verse is so precisely because it does lend itself to citation and could scarcely have been better designed for reproducibility and mass citability.[43]

In this regard Kraus emphasizes that citation without quotation marks is not simply plagiarism, for the very originality of such appropriation is the deletion of these marks: "It is precisely this appropriation which has original value and the production is not consummated here in the words themselves but rather in their application, their incorporation."[44] By incorporating an excerpt from *Hamlet* into his text, Kraus in effect grants these words a new originality instead of the mere status of "adornment" which inclusion of quotation marks would have effected. But Kraus insists that there yet remains a tense nonrapport between the fragment and his own discourse, a tension he feels is in this case even heightened, indeed, made possible, by the omission of citation marks. And this tension aims further to strike his foes. For Kraus incorporates Hamlet's words in order to denounce those powers which he sees as his principal enemies, the forces of institutionalization and the press. Kraus does not use them for their content alone, however, but also, and at the same time, for their status as citation. In listing the target range of his critique and defense, Kraus explains, he had left out those two in which he retains the greatest investment; it was into this "gap" inflicted by his enemies that this citation without citation marks "had to be" incorporated.[45]

By relying on plagiarism—or improper burial—to effect his satire, Kraus is racing to overcome the effect of inoculation. Kraus's peculiar view of language as a cycling of lifeblood ever in danger of being interrupted or spilled is not, he emphasizes, to be taken metaphorically. And indeed, Kraus sees himself as something of a vampire: "And once I am lying on the bier / traveling to unknown territories, / it is then that I enter life."[46]

Kraus belongs to that select circle consisting otherwise of Kafka and Nietzsche that built anti-inoculation systems of defense against those "monsters of nihilism" who, in Nietzsche's words, were waiting at the portal, and in Kafka's were already knocking at the door. Yet Kraus alone would live to face directly that most formidable enemy, Hitler. Kraus must concede defeat in the race against the inoculation effect, which, however, secures its cumulative effect and culmination in Hitler's unchallenged rise to power. With the advent of Naziism it is, Kraus warns, no longer "possible for the art form of language satire to deliver us from the magic by means of which blood erupts out of phrases."[47] Any Nazi slogan such as "Juda verrecke" conceals nothing and is thus unreadable, unbelievable, and cannot, then, be fazed by Kraus's satiric art. Emptied out by journalistic citation, the German language, which is in 1933 already a dead language,[48] rises from the grave ravenously hungry for what Kraus calls the former content of words: "And what revelation would be more surprising and what view more stunning than that of the word hull which fills itself anew with blood which was once its content? . . . Gorgonlike, since it is the eruption of physical blood which begins to flow out of the crust and scabs of language."[49]

Before his heart stops, however, in consequence of that "conceptual paralysis" which Naziism brings with it, and the very word dies on his blood-drained lips, Kraus derives pleasure from the possibility that his satire somehow surpasses its prophylactic potential and shapes current events: "Indeed I laugh night after night, these past twenty-six years, when the raw material of current events sets about taking up my form."[50] While during World War I Kraus was yet empowered to reveal the then prevailing "union of the linguistic with the material" to be one of phrase and blood, and the empty word to have engendered the deed,[51] with the advent of Naziism Kraus realizes that the satiric methods at his disposal have been rendered superfluous: "There prevails a secret understanding between things which exist and their denouncer: Autonomously they produce satire and the material so completely has the form which I once had to gather from it in order to make it transmittable, believable, and, again, unbelievable that it no longer requires me and nothing further regarding Hitler occurs to me."[52]

The race between vampires that culminates in the endpoint or Apocalypse of citationality can only describe a race destined to be lost. But Kraus, like Nietzsche, is no loser. To characterize Kraus's satiric art as a mode of incorporation effected, for example, through plagiarism, it thus proves necessary to join Benjamin, who finds Kraus's other and god in Mickey Mouse.[53] As premier talking animation of cartoon cartouches, Mickey Mouse embodies, as its culmination, the original coemergence of two typographical analogues or props of satire: caricature and quotation marks. In caricature, as its etymology attests, notions of animation, of charge and exaggeration, have always inhered; quotation marks—first called quotation quadrats—not only preserved phrases from the acts of plagiarism they first introduced, but even put ears on phrases. As Mickey Mouse and the quadrats make clear, citation also amounts to reanimation of a voice though always on the other track.

Benjamin sees both Kraus and Mickey Mouse as embodying a cannibal's "kind of experience: incorporation," an experience which reaches outward from the child who wields rhyme to the nonhuman who is responsible for the name. According to Benjamin, both Mickey Mouse and Kraus push aside mythic man, including superman, and replace the old creature concept, according to which man's relation to his fellow man was purified concurrently with the satisfaction of the sex drive, with a new creature concept in which the cannibal purifies his relation to his fellow man at the same time as he satisfies his hunger. This "nonhuman" dislodges mythic man—that is, guilt itself—by allying himself with the destructive aspect of nature and developing a new relation to technology previously blocked by mythic man's belief in creative, constructive labor.[54] The primary court (*Gericht*) which stands behind Kraus's citational praxis and to which this praxis would restore language is, literally, a meal (*Gericht*), the meal Benjamin, echoing Freud, calls cannibalism.

Kraus's employment of citation as a means of punishment that also effects restoration reflects Mickey Mouse's "kind of experience." Kraus's entire conception of language, from *Gericht* to *Gericht,* is, according to Benjamin, organized around this double track of citation. Citation lies at the very origin of language, which it both preserves and destroys. And the outer reaches of this origin, which citation ever renews, are rhyming at one end, and naming at the other. To cite citation is to remove the phrase from its "envelope of opinion" and send it back to its original address as name. Thus the delivered phrase is made to stand alone and expres-

309

sionless on the one hand and, on the other, to attract, through rhyming—its reanimated voice track—a new context of similar names.[55]

In the essay on plagiarism, Kraus insists that the thought behind his having put Hamlet's verse into his own verse lies not in the two verses themselves but rather in their not being his own, in their take-over, their *Übernahme*.[56] In what may be a Nietzschean vein, Kraus seeks through his citational praxis to restore language to the *Übername,* the supername, to make the superego omnipotent. Only in this way could full-fledged incorporation of a body, for example the body of the mother, be possible.

Freud addresses, in a footnote to resistance to cure, the emergence of the supername alongside repression of *Schuld* and loss. In certain patients resistance stems from an unconscious sense of guilt. This sense of guilt is a "borrowed one," "the product of an identification with some other person who was once the object of an erotic cathexis. Such an assumption [*Übernahme*] of guilt is often the sole remaining trace of the abandoned love-relation and not at all easy to recognize as such. (The likeness between this process and what happens in melancholia is unmistakable.)" The *Übernahme* can be busted, Freud suggests, if the analyst is placed by the patient in position of ego ideal, though, Freud is quick to add, this scenario lies outside psychoanalysis as one of the limitations of its effectiveness.[57] Assumption of the position of ego ideal, which gives ready access to the institution of broadcasting, its adjunct, underlies the successful takeover by dictator, prophet, or redeemer of power exercised unconditionally over the masses.[58]

In Fritz Lang's *Dr. Mabuse the Gambler,* of the countless disguises Mabuse assumes, two mask through revelation. As the hypnotist Weltmann, Mabuse attains his greatest power over men and beasts, which he demonstrates by effecting the mass suggestion that the oriental tribe advancing in the film projected on stage will march on into the audience. Mabuse tells the police that a certain Count Told is under Weltmann's influence; in fact Mabuse exercises, in his own name, complete control over the Count in another guise, that of psychoanalyst. Dr. Mabuse's psychoanalytic technique retains similarities to hypnosis, which in turn holds the place of film. But film and mass suggestion do not guarantee the kind of control Dr. Mabuse the psychoanalyst seeks to administer: the Count must not leave the house nor is he allowed to see or speak to anyone who might thus remind him of his former self. Leaving film behind, Mabuse treats his patients only in their homes, as he informs the Count by phone. Henceforward, Told is told, he cannot place or receive phone calls. The Count is thus at the mercy of the telephone, which issues only Mabuse's one-way broadcast. By taking hold of the position of ego ideal—of the missing phone—Mabuse takes charge of Told. But Freud stresses that such a takeover, whereby dictation is given rather than taken, is precisely out of the psychoanalyst's reach, though only to the extent that it remains the constitutive temptation or breakdown of psychoanalysis. What resembles to the point of resisting, and yet being effaced by, this takeover is the *Übernahme* displayed, for example, by melancholic identification.

The *Übernahme,* which prevents the superego from developing to the point of "surmounting" the Oedipus complex, does not inflict "bites of conscience" (*Gewissensbisse*) as does the conscious reception of guilt, but reflects instead a certain need for punishment.[59] Such p-unitive wishes can, according to Freud, refer only to the father, whose dread penetration was first reversed by identification. To block incorporation of missing persons other than the father, the superego repeats its context of origination, proffering, like some incubus, sexual penetration from one end and, from the other, incorporation.[60] In place of the "overcoming of the Oedipus complex" (*Überwindung des Ödipuskomplexes*) we find an *Überwunde* secretly incised by fangs belonging not to father or incubus—nor to psychoanalysis, which, according to Freud, bares "poison fangs."[61] As Karl Abraham argues, for example, biting in melancholia holds the place of the maternal body it holds in place.[62]

As Freud puts it in "On Narcissism: An Introduction," though the ego ideal promotes sublimation, it cannot command that sublimation be carried out. The self-regard and self-observation of the ego can only demand the shortcut of repression for implementation of the ideal's commands.[63] Sublimation, which first circumvented by building this observation post, continues to offer, with each identification, a detour around repression. But sublimation can also always succumb to the desexualizing simulation it applies.

According to Adorno and Horkheimer, life in and according to the culture industry is a constant initiation rite: everyone must show that he identifies himself with the power which is belaboring him. As in the constitution of the superego according to Freud, however, the incorporation, which mass media culture brings about and reflects, consumes products that were never really alive. The serial productions of the culture industry center on that which must never take place, sublimation or incorporation of the mother's body. The mass production of this invitation to identify, which the culture industry issues but withdraws, automatically achieves its repression.[64]

On the other side of the culture industry according to Cargo Cult, secular education—the modern university—is also mimicked in its absence. In the warehouses the good "thinkthink" requisite to the successful homecoming of the cargo-bearing ancestors was taught and practiced. Outside these stations of identification only missionaries had given instruction to the Melanesian populace. Thus the Bible—"Talktalk belong Baibel"—was the point of access to the white man's secret. Some believed that the secret was contained in the first page of the Bible, which had been torn out of the copies the Melanesians received. Indeed, these Bibles were abridged to the extent that they were translated; did the white man ever translate the whole Bible?

The translation scene in Goethe's *Faust* accordingly repeats and rehearses the primal scene of the modern university as sealed by the devilish pact between professor and his double, the bureaucratic administrator of his wishes.[65] But by a kind of double take, the other double, the professor, always turns away from taking responsibility for the literalization of his Faustian desire. Faust's free translation of *logos* is inspired, even dictated by the spirit or ghost rather than the dead letter; by replacing "word" with "deed" Faust introduces in place of literal translation of the Bible a hermeneutical reading which remains literary even when it is the Bible that is thus better read than dead. The professor of free translation or literary interpretation is one of the two souls crowding Faust's breast; the other belongs to the literal-minded functionary who wears the "farce face" of Faust's signature.[66] Mephistopheles pops up rolling his eyes in the corner of every scene of Faustian striving.

As with every contractual relation with the devil, according to Freud, so the Faustian pact must also always be sealed twice to secure its tenure. Thus to gain access to Margaret through her close friend, the local gossip Marthe, Mephistopheles and Faust must first bear false witness and sign a death certificate rendering Marthe's missing husband, as per her request, properly and permanently absent. When Faust at first refuses to join in the ruse, Mephistopheles charges him with always having borne false testimony: by signing a death certificate in the absence of even a glimpse of the corpse, Faust would only, as always, be professing and playing doctor without material guarantees. It takes the two souls in Faust's breast, the professor and the bureaucrat, to produce the effect of a true and negotiable death certificate.

Before Faust thus follows to the letter the contract of the modern university professor, another contract or deed has come due: what has come to a conclusion from which it can only rebound is the suicide pact between Faust and his father, the family physician who unwittingly administered poison to plague victims who died not of one thing but of another. The suicide pact covers that relationship to the dead which Freud pursued under the rubric, borrowed from Ratman, of omnipotence of thoughts. The technical media are applications of omnipotence of thoughts also to the extent that this omnipotence—since it always turns around into a death wish—must be shared with a dead person. The underworld slave labor camp, where, according to the Cargo Cult, all telecommunications devices are made, contains the mournable deaths which have always taken the dead father as model. In Faust's case, the dead father reemerges as Mephistopheles, the bureaucrat who must slave to realize Faustian desire.

Thus it is the mother who can only be found missing in a death-wish pact which commences, in the series of its institutionalization, as the eighteenth-century coemergence of childhood, the technical media, and the modern university. The pact forged between university and state was first rehearsed in yet another contractual relation. In the eighteenth century the state required that at every German birth a physician be in attendance. According to Dr. Semmelweis's confession in the mid-nineteenth century, the century-old decree that put physicians in the place of midwives at the primal scene of birth had also conveyed death to the mothers via the doctors' dirty hands. "Semmelweis noted that because of the great emphasis placed on the study of pathology in the Vienna Medical School, professors, assistants, and students all had frequent contact with cadavers. In the days before rubber gloves, 'cadaveric particles' clung to their hands and were not entirely removed by washing with soap, as was demonstrated by the persistence of the 'cadaveric odor.' Later, during vaginal examinations, the contaminated hands introduced cadaveric particles through absorption into the vascular system of the women examined."[67]

Every modern master and builder of mediums accordingly advances to degree candidacy: Doctors Frankenstein, Caligari, and Mabuse. Dr. Semmelweis's confession belongs to the target range of every monster's shifting identity. Every monster is mummy; but every monster also assumes the cover of the repressed—of the primal father. *Doktorvater* emerges in the place of the fostering mother and midwife. Only upon driving away the Shamanska did the Shaman first adopt maternal attributes; henceforward he embodied, on stereo or bisexual tracks, the scene of the primal father's murder and consumption. But, as also witnessed by the Marquis de Sade's scenarios, this eighteenth-century primal scene requires that the mother be killed off, left over, or reconstituted. The body—which is also always the maternal body—is replaced and reanimated through the prosthetic encryptment of missing parts: a monstrous corpus built of substitutions for mourning.

"Made in Germany" is Freud's example of the sort of legible label the repressed, too, must bear even as it works under cover. As Freud argues in another place, the modern university—another German product—has shaped the institution of psychoanalysis by excluding it. But this logic of relocation and projection belongs to ever more primal precincts.

In Melanesia graveyards had been left behind as each village, under the new economic pressures and attractions, moved over and again to more suitable locations. In anticipation of the return of the mourned dead, these cemeteries had to be brought back into closer range of the living. Once the relocation project or projection had begun in a certain village, once the bones of the dead had been gathered, cleaned, and kept for a time in the homes of the descendants, a "teacher" would appear to the villagers.

The secrecy that must accompany the articulations of Cargo Cult—which thus responds in kind to what the Melanesians took to be the withholding of real education by the whites—in turn required "teachers" to provide revelations and other validating signs of the nearness of ghosts and Cargo. Thus in one case visions and dreams of a dead father announced his imminent return as "teacher." At one end of their neo-Melanesian conception, "teachers" are the transitional leaders who take control of the cult following the first active phase of possession called "Noise"; at the other end the "teachers" of the Second Cult are, quite simply, ghosts.

So far only "teachers" have returned from the underworld where the mourned dead slave for the reconstituted *mater:* the amalgam of unmournable death at the controls of this cult intercepts and puts on hold even the messages the mourned dead send to the living. The full return of the mourned dead—of which "teachers" are the advance emanation—can be met only with total annihilation: only a stricken world reduced to "rubbish" can attract the cargo it will in future store. Before this return of the mourned dead—and in the midst of interference and control which unmourned death exercises in consumerist scenarios of dissatisfaction—psychoanalysis would intervene, but only, according to Kraus, by injecting the death of the father into the grieving body to abort the unmournable deaths of mother, child, and sibling. Thus Kraus counsels that the telephone be kept out of Freud's reach.[68]

As is the case with Dr. Frankenstein and his monster, incorporation by the ego of a lost object, of the departed mother, for example, creates a fiend that destroys and puts to rest both the ego and the object inside the ego. The ego that incorporates a dead object cannot help but lose the race it thus initiates against the superego; near the finish line, sublimation always reverses itself to reveal close-up the vampire it had hitherto veiled and pushed back. Through a reversal which transpires, then, over time, the superego drops the veil of sublimation and becomes indistinguishable from the return of the repressed. For, as Freud argues in "The 'Uncanny,' " although derivatives of what is repressed are foremost among the items reprehended by the ego-criticizing faculty or conscience, the division between this critical faculty and the rest of the ego is not superimposable onto the antithesis between the ego and what is unconscious and repressed.[69] The reversal built into sublimation, which renders the superego first subliminally effective and then cruelly destructive, does not only unfold over time. As is the case with citation in Kraus's conception, both aspects are also copresent and await their simultaneous or stereo broadcast at once under and over the threshold of repression. In this way sublimation would attain what Nietzsche described as the sublime simultaneity of both meanings of *Sinn*, of both sensuousness and chastity, a simultaneity which would attest to the circumvention of that threshold of repression which would otherwise prohibit their co-occurrence.

Following the death of his mother, whose memory he kept current with a lock of her hair, a letter, and a leaf from her grave, Kraus committed himself to the study of Latin, through which, he maintains, he first learned German; that is, after his mother's demise he retroactively recommenced his rapport with the mother tongue by taking a detour via a dead paternal language, indeed, the superlanguage. In the name of language, that is, from the position of the superlanguage—a language which is both sheer citation and without citation—Kraus carries out the detonation of the journalistic phrase and its restoration to the status of name: "For there appeared unto me an angel, and the angel said unto me: Go hither and cite them [the journalists]. And so I went and cited them."[70] In the name of language: the pseudonym Kraus adopts for his first publications, Crepe de chine, is that veil-name he would restore to the mother tongue, the veil which citation and *hymen* otherwise first suspend and then destroy. Kraus arrests his sexual explorations, his critique of language and his satire—satire being for him an exclusively masculine activity[71]—at the very threshold of the mother tongue. The position he takes up with regard to this threshold permits him to be simultaneously on both sides of the veil of citation, at one and the same time enchanter and among the enchanted. Kraus aims to be "the creator of citation" or, as he also claims, "the first case of a writer who at the same time experiences his writing theatrically."[72]

Mickey Mouse and Kraus, cannibal and vampire: these subhumans, which both embody and dispense with the superego, can incorporate without residual criticism or guilt. And, as Friedrich Kittler has shown, Count Dracula can be defeated only by the synchronized operation of various technical media including dictaphone and typewriter, whereby all information about the Count and even about his pursuers is stored in triplicate.[73] Only through such total media control, which doubles the lives of vampire and vampire killers alike, can Dracula's telecommands, which reach from prehistory across the distance between Transylvania and England, be withstood. Thus, Kraus counsels, the radio must be detached from its limited goal of replacing the stage and, together with a device for visual superintendence, be directed against the press:

> But even technical progress might be pressed into the service of mankind if radio would replace the editorial offices rather than the stage, and would in this way bring about an unmasking of the voices of the press, though to this end it would prove necessary to develop and add on a new telescopic device through which the individuals who represent public opinion could be observed. . . . This is the last hope that time-bound life has left me. Technology cannot be so utterly the work of the devil that it could not also paralyze through one of its possible manifestations the damage which it brought about and thus put an end to the enchantment through an even more precise disenchantment.[74]

NOTES ON VAMPIRISM AND FILM

Already in ancient Rome a college of clairvoyant priests was established for combating Lamiae, those blood-sucking ghosts of loose women to whom the Romans were forbidden by law to expose or deliver their dead. Ever since its foundation, the institution has kept vampirism, alongside citation, in some other place only to find it pop up, close up, as its own uncanny caricature and portrait. In determining what must be included in and excluded from its functioning, the university at once rejects and appropriates that which is "outside," "different," and "not-self." All these targets, whereby, in taking aim, the man of resentment constitutes himself, are placed by Nietzsche in quotation marks.[75]

The vampire covers trace structure from his citation bites to the hammering, like typewriter keys, of his fangs.[76] In the corner of every breakdown of defense or immunity, vampirism is there, always attached, of course, to those on the wrong side of lines of segregation. The slippage of these lines and hence of vampirism is everywhere in evidence. While the threat of communist expansion

317

and infiltration elicits allegorizations of Stoker's *Dracula* by Mc-Carthy supporters, the enemy in World War II is brought into focus by distributing copies of *Dracula* among the GI's.[77] In vampire literature popular in twentieth-century Germany, the Jewess is the original source of the blood lust which has contaminated an entire nation.

The intense interest in vampirism in the eighteenth century emerged alongside massive evidence of premature burial uncovered in the course of relocating the dead to segregate them from the living: exhumed corpses which had gnawed the shroud with blood-stained mouth and clawed the coffin with bloody fingers. As witnessed by the large number of scholarly treatises on vampirism published at the time at French and German universities, the evidence also prompted university professors to speculate on a problem that for the academic begins at home. The diagnosis of those buried alive—and, according to Montague Summers, in the first half of the twentieth century in the United States no less than one case a week of premature burial was discovered and reported—often turned out to be hysterical catalepsy, a form of playing dead whereby the exhausted body recoups its expenditures.[78] Even in a strict sense, then, vampirism and psychoanalysis can be seen as rival sciences of the undead.

The eighteenth-century relocation of death summoned, close range, the phantasm of premature burial; long range, the automatic return of the repressed brought back eyewitness reports from Eastern Europe of the vengeful dead maltreating the living. As one French journal reported: "The vampires appeared after lunch and stayed until midnight, sucking the blood of people and cattle in great abundance. They sucked through the mouth, the nose but mainly through the ears. They say that the vampires had a sort of hunger that made them chew even their shrouds in the grave."[79] On this Eastern front of journalism, Vampire courts run by Imperial Army officers delayed burial of suspect corpses: after seven weeks the yet ruddy dead were decapitated and burned. Back home, academic disquisitions took issue with journalism's vampire without, however, divorcing journalism, which did the research.

This reading of the other's unconscious in place of one's own, which remains hidden, summoned the first vampire literature. In-

318

deed, the vampire from Transylvania was a German fabulation: Saxon traders colonizing the environs of Transylvania in the fifteenth century sent back to Germany horror stories about Vlad Dracul the Impaler, Prince of Walachia, who was attempting to push back German influence in his territories. These Vlad the vampire stories, which became the bestsellers of the printing-press culture newly established in Germany, set the terms of a contest between those who would devour and exploit a people and the crew of cannibals they take this people to be.

In Stoker's novel, the "new woman" is the object of dread. She emerges as vagina dentata, the woman who is all teeth: all her orifices are superimposable one onto the other, and all of them have teeth. The teeth must thus be extracted from the new woman before she, too, can become happily married. As is also the case in psychoanalysis—which parallels to the point of being included in Stoker's exhaustive study of vampirism—the ancient images of the dread woman have shifted in *Dracula* from the metaphorical to the clitoral. What has thus been covered by Stoker is the first emergence of the mother tongue. The bearer of this tongue is new also because she has married the new technologies which nevertheless keep her, like Psyche, in the underworld of her newfound repression: she is at the switches of these technologies only to the extent that she is also bride of death.

Hence the normal cycle of reproduction is mimicked in its absence. Since he does not kill his victims but grants them instead a kind of posthumous birth, Dracula is a mother: according to that logic in evidence in countless folk tales, biting, also in Dracula's case, replaces reproduction. But Dracula is the mother of corpses he keeps alive or of living beings who, following his example, imitate corpses. And this mother-and-child blood bond which preserves loss is itself never lost. All the characters in Stoker's novel come to be linked together through transfusions, suckings, and nursings within a circle of recycled blood.

In Stoker's case, vampirism embraces a primal scene. At the paternal end, Dracula's first point of entry and biting in England is inserted into a cemetery which contains notably—and at odds with the tombstone inscriptions which mark them—many empty graves, memorials to lost seamen.[80] These tombs transmit advance signals of Dracula's approach from across the sea; the ship *Demeter*, which conducts Dracula, has in turn lost at sea all but one of its seamen corpses. Thus loss—of fluid, for example—is lost. Ernest Jones notes in his reflections on vampirism the equivalency in the unconscious of blood and semen;[81] but in the vampire these fluids are interchangeable to the extent that both are recycled or utterly absorbed, lost without remainder. Thus the Rumanian designation for vampire, *nosferatu* or *nosferat,* covers what is always the case by referring only to a special case of vampirism that causes a husband to become impotent or, at the same time, to model himself after corpses.

The phantasm of vampirism is a primal scene witnessed from crib or crypt. The Count, in turn, has a child's brain. Count Dracula is Stoker's self-portrait as child: "In my babyhood I used, I understand, to be often at the point of death. Certainly, until I was about seven years old, I never knew what it was to stand upright."[82] Count and count: these seven years also saw the complete growth of the Stoker family which closed with the birth of George, the last and seventh of the Stoker children.

In a letter to Freud dated October 15, 1924, Karl Abraham points out that the number 7 is always the cipher of self-restraint and hence also expression of taboo, just as it is central to the rituals of obsessional neurotics. Abraham must thus conclude that 7 is a hybrid comprised of 3, which stands for the father, and 4, the symbol of the mother. Seven has accordingly always served as the numerical unit most readily portable in memory. Hence the always seven digits of the telephone number: dial D R A C U L A.

"If there had been no railway to conquer distances, my child would never have left his native town and I should need no telephone to hear his voice." At the other end of this phone call, Freud inserts yet another portrait of the child: "What is the use of reducing infantile mortality when it is precisely that reduction which imposes the greatest restraint on us in the begetting of children, so that, taken all round, we nevertheless rear no more children than in the days before the reign of hygiene, while at the same time we have created difficult conditions for our sexual life in marriage, and have probably worked against the beneficial effects of natural selection?"[83] Next to the distance to be conquered and yet retained by the telephone, infant mortality thus emerges in Freud's reflections as the other primal content of that to which Freud is building up here: the prosthesis god.

As Bierman discovered, a spectacular error in multiplication in Stoker's children's story about animated numbers—"How 7 Went Mad"—shows that here, too, 3 and 4 carry a weight in excess of correct coupling. Holding the place of little Stoker we find 7 being examined and bled by the doctor. At this point of bleeding a double pun emerges which includes, alongside stethescope, telescope, and microscope, also horoscope, which a child mishears as horrorscope. Occult and technical media together deliver, via a child's stammering lapsus, the secret definition of the horror genre.

In "How 7 Went Mad," 7 is now wished dead, now, through change of heart, wished alive again. In an adjacent story, "The Wondrous Child," we find an imaginary baby shared by siblings in place of their new baby brother back home: angry thoughts cause this effigy to die; good, repenting thoughts bring it back to life. Like the Count, this baby brother comes from across the sea.

Bierman detects death wishes directed against George, the seventh child in the Stoker family, in every multiple of seven in Stoker's works, even in the seventh astrological sign presiding over these works—that fateful crab devoured by Stoker prior to his dream about the vampire king rising from his grave—under which George had been born. But this cannibalistic indigestion and ventriloquism includes Stoker: the crab moves backwards. Thus by emerging from his coffin bed after seven years, shortly after George's birth, Stoker inserted himself into the family as the seventh, youngest child. At this end of identification, the vampire's mouth or grave opens onto, as Bierman instructs, "the wish to eat, be eaten, and sleep."

The dream of the vampire king rising from his coffin bed conducts a death wish all the way to its vampiric deadlock; the bond and bondage of identification is fratricidal in scope also to the extent that the brother can never go. "To find relief," Bierman writes of this death wish, "Stoker had to write his novel in which the vampire's victim could rise, disgorged from the tomb, while the Dracula in Stoker could be laid to eternal rest, unable to rise again to go about his ghastly business."[84] But a kind of ghostly business nevertheless remains. George, a physician like all his brothers but one, did a stint of transporting the dead during the Russo-Turkish war. For dramatic purposes Stoker and Irving needed to know just how one carries a corpse; they pressed George for a demonstration. George automatically complied, as did Stoker—also on automatic—playing, as always, the corpse. As youngest and seventh child, Stoker remained his brothers' perpetual patient and cadaver in games of playing doctor and playing dead.

One of the writing projects which prepared Stoker for the fable of living death was George's contribution: Stoker helped his brother write down an eyewitness account of the Russo-Turkish war which the witness and ghostwriter together entitled *With the Unspeakables*. And yet it was another eyewitness account which had already inaugurated Stoker's oeuvre. Foremost among the stories Stoker's mother told her bedridden son were her recollections of a cholera epidemic in the course of which many of the afflicted were buried alive. Though he put her reminiscences to use in one of his early literary efforts, it was not until he wrote *Dracula* that he received his mother's recognition, her assurance that he was already immortal.

In addition to *Dracula* Stoker saw through to publication only one other vampire tale, "The Lady of the Shroud," in which he also applied a style of sheer citation, consisting of journal, diary, and newspaper excerpts. Around citation-marking fangs an insatiably hungry mouth opens in the absence of any voice. Stoker's *Dracula*-style was first rehearsed at the limit point of journalistic citation: Stoker had earlier helped found a newspaper which was entirely citational to the extent that it—the first in Dublin—did not air any political views of its own.

Stoker's *Dracula* concludes with the reflection that the archive—which, amassed in busting the vampire, remains interchangeable with the novel itself—includes no "authentic document" but only a "mass of typewriting." The terror that overwhelms Mina upon listening to voice reproduced by dictaphone—"That is a wonderful machine, but it is cruelly true"[85]—drives her to transfer everything to typewritten record. The vampire which thus emerges only in the absence of authentic documentation of voice is, as Goerres already pointed out, essentially the incarnation of exteriorization and telepathy.[86] Even when the Count is granted a voice, in

Browning's *Dracula*, for example, he speaks with the lilt of citationality: "I like to drink uh wine." The audio portion of the
vampiric suspension of life and death between quotation marks
holds out the possibility that someone be "uh dead."

In the twentieth century the phantoms of the printing press
leave literature behind and secure entry into psychoanalysis and
film. Also in this sense, then, film remains, as McLuhan argues, a
late application and extension of the printing press.[87] The sheer
citationality of Stoker's novel—Minna's mechanically amassed
archive—accordingly finds its analogue, in the film versions of
Dracula, in the technical aspect and apparatus of the film medium. Since all the references to technical media which crowd the
novel have been left out of the transfer to film, the projector is
nevertheless evoked in the film versions by metonymy and absence.[88] By focusing in turn on the telehypnotic control a phantom exercises over and through its medium, these movies cannot
stop short of projecting their self-reflection.

In Murnau's *Nosferatu*, the telepathic bond between the vampire Nosferatu and Nina, which is so strong that it is unclear who is
telecommanding whom, is first established with the circulation of
Nina's portrait as it passes into Nosferatu's hands. Like Nina's
portrait, which is animated through circulation—and this is consequently Nina's own status—Nosferatu is animated still life. Nina's
self-sacrifice at the end of the film recalls both from the circulation
of blood and money which has remained invisible throughout.[89]

The relation between still image and motion picture in
Nosferatu comes into focus only by going out of control each time
the film crosses over into the realm of the undead. Acceleration of
the apparatus and deletion of individual stills produce the rapid,
lurching movements of Nosferatu as he drives his carriage, piles up
coffins, and rises from his crypt. The vampire has always risen
from his grave in anticipation of film, which attains through its
doubling and suturing of shadows what was otherwise only legend:
the vampire lacks a proper image which a mirror would in turn
reflect.

Monster movies thus represent the dual nature of film composition in primal scenes of unnatural creation: film, like monster
making, animates through technology the amalgam of parts that
were edited by hand—dissected and sutured together. Film recog-

nized itself in stories of monster animation to the point of including in its versions the added attraction, which it alone could offer, of doubling. In the first film version of *Frankenstein* the doctor recognizes the monster as his own reflection in the mirror.

What is thus in a state of dispersion is also always a means of control that goes out of control. In Lang's *Metropolis,* doubling and division govern both the segregated polis and, at closer range, woman's place; in each case a disturbed relation to the dead body emerges spectacularly as the ground for building in place of burying. In *Metropolis* we find a fully established Babel, at the heart of which lies a robot cast in the image of a woman. This robot remains attached to its creator, who took a robot hand to replace his own, lost in the course of constructing the replica android. As a country-and-western refrain once put it: "When love dies it goes to hell." Hel—whose name was too close to "hell" for the American editors to include her in the 1927 version of *Metropolis*—is the dead woman doubly missing from this frenzied building of cities and bodies in the place of dispersion or loss. What organizes *Metropolis* is this absence, between "brain" and "hands," of a mediating "heart," which also covers a missing womb. Enter Freder, the saving son who supplies this missing heart also to the extent that his birth doubled as cause of Hel's death.

The robot reconstitutes this dead woman, and the bond between the resurrected woman and the robot builder is the hand he had offered her in marriage, which could not be accepted live. Even when the heart joins hand and brain at the close of the film in a marriage ceremony that reconciles all citizens of this new Babel, this union is but the repetition of the exchange of hands between the robot and its creator, a bond of incorporation that joins the Babel tower and its underworld, where workers labor solely to generate the electricity which illumines and animates Metropolis, the city and the film.

Lang was destined to be an architect; his turn toward film was part of a vaster context of return—to death-cult precincts. Architecture became the first thought experiment to address the newly discovered masses: the first issue of this encounter was a new conception of dramaturgy matched by a hundredfold increase of theaters. But the increase in architects still exceeded every total theater project. Only film could thus supply the housing projects for the masses who, as in *Metropolis,* entered the underworld of film. For *Metropolis* Schüfftan developed a mirroring process for the transformation of architecture from stage props into the death-cult illusions proper to cinema.

In Lang's *The Testament of Dr. Mabuse,* underworld hands serve a "dead brain" which has come back to life with enhanced telehypnotic powers. Even his cohorts find Mabuse "uncanny": that which exercises absolute control over them has no corporeal identity that might bear the name. Sheer name without corpse, "Mabuse" remains, ultimately, a cinematic projection: a veiled wooden silhouette and record player which issue commands to gang members on the other side of the screen in a windowless vault to which typewritten notes have summoned them. Only the gang member who has—as his fianceé alone can remind him—already done time for murder and thus brought to completion a certain labor—of mourning—can escape this underworld; he floods Mabuse's mined crypt and movie theater, which he thus defuses and puts to rest.

Lang's reflections on certain German substitutions for mourning thus come into focus by coming to a close—in time for his move to Hollywood—as mourning and testament. But this testament also rebounds from the narrative frame Lang added to the original story of *The Cabinet of Dr. Caligari;* according to Siegfried Kracauer, Lang's frame-up delegates Hitler's phantasmic control over the German medium, which, like every medium, is the willing and active partner in telehypnotic relations. But the frame Lang adds to *The Cabinet of Dr. Caligari* does not contain the original indictment directed against those in charge of institutions; instead, the institutional or representational frame emerges spectacularly as the mad or unhinged focus in a film turning on containment.

From the cabinet and coffin to the mental asylum and university—the Caligari phantasm is charted back to a book which is the property of the University of Upsala—the frame that, in exercising control, goes out of control, also covers an unmourned corpse. At one end a murderer would frame his crime as part of a preexisting series of murders; unable to keep himself out of the picture, he finds himself framed for perpetrating the whole series. At the other end, the benign psychiatrist inhabiting the outer narrative frame can detach himself from the Caligari inside the framed delusion of a madman only by removing his glasses; what is thus brought into focus as the ultimate frame is the evil eye, the eye of some murder victim who retains the power to inflict vengeance with his Medusean gaze. Caligari's series of murders accordingly commences by fulfilling a common death wish: the rude official must die.

What follows this death-wish scenario in the series of Caligari's repetition compulsion is the murder of Alan, which thus remains adjacent to its origin and meaning. The threesome comprised of Jane, Francis, and Alan—which we see convened between a title announcing, in conjunction with the first murder, "Murder Reward" and the scene of Alan's knifing—is untenable in terms of the logic of the frame which, in the case of the marriage contract, dictates that odd man must go. Within Francis's narrative Alan is that goner who can thus not be buried or framed: he alone is missing from the recycling of the figures who, though killed off in Francis's story, nevertheless reappear in the outer frame. Alan's missing corpse accordingly keeps the narrative frame from assimilating the improper burial in the film to an asylum of the mourned dead.

Already before World War I, Expressionism was established as a recognizable style: German Expressionist film, as Expressionism on loan, thus borrows from across the war zone that shadows it a certain resistance to framing. At the other end of the war, Expressionism is recycled to cover losses which are embalmed or projected without proper burial. Expressionist artists had joined in the frenzied acclaim for a world war they too had seen as externalization of an inner combat zone. The *Blitz* of the war came to deadlock in facing graves where the cohabitation of soldiers and the unburied was sustained even beyond the time alotted for proper mourning.

Thus Max Beckmann, who before the war was a highly successful portrait painter working in a conventional idiom, turned to Expressionism only in the midst of this pile up of corpses in place of combat. In 1914 an Expressionist painter could confide to his diary that he had long carried "this war" inside him, such that "inwardly it was no concern of his." In 1915 Beckmann writes: "I want to digest all this, so that afterwards I shall be quite free to make almost timeless things: this black human countenance, looking out from the grave, and the silent dead who approach me are dark salutations from eternity, and as such I want to paint them later."[90]

In turn, the recognizably Expressionist style of *The Cabinet of Dr. Caligari* was adopted so that the film could break out of Germany: only art films were allowed to circulate outside German borders. The repressed, Freud advises, must, while working under cover, always also bear a legible label, like "Made in Germany." Under the cover of the label of repression, borrowed Expressionism would "digest" that which continues to look "out from the grave." On this side of resistance to burial, the drive to assimilate within a collective of survivors can yield only monster making.

In *Civilization and its Discontents,* Freud's thorough rundown of technical media and means of transport, which even juxtaposes the uncanniness of *tele* with that of infant mortality, leaves out only film, which is also always the one analogy which, for Freud, goes without saying. But the theory of projection—which can only be found missing in Freud's works—is in turn controlled by the missing analogy with film. In the wake of World War I, film and occult research each in turn proposed some form of alliance with psychoanalysis. But Freud accepted only the occult challenge in place of—and as the secret meaning of—the film offer, which he turned down.

> It no longer seems possible to keep away from the study of what are known as "occult" phenomena—of facts, that is, that profess to speak in favor of the real existence of psychical forces other than the human and animal minds with which we are familiar, or that seem to reveal the possession by those minds of faculties hitherto unrecognized. The impetus towards such an investigation seems irresistibly strong. During this last brief vacation I have three times had occasion to refuse to associate myself with newly founded periodicals concerned with these studies. Nor is there much doubt as to the origin of this trend. It is a part expression of the loss of value by which everything has been affected since the world catastrophe of the Great War.[91]

Anticipating scandals detrimental to the establishment of psychoanalysis, Freud emphasized that his interest in the occult was, like his Judaism, his private concern outside the public published program of his science and legacy. Following World War I, a projective trajectory emerges which links the occult to psychoanalysis but keeps film in some other place; in its place another side of image

327

making—assimilation—conjoins Judaism and the occult. Expressionist film covers this trajectory. Rye's *The Student of Prague* pushes the drive to assimilate to the limits of becoming simulacrum: the student seeking entry into high society must confront his own animated mirror image, which he has sold to a sorcerer for a premium—the price, at the other end of assimilation, of the entry ticket. This uncanny confrontation comes into focus by reconvening in the Jewish cemetery, which then returns as the end of the film: the silent double or image sits above its title, the student's grave inscription.

The phantasm of effacement by one's own image is transferred by Wegener, who both commissioned and acted in Rye's film, to the Golem films in which he starred, on the final rebound under his own direction; in subsequent remakes the doubling puts Wegener, in his Golem suit, in a movie theater featuring the earlier Golem film, which Wegener thus watches. The spectral props of Jewish burial, image making, and assimilation thus hold interchangeable places with the out-of-control doubling of film. In the 1920 version, *The Golem: How He Came into the World*, Rabbi Löw, at the behest of the emperor, conjures up spirits from the past in a magic show which, represented as a film within the film, carries with it Löw's warnings of the dangers of the show: warnings which, since not heeded, materialize in catastrophic fashion. By rescuing the emperor and his court from cinematic necromancy, the Golem-robot secures a respite for the Jews from the emperor's decree of banishment.

To safeguard against crisis, the Jews were granted, according to the Golem legend, a single media support system, though under the constraint of numerous restricting clauses and terms. Golem making thus exploits those powers of image making and nomination otherwise interdicted by Old Testament law. At the heart of this visual medium lies a label inscribed with one of God's names, aemaeth or "truth." The Golem can be put to rest only by removing the written label from the robot's heart or by deleting the letter that links and separates aemaeth and *maeth*, which spells "dead." In a context of monstrous consumption or creation which is also consumerist, the label, which always designates citizenship in the repressed, covers the placement of the double legacy of father-god and death inside a monster created—in the film—in the missing place of the mother. Although, like Adam, Golem—literally, "un-formed mass" or embryo—is animated only by the breath or name of God, the robot is also created out of the earth; as Gershom Scholem points out, the tellurian powers the Golem thus receives deliver the dangerous consequences of his creation. The ground out of which Golem is formed is also burial ground: the animated image cannot speak or reason, nor can he procreate. According to at least one account of Golem making, the Golem was first to be buried in the earth before he could be animated.[92]

In Wegener's film, Rabbi Löw, in response to the emperor's decree that all Jews be banished from the realm, creates together with his male assistant a son to be the savior of his threatened people. The mother is doubly absent from this laboratory, missing without commemoration. The daughter in turn responds to the threat by initiating negotiations, largely sexual in nature, with the Christian messenger from the emperor's court. Both the daughter and the animated Golem are attracted to the outside of the ghetto, to the Christian exterior inhabited by the saving mother and child. At the end of the film Golem, on the loose and out of control, makes a break for the outside of an unattainable exterior. When he knocks down the gates and joins the Christian children picking flowers outside the ghetto walls, one child lingers unafraid to play with Golem: the word made flesh meets the product of a dead reading and writing tradition consisting entirely of male-to-male transmissions. As they play, the innocent but knowing child re-moves from Golem the written label which animates him. The removal of the label introduces a second—and total—death; the urge to annihilate the victim always seeks the destruction also of his grave inscription.

German Expressionist film's short-lived legacy—essentially carried on only by Hollywood's monstrosity films of the 1930s[93]—includes a warning about the limits of assimilation, a warning the Golem, as much a threat to assimilation as he is an amalgam of its aspirations, embodies. Hollywood monstrosity films continued to transmit these warnings at a time when the German film industry had, already since 1927, come to be dominated by anti-Semitic nationalistic concerns. The transfer of German-Jewish involve-ment in filmmaking, which preceded the Nazi takeover of the Ger-man state, amounted to a warning signal which only Hollywood could have received. Indeed, many of those who had left for Hollywood before 1933 were active in arranging the movie contracts which would save imperiled Jewish intellectuals by granting them entry tickets into Hollywood, where largely secularized Jews were in control.

Entry into the culture of assimilation capitalized on by Hollywood, which in turn served as its capital, had already been memorialized in *The Jazz Singer,* which lapsed Jews produced to celebrate and cover their own assimilation into a kind of non-denominational, yet essentially Christian, American society. Jakie Rabinowitz, the son in Hollywood's first sound film, abandons Jewish family traditions when he ignores his father's wish that he, too, should serve as cantor. Instead, Jakie changes his name to Jack Robins, just as he exchanges his patrimony for a career as jazz singer. *The Jazz Singer* thus marks a descent from *Gesang* to *Gerede,* from the voice to the *vita-phonē* on the one hand, from silent films with musical scores to "talkies" on the other. Jack Robins becomes a successful mammy singer and, once back home again, wounds his father by babbling on about having made a name for himself. Since the mortally ill father must be replaced as temple cantor on the Day of Atonement, Jack cannot help but accept this invitation to identify with his father: as he receives his dying father's blessing, Jack sings the Kol Nidre. Jack's show of piety remains, however, a one-time stint as cantor, a brief delay injected into his career as jazz singer. The culture of assimilation represented by Broadway and Hollywood thus prevails to the point of securing the blessing of that which it then eradicates. The seductive alternative to the Jewish patrimony, which Jack's mother Sarah "understands," consists of a series of "marys," including Mary Dale, whom Jack Robins hopes to marry, and the injunction to assimilate through intermarriage which "America" harbors.

The programming of Jews to adopt, take over, or internalize the drive to assimilate is traced by Hannah Arendt back to the new eighteenth-century culture of *Bildung,* which was formulated from the start as a response to the Jewish question. According to Arendt, it became the earliest proof of *Bildung* that the oriental in the midst of educated Europe—the Jew—could be shaped into a paragon of edification. The most famous example of eighteenth-century Golem*Bildung* was Moses Mendelssohn, the "Jewish Socrates." The culture of *Bildung* built the "exception Jew," who would both be and yet not be a Jew; never an "ordinary Jew" since always emancipated through education from Jewish "superstition," "exception Jew" would retain the extraordinary, exciting allure of nevertheless being, after all, a Jew. Thus, Arendt concludes, the former parasite was recast through an impossible demand into the new stereotype: the "virtuoso," actor, or jazz musician.[94]

Inaugurated in the Enlightenment to promote the assimilation of Jews into secular society, the new culture of *Bildung* meets, under National Socialism, with its utter literalization and reversal in the so-called "Enlightenment Project" (*Aufklärungsreferat*). Its aim: the construction in Prague of the largest museum of Jewish history on earth, an archive which would put on display comprehensive documentation of the race Hitler had effaced.[95] In preparing to demonstrate, after annihilation of the Jews, that he had in fact had humanitarian interests in mind all along, Hitler sought to make himself the guardian and curator of the artifacts and remnants of those whose existence he would confine to the past. But does not the museum in fact occupy while refusing to occupy the place of a tomb, an empty tomb without survivors and without mourning? Without commemoration this collection of artifacts would, as mere display, mere image, and mere name, embody, at the other end of Golem making, that eidetic crisis which Judaism has ever sought to push back.

In the first half of the twentieth century two prominent, popular discourses—Freudian psychoanalysis and film—momentarily place a certain Jewish need or desire to assimilate at the very controls of assimilation, including the assimilation of secularized Christians into their own culture. Though film in particular was active in getting Jews out of Hitler's museum of Jewish history, it should be stressed, lest this Jewish indebtedness to film remain a screen memory, that the drive to assimilate has always pushed Jews into the positions which influence assimilation of all persons within a given collective. This drive to assimilate finds its points of derivation alongside Marx, Spinoza, the picaro, and, indeed, Christ, who is thus the model of Jewish assimilation which, springing from a transgression, creates a discourse at once esoteric and popular, which in turn wields great powers over the host culture. Indeed, ever since Christ's break with Jewish tradition, which led not to assimilation into any extant non-Jewish society but instead rerouted the drive to assimilate around new models, the media in the broadest sense have proferred Jews an alternative to the Enlightenment project and projection. In the wake of his defeat, Hitler had planned the construction of *Todesburgen,* "Death Castles," which would have occupied interchangeable places only with one other memorial, Hitler's endless documentation in film of total war and genocide. World War II: a war in film and of film.

CHAPTER NINE
THE UNBORN

In his ultimate reckonings with melancholia, Freud found himself pushed back against the threshold of the womb. Two melancholics, Wolfman and Rank, delivered, on separate occasions, fantasies of traumatic birth and prenatal existence which threatened, in theory, to preempt Freud's Oedipal interpretation of anxiety. The patient and the colleague each in turn introduced into psychoanalysis the unborn child who, because either normal or neurotic on arrival, depending upon the impact of arrival, never runs up against the Oedipus complex. By thus anchoring neurosis in the unborn state, Rank leaves out the father, which was his aim and inspiration, but only by effacing, as in all fantasies of the unborn, the influence of the mother. In the course of demonstrating the mother's exclusive rights to the child—his other aim, according to Jones—Rank removed the mother entirely, a secret assassination attempt which prompted Freud to keep in place—while acknowledging for the first time—the centrality of her role in early childhood.[1]

Taking up Rank's challenge, Freud traced the anxiety that betokens, up front, the double urge to return to the womb and be born again away from the prenatal zone to the maternal province of *fort/da*. Freud detects in the typical anxiety-producing situations, which range from birth, to separation from the mother, to dread of castration, removal in each case of some cherished object which the mother was thus the first to embody. Separation from the mother, which, in the *fort/da* game, finds mournful commemoration through reversal of its administration, not only anticipates castration, which represents it, but also faces the other way to produce the fantastic past of prenatal existence to which the child henceforward seeks and fails to return, either as whole body or as genital part.[2]

Whenever Freud had hitherto touched on the infant's maternal bond, he had contrasted the young child's innate narcissism with the anaclitic outlet onto the other which the mother first proffers. Through anaclisis, sexuality proper emerges only by "leaning on" a relation already established solely for the purpose of satisfying the hunger of the little narcissist, who remains concerned only with his autoerotic self-sufficiency and survival. The other thus first appears when the breast that feeds the infant becomes, through anaclisis, exciting as well. Though at this juncture the infant, who does not yet distinguish between the breast and his own body, retains and secures his narcissism, a separation has emerged between the urge that sucks for pleasure and that which sucks for nourishment.[3]

The infant cannot help but develop along lines of anaclisis to the point of taking the *fort/da* line into his little hands; inversion, however, may at this point turn around the perspective of a scene that otherwise remains the same. In "On Narcissism: An Introduction," Freud contrasts to anaclitic selection the narcissistic choice which also takes the mother-infant relation as model, only to do a double take: the child assumes the mother's position by identifying with her to the point of always choosing images of that part or version of himself his mother adored. What is born again, in any case, is the narcissism of the parents, whose hard-pressed conviction that the ego is immortal, for example, takes refuge in the infant, their prosthetic part and portrait. While the infant approaches or departs anaclitically, the parents adore or grieve over the little placeholder of their own narcissism.[4]

The "caesura" of birth, Freud argues, hardly punctuates the continuum covering pre- and postnatal existence. The maternal body is the fetus's object to the extent that it has no objects within its maternal surround. The mother thus emerges as full-fledged object for the child's psyche because she already embodies the child's fetal, objectless past.[5] Günter Grass has defined melancholia as utopian objectlessness,[6] a conjunction of ahistorical zones which, as transmitted through Grass's *The Tin Drum*, for example, returns to that commencement of a modern history of melancholia which, in the eighteenth century, finds the melancholic and the unborn each the other's analogue and condition. At the other end of this history we find Oskar, the now midget, now dwarf protagonist of *The Tin Drum*, taking pictures: "real sorrow is in itself already objectless. . . . If there was a possibility to flirt with our sorrow then only with respect to the pictures, because in these serially produced snapshots we found ourselves, though admittedly not clearly discernible, nevertheless, and what was more important, passive and neutralized."[7] As in the case of the female paranoid analyzed by Freud, the maternal context of the melancholic and unborn issues in a photographic *Kasten*.[8]

The "caesura" of loss which produces the fantasy of return to womb first emerges within the *fort/da* bond with the mother which, in Freud's own recollection from early childhood, a *Kasten* guaranteed. Before this *Kasten* marks the withdrawal of the mother at the father's behest, it embraces the caesura left behind by a missing brother. The cut of caesura was the initiating trauma boxed in in the Caesar name: Caesarian section, whereby baby is not born but taken from the incised womb of the mother, attended the arrival of some ancestor of the Caesar family, most likely Julius Caesar himself. Fantasies of intrauterine existence, often represented, according to the theory of the uncanny, by dread fear of being buried alive, leave out, together with father and mother, the sibling, who is retained as the twin that lives alongside each fetus until birth separates the dead from the living.

According to Freud, the double doubles, upon arrival, as rival. This view is summed up in close up in a dream Freud cites in *The Interpretation of Dreams*: the competitive wish that one's brother restrain himself (*sich einschränken*) places this brother, in his rival's dream, now into a *Kasten*, now into a closet or *Schrank*.[9] This ghost or skeleton in the closet haunts in turn Freud's theories of homosexuality, which see incorporation of the dead mother or of the mother's always narcissistic and, hence, unacknowledgeable grieving for a lost child as installing in the survivor inversion as the reanimation of the other's desire.

Thus, to follow Freud by coming full circle, the mother's crucial importance for the infant is, once Freud comes around to affirming it as such, twofold: she not only feeds the infant her breast and milk but also trains, cares for, and, in effect, seduces his little body.[10] Sibling rivalry transpires over the mother who is left behind to bury, secretly, the dead double. The *Kasten* is in place in a young child only to the extent that, at some level, the mother alone knows its secret location. The child that must carry the *Kasten* only follows its closeted commands.

In the case of Wolfman, the conjunction of born-again and back-to-the-womb fantasies corresponds, according to Freud, to his patient's fully orchestrated bisexual disposition: to return to the womb is to await penetration by the father, while rebirth issues in incest with the mother. The underlying fantastic structure, which Freud thus points out only to swerve from it by concluding with the father, leaves Wolfman his own double perpetually pregnant with himself.

The step aside that seeks refuge from the dread fantasy of return to the womb and return of the double is always taken toward the father. Thus Abraham's elaborate Oedipal reading of street anxiety—where the street represents the mother or, when the child is taken on walks by the governess, exile from the mother or, when the father is away from home, the place where a son's death wishes strike the father down[11]—had commenced, four years earlier in his correspondence with Freud, inside the pre-Oedipal zone.

In a letter dated May 16, 1909, Abraham writes to Freud, on Freud's birthday, about his own interest in that shrinking feeling encountered in states of street anxiety, which is reflected in the enormity of everyone else, and which represents, ultimately, the fervent wish to be an embryo. In response to Abraham's conclusion that this wish is but an effect of fixation on mother or father, Freud replies on May 23: "I am familiar with the indubitably significant derivation of street anxiety from infantile impressions of space. Nowhere will you be more likely to miss the father-mother-fixation. Anxiety regarding space seems to refer specifically to extinct fantasies of ambition." Abraham would chart omnipotence of thought back to the omnipotence the infant ascribes to its excremental functions and products.[12] Like Freud, Ferenczi pushed the pedigree of overweening ambition and pride back even further, though still within the context of the double, when he ascribed omnipotence of thoughts to the impression the fetus gets from its existence; the craving for instant wish fulfillment always hearkens back to, while hankering after, the fetal state.[13]

In accordance with Freud's speculations on homosexuality in terms of mourning and not mourning, Wolfman's simultaneous broadcast of bisexuality suggests the internal cohabitation of and demarcation between Wolfman and some encrypted other. Wolfman, like the werewolf Freud's name for him translates as, is the victim of a sin of incest he commemorates not by becoming on occasion an animal but by wearing reversible skin, at once his own and an other's. When in human form the werewolf bears its hirsute cover on the other side; when it shows its fur the werewolf must feed on children.

Lycanthropy has always designated another cannibalistic variant of melancholia. Though Jones claims that hatred of the father informs every case of lycanthropy he has ever encountered, in the case of Wolfman, the breakdown of mourning his name already conjures is detonated by a sister's suicide. As Jones notes, the dreamlike capacity of the werewolf to be double turns around the only known cure: call the werewolf by his Christian name, and tell him that he is a werewolf.[14] But to bust the ghost one must know both his names.

Freud postulates for Wolfman's womb and rebirth fantasies the common ground of a primal scene which cannot be seen but only bypassed by the urge to see oneself being engendered and born. The other nonfantasy, Freud emphasizes, is Wolfman's recollection from early childhood of his seduction by his sister. And yet Freud lines brother and sister up in such a way that they must race to secure sole access to their father's affection, this finish line being the basis of their sibling bond. The detour Wolfman must take to let out his grief over his sister's departure borrows from the *Trauerarbeit* conducted by the father, who had compared his cherished daughter to the poet at whose grave Wolfman finds himself

337

weeping. The father thus supports, slaves for the cargo-cult relationship between Wolfman and his phantom sister, who oversees the father's work, and contains his superegoical broadcasts.

Rank returns Freud to the womb to reconsider anxiety or loss in terms of a trajectory of the *Kasten* which castration, like birth trauma, only commemorates. Rank, who was completely dependent on Freud for his livelihood, was alone privy to the full diagnosis of Freud's wounded jaw at the time this verdict of cancer was first reached. The insertion into Freud of the prosthetic device thus drives Rank doubly insane: his manic phase delivered the born-again revisions of psychoanalysis, his melancholia for exhausted confession and restitution to Freud. The cyclical, migratory pattern of Rank's cannibalistic commemoration of Freud's corpus begins, then, with and as the first broadcast of the *Kasten* in Freud's mouth. The first rehearsal of Rank's mania and melancholia, however, had transpired as a frenzy of sibling rivalry against Jones and Abraham, a desperate drama which, the brothers feared and predicted, would ultimately reach its proper target, the father Freud.[15]

The father, according to psychoanalysis, subsumes many roles. His death is the model for every other death: every dead person is represented by the father's corpse. To this extent the father covers both the mother and the little sibling rivals. Once the rival—who is ultimately, according to psychoanalysis, also the father—is eaten, his person becomes, as Róheim argues, maternalized.[16] Because cannibalistic identification always maternalizes the corpse in question, the father, when he offers himself up to be devoured, diverts incorporation from the mother to his own corpus. The superego thus emerges both through incorporation or sublimation of the wrong object and in order to put a stop to incorporation, for example of the mother. The father pretends to be the mother or even the monster, just as the vampire in turn pretends to be a father with legitimate rights to transference and proper burial. Only when Count Dracula, who otherwise resembles the primal father to the extent that the league of vampire killers resembles the primal band of rival sons and brothers, is caught breast-feeding one of his victims can his motherhood no longer be covered by paternity.

The father exercises undead or unborn control over those

drawn to devour him also by assuming, like the phantoms of the modern media, vast or tiny proportions. The little men who populate Schreber's delusional revision of the technical media, like the hieroglyphic determinatives Freud cites in his review of primal words, share with the primal father what is in their case also a reference to size. Freud refers to the primal father always as *Männchen*, a generic designation reserved for classification of the nonhuman and prehistoric male. But who can help but overhear in *Männchen* the first father's uncalled for tininess? According to a logic as primal as the first father, the very small always also represents immense magnitude. This is particularly apparent in the melancholic who is afflicted by shrinkage of his wounded ego only to the extent that in the manic variation on the same narcissistic disorder he, like the humorist, pushes back anything that might miniaturize or even put into perspective his all-encompassing ego.[17]

The primal father was the overman, Freud concludes,[18] thereby sending Nietzsche back home from the institutions he critiqued along the very route of that critique. The educational institution, for example, allows the father to pretend to be the mother, death to be life, the Oedipal edible. Every father is primal, according to both Nietzsche and Freud: the father covers the past by becoming, in the guise of mother or sibling, the child's premier repast. The telepathic lines to her unmourned dead which the mother lays down in the living child are accordingly incessantly undergoing Oedipal scrambling and tampering. Freud speculates that Nietzsche's thought amounts to yearning for his own dead father inside one context where Schreber's dead brother cannot go unacknowledged, and adjacent to another in which Nietzsche's brother must go, in place of Nietzsche, to join the father's phantom.[19]

Nietzsche, as Derrida has shown, amplified and overturned the inherited, testamentary relation to the father, whose broadcast is always posthumous—over-and-out and yet ongoing—by going into the ear and its relation to the proper name.[20] Among the anaclitic expansions that demonstrate, in the mother's absence, the infant's maternal bond, Freud cites not only sucking movements of the mouth but also the infant's tugging at its earlobes, a signal which rises above the ambiguity of sucking to commemorate the mother solely as seducer and not also as food source.[21] The maternal bond first emerges at the ear but does not stop at the lobe; it penetrates to and rebounds off the eardrum. Between these limits of reverberation there emerges a space of incorporation. The oral/aural *Kasten* is the premier source and receptacle of phantom doubling. Only the voice attains and transmits, through the recording media as through their superegoical and occult analogues, its absolute double. Every name reserves, alongside its paternal connection, the full range of incorporation: it too bears an ear, the vibratory space of the name's stammering profusion and preservation.

THE TIN EAR

The Tin Drum borders on the picaresque while taking aim at the *Bildungsroman*, the novel of development.[22] The ironic distance *The Tin Drum* thus covers can be measured in terms of its different take on America; whereas Wilhelm Meister's *Bildung* can be vouchsafed and reflected back only through assimilation within the American collective, Oskar reveres America as that forever far-off place where presumed dead grandfathers are preserved (29). Oskar's phantasmic safety zone lies beyond assimilation as its beyond. In turn, the picaro always remains displaced with respect to that development to the point of assimilation which the photogenic hero of *Bildung* achieves.

The earliest picaresque novels were written by *conversos*, Spanish Jews who, upon securing assimilation through religious conversion, found that they had attained equal status only to the extent that they, as "new Christians," remained segregated from "old Christians" whose putative "purity of blood" was thus conserved inside the circulatory system of money which, however, had to be kept from seeping into Christian blood lines.[23] The unprofitable conversion rate from culture to culture thus became the premier picaresque theme injected into a popular medium. But the picaresque novel advanced toward the media controls of the drive to assimilate only by leaving the *conversos* behind. The *converso* writer Aleman was finally allowed to leave Spain for Mexico in exchange for the rights to part two of his popular novel *Guzmán*. The picaresque novel left itself behind by succumbing to the logic of identification it sought to exorcise. The urge to become like someone else always summons a blood bond of identification— with a corpse. Hence doubling and repression followed the *converso* picaresque novel as its follow up. In Queredo's *El Buscón* the picaresque is mimicked to the point of its reversal: the inherently corrupt picaro cannot advance beyond the impurity of his blood by reaching America, where he encounters only greater hardships.

Already in the premier picaresque novel, *Lazarillo de Tormes*, the eponymous picaro is linked by name to two New Testament accounts in which dead persons return from the grave. Essentially the chronicle of Lazaro's ongoing struggle to gain illicit access to the food his masters would keep from him by storing it in locked containers, *Lazarillo de Tormes* juxtaposes this quest for nourishment with the powers of the dead. Having been sent by his master to buy them a meal, Lazaro overhears a dead man's widow lamenting that her husband is being taken to the sad and gloomy place where no one ever eats and drinks. Sad and gloomy is precisely how Lazaro had already characterized his master's home because it was bare of all provisions; he had also observed that his master had less desire to eat than a dead man. Upon overhearing the widow's words, Lazaro immediately rushes back to the house and bolts the door lest the mourners enter with the corpse. According to the etymological transmission which associates picaro with "gnawing around on food" and the German word for picaro, *Schelm,* with "corpse," a picaro's ever empty, yet ever gnawing mouth, like the ever-hungry, ever-widening mouth of the vampire, opens onto that indigestion which the juxtaposition of burial and nourishment can, if unaccompanied by the ingredient of proper mourning, leave behind.

Nietzsche is something of a picaro—according to certain modernist recyclings of the picaresque in terms of refusal to become assimilated within a collective of mourners. As he declared in *Ecce Homo*, Nietzsche divested himself of his biological heritage by identifying with his parents to the point of becoming what he had cannibalized; by surviving himself, he disgorged both his dead father, for example, and that part of himself which would have been afflicted or contaminated by this loss.

The view of history as Eternal Return of the Same can still be acknowledged as the premier Nietzschean element in *The Tin Drum* and *Doctor Faustus*. In sync with this Nietzschean review of history, modes of citationality first established for the technical media provide the background music. The reader must listen to tribal background rhythms as he awaits the connection to Nietzsche rung up by Mann or Grass. Among the hit tunes drummed out in the background can be overheard eternally the same opinions about Nietzsche as promulgator of some literal will to power, or as celebrator of the essential relation of deformity and illness to all creative efforts associated with genius. What emerges out of this background beat is the allegedly ironic connection, established, for example, in *Doctor Faustus,* between the suffering creation of the Nietzsche figure and the emergence of National Socialism. But these connections were already installed by Hitler, who conceived of himself as being in the first place an artist, though, before he was the *Führer,* he had in fact been known in Germany, since 1922, as "the drummer."

Nietzsche harnassed the drum power of the tiny ears he was so proud to possess. He first put his ears on when near-blindness endowed him with the maternal instinct of philosophy, which he henceforward applied by sounding out hollowness with his little hammer. According to Nietzsche, both ear and womb, those labyrinths of becoming, are the premier organs of Eternal Return.[24] And indeed, Nietzsche fancied himself pregnant when philosophizing with his miniature ears: he was pregnant with the doctrine of Eternal Return when he drummed it out. This aural medium of return embraces, in turn, fingers, umbilical cord, and the pregnant womb—the body rendered a drum.

When projected onto the screen, some enigmatic force of nomination earned *The Tin Drum* an Oscar, at once the first or primal prize to be presented in the place of a technical medium and the perfectly proportioned miniaturization of a man. The name which thus rebounds at the other—projective—end of its tiny embodiment already embraces, etymologically, spirit or demon at its opening, and closes with the ancient word for spear. The demon that has piercing powers also emerges from its homonym, the os or mouth. In consonance with the interrelation of miniaturization and magnification, the perpetual three-year-old Oskar is the veritable embodiment of amplified sensory abilities: his scream can shatter glass, while his nose responds to the slightest scent. Owing to the near invisibility his diminutive size affords him, scarcely anything falls outside his surveillance, and his sense of touch is so keenly developed that his drum sticks are veritable extensions of his tactile sense—indeed, they surpass his fingers in sensitivity. And yet, most conspicuously, Oskar the drummer is an ambulatory ear; his sense of hearing is, already at birth, so acute that, Oskar concludes, he is one of those infants born fully conscious (35). The ear is the only organ that from birth on cannot develop; its hammer, anvil, and stirrup are, right from the start, already in place, tiny and perfect.

Shortly after birth Oskar overhears his mother's promise, which he immediately accepts, to present him with a tin drum on his third birthday. The father's plan that the son take over the family store is also overheard but circumvented in the proposed return, vouchsafed by the bestowal of the drum, to the protection of the womb. Remarking that his umbilical cord had been his first drum stick (145), Oskar acknowledges the womb as drum, or his drum as womb, inside which the unborn registers those higher pitched sounds of the mother's voice as a muffled drumming.

Oskar's birth instills in him not only the desire to cease growing at age three but also an affinity at once to drumming and to the fragility of glass. This double rapport is emblematized when, at Oskar's birth, a moth beats against a light bulb. The moth's unyielding attempt to penetrate to the light—which would, of course, be its undoing—is frustrated by the vitrious membrane: the moth's perpetually failed attempts, its drumming, can be seen as striving after that which it must defer if drumming is to continue, however briefly. As with the moth's and Oskar's own perpetual drumming, in the ear the beating of the hammer against the drum must ceaselessly proceed lest the eardrum itself be impaired; it is, after all, by rendering sonic vibrations in gradual succession that any overwhelming concussive effect is circumvented, and the labyrinthine inner ear protected. In Oskar's case, his piercing sheer voice applies long-range that penetration of the membrane his drumming defends against up close. Oskar witnesses the moth's drumming against a light bulb at the same time that he is penetrating to the light outside the womb, and, from this point onward, drumming offers Oskar a way of deferring ultimate penetration or birth.

Oskar and his mother attend a dramatization of the Tom Thumb story in which the miniature being can be represented on stage only by the broadcast of its voice (87). For the remainder of the Christmas holidays, Oskar's mother calls her diminutive son "now jocularly, now mournfully: Tom Thumb. Or: My little Tom Thumb" (88). Tom Thumb fits both in hand and ear where the sensuous appeal of diminutive beings and things have ever found their measure and sheltering receptacle. According to the fairy tale of Tom Thumb, the miniature size of this child is the literalization of its mother's wish that she conceive a child, even if that child be but thumb size. And Tom Thumb's mother in no wise receives this literalization, her miniature son, as a punishment contrary to her desires.

The miniaturization Tom Thumb embodies thus only intensifies what already inheres in the concept of childhood. According to Susan Stewart, childhood is an intense and tiny condensation of the life history it opens: Limited in physical scope, childhood is also always fantastic in content. The celebration of childhood as the miniaturization of adulthood—informing the fashion doll, the doll house, and Tom Thumb weddings—has ever been an adult amusement or had at least originated as one. The origin of the doll house, Stewart points out, lies in the crèche.[25] Thus, on Christmas, Wilhelm Meister receives from his mother in the form of its miniaturization what will become his overriding fascination with the theater. The gift of a puppet theater thus installs in him his own childhood as the reduced scale model of the full range of his—or his mother's—desires.[26]

Christianity leaves out childhood to the point of introducing the apotheosis of the child. Christ, the issue of intercourse through the ear, was even as infant the Incarnation in every sense. Christ was at the same time Mary's Heavenly Bridegroom, the infant spouse, who, having chosen her for his mother, was choosing her for his eternal consort in heaven. Indeed they were already wed when the word was made flesh in Mary's virgin womb.[27] To the extent that womb and bridal chamber remain thus interchangeable, Christ in a sense never left the womb, and as one of the

344

unborn always enjoyed a heavenly rather than any ontological status. Christianity has always spoken in the name of the unborn; Christ himself is the perpetually unborn.

Oskar accordingly recognizes in a statue of the baby Jesus—whose hands are raised as though holding invisible drum sticks—his rival double. But when he places his drum around the baby's neck and the sticks in his hands, Oskar witnesses not the drumming he demands but another miracle instead: enraged by the figure's refusal to react and perform, Oskar aims his voice at one of the cathedral windows only to experience for the first time the failure of his voice to shatter glass. Miraculously, then, the Christ child's membranous enclosure—the glass which Oskar ever associates with virginity (107)—resists every attempt to penetrate it.

According to the terms of his contract with his mother, Oskar must become an artist, a genius, a savior: the apotheosis of the son. To this end the only son must be the end of his line. In exchange for his mother's efforts in obscuring his indebtedness to one father, which she has replaced with what is referred to as the trinity, her marriage conjugated with her adulterous attachment to her cousin Jan, Oskar must make sure that any product of his sexual encounters would in turn, as was the case with his own engendering, have at least two fathers. The uncertainty of his paternity grants Oskar's mother a kind of chastity—no one had ever entirely possessed her, Oskar reflects (140)—and himself an immaculate conception.

The drum, which serves as constant reminder to his mother of their contract, accordingly already resembles her coffin once she discovers that she carries a second son. The drum, which, unlike a mother, Oskar reasons, can be replaced over and again (141), holds the place of the mother just as it ultimately holds her in place. Oskar contemplates following his dead mother under the sod to render her coffin his supreme drum. For this coffin-drum is the most perfectly proportioned reduction Oskar has ever witnessed:

> The coffin . . . got narrower (*verjüngte sich*) in a wonderfully harmonious fashion as it tapered to the foot end. Is there in this world a form which corresponds to the proportions of man in a similarly successful fashion? . . . Oskar wanted to climb up onto the coffin. He wanted to sit up on it and drum. Oskar didn't want to beat his drum sticks on the tin, but rather on the

cover of the coffin. . . . . Oskar wanted to go into the pit with his mother and the embryo . . . he wanted to sit on the narrowed (*verjüngten*) foot end, to drum—if possible, to drum under the ground. (133–34)

This drum roll accompanies Oskar's every retreat and return—his picaresque nondevelopment. Oskar's *Bildung* accordingly consists exclusively of two texts, a biography of Rasputin and Goethe's *Elective Affinities*. *Elective Affinities* is notably not a *Bildungsroman*, combining as it does a chemical notion of nondevelopment with the notion of fixed contractual relations, thereby creating the sort of laboratory setting which might allow for the creation of a Homunculus or an Oskar. Although Rasputin and Goethe are received by Oskar as his own contradictory principles, as Dionysus and Apollo, for example (266), by the end of the novel the "black cook" (*Schwarze Köchin*), that phantom incarnation of melancholia which haunts Oskar, is none other than Goethe himself (487), that "Goethe," in other words, who is interchangeable with Rasputin. What Rasputin shares with Goethe as well as with the picaro is a certain refusal to die. Rasputin survives multiple murderous attacks only to die suddenly of a side effect of these murder attempts—exhaustion. Similarly, the picaro incidentally ends or interrupts the chronicle of his multiple batterings and rebounds as though out of exhaustion and not because he has come to any conclusion. Like some cartoon character which, though unceasingly battered, remains unscathed, the picaro survives to the point of exhaustion, not of death. Oskar shares with the picaro his unborn insularity, his indestructible nondevelopment.[28]

Oskar identifies with that originary media-*converso*—Christ— also to the extent that he must, in order to survive his position of outcast, set himself up as model from which an audience can be cast.[29] As soloist drummer in postwar West Germany Oskar is ultimately acclaimed as "Messiah" (464). Yet Oskar abandons his stardom and returns, retreats to the realm of the secret and imperceptibly small. Together with a close friend who is also, Oskar emphasizes, the end of his line, Oskar, in his thirtieth year, stages, with respect to a murder of which he is innocent, his own flight and arrest. During his flight the past he writes down and drums out in his arrested state had taken on the single menacing shape of the black cook, a specter which in retrospect pervades his entire life. Before thus assuming the attributes of all the negativity of Oskar's existence, the black cook had manifested itself as a "chewing triangle" (316), the shape a girl's chewing mouth assumed as she placidly stood witness while the boys she had denounced to the authorities were sentenced to death. The most horrible image he had yet beheld—veritable vagina dentata—now, at the end of *The Tin Drum*, faces Oskar, comes toward him, and awaits Oskar's penetration or release. Oskar must beat back with his drum this incarnation of birth and development. As Zarathustra advises, it is difficult and terrible to be an *Erbe*, at once orphan and heir. Even to be born, according to Oskar, is the most horrible inheritance.

Shortly after his mother's death, Oskar, together with Jan—his uncle or possible father—enters the Polish post office, hoping to replace his damaged drum or have it repaired. On the day of the Nazi invasion of Poland, the red and white drum thus pulls Oskar into territory with which his maternal line had ever sided. Oskar links the destiny of his drum to the supernatural place of address where Jan had already sought to realize, by transferring his childhood delight in stamp collecting to his employment as postal official, his far-reaching affection for the miniature. As the fatherland continues to penetrate this realm of postness and tininess, Oskar and Jan retreat and return to a windowless mail sorting room where Oskar "buries" his drum beneath the piled-up post. In this place of commemoration Jan converses with Oskar's dead mother while constructing fragile monuments out of the miniatures he has rescued: his playing cards and family photographs.

The windowless mail sorting room returns as part of that attraction to nurses which compels Oskar absolutely, beginning with his hospitalization immediately following the fall of the Polish post office. Later in West Germany the nurse he becomes most obsessed with, and whose severed ring finger will eventually come into his possession fortuitously, lives, as he had anticipated, in a windowless room (406). The recurrent figure in German films, projected within windowless rooms, is, according to Oskar, the nurse (401). The nurse thus appears once again alongside the fall of the Polish post office, the event that opened World War II also to the extent that it was instantly transformed into a film, a newsreel shown in all the movie houses of Germany (199–200). Oskar's mother was a nurse when she inaugurated the trinity that would engender Oskar. In his thirtieth year, which, according to the logic of return to womb, is also the year of his third birthday, Oskar receives the nurse's wedding ring finger of recurrence.

At once the center of circulation of Polish post and the dwelling of the nurse whose ring finger will be Oskar's most cherished possession, the windowless room, before hearkening back to his mother's womb, must first be superimposed onto that inner chamber of movie houses which is also always a camera. When leaving behind Poland on his way to West Germany, Oskar secures and takes with him the family photo album. His fascination with photography thus begins with the emergence of his chthonic dwarfishness. Photographs, which Oskar sees as comprising a "family grave" (37), recall the post to the extent that Oskar's own premier photograph, his baby picture, was a post card (45).

Though Oskar would appear to traverse a whole series of phallic members, from the umbilical cord, to the drum sticks, to his own "third drum stick" (229), the culmination of this series is not, however, Oskar's sexual member, which, following the death of his other presumed father, Matzerath, grows to full size at the same time that his back hunches up. Rather, it is the severed ring finger he later discovers and conserves in a glass jar. Every recurrence of drum stick or umbilical cord in his life has guaranteed, Oskar exults, that this ring finger, this wedding ring of recurrence, would be his own (475). Even as he writes down and drums out his memoirs, Oskar worships and consults this ring finger.

Oskar's perusal of photographs is marked in turn by his attention to fingers, finger tips, finger nails, and index fingers (44). As Roland Barthes has shown, the photographer's primary sense organ is not his eye by rather his clicking finger, just as the model of photographic signification is the pointing finger.[30] By virtue of its being a vestige, an impression—as is, for example, a footprint in the sand—the photograph is therefore not an iconic representation, as is a painted portrait, but rather, as Peirce already established, an index, a pointing sign.[31] Fingerprints and anthropometric photographs thus manifest the indexical origin of photography.

As demonstrated by braille, one can see—that is, read—with fingers alone; photography, unlike painting, is dominated by the finger's capacity to point, trace, and read. According to Barthes, the photograph is in this sense invisible: though the photograph amounts to pointing one's finger at something and saying "There it is," what one sees, in place of the photograph itself, is the presence of that thing's absence. Barthes can thus conclude that every photograph marks the return of the dead to the extent that, even while still alive, every person photographed instantly becomes a specter. *The Tin Drum* in turn describes the reading of photographs as the ultimately cinematic attempt to bring the dead back to life by reanimating image or corpse. The photographer's ultimate aim, then, is to create not new life but still life—still alive—by recomposing and reanimating decomposition. At one end "Oskar's love for the labyrinthine" is "nourished" by his family photographs (38); at the other end this allegiance to flight, retreat, and return must find protection and projection within the windowless room of the post. In this place of burial and nursing back to health, the maternal specter must mourn in place of the son, who never mourns.

PFORTA-GRAPHY

Nietzsche, under the name Nietzsky, guarantees that, through his continued existence, Poland, already lost, is not yet lost.[32] Oskar comes to this conclusion when, by drumming out O sound-shapes, he conjures the spectral return of the Polish cavalry to rescue a hard-pressed survivor of the Nazi invasion of the Polish post office (481). The O sound-shapes, which, like "Nietzky," pronounce Poland both not yet lost and always already lost, orchestrate the temporal paradox Barthes ascribes to the photograph:

> I collected in a last thought the images which had "pricked" me. . . . In each of them, inescapably, I passed beyond the unreality of the thing represented, I entered crazily into the spectacle, into the image, taking into my arms what is dead, what is going to die, as Nietzsche did when, as Podach tells us, on January 3, 1889, he threw himself in tears on the neck of a beaten horse: gone mad for Pity's sake.[33]

Yet this embrace in turn marks a return in Nietzsche's autobiography. Six years before his collapse, Nietzsche had formed, together with Paul Rée and Lou Salomé, the group dubbed the

"Trinity" mutually to promote and superintend their intellectual development, though principally, as far as Nietzsche was concerned, to insure the transmission of his doctrine of the Eternal Return of the Same. On one notable occasion this threesome was photographed. In this photograph of the Trinity group we find, consonant with Nietzsche's wishes, Rée and Nietzsche harnessed to the cart in which Lou stands brandishing a whip. In this portrait of Nietzsche as a horse, doubled by Nietzsche's embrace of the horse once again being whipped, we join Barthes in witnessing what has been and what will be.

Riding springs from the blood drops that fall from Medusa's severed head. The same blood with which Poseidon creates Pegasus, that first horse to bear a rider, seeps, as Bernard Pautrat has shown, into Nietzsche's reflections on Eternal Return.[34] Ever since Pegasus vied with Hermes, riding has stamped the post with a return address: "post horse of the side roads" was the original meaning of *Pferd*. And yet the sacrifice of the horse always commemorated a race to the end—to the other end—of scheduled indebtedness or saving. Sailors sacrificed a constructed horse, which they set aflame and cast into the sea, to mark the receipt of advance payment and the end of a period of unremunerated labor. The ancient Roman sacrifice of the October horse celebrated, at the close of a race run on the field of Mars, the very death of death. To Wolfman and little Hans, the horse accordingly conveys identification with the father; they take dread delight in torturing horses only to the extent that they swoon when they witness a horse being beaten. One of Abraham's melancholic patients thus includes himself, in dreams of the horse-drawn haul, as the casualty, strapped beneath the cart, of his parents' coitus.[35] But Nietzsche becomes a horse, the October horse, by always delivering yet another anniversary of the return of the same in October, the month of his birth.

As with Nietzsche, Oskar's various literalizations and identifications leave no gap or overlap between a manifest story and its latent content which would allow psychoanalytic hermeneutics to peel one off the other. There are no zones of imbrication in *Ecce Homo:* Nietzsche is his living mother and his dead father. In turn, the drummer Oskar is—inside his mother's womb which he also carries—indefinitely pregnant with himself.[36] Oskar must repeat himself eternally as the same, as a stillborn beginning which does not develop but is its own end. *Wieder* means both "again" and, at the primal level, "against" (*wider*). Repetition of the same follows out the logic of identification to the point of acquiring, beyond identification, release from the father's death. As Rodolphe Gasché shows, *Wiederholung,* in Nietzsche's case, issues in *Erholung,* that restorative recovery which always alternates with yet another disabling fall from the horse. Repetition of the same thus affords recovery from the Oedipalized past which the same *Wiederholung* literally hauls: Nietzsche's Trinity photograph reaches back to Rossleben—literally the "stallion life"—the site of his father's theological seminar and, hence, of a certain insemination of Nietzsche by Death.

The emergence of motion picture technology out of photography was propelled by horse power. Having been commissioned to ascertain whether, when running at full speed, all four of a horse's feet were ever simultaneously off the ground, Muybridge, in the course of proving the correctness of this claim, took a series of consecutive photographs of the horse in motion. Nietzsche and Oskar take off in Pegasean flight by photographing and literalizing, in rapid succession, the component parts of the Oedipalized past. According to Karl Abraham, the Oedipal zone accordingly guards against the Medusean gaze of photographic recall. Certain patients otherwise compelled to recall every sight as photographic souvenir, can never summon up the faces of their absent parents.

Photographic recall is always scopophilic to the extent that it emerges only by keeping in some other place the physiognomy of one's faceless parents. The repression of scopophilia, which photographic recollection represents, can lead, as in the case of one of Abraham's obsessional patients, to incessant brooding over the appearance of that which must remain invisible, including, Abraham notes, consciousness and the unconscious or the patient's own neurosis. "He wanted to see everything including, for example, his own birth. He envied Pythagoras, who had thrice experienced his own birth."[37] Abraham links this displacement of the urge to see back to incestuous fixations reflected, in turn, in the Biblical interdiction against representing God. The vaster picture of the parents and their divine counterparts is circumvented and exceeded by the tininess that must be assumed in order to see one's own birth or the unconscious.

Freud populates the nonrepresentability of the distinction he must nevertheless draw between consciousness and the unconscious with little beings. Enter what Freud calls the id, "in Anlehnung an den Sprachgebrauch bei Nietzsche."[38] Freud introduces the id by borrowing from Nietzsche, to whom he thus enters into anaclitic relation. Through anaclisis, which the introduction of the id represents, sexuality grafts the little narcissist, now doubly insatiable, onto the other.

The ego is a test-tube creature, the effect of defense strategies the id, which is unreasonably affirmative to the point of self-destruction, requires. Like all artificial beings the ego yearns for life and libido; it therefore identifies with the objects it must simulate in order to attract the libidinal attachments of the id.

The id makes all libidinal investments, which the ego "registers" or drums out;[39] indeed, the ego is stretched between reality and psychic apparatus like a protective "membrane." The ego must beat this drum to protect the id: it controls access to motility by inserting between need and action the delay of thought.[40] But the ego controls the id the way that, according to Freud's analogy, a rider controls his horse, which not only supplies the energy for the riding couple but often gives the direction which the rider can only pretend to destine. The ego is—always in relation to the id—a little man on horseback who, "like the little brain man of the anatomists," wears his acoustic cap at an angle.[41] The ego introduces delay into the equine energy he cannot control but only protect.[42] The ego spreads and embodies the membrane it also beats. But this ego drum also beats out the funereal music of identification.

According to Freud, every infant is an Oskar to the extent that both ride and drum out the anaclitic relations binding ego and id in isolation from the superego. Like the overman, according to Freud, the infant is "absolutely narcissistic" and "amoral."[43] The little narcissist and cannibal only identifies with objects. The infant lacks a superego to the extent that its sensorium is utterly open— and impervious—to every parental broadcast. The young child knows only death wishes and ghosts; the superego emerges out of a mournful repast taken in lieu of an Oedipal choice that was interdicted. The process of identification which nourishes baby also builds the superego, but on different sides of the Oedipal schedule. The superego belongs to the mourning after an Oedipal phase which the perpetual infant, who eats the objects it need not choose, never reaches. Everyone remains in part this perpetual infant or unborn, as witnessed, says Freud, by the ritual requirements which attend sleeping and dreaming.[44] According to these back-to-the-womb rituals, dreaming holds interchangeable places with the mass media sensurround to the extent that, as Freud stresses, every prosthesis must be dropped before the fetal position can be assumed and oneiric projections viewed.

In *The Interpretation of Dreams* Freud already provided the missing link that always brings reflections on return to the womb full circle: "we should picture the instrument which carries out our mental functions as resembling a compound microscope or a photographic apparatus, or something of the kind. On that basis, psychical locality will correspond to a point inside the apparatus at which one of the preliminary stages of an image comes into being."[45] The cremation fire in the photo-magnifier has already been overheard. Photographic or microscopic detail always exchanges its tiny indiscernibility—like Oskar wielding his glass-shattering voice in place of his Tom-thumb invisibility—for blown-up proportions.[46] Photography thus includes, alongside the melancholy shrinkage it also always applies, that moment of libidinal exhiliration which, as Abraham stressed in finding the regular counterpart to mania, interrupts and overwhelms the mourner.[47] But the blowup and cremation on the other side of photographic miniaturization remain another side of photography's double achievement: secret mummification inside a camera—a room or tomb—which expands and empties out to admit phantoms. The photographic *Kasten* thus conceives the return to the womb out of the uncanny meaning—the negative—of this return: live burial.

REWIND

Hand and fingers enclose, as Abraham clarifies, an erogenous zone which translates into digits, the primal currency of the unconscious.[48] The unconscious, Jones confirms, is the supreme reckoner.[49] Taken out of circulation, numbers congeal into omens which, like Freud's 1900 telephone number, can portend the year of one's own death. And yet the telepathic ring of Freud's telephone number, for example, need never ring true since it already finds conviction and resonance, according to Freud's interpretation of the occult, in the unconscious. Thus Freud did not have to agree with Ferenczi's conclusion that the horse "clever Hans," which could add, subtract, and draw circles, demonstrated special telepathic prowess; above and beyond any occult perspective, the psychoanalytic understanding of the unconscious already explained the extrasensory intelligence of animals.[50]

Though Freud otherwise presses into service references to archaeological excavation of sites of burial and mummification when it comes time to evoke the psychoanalytic exploration of unconscious precincts, in "A Note on the Unconscious in Psychoanalysis" Freud explores this underworld of the unconscious to the point of unsettling certain occult implications also harbored by the technical media. In this note Freud finds analogies for the unconscious first in one kind of medium, then in another. One proof that the unconscious exists is posthypnotic suggestion, whereby a command received while under hypnosis can be carried out even after the medium has returned to a fully conscious state. The unconscious would be, then, that source of remote control that slips away from consciousness even as its effects assert themselves. Slipping from the hypnotic to the technical medium, Freud sees photography as holding the place of the relation between unconscious and conscious thought: since every photograph must, in order to become developed, pass through the negative state, and since only certain negatives are selected for positive development, the photograph can, Freud concludes, represent the relation of conscious thought to the unconscious.[51]

As Freud advises in a note to *The Ego and the Id,* there are still a few recalcitrants out there who, though otherwise sympathetic to psychoanalysis, reject the notion of the unconscious. Their argument: the unconscious simply lies at the end of varying degrees in clarity and intensity of conscious thought. The so-called unconscious is, then, a thought which is at present only weakly conscious. That gradations of consciousness should lead to the conclusion that the unconscious as such does not exist reminds Freud of the argument that, since there are various degrees of vitality, there is, therefore, no such thing as death. A consciousness that one does not, however, know—Freud concludes—is hardly an alternative to the concept of the unconscious. For whatever consciousness does not at first notice will, when it receives full attention, withdraw from full recognition while advancing as something alien.[52]

This figure of unconscious thought—knowledge that does not know—is, in one of Freud's absurd dreams in *The Interpretation of Dreams,* the dead father's return ticket. But that the dead father makes a ghost appearance in his son's dream only because he, the father, does not know that he is dead, is anchored by Freud in the wish that went without saying in the dream: what the father does not know is that his son at one point wished him dead.[53] In an adjacent absurd dream a dead father continues to serve as premier target for his son's death wishes which here, in the form of a scar, exhibit a displacing power that the photographic process, by putting itself into reverse, registers and inflicts. The scar that mars the dreamer's injured father, who had in fact died six years earlier, first appears, on the other side of the dream, as the scar cut just the other day into the photograph the dreamer had taken of his young daughter. Superstition, Freud stresses, attended this photographic displacement: some time back, the dreamer's mother had died shortly after the photographic plate harboring her image had been damaged.[54] The fatal shot in telepathic zones thus achieves development only in some other place as the wound every death wish inflicts upon the dead father.

According to the analogy in "A Note on the Unconscious in Psychoanalysis," conscious thought corresponds to the developed photograph only to the extent that both give the complete picture by leaving out of the picture the unconscious, inverting shot to which they owe their conception. In this regard, Barthes argues, photography is *fort/da*, where the *fort*, the death wish, predominates to the extent that it, like the inverting shot of photography can, like a separate, primal ritual, be played on its own, independent of any development into *da*.[55] By thus shifting between two psychoanalytic analogues to the unconscious—between photography and *fort/da*—Barthes yet remains within the single laboratory which produced what are, in effect, doubles coextensive with the unconscious.

Barthes' point becomes deeply psychoanalytic once it has been driven home: *fort/da* was first played where psychoanalysis first encountered it, in the household of a professional photographer, Freud's son-in-law Max Halberstadt. Through *fort/da* the young child develops the negative only to the extent that he repeats and inverts a scenario of deprivation and loss. Death wishes thus cover over separation with the simulation of some terrible control the child exercises over all transit between life and death.

The telepathic power wielded here by the child reflects, as always, only a share in someone else's omnipotence of thoughts, that share a survivor must extend to the dead. The advent of childhood in the eighteenth century covered the holding pattern between infancy and maturity which the new literacy requirements introduced. But the colossal rate of infant and child mortality did not recede with the establishment of childhood. This lag between the advent of childhood and the decrease in mortality rates for the very young produced what it ended up introducing—the unmournable death of the child. Hence the bond between childhood and ancient death cults: the accoutrements of childhood, like those found in temples of the dead, are lightweight, small-scale reproductions of items used in everyday life.

The unmournable death of the child emerges alongside the recasting of the image of death: the skeleton residing—even in Arcadia—in the midst of the polis came to be replaced in the eighteenth century by the beautiful twin of sleep; in turn, the place of the dead remainder was henceforward kept segregated from the realm of the living. And yet the relocation of the dead to the newly instituted cemeteries yielded evidence of premature burial which the eighteenth-century preoccupation with vampirism sought to contain. Thus in the trail of death's removal, death reemerged at even closer range. The doubling of death and sleep both pushed death outside the polis and kept it pervasively and invisibly at home, where, as the uncanny, it would henceforth belong. At one end the slide from stillness into death was, as in sleep apnia, the main exit chute of the infant; at the other end of this mirroring of animate and inanimate states, hysterical catalepsy—a form of melancholic identification with the dead—embodied that most uncanny model of rebirth or return to womb: the awakening out of deep sleep to the evidence of one's own premature burial.

To represent the realm of the dead, miniaturization and desubtantialization of appearance always first proceeded along an axis of specular inversion. Cities of the dead were always entered from the west rather than, as with the cities of the living, from the east. To this day, mourning ceremonies continue to dramatize this mirror reversal that links and separates life and death: mourners wear black in place of lighter-colored attire. The dead were always first represented in miniature and identified with by undergoing or marking some reversal: in certain primitive or primal cultures the mark of mourning is carved into the bereaved's left hand or foot.

Photography, an acknowledged late arrival of ancient death-cult practices, doubles—first by reversing from right to left—the original it also shrinks and embalms. The place of the wallet-sized photograph was held, in nineteenth-century Anglo-American culture, by so-called "mourning pictures," which commemorated the deceased on paper or silk also by miniaturizing as "pocket grave" their monumentalization in stone. Once photography achieved currency, even and especially dead babies now found commemoration. In cultures where photography is not customarily used to adorn graves, the grave of an infant can nevertheless mark an exception; in Princeton's central cemetery the only photograph to be found decorates the tomb of Baby Norman. This retreat and return to the realm of the tiny and indiscernible was already in focus as the focus of the child's first emergence in the wake of his disappearance. When, with the advent of the printing press, dead children were for the first time included in the family portraits which decorated the tombs of parents, they were rendered slightly smaller than the children still alive at the time the portrait was executed. The other identifying mark of the dead child: a skull carried in the left hand.

Photography has always conceived a funerary image of childhood the printing press first imprinted. In turn, however, the relation of child to parents—that transportable rapport Freud called transference—could only be conceived by Freud in terms of reprinting. Though the clichés of transference reach back into the printing-press past each time they are, as Freud puts it, "reprinted," they also line up with the meaning of photographic negative the term cliché was subsequently borrowed to cover. While "transcendental photography" offered testimony that the camera could conceive images of the otherwise indiscernible phantoms conjured in séances, Freud responded by linking and limiting the occult effects and analogues of the technical media to the workings of transference. But Freud discovered the mechanism of transference only to the extent that he recognized in his own friendships—for example, with Fliess and then with Jung—the phantom presence of nephew John. Fliess and Jung were thus the reprinted *imagines* or clichés of this early rapport with John; indeed, as Freud puts it in his case, they doubled as *revenants*, as phantoms.

In the dream which announces to Freud that Fliess is but a *revenant* from his own childhood past, Fliess returns to Vienna in the month of July—of Julius, Freud translates.[56] And, Freud recollects, when John returned to Vienna on a visit, they performed an improvisation of the murder of Julius Caesar in which Freud played Brutus. "My heart is in the coffin here with Caesar" Freud cites in a letter to Fliess dated April 27, 1895. Freud thus left out what he would always keep inside. Michelangelo's statue of Moses, on which Freud had written—as though on a monument to his own name—anonymously, was originally commissioned as cornerstone of the tomb of Julius.

In Freud's analysis of a female paranoid, a photographic *Kasten* is the vehicle of a mother's transmission and control. The analogy Freud summons to illustrate the way in which the eidetic memories of a two-year-old, though inaccessible to the child, nevertheless emerge later in life is borrowed from this photographic *Kasten:* "It may, however, be less well known that the strongest compulsive influence arises from impressions which impinge upon a child at a time when we would have to regard his psychical apparatus as not yet completely receptive. The fact itself cannot be doubted; but it is so puzzling that we may make it more comprehensible by comparing it with a photographic exposure which can be developed after any interval of time and transformed into a picture." Repression introduces a delay into this photographic process by leaving behind a "scar of repression" which blocks the path to one satisfaction only to open up another path to what Freud calls a substitutive satisfaction, which comes to light as a symptom.[57] The death wish travels and etches the route of displacement between scar and symptom. The scar scratched into the photograph taken of a daughter ends up on the face of the phantom father. The father in the absurd dreams is a phantom only to the extent that his son's death wishes, which animate him, go unacknowledged.

The death wish is located on one side of the photographic process, displaced with respect to the developed image. But the death wish rebounds off photography's other end, which does not end. As Derrida adds to Barthes' reading of photography as commemoration of that which has been shot: though it would appear to achieve, in the complete picture, a kind of proper burial, the mournful inversion that characterizes the relation of image to referent in photography is nevertheless skewed and exceeded on the other side of the developed negative by the seriality, the out-of-phase self-referentiality which governs interphotographic relations.[58] Work on the photographic copy itself—as in retouching, or when a photograph cites or consists of other photographs—opens onto a serial proliferation, along an axis of inversion, of frames within frames. This seriality of the photograph in isolation from vestigial relations admits the phantoms of photography which thus emerge on the other side of their pocket graves always and already in anticipation of their filmic projection.

Count Dracula enters England at the town of Whitby, where his advance signals were already received in a cemetery crowded with empty tombs commemorating lost seamen. But Dracula's destination is also a caption to popular photographs taken by Frank Meadow Sutcliffe, who portrayed local seamen and fishermen in such a way, his admirers claimed, as to leave them animate in appearance. Only a town consisting of the photographs or empty tombs that have replaced it can anticipate and welcome the arrival of the vampire king.

In *Totem and Taboo* Freud announced that haunting belongs in the movies; it is the projection of hostile feelings harbored even against someone close who goes away. The death of someone close is that close call that always and originally summons the first ghosts just as it creates for the first time the need to mourn. Unlike the slain enemy, who bears the sheer target of exteriority, the dead loved one is also, since other, another inimical alien, but at the same time that part of oneself that must also go. In the savage and childhood context, where there is no conception of natural death

or departure—to go is to be a goner struck down by death wishes—
every dead person ends up, Freud instructs, a vampire. The premier and primal response on the part of the survivor of "the near-
est and dearest" is to project onto the animated image or corpse
death wishes which come into focus up close as vampiric, in the
long shot, at the other end of mourning, as worthy of some ancestral spirit or friendly ghost.

The death wish gives rise to ghosts. As premier application of
what Freud called the omnipotence of thoughts, the death wish
accordingly corresponds to belief in and practice of magic. But
that's not all: the modern technical media, Freud concludes, have
their origin in the omnipotence of thoughts. The death wish thus
inaugurates a primal structure represented and run by death cults,
including, to this day, the modern technical media. The death wish
is effective only by taking total credit for every accident in its range
and only to the extent that it also opens up a joint account with—
and shifts the balance to—the dead.

What Freud discovered in *Totem and Taboo* was also discovered that same year by anthropology, though in some other place
under the name of Cargo Cult. Because he stands at the switches of
telecommunications, the white man is what Freud calls a "prosthesis god"; that is, he is a god, according to the Cargo Cult, to the
extent that he is living dead. Insofar as his sensorium consists only
of devices which the dead build to keep in touch with the living, the
white man controls a phantom zone he also embodies. The first
telecommunications prosthesis which the Cargo Cult put at the
center of their blocked relation to the dead was the flag pole
through which, they believed, the white man received only to keep
to himself messages from the dead who must slave for the white
man's every wish.

According to Freud, every prosthesis represents not so much
an addition as the replacement or castration of that which it extends. But castration and death, according to Freud, cannot be
represented but only embodied—for example, by some dead person. Thus every point of contact between a body and its media
extensions marks the site of some secret burial. The white god of
the Cargo Cult holds the place of unmournable death. The underworld slave labor camp contains the mournable deaths which, from
the cult of Isis to psychoanalysis, have always taken the dead father

as model. In Freud's Ratman case—where Freud first borrows the phrase "omnipotence of thoughts" from Ratman, who coined it to describe the efficacy of his death wishes—the dead father must pay, must slave for Ratman's every wish. Ratman's dead sister is the rat at the controls of his Cargo Cult. In exchange for the total thought control her brother thus grants her, the rat never conveys to him the messages of the mourned dead. The mourned dead know Ratman's thoughts only to the extent that he does not know it; the dead, however, must slave for Ratman's every thought.

Death cults thus operate on two levels which correspond to two irreconcilable zones of theorizing in Freud. In the Oedipal zone, repression—of the death wish—animates the dead, who return as vengeful phantoms but recede, at the end of mourning, as friendly ghosts or fond memories. And yet, what can never be acknowledged is that these mourned dead in fact enter an underworld they never leave. At this level the mourned dead continue to receive and slave for every death wish. In the zone of Narcissus, ancient childhood conceptions of death or the dead, conceptions otherwise believed surmounted, return. These ghosts from childhood, which correspond to the unmournable deaths of children, always love the haunted survivor—to death. But these ghosts are menacing or vengeful only to the extent that the survivor must, in order to keep his secret and have it too, put on a show of reproachful combat with some demon or even stage his own self-reproach.

In "On Narcissism: An Introduction," that first psychoanalytic inquiry to give a fully orchestrated theory of childhood—in which both anaclitic and narcissistic choices are accounted for, and all the resulting positions are in place—Freud contemplates the destiny of childhood narcissism in terms of a convergence of simulation and repression for which even Freud finds only mass-media analogues. The essay on narcissism follows out by multiplying the logic of inversion to the point that childhood narcissism is retrieved and protected only by internal institutions or courts also called, for example, conscience, dream censor, or ego ideal. These censorial institutions, which, as Freud advises, transmit and hold the place of not only early parental criticism but even public opinion, thus repeat and rehearse the so-called influence of the technical media.

When, in a letter dated March 16, 1914, Freud confides to Abraham that "On Narcissism: An Introduction" had been a "difficult birth," and accordingly displayed upon delivery certain "deformities," he immediately turns to photography to record and push back this terrible birth or stillbirth: "It still very much requires retouching," Freud concludes. This curious turn to the photograph continues to return. Children, when they die, do not die but are made to shrink and blow up on the photographic horizon of Oedipal and superegoical precincts shaped by the subliminal consumerism—the sublimation or incorporation—of the wrong objects.

To this day we have been receiving in the mail—through the post—countless advertisements asking the whereabouts of children who are neither living nor dead but missing. Each notice provided by "ADVCO-SYSTEM, INC., america's direct media company" opens with the demand, "Have you seen me?," which it follows up with a photograph and list of identifying information. In the supermarket, milk cartons bear for the mothers and children most likely to look at them the shadowy photographs of missing children. The subliminal force of their phantomization derives from the anaclitic angle at which the children must get the picture.

A death cult is always coextensive with the media extensions of the senses current in a given culture. Childhood occupies interchangeable places with the technical media to the extent that today, for example, childhood has not so much been effaced as replaced by television, which holds its place. In Santa Barbara certain stores selling the latest products and devices of the technical media have offered to video-tape, free of charge, all of Santa Barbara's children, who thus can only be protected against their absence within the search for their missingness.

FINALE: WITH BACKGROUND MUSIC

In Stoker's *Dracula*—to give the classic example—the inevitable convergence of sheer citationality and technologization is already in place. For Thomas Mann this double track becomes a rule or principle he calls montage: he thus borrows from one technical medium a term he uses to describe the approximation of *Doctor Faustus* to another contemporary medium, the music his novel has become, Mann claims, in the course of being about it.[59] Film and music—or film music—the late arrival or culmination of Wagner's endless melodies, thus provide a certain model for Mann's conception of a work that is citational to the extent that all life, he now believes, is a series of mythic clichés.[60] But in the background of Mann's account of the genesis of *Doctor Faustus*, one cannot help but discern muffled, choked breathing. His own lung operation allusively fulfills, as he puts it, the prophecy he made to himself that he would die at age seventy, the age his mother attained just before departing.

The return of the death wish, which this kind of suicide pact always embraces, emerges, then, as constricted breathing.[61] Thus we find already inside the corpus an endlessly repeated context of broadcast that marks the California portion of Mann's exile. The artist, like the philosopher, is, according to Mann, a transmitter or medium[62] to the extent that Mann himself, during exile in California, always had to rush, upon delivering one of his countless speeches, to some studio to repeat into a recording device a shortened version for public broadcast. The talk itself was delivered before "a double auditorium," in one chamber live, in the other via loudspeaker.[63] The news of Roosevelt's death can only resonate within this double auditorium of technologized audition and impeded breathing: "We stood stricken in the feeling that all around us a world held its breath. The telephone rang. I had to decline the improvised radio broadcast they requested. We revised a telegram to the widow of the deceased and listened all evening to the loud speaker."[64]

In the contemporary setting of the culture industry, in which Mann composes his music novel as montage while listening to the radio, all music, according to Adorno, is background music also to the extent that it occupies interchangeable places with silence. The coauthor of *Doctor Faustus* thus summarizes, by keeping in a separate, late time zone—some call it California—the primal reception of music which Freud tuned in by turning the pleasure principle around to its other side. "Music indwells the gaps of silence that emerge between men malformed by anxiety, bustle, and unprotesting submission. It assumes everywhere and unnoticed the deadly sad role which it had in the era and specific situation of silent film. It is now apperceived only as background."[65]

According to Mann, citation is at once mechanical and intrinsically musical;[66] in turn, all musical language, Adorno argues, has always been ruled by citation: from deliberate citation of children's songs to completely latent borrowings.[67] And yet, if music reaches its reversal and reduction only by virtue of having always been, right from the start, ruled by citation, the citational praxis of modern mass music amplifies by returning to a primal source of inspiration. The contemporary praxis whereby entire pieces from the classical repertory are adopted and adapted reflects the ambivalence of what Adorno calls infantile or regressive listening. The citations are at once authoritarian and parodistic, much in the way a child mimics his teacher.[68]

It is thus not so much music that has become fetishized within the culture industry as childhood itself: "But the configuration in which such a children's song appears: the masochistic derision of one's wish for lost happiness, or the compromising of one's wish for happiness through retroversion into a childhood, the unattainability of which guarantees the unattainability of happiness—this is the specific accomplishment of the new listening, and nothing that strikes the ear is spared inclusion within this scheme of appropriation."[69] Within the culture industry dance and music are sado-masochistic parodies of affirmation which take sexual excitement as model only in order to deride its effects. The jitterbugs, who affirm only to the point of deriding their metamorphosis, destroy what drove them to ecstasy the day before, as though exacting revenge for the recognition that their ecstasy was only simulated.

No one really trusts or believes in the pleasure obtainable through the culture industry. Every new stimulus offered turns out always to be the same thing.[70] As in Kafka's "Josephine the Singer," mass art becomes the parody of childhood in a culture where there is no childhood only to the extent that all remain child-like. Identification is made only with members of the group, not with any ego ideal. This is America's problem, Freud notes in *Civilization and its Discontents*.[71] In the culture industry, Adorno clarifies, the superego can only be simulated and summoned through nonstop consumerist identification with the products themselves in sado-masochistic scenarios where advertising turns around into terror. The fetish character of music, for example, withdraws from conscious recognition through this identification of the listeners with the fetish: "This identification first confers on the hits the power over their victims. . . . The writing under the tonal image, however, which permits the identification, is nothing other than the manufacturer's label of and in the hit."[72]

The subliminal message secretly etched into this background of music numbs and veils the consumerist identification it commands absolutely. Sublimation and subliminal, identification and consumerism: according to the logic of endopsychic perception, the technical media always double as delusional formations only to the extent that in the theory of the psychic apparatus they in fact occupy interchangeable places. What is thus heard in place of the silent command was projected, beginning in the eighteenth century, as communication with the living dead. "Chewing thinking," the simulation of speaking and hearing which Samuel Heinicke devised for deaf-mutes, repeated and rehearsed a technical medium as an occult medium. Just as the telephone communicates with the occult, according to Freud, so chewing thinking finds its close-range analogue, in 1728, when Michael Ranft published reflections on the sounds of chewing and lip-smacking which reportedly issued from graves. Freud's aversion to music has been linked and limited to his distrust of its orchestrated resistance to intellectual comprehension. But there remains, as Jones recollects, a primal meaning and scenario to Freud's dread reception of music: "One well remembers the pained expression on his face on entering a restaurant or beer garden where there was a band and how quickly his hands would go over his ears to drown the sound."[73]

Inasmuch as it is always a station of identification, background music broadcasts what Theodor Reik calls the "haunting melody": this background tune or lyric, which one cannot stop hearing recur out of sync with any matching context, announces, according to Reik, the imminent return of a death wish which must be kept in some other place.[74] Both the sado-masochistic scenario and its background music summon and represent, in the series of hit songs, that which is otherwise unrepresentable. The death drive always remains mute, according to Freud, though only to the extent that it remains in the background of what Freud also calls the "all-powerful melody of the drives." "There is going through my head," Freud writes to Marie Bonaparte in a letter dated August 13, 1937, "an advertisement which I think is the boldest and most successful American one I know of. 'Why live, when you can be buried for ten dollars?' "

What goes through not only Freud's head is that phantasm of attending one's own burial which only the technical media can, by institutionalizing Freud's discovery of the mechanisms of repression, stage live. By introducing reversal into the physiological functions they also amplify and accelerate, the technical media tap into the unconscious at one end and, at the other, hold the place of our missing death cult. Following Schoenberg's psychological conception of tone-color as the sheer effect of repression such that the unconscious alone hears the high overtones which have otherwise, in recognizable music and speech, undergone repression, Anton Ehrenzweig discovers that only since the advent of recording devices, which add to our sensorium the new dimension of play back in reverse, can the noise of the unconscious be heard:

> If we destroy the order within time, the articulation as well as part of the repression is also destroyed; the inarticulate transitive sounds will then emerge from the unconscious. This reversal is done by reversing the course of the gramophone needle so that it runs from the centre of the disc towards its periphery . . . so that every sound is reproduced in exactly the reverse order of time. . . . A multitude of little smears, grunts, and squeaks obtrude on our attention which previously had been passed over as mere transitive sounds. But also the brilliance of the sound quality, so cherished in dance music, has gone. 'Reversed' music as a rule sounds muffled and flat.[75]

The audio portion of reversal always discloses muffled breathing, which sounds out in certain contexts the primal scene, which, as Freud already assured Fliess in a letter dated May 2, 1897, refers to things heard, not seen. Ferenczi, for example, interprets asthma as the self-effacement an unwanted child enacts by embodying the heavy breathing of his copulating parents.[76] Thus in the psychoanalytic view of language origin advanced by Hans Sperber, the first word emerges when primal man repeats his grunt of sexual pleasure in a context where some technically nonsexual activity—tilling the soil, for example—nevertheless resembles sex to the point of calling forth the heavy breathing which now signifies both sex and the work to be accomplished.[77]

Primal language thus resembles the muffled air flow it also brings about. But constricted breathing emanates from primal scenes only to the extent that it has already been simulated in the gastrointestinal zone. The central tenet of psychoanalysis, which goes without saying in the same measure that it attracts tamperings with the institutional name itself, holds that every beginning has already been displaced upward—projected—from the anal under- world where it lies buried. As Jones notes: "In the ideas histori- cally moulded on that of breath we recognize again what in the unconscious are symbolic equivalents of intestinal gas: thus, wind, fire, speech, music, thought, soul, etc."[78]

The heavy, constricted breathing in the background of speech and music thus broadcasts, at the other end of chewing thinking, the primitive rhythms of retaining and then expelling. In singing, for example, Ehrenzweig clarifies, "the breath is not allowed to flow away freely, but is stored under increasing tension and then given off gradually in little explosions."[79] The logic of the reverse or back side nevertheless continues to prevail: no matter at what level their blast or roar is interpreted and located, trumpet and thunder alike ultimately wield the power of resurrection.[80] Primal breathing thus fills air waves and inflates ghosts: It was the movement of air, Freud instructs, which first gave rise to spirituality and spirits. Freud con- tinues: "Observation found the movement of air once again in men's breathing, which ceases when they die. To this day a dying man 'breathes out his spirit.' Now, however, the world of spirits lay open to men."[81]

In the legend of the Pied Piper of Hamelin, rats and children are interchangeably disposable only to the extent that their depar- ture holds the place of piped music. In the midst of discussion of slips of the pen which admit "preoccupation with priority"—that harbinger of castration and death—Freud slips down to the foot- note of the other to receive "music phantoms," which, as elabo- rated by Christoph Ruths, are "unconscious" apparitions which music animates via a mode of transference always akin to photo- chemical processes.[82] Although music cannot in fact "transfer pho- tographs . . . to the brain," says Ruths, elements of photographic recall can nevertheless be found spliced together in music phan- toms; the mental images and associations music summons thus compose themselves, in the series of their projection, into alien bodies.[83]

The only music phantoms which Ruths characterizes as disturbing, unsettling, even uncanny cover a kind of double exposure. In one case, "especially sharply developed" phantoms of children crowd in on the observer following a performance of *Hänsel and Gretel*. Suddenly the face of the deceased Mr. G. comes into focus on one of the tiny ghosts.[84] Although, Ruths emphasizes, specific recollections do not return in music phantoms, the anniversary or return of Mr. G.'s death has thus been marked: he returns as the phantom ultimately of his mixed reception, having served in life as the observer's moving target in that cross fire of respect and anger we call ambivalence.

The intensity of ambivalence is always matched, according to Ruths, by the efficacy of its phantoms. Originally imprinted through what Ruths calls "progressive substitution" of stronger for weaker images, the phantom is transferred subliminally or telepathically from the composer or conductor to the listening observer. At the receiving end, the phantom literally "develops" by reversing light and dark, front and back. The photographic process that thus conjoins motion picture and music yields film music or background music. Ruths writes: "To our observers music often appears only as an accompaniment to their phantoms."[85] Music phantoms are unconscious, according to Ruths, to the point of being as ancient and all-pervasive as only the effects of simulation can be: even public opinion and advertising, Ruths concludes, circulate only by gathering momentum in ever more exagerrated restatement.[86]

Coined by analogy with Kodak: Muzak was first created in 1922 to provide music over the telephone. By 1939, when it was introduced, Muzak had extended its aim and range: background or atmosphere music soon pervaded every public enclosure for which the shutdown of context that always provides an invisible vault around the phone call now served as model. Muzak is also called canned music, originally by analogy with film, which cans to the extent that it is found in cans. In an example the OED includes, canned music has been "embalmed upon gramophone records."

In the year of Muzak's introduction, Géza Róheim treats a male hebephrenic, thirty-two years old, who hears voices and music in the background as he consumes that which in turn consumes from within all nourishment such that he starves, but not really, he stipulates—only inside.

> The sound came from the back of my head—or as if I had food in my mouth.
>
> The voices inside me are connected in some way with my difficulty in making myself understood. Once, when I was at home, I asked my mother for supper and she said that I had had my supper already! The trouble was not the actual food—it was the *work in the food*.
>
> I have a photographic machine that takes pictures of people eating. This machine is like the one in the movies. The doctors built it—to see who was putting his head inside me and eating my food.[87]

According to the thirty-two-year-old, the doctors superintend his every identification and projection by tapping into his superego, which they simulate with recording devices. On both sides of its endopsychic construction the superego thus guarantees and requires that in the frenzied drama Róheim's hebephrenic calls "work in the food" and others call consumerism, always the wrong object will have been eaten: "Perhaps all these stories are the same story. That somebody was starved, but not really—only in his insides."[88]

The thirty-two-year-old's greatest trouble and concern is what he calls the "speed" or "gravitation" inside him. A certain velocity always brings about a reversal which he struggles to reverse in turn. Thus by fantasizing that his dinner is his breakfast he tries to keep ahead, ahead of time, of his inner reversal of time in fast forward. But "then the whole trouble started by somebody's eating the soup that I was eating, but eating it in the opposite direction."[89] Enter Little Depth Koda, who emerges out of the profound noise that reversal always brings about.

> She is called Depth because 'depth' is like 'deaf,' and I sometimes felt deaf with all the noise around me. . . . Depth means something deep, like the ocean. Koda is an island in the ocean, or a photo—like Kodak. There is something like a diluted reel of film in my brain, and the reel and the photo are like the doctors—trying to tell me what to do.[90]

The background music featuring the doctors, reels of film, Little Depth Koda, and Angel Love holds the place of the noise it would hold in place.[91] But the hebephrenic hears only the reversal of music, the noise of death wishes—the sound in the back of his head as he eats the wrong way.

Depth is also like death. The superego attracts and directs death wishes which are thus contained only to the extent that they rebound off the superego and its censorial institutions of broadcasting in the recognizable form of fear of death. According to the thirty-two-year-old, ancestors—the mourned dead—reside on one side of the superego. The doctors are in control also to the extent that they keep the patient from accepting, on the other side, "the job of Angel of Death," the controlling position in his media-technical death cult.[92] At the controls of this delusional system we find a primal "bug," also called "teethy," which the doctors and Little Depth Koda contain only by simulating and serving. In addition to representing a point of breakdown in any apparatus, a bug also ultimately symbolizes a sibling in phantasmic scenarios animated by death wishes.[93] Close-range, the hebephrenic's death wishes were first realized in his sister's departure, which originally sent him to the hospital. The bug flies out of his dead sister's stomach into his own, which instantly fills up with hot air.[94]

Cargo Cult refers to its point of inception and supernatural meaning as "noise." In turn, each cult follower commences picking up messages from the returning dead in fits of trembling also called "noise." Possessed individuals receive in their stomachs wisdom emanating from the ancestors. To induce possession through a literal kind of vetriloquism, the believer pounds and fans his stomach: "belly he think." Out loud communication with the ancestors was conducted not in English, the language of interference and scrambling, but in "Djaman" or German, the idiom of the dead.

Prior to the advent of Cargo Cult, mankind's most ancient and popular sacred instrument or symbol, called bullroarer or buzzer or, in Dionysian circles, rhombus, was also used by the Melanesians to produce spirit voices in initiation ceremonies designed to separate men from the women and children who were taken in by the ghostly spectacle of death, castration, and rebirth. While anticipating and making room for cargo, the buzzers are derisively exhibited, indeed, parodied, in front of the women and children: "Throw'em away bloody New Guinea something." Instead, the cult followers erect telegraph poles to communicate directly with their dead. Messages come down the pole into a medium's stomach where they are received; out of the medium's mouth come meaningless songs, which the bystanders waiting around in turn pick up and sing.[95] Phantom whistling and heavy breathing announce the time of arrival of the cargo-bearing ancestors. On the appointed day of their arrival everyone hears, while waiting to be taken off hold, the sounds of cargo—ships approaching, anchors being dropped, the clank of sheet metal being unloaded, the buzz of planes, the static of a broadcast on the verge of being put through. As Róheim's hebephrenic concludes: "It was like phantom lyrics, like a ship approaching—coming nearer and nearer, but you never catch it."[96]

NOTES

INTRODUCTION

1. Cited in *Von den Vampiren oder Menschensaugern. Dichtungen und Dokumente*, ed. Dieter Sturm and Klaus Völker (Munich: Carl Hanser Verlag, 1971), 520.
2. See the closing line of "On the History of the Psychoanalytic Movement."
3. Sigmund Freud, *The Standard Edition of the Complete Psychological Works,* ed. James Strachey (London: The Hogarth Press, 1960), 14:306. Hereafter cited as *SE*. The German original can be found in Sigmund Freud, *Studienausgabe,* ed. Alexander Mitscherlich et al. (Frankfurt a/M: S. Fischer Verlag, 1975), 10:226. Hereafter cited as *SA*. Since the English translation is, as its title suggests, the standard edition of Freud's works, references are always also given to this edition. No translation policy has, however, been observed: I either offer my own translations of Freud or borrow from Strachey's translation. English translations of all other German texts, unless otherwise noted, are my own.
4. *SE* 14:289–300; *SA* 9:49–60.
5. See John Bowlby, "Pathological Mourning and Childhood Mourning," *Journal of the American Psychoanalytic Association* 11, 3 (1963): 500–541.
6. Bowlby points to Freud's "A Religious Experience," in which a young man is overwhelmed, upon viewing a woman's corpse, by longing for his mother, a chain reaction which springs from his Oedipus complex. All this remains in the realm of the "typical."
7. *SE* 14:249; *SA* 3:203.

8. *SE*, 19:31; *SA* 3:299.
9. Karl Abraham, *Gesammelte Schriften*, ed. Johannes Cremerius (Frankfurt a/M: Fischer Taschenbuch Verlag, 1982), 2:50.
10. Abraham, *Gesammelte Schriften* 2:49.
11. Abraham, *Gesammelte Schriften* 2:270 ff.
12. *SE* 11:105–6; *SA* 10:130–31.
13. Abraham, *Gesammelte Schriften* 1:14–21.
14. Viktor Tausk, *Gesammelte psychoanalytische und literarische Schriften*, ed. Hans-Joachim Metzger (Wien and Berlin: Medusa Verlag, 1983), 231–35.
15. *SE* 14:306; *SA* 10:226.
16. *SE* 14:249–50; *SA* 3:203.
17. Abraham, *Gesammelte Schriften*, 2:76–77.
18. *SE* 14:306–7; *SA* 10:226–27.
19. *SE* 13:65–66; *SA* 9:356.
20. *SE* 20:172; *SA* 6:308.
21. *SE* 18:19; *SA* 3:228.
22. Ernst Simmel, *Kriegsneurosen und "Psychisches Trauma"* (Leipzig and Munich: Verlag von Otto Nemnich, 1918), 25.
23. These images, which always apply to manifestations of the repetition compulsion, abound in "The 'Uncanny' " as well as in the fifth section of *Beyond the Pleasure Principle*.
24. See *Massive Psychic Trauma*, ed. Henry Krystal (New York: International Universities Press, 1968). In characterizing the ambivalence of these policies, Alexander and Margarete Mitscherlich, in their *Die Unfähigkeit zu trauern* (Munich: R. Piper & Co. Verlag, 1967), 81, argued that "There is no difference in principle between this *form* of administered restitution and the forms of administered murder of an entire people."
25. *SE* 23:67; *SA* 9:516.
26. *SE* 22:50; *SA* 1:489.
27. Ernest Jones, *On the Nightmare* (New York: Liveright, 1951), 92 ff.
28. *SE* 20:129–31; *SA* 6:271–72.
29. See "Deuil ou mélancolie, introjecter—incorporer," in Nicolas Abraham and Maria Torok, *L'écorce et le noyau* (Paris: Aubier-Flammarion, 1978), 259–75.
30. *SE* 13:105; *SA* 9:392.
31. Abraham, *Gesammelte Schriften*, 2:67–68.
32. Letter to Fliess (May 31, 1897).
33. Letter to Fliess (October 3, 1897).
34. *SE* 17:151; *SA* 10:261.
35. See Stephan Broser, "Kästchen, Kasten, Kastration," in *Confrontation* 8 (1982): 87–114.
36. See Freud's early draft on melancholia forwarded to Fliess on January 7, 1895.
37. These phantoms, ultimately of Julius, appear via Freud's ambivalent rapport with his nephew John, one year Freud's senior. He ascribes his fainting spells alongside Jung to his recognition of the return, in his relations with Jung, of this childhood rapport. But in a letter to Ferenczi, Freud also draws the ultimate connection by tying his dead faints to Julius's death; Freud was one of those wrecked by success—the success, in fact, of his death wish directed against Julius. See Ernest Jones, *The Life and Work of Sigmund Freud* (New York: Basic Books, 1953), 2:146.
38. Freud thematizes the conversion rate dictated by the terms and conditions of analysis in a footnote to his case study of Ratman. *SE* 10:207; *SA* 7:73.

39. *SE* 19:85ff.; *SA* 7:299ff.
40. *SE* 21:155–56; *SA* 3:386–87.
41. *SE* 19:53ff; *SA* 3:319ff.
42. *SE* 4:254n.1; *SA* 2:259n.1.
43. Nicolas Abraham and Maria Torok, *Cryptonymie. Le verbier de l'Homme aux Loups* (Paris: Aubier-Flammarion, 1976). Derrida's introduction, "Fors," provides the indispensable supplement.
44. *SE* 17:23ff; *SA* 8:142ff.
45. Cited in Bowlby, "Pathological Mourning and Childhood Mourning," 530n.10, where a discussion of Freud's curious split reception of Wolfman's sister's death—curious also given certain contexts within which the split emerges—is already in place.
46. See Derrida's analysis of Hegel's Antigone in *Glas* (Paris: Editions Galilée, 1974).
47. See Robert H. Koff, "A Definition of Identification," *International Journal of Psycho-Analysis* 42 (1961): 362.
48. *SE* 13:59; *SA* 9:350.
49. See Abraham and Torok, "Deuil ou mélancholie, introjecter—incorporer," 274–75.
50. Avital Ronell has initiated the cryptonymically precise reading of *Frankenstein* in a series of lectures which will become part of *Telephony*.
51. Mary Shelley, *Frankenstein. Or, The Modern Prometheus* (New York: Signet Books, 1965), 88.
52. *Frankenstein,* 57, 192.
53. Sándor Ferenczi, *Schriften zur Psychoanalyse*, ed. Michael Balint (Frankfurt a/M: Fischer Taschenbuch Verlag, 1982) 1:12–47.
54. *SE* 12:66n.1.
55. *SE* 14:106n.1.
56. *SE* 14:224.
57. Tausk, *Gesammelte psychoanalytische und literarische Schriften,* 245–86.
58. *SE* 9:51; *SA* 10:49.
59. *SE* 13:92; *SA* 9:380.
60. *SE* 12:79; *SA* 7:200.
61. *SE* 12:115–16; *SA* Ergänzungsband: 175.
62. *SE* 22:55; *SA* 1:494.

CHAPTER ONE

1. See Philippe Ariès, *L'enfant et la vie familiale sous l'ancien régime* (Paris: Plon, 1960) and Neil Postman, *The Disappearance of Childhood* (New York: Delacorte Press, 1982). Postman stresses the link between the printing press and childhood, arguing that the eventual decrease in infant mortality rates did not, as Ariès suggested, contribute to the establishment of childhood since the decrease went into effect only some time after the invention of the child. The citation from the midst of Ariès' discussion of funereal representation can be found in *Images of Man and Death*, trans. Janet Lloyd (Cambridge: Harvard University Press, 1985), 247.
2. See Jacques Lacan's "L'intervention sur le transfert," *Ecrits* (Paris: Seuil, 1966).

3. *SE* 12:100; *SA* Ergänzungsband: 159.
4. *SE* 20:92; *SA* 6:238.
5. *SE* 22:55; *SA* 1:494.
6. *SE* 12:154; *SA* Ergänzungsband: 214.
7. Freud borrowed the term introjection from Sándor Ferenczi, who introduced it in the course of discussing hypnosis and transference in terms of prior "introjections." See "Introjektion und Übertragung," *Schriften zur Psychoanalyse*, ed. Michael Balint (Frankfurt a/M: Fischer Taschenbuch Verlag, 1982), 1:12–47.
8. *SE* 23:77; *SA* 9:525.
9. *SE* 28:105; *SA* 9:98.
10. Abraham, *Gesammelte Schriften* 2:70, 28.
11. *SE* 18:198; *Gesammelte Werke*, ed. Anna Freud (London: Imago Publishing Co., 1952), 13:167. Herafter cited as *GW*.
12. See "Die Stellung der Verwandtenehe in der Psychologie der Neurosen," *Gesammelte Schriften* 1:14–21.
13. Jones, *The Life and Work of Sigmund Freud* 1:3, 11, 25.
14. I am following Paul Roazen's account, in which this shift to Freud's essay on Dostoevsky was already in place. *Freud and His Followers* (New York: Alfred A. Knopf, 1975).
15. *SE* 12:294–96; *SA* 10:186–88.
16. *SE* 20:129–30; *SA* 6:271–72.
17. See Stephan Broser, "Kästchen, Kasten, Kastration," 87–114.
18. Jones, *The Life and Work of Sigmund Freud* 1:13. These early travel experiences, which may have been separated by years, most likely occurred, Jones suggests, many years after Julius's death. But Freud nevertheless recollected his travel souvenirs as having followed closely his brother's departure. Freud's eldest brother Emmanuel, father of John and Pauline, died in a train accident; shortly thereafter Freud commenced working on "Mourning and Melancholia."
19. *SE* 5:424–25, 483; *SA* 2:411–12, 465.
20. See Jacques Derrida, "Télépathie," *Furor*, February 1981, 5–41.
21. *SE* 5:424–25; *SA* 2:411–12.
22. Jones, *The Life and Work of Sigmund Freud*, 2:366.
23. See Konrad Burdach, "Faust und Moses," *Sitzungsberichte der Königlichen Preussischen Akademie der Wissenschaft*, 1912, 1:358–403; 2:627–59; 3:736–89. Goethe's early speculations on Moses are cited in 1:377. In this study Burdach argued that the death of Faust was most likely patterned after that of Moses.
24. See Erik H. Erikson, *Young Man Luther: A Study in Psychoanalysis and History* (London: Faber and Faber, 1958), 21ff.
25. *D. Martin Luthers Werke. Kritische Gesamtausgabe* (Weimar: Hermann Böhlau, 1883), Bible, 10, 1:100. Hereafter cited as *WA*.
26. Cited in H. G. Haile's *Luther: An Experiment in Biography* (Garden City, N.Y.: Doubleday, 1980), 74.
27. Cited in Haile, *Luther*, 229.
28. See *Open Letter on Translation*.
29. See *Tischreden* (Weimar: Hermann Böhlau, 1912–1919), 3:23. See also *WA* 25:138.
30. Letter to Nicolas von Amsdorf dated January 13, 1522.
31. *WA* 8:685.
32. *WA* 44:446.
33. *WA* 50:158.
34. See *WA* 50:137.

35. See Bernd Moeller and Karl Stackmann, "Luder—Luther—Eleutherius: Erwägungen zu Luthers Namen," *Nachrichten der Akademie der Wissenschaften in Göttingen, I. Philologisch-Historische Klasse* 7 (1981).
36. *WA* 30, 2:637.
37. *SE* 23:103; *SA* 9:550.
38. *SE* 23: 52; *SA* 9:501.
39. *SE* 23:39; *SA* 9:489.
40. *SE* 23:43; *SA* 9:492.
41. *SE* 23:118; *SA* 9:563.
42. *SE* 23: 113; *SA* 9:559.
43. *SE* 20:125–26; *SA* 6:268.
44. This Freud confides to Lou Andreas-Salomé. Cited in Rudolph Binion, *Frau Lou: Nietzsche's Wayward Disciple* (Princeton: Princeton University Press, 1968), 392–93.
45. *SE* 23:104; *SA* 9:551.
46. *SE* 23:94; *SA* 9:542.
47. *SE* 23:25; *SA* 9:475.
48. *SE* 6:82n.5; *GW* 4:92n.1.
49. Derrida overhears this paronomasia of the name in the course of uncovering the drive of the proper in *Beyond the Pleasure Principle* (see *La carte postale*).
50. *SE* 23:121–22; *SA* 9:567.
51. *SE* 23:62; *SA* 9:511.
52. *SE* 22:48; *SA* 1:487.
53. *SE* 23:113; *SA* 9:559.
54. *SE* 21:92; *SA* 9:222.
55. Avital Ronell, "Goethezeit," in *Taking Chances: Derrida, Psychoanalysis, and Literature*, ed. Joseph H. Smith and William Kerrigan (Baltimore: The Johns Hopkins University Press, 1984).
56. *SE* 20:188; *SA* Ergänzungsband: 280.
57. See Jones, *The Life and Work of Sigmund Freud*, 2:152–67; 3:213.
58. Ursula Sigismund, *Zarathustras Sippschaft* (Munich: Franz Ehrenwirth Verlag, 1977). Subsequent references are noted in the text.
59. Michel Foucault, "Nietzsche, Genealogy, History," in *Semiotexte: Nietzsche's Return* 3, 1 (1978): 78.
60. Lou Andreas-Salomé, *Lebensrückblick* (Frankfurt a/M: Insel Verlag, 1968), 242n.85. See also 128.
61. See Binion, *Frau Lou*, 54, 57, 118, 154.
62. *Ecce Homo*, 1, §3.
63. *SE* 18:123, *SA* 9:115.
64. See Freud's letter to Jung dated October 13, 1911.
65. See the third section of "The 'Uncanny' " ("Das Unheimliche").
66. See, for example, the final paragraph of *Inhibitions, Symptoms and Anxiety* (*Hemmung, Symptom und Angst*).
67. See Curt Paul Janz's *Friedrich Nietzsche. Biographie* (Munich: Deutscher Taschenbuch Verlag, 1981), vol. 1, pt. 1.
68. From a poem Nietzsche composed in early childhood.
69. Janz, *Friedrich Nietzsche*, 33, 102.
70. Cited in Binion, *Frau Lou*, 95, 79.
71. See Tobin Siebers, *The Mirror of Medusa* (Berkeley: University of California Press, 1983), 3–11.
72. *Gesammelte Schriften*, 2:233.

73. Cited in Kittler, "Nietzsche, der mechanisierte Philosophe," *KultuRRevolution* 9 (1985): 26.
74. Cited in Binion, *Frau Lou*, 104.
75. See Friedrich Kittler's "Draculas Vermächtnis" in *Zeta 02/Mit Lacan* (Berlin: Rotation Verlag, 1982), 103–33.
76. Marshall McLuhan, *Understanding Media: The Extensions of Man* (New York: Signet Books, 1964), 227–32.
77. See Nietzsche's letter to Overbeck dated Christmas 1888.
78. See H. F. Peters, *Zarathustra's Sister: The Case of Elisabeth and Friedrich Nietzsche* (New York: Crown Publishers, 1977), 61. See also Nietzsche's letter to Overbeck, Christmas 1888.
79. See Janz, *Friedrich Nietzsche*, 1:474.
80. See Derrida's investigation of the politics of the proper name in Nietzsche: "Otobiographies," trans. Avital Ronell, in *The Ear of the Other*, ed. Christie V. McDonald (New York: Schocken Books, 1985).
81. October 16, 1895.
82. See Walter Benjamin's essay "Karl Kraus."
83. *Ecce Homo*, 1, §3.

CHAPTER TWO

1. *Nietzsches Werke* (Stuttgart: Alfred Kröner Verlag, 1921), 2:14.
2. *Gotthold Ephraim Lessings sämtliche Schriften*, ed. K. Lachmann and F. Muncker, 3d. ed. (Stuttgart: G. J. Göschen'sche Verlagsbuchhandlung, 1886–1924), 2:383–84. Further references are cited in the text.
3. *Nietzsches Werke*, 2:8.
4. 11, 14, 16.
5. 4.
6. Friedrich Schlegel, *Kritische Schriften* (Munich: Carl Hanser Verlag, 1956), 242–44.
7. See Jürgen Schröder, *Gottfried Ephraim Lessing. Sprache und Drama* (Munich: Fink Verlag, 1972), where the discussion of *Wortgrübelei* is already in place.
8. Schröder, *Lessing*, 206.
9. Karl Abraham, *Gesammelte Schriften*, 1:24ff.
10. See Wolf Lepenies, *Melancholie und Gesellschaft* (Frankfurt a/M: Suhrkamp Verlag, 1969), 22–45.
11. See Hans-Jürgen Schings, *Melancholie und Aufklärung. Melancholiker und ihre Kritiker in Erfahrungsseelenkunde und Literatur des 18. Jahrhunderts* (Stuttgart: J. B. Metzlersche Verlagsbuchhandlung, 1977), 110–23.
12. Manfred Durzak, "Das Gesellschaftsbild in Lessings *Emilia Galotti*," *Lessing Yearbook* 1 (1969): 67. In *The Enigma of Emilia Galotti* (The Hague: Marinus Nijhoff, 1963), Edward Dvoretsky has collected the more prominent instances of the ambivalent critical response to *Emilia Galotti* which always finds its point of articulation in machine analogues. See 58, 68 n.4, 87.
13. McLuhan, *Understanding Media*, 135–144.
14. See the chapter on anti-Semitism in Theodor W. Adorno and Max Horkhei-

mer, *Dialektik der Aufklärung*, in T. W. Adorno, *Gesammelte Schriften*, ed. Rolf Tiedemann (Frankfurt a/M: Suhrkamp, 1981), vol. 3.

15. "On Deliverance" in *Thus Spoke Zarathustra*.

16. *SE* 21:99; *SA* 9:229.

17. Sheridan Le Fanu, "Carmilla," in *The Dracula Book of Great Vampire Stories*, ed. Leslie Shepard (Secaucus: The Citadel Press, 1977), 26, 42.

18. 48.

19. 52–53.

20. 35.

21. 42: ". . . life and death are mysterious states, and we know little of the resources of either."

22. Friedrich Kittler demonstrates the convergence of *Bildungsroman* and psychoanalytic hermeneutics in Gerhard Kaiser and Friedrich Kittler, *Dichtung als Sozialisationsspiel* (Göttingen: Vandenhoeck & Ruprecht, 1978). Kittler's portion is devoted to *Wilhelm Meisters Lehrjahre*. In this section I am following closely Kittler's article on the conjugation of paternity and transference, and on the return of phallic motherhood: " 'Erziehung ist Offenbarung.' Zur Struktur der Familie in Lessings Dramen," *Jahrbuch der deutschen Schillergesellschaft* 21 (1977): 111–37.

23. *SE* 10:193; *SA* 7:63.

24. See John Bowlby's section on psychoanalytic theories of the mother-infant relation in volume 2 of *Attachment and Loss* (New York: Basic Books, 1980).

25. Emil Staiger, "Rasende Weiber in der deutschen Tragödie des 18. Jahrhunderts," *Stilwandel: Studien zur Vorgeschichte der Goethezeit* (Zürich: Atlantis Verlag, 1963), 25–83.

26. Goethe made his remarks in 1809 in a letter to Johann Daniel Falk.

27. *SE* 22:122; *SA* 1:551.

28. *SE* 22:24; *SA* 1:466.

29. *SE* 22:130; *SA* 1:560.

30. *SE* 22:134; *SA* 1:564.

31. *SE* 14:264, 266; *SA* 7:208, 210.

32. *SE* 18:226; *SA* 7:222.

33. Cited in Volker Nölle, *Subjektivität und Wirklichkeit in Lessings dramatischem und theologischem Werk* (Berlin: Erich Schmidt Verlag, 1977).

34. Johann Gottfried Herder, *Sämmtliche Werke*, ed. Bernhard Suphan (Berlin: Weidmann, 1881), 17:185–86.

35. Immanuel Kant, *Anthropology from a Pragmatic Point of View*, trans. Victor Dowdell (Carbondale and Edwardsville: Southern Illinois University Press, 1978), 102–4.

36. 105–6.

37. 115.

38. This is Freud's first theory of melancholia, worked out in the course of his correspondence with Fliess. See the second part of Victor Tausk's "Diagnostische Erörterungen auf Grund der Zustandsbilder der sogenannten Kriegspsychosen."

39. In "Introjektion und Übertragung" (in Ferenczi, *Schriften zur Psychoanalyse* 1:32).

40. A. W. Schlegel makes this observation in "Vorlesungen über dramatische Kunst und Literatur," *Kritische Schriften und Briefe*, ed. Edgar Lohner (Stuttgart: W. Kohlhammer Verlag, 1967), 6:274.

41. Norbert Haas, "Lessings Emilia," in *Der Wunderblock* 7 (1981): 12–28.

42. Otto Weininger singled out the letter I as the most meaningful and charged of all the letters of the alphabet.

43. The naked name as the site of everything and nothing is one of Derrida's topics and discoveries. See, for example, "No Apocalypse, Not Now," *Diacritics*, Summer 1984, 20–31.
44. Géza Róheim, *Magic and Schizophrenia* (Bloomington: Indiana University Press, 1970), 115.
45. See Mark Waldman, *Goethe and the Jews: A Challenge to Hitlerism* (New York: G. P. Putnam's Sons, 1934), 157.
46. Goethe to Zelter, March 27, 1830. Unless otherwise indicated, the background information on the intertextual triad *Emilia Galotti*, *Götz von Berlichingen*, and *Die Leiden des jungen Werther* can be found conveniently collected and documented in Ilse Graham's *Goethe and Lessing: The Wellsprings of Creation* (London: P. Elek, 1973).
47. *SE* 10:297.
48. *SE* 10:207n.1; *SA* 7:73n.2.
49. *SE* 10:299.
50. *SE* 10:276.
51. *SE* 10:297.
52. *SE* 10:309.
53. *SE* 10:278.
54. Róheim, *Magic and Schizophrenia*, 209–10.
55. *SE* 10:284.
56. *SE* 10:264.
57. *SE* 13:154n.1; *SA* 9:437n.1.
58. *SE* 13:85ff; *SA* 19:374ff.
59. *SE* 23:113–14; *SA* 9:559–60.
60. Róheim, *Magic and Schizophrenia*, 161.
61. Róheim, *Magic and Schizophrenia*, 171.
62. *SE* 13:54–56; *SA* 9:345–47.
63. Róheim, *Magic and Schizophrenia*, 96.
64. Avital Ronell, *Dictations. On Haunted Writing* (Bloomington: Indiana University Press, 1986), ix–x.
65. *Goethes Werke*, ed. Erich Trunz (Munich: Verlag C. H. Beck, 1974), 4:173.
66. *Goethes Werke* 6:76, 65. Subsequent page references are given in the text. Whenever this section closes in on *Werther*, and the intersection of silhouette, dash mark, and little Hans in turn asserts itself, Peter Connor, who was my research assistant at the time I first worked on *Werther*, guides my pen.
67. See Graeme Tytler's *Physiognomy in the European Novel: Faces and Fortunes* (Princeton: Princeton University Press, 1982), esp. 56ff.
68. *Gedenkausgabe der Werke Briefe und Gespräche*, ed. Ernst Beutler (Zürich: Artemis-Verlag, 1952), 17:642.
69. *Gedenkausgabe* 18:911–17. "Meteore des literarischen Himmels" thus appears, in this edition, in the second volume of Goethe's scientific writings.
70. See Derrida's *L'oreille de l'autre* (Montreal: Vlb Editeur, 1982).
71. See J. Hillis Miller on *Elective Affinities:* in *Glyph* 6 (1979): 1–23.
72. In one of the decorations printed in 1813 or 1815 in celebration of the end of the Napoleonic Wars and of Karl August's return home we find an armoured arm covering certain books which it shields from the inclement weather. Beneath the image portion of this album page—a kind of souvenir which Goethe bestowed on visitors—we find four lines of verse followed by the signature "Goethe" in facsimile. Reproduced on p. 87 of Peter Boerner's *Goethe* (Reinbek bei Hamburg: Rowohlt Taschenbuch Verlag, 1964).
73. Róheim, *Magic and Schizophrenia*, 172.

CHAPTER THREE

1. See both Max Baeumer's *Heinse-Studien* (Stuttgart: J.B. Metzlersche Verlags-buchhandlung, 1966), esp. 55–57, and his "Nachwort" to *Ardinghello und die glückseligen Inseln*, ed. Max Baeumer (Stuttgart: Philipp Reclam, 1978), 641–718.

2. *Sämmtliche Werke*, ed. Carl Schüddekopf (Leipzig: Insel Verlag, 1902–1925), 10:328. Future references to this edition are given in the text.

3. See Emil Petzold, *Hölderlins Brod und Wein. Ein exegetischer Versuch* (Darmstadt: Wissenschaftliche Buchgesellschaft, 1967), 27.

4. Paul de Man, "Phenomenality and Materiality in Kant," in *Hermeneutics: Questions and Prospects*, ed. Gary Shapiro and Alan Siza (Amherst: University of Massachusetts Press, 1984), 121–44, esp. 141–44.

5. In "Goethezeit," in *Taking Chances: Derrida, Psychoanalysis, and Literature*, Avital Ronell establishes the resonance of what began, in *The Interpretation of Dreams*, as Freud's punning resolution of that part of a patient's dream dedicated to Italy (*SE* 4:232; *SA* 2:239).

6. See Craig Owen's "Detachment from the parergon," *October* 9 (1979): 47.

7. In *Der junge Heinse in seiner Zeit* (Munich: Wilhelm Fink Verlag, 1980), 89ff, Manfred Dick explores the untimely way in which the arousal of the senses asserts itself in Heinse's reflections on the irrational means of art.

8. This is a close paraphrase of Friedrich Kittler's elegant formulation of the difference between semiologies of art and art's media reception: "Weltatem: Über Wagners Medientechnologie" in *Diskursanalysen I: Medien*, ed. Friedrich Kittler, Manfred Schneider, and Samuel Weber (Opladen: Westdeutscher Verlag, 1987). In "Lessing und Heinse: Zur Wirkungsgeschichte des *Laokoon*," *Lessing Yearbook* 2 (1970): 56–89, and in *Wilhelm Heinses Ästhetik* (Munich: Wilhelm Fink Verlag, 1972), Rita Terras has amply demonstrated and documented Heinse's simple but subtle aesthetic criterion: art must always supply a direct connection between the perceiving organ and the representational means.

9. See Emil Ludwig, *Goethe* (Berlin: Paul Zsolny Verlag, 1931), 320.

10. The terms that usually cover nakedness in German were already ontologized by Winckelmann, who addressed what he called *das Nackende*. Heinse strips down *das Nackende* to the point that, in its name, the auditory sublime can be celebrated.

11. Cited in Albert von Lauppert, *Die Musikästhetik Wilhelm Heinses. Zugleich eine Quellenstudie zur Hildegard von Hohenthal* (Greifswald: Julius Abel, 1912), 96.

12. Heinse distributes the potency of voice in terms of a logic of quantifiable sexual difference which takes off from the male genitalia. Though women are accorded the vote (*Stimme*) in the utopian island society attained in *Ardinghello*, their vote or voice is restricted in power to the tenth part of the male voice (4:393). This logic of sexual and vocal difference is representational to the extent that absence does not alter it; castration puts the apportionment of privilege into reverse without, however, reversing it. Though the male voice can be embodied as perfect only through castration, woman can simulate the unmatched castrato voice only by assuming a disguise that, once dropped, reveals a double castration. Even though the heroine Hildegard obtains, in the guise of a castrato singer, the acclaim of the Roman audience, and thus the proof she seeks that the female soprano is equal to the allegedly supreme castrato voice, her success in this contest is eclipsed by what for her is an even

Notes to Pages 108–17

greater triumph: namely, her eventual marriage to the man who recognized that she was in fact a woman costumed as castrato. But just as her disguise is thus removed so her voice must soon follow: according to the novel, marriage, or rather childbirth, bears with it the impairment of the female voice (5:49). Directly explicit against Rousseau's plea for an end to the cultivation of castrato voices, Heinse's appreciation of the unique type of voice that only castration can project offers a stay against the reception of his works as harboring intact some Rousseauistic element.

13. In *Understanding Media* McLuhan uses these terms; the argument is Freud's and can be found in *Civilization and its Discontents*.

14. Cited in Karl Detlev Jessen, *Heinses Stellung zur bildenen Kunst und ihrer Ästhetik. Zugleich ein Beitrag zur Quellenkunde des Ardinghello*, in *Palaestra* (Berlin: Mayer & Müller, 1901), 21:82n.1.

15. Cited in Lauppert, *Die Musikästhetik Wilhelm Heinses*, 77.

16. Joachim Gessinger has been developing some of these connections, for example in a paper delivered at the Third International Conference on the History of the Language Sciences.

17. See Terras, *Wilhelm Heinses Ästhetik*, 77.

18. 7:259–60 and 8.2:246.

19. See Theodor Reik, Introduction to *The Haunting Melody* (New York: Farrar, Straus and Young, 1953). Freud brings up the melody of the drives as something Jung had missed (in "On the History of the Psychoanalytic Movement").

20. Anton Ehrenzweig, *The Psycho-analysis of Artistic Vision and Hearing: An Introduction to a Theory of Unconscious Perception* (New York: The Julian Press, 1953), 99, 153ff.

21. Ernest Jones, "The Problem of Paul Morphy. A Contribution to the Psycho-Analysis of Chess," *The International Journal of Psycho-Analysis* 12, 1 (1931): 7.

22. See Reuben Fine, "Psychoanalytic Observations on Chess and Chess Masters," *Psychoanalysis* 4, 3 (1956): 7–77.

23. "The Problem of Paul Morphy," 4, 21. One of the chess strategies described in Heinse's novel can be found in dictionaries of chess under "Anastasia's Mate." Heinse's strategy consists here in sacrificing the white queen; once the black king has been forced to take the white queen, he stands in the line of fire of the white rook, who takes the king.

24. Ernest Jones, *Essays in Applied Psychoanalysis* (London: Hogarth Press, 1951), 1:368.

25. *SE* 12:54; *SA* 7:179.

26. Diderot comes up with this one in "Entretiens sur *Le fils naturel.*"

27. Frances Ferguson, "The Sublime of Edmund Burke, or the Bathos of Experience," *Glyph* 8 (1981): 64.

28. See Hans-Jürgen Schings, *Melancholie und Aufklärung*, 52–54, 69–70. In *L'Homme machine*, de la Mettrie links up the deaf and the blind, imbeciles, madmen, savages, animals, and those who have lost their imagination through or to melancholia and hypochondria.

29. Stuart A. Ende, *Keats and the Sublime* (New Haven: Yale University Press, 1976), 129–30.

30. Jones, *Essays in Applied Psychoanalysis*, 1:320.

31. *Sämmtliche Schriften*, ed. Heinrich Laube (Leipzig: Verlag von Volckmar, 1838), 4:143.

32. See Norman Brown, *Love's Body* (New York: Random House, 1966), 55. Ned

Lukacher applies Brown's notion to the case of Schreber in a particularly illuminating way: "Schreber's Juridical Opera: A Reading of the *Denkwürdigkeiten eines Nervenkranken,*" *Structuralist Review* 2, 2 (Winter 1981): 16. Goethe's and Wagner's respective receptions of Heinse's *Ardinghello* thus come into focus as negative and positive of the same impression. This impression can be pursued to the extreme end of its development where we find Schreber taking from Wagner a certain conception of the castrato as model for his own reconstitution (see Lukacher). In this way Schreber offers the summary of Heinse.

33. *Briefe aus der Düsseldorfer Gemäldegalerie,* ed. Arnold Winkler (Leipzig: Edmund Schmid, 1914), 116–18.
34. *Briefe aus der Düsseldorfer Gemäldegalerie,* 106 ff.
35. See Lauppert, *Die Musikästhetik Wilhelm Heinses,* 14ff.
36. *Briefe aus der Düsseldorfer Gemäldegalerie,* 112–15.

CHAPTER FOUR

1. See Gilles Deleuze and Felix Guattari, *L'anti-Oedipe* (Paris: Les Editions de Minuit, 1972) and Friedrich Kittler, "Flechsig/Schreber/Freud: Ein Nachrichtennetzwerk der Jahrhundertwende," *Der Wunderblock* 11/12 (1984): 56–68.
2. McLuhan, *Understanding Media,* 263–64.
3. All Artaud references are to the *Oeuvres complètes d'Antonin Artaud* (Paris: Editions Gallimard, 1956–).
4. Regarding Artaud's persecutors, see Jacques Prevel, *En compagnie d'Antonin Artaud* (Paris: Flammarion, 1974). Other sources upon which I have drawn for information, often biographical in nature, which was not otherwise accessible to me include Martin Esslin's *Artaud* (London: Fontana Modern Masters, 1976), Naomi Greene's *Antonin Artaud: Poet Without Words* (New York: Simon and Schuster, 1970), Ronald Hayman's *Artaud and After* (Oxford: Oxford University Press, 1977), Elena Kapralik's *Antonin Artaud* (Munich: Matthes & Seitz Verlag, 1977), and Bettina Knapp's *Antonin Artaud: Man of Vision* (New York: David Lewis, 1969).
5. By the end of the eighteenth century Niebuhr had already recognized the "lesser characters" (letters) in hieroglyphics and, in 1797, Zoëga discovered that the cartouches contained names.
6. *SE* 9:40; *SA* 10:39–40.
7. *SE* 10:176–77; *SA* 7:51.
8. Marthe Robert, *The Psychoanalytic Revolution: Sigmund Freud's Life and Achievement,* trans. Kenneth Morgan (New York: Harcourt, Brace & World, 1966), 271.
9. *SE* 9:149; *SA* 10:176.
10. *SE* 9:41; *SA* 10:49.
11. Géza Róheim, "Nach dem Tode des Urvaters," in *Imago* 9 (1923): 83–86.
12. See Derrida's reading of the hieroglyphic nonorigin of language developed in his introduction to Warburton's *L'essai sur les hiéroglyphes* (Paris: Flammarion, 1978) entitled "Scribble (pouvoir/écrire)."

13. Denis Diderot, "Lettre sur les sourds et muets," in *Oeuvres complètes*, ed. J. Assezat and M. Tourneux (Paris, 1875–77), 1:371–74.
14. Diderot, *Oeuvres complètes* 10:520.
15. *SE* 13:177; *GW* 8:404–5.
16. See Freud's review of Karl Abel's *Der Gegensinn der Urworte*. But also see Karl Abel, "Über den Ursprung der Sprache" in his *Sprachwissenschaftliche Abhandlungen* (Leipzig: Verlag von Wilhelm Friedrich, 1885).
17. *SE* 13:177–78; *GW* 8:405.
18. Hans Sperber, "Über den Einfluss sexueller Momente auf Entstehung und Entwicklung der Sprache," in *Imago* 1 (1912): 405–53.
19. *SE* 20:93; *SA* 6:239.
20. *SE* 11:16–17; *GW* 8:11–12.
21. *SE* 14:229; *SA* 3:185–86.
22. *SE* 14:223–24; *SA* 3:180–81.
23. Jacques Derrida, "Le Théatre de la Cruauté, " in his *L'écriture et la différence* (Paris: Seuil, 1967).
24. Cited in Ernest Jones, "The Madonna's Conception through the Ear," in his *Essays in Applied Psychoanalysis* 2:292–93.
25. Another discursivity could, by all accounts, be linked up to that festival of name change which is cinema: Eisenstein, who first developed his theory of montage using analogies drawn from hieroglyphics and ideograms, planned to film *Das Kapital*.
26. *SE* 20:129–31; *SA* 6:271–72.
27. This was Kenneth Burke's pun.
28. Karl Abraham, *Gesammelte Schriften* 2:39–40.
29. 2:54.
30. 2:101.
31. 2:43–44.
32. Abraham, *Gesammelte Schriften* 2:59–60.
33. Abraham, *Gesammelte Schriften* 2:54, 91–92.
34. 100.
35. Abraham, *Gesammelte Schriften* 2:49.
36. See Jones, *The Life and Work of Sigmund Freud*, 3:116.
37. Otto Rank, "Der Doppelgänger," *Imago*, 3 (1914): 97.
38. See Uwe Gaube, *Film und Traum* (Munich: Wilhelm Fink Verlag, 1978), 28–38.
39. Rank, "Der Doppelgänger," 155–56. Rank is following J. B. Schneider's "Das Geschwisterproblem."
40. Abraham, *Gesammelte Schriften* 2:55, n. 2.
41. See U. C. Knoepflmacher, "Thoughts on the Aggression of Daughters," in *The Endurance of Frankenstein*, ed. George Levine and U. C. Knoepflmacher (Berkeley: University of California Press, 1979).
42. Vladimir Nabokov, *Despair* (New York: Putnam, 1979), 25.
43. 37, 69, 201.
44. 45–47, 128.
45. 96–97.
46. See the subsection of "Taboo and Emotional Ambivalence" entitled "The Taboo upon the Dead."
47. Cited in David Bordwell, *The Films of Carl-Theodor Dreyer* (Berkeley: University of California Press, 1981).

48. *SE* 13:97; *SA* 9:385.
49. Lou Andreas-Salomé, *In der Schule bei Freud. Tagebuch eines Jahres (1912/ 1913)* (Frankfurt a/M: Ullstein, 1983), 102–3.
50. *SE* 13:92; *SA* 9:380.
51. *SE* 12:79; *SA* 7:200.
52. Viktor Tausk, "Über die Entstehung des 'Beeinflussungsapparates' in der Schizophrenie," in *Gesammelte psychoanalytische und literarische Schriften*, 246.
53. 247, 253–54.
54. See Helene Deutsch's case study in *Internationale Zeitschrift für ärztliche Psychoanalyse* 5 (1919):41–45.
55. Tausk, "Über die Entstehung des 'Beeinflussungsapparates' in der Schizophrenie," 249, 273–74.
56. 252–53.
57. 257, 275–76.
58. 262–69.
59. *SE* 14:222; *SA* 3:179.
60. Tausk, "Über die Entstehung des 'Beeinflussungsapparates' in der Schizophrenie," 261.
61. 251.
62. 256.
63. 254–55.
64. 256, 278–79.
65. 259–60.
66. 256.
67. 282–83n.8.
68. 271–72.
69. 277–78.
70. 283n.8.
71. 281n.4. On the linguistic moment in psychoanalytic interpretations of paranoia, for example, see Joan Copjec, "The Anxiety of the Influencing Machine," *October* 23 (1982): 43–59.
72. *SE* 14:95–98; *SA* 3:60–64.
73. *SE* 14:20, 25; *SA* 3:290, 293. In the second paragraph of his new introductory lecture on femininity, Freud quotes from Heine's *Nordsee* a stanza beginning with the line "Heads in hieroglyphic bonnets."
74. McLuhan, *Understanding Media*, 261.
75. See 12:35ff. See Hayman, *Artaud and After*, 5. See also Kapralik, *Antonin Artaud*, 11.
76. Cited in Hayman, *Artaud and After*, 14.
77. In his other essay on Artaud, "La parole soufflée," also in *L'écriture et la différence*, Derrida situates Artaud's preoccupation with excrement alongside Artaud's intense wish to distance himself from the *organ*, whether as work, masterpiece, or bodily organ. For every organ-ized body is at once expropriated and dismembered. Though Derrida does not name the fart, he has, I believe, left behind a place for it in his reading of excrement in Artaud against and alongside the semantic congeners of the etymons of *souffle*, including, for example, breath, whisper, stealth, theft, and prompter. For another discussion of Artaud's pursuit of fecality, specifically his translation of "Jabberwocky," see Gilles Deleuze's "Du Schizophrène et de la petite fille," in *Logique du Sens* (Paris: Editions de Minuit, 1969).

78. In a letter to Henri Parisot, dated December 6, 1945, Artaud elaborated his relation to his double Nalpas. He, M. Artaud, had been crucified and resurrected two thousand years ago on an insanity charge. The so-called Christ was Antonin Nalpas, a cowardly impostor who sometimes in the form of a ghost sought to insinuate himself into Artaud's body and magnetize his testicles and bewitch his excrement. For an analysis of Artaud's thematization of matriarchal affiliation in *Héliogabale*, see Carol Jacobs's chapter on Artaud in her *The Dissimulating Harmony* (Baltimore: The Johns Hopkins University Press, 1978). That Artaud would henceforth inscribe the shards of his demolished name within his late poetry, in which glossolalia and the explosive syllabification of words yield hieroglyphs, is evidenced, for example, by the inclusion in one such poem of the hieroglyph AR-TAU. The proper name thus destabilized, all names or words must follow suit. For instance, Artaud's Toledo sword may well derive its importance from its partial homonymic convergence with Artaud's allegation that at age nineteen he had been stabbed in the back (*dos*). Esslin, for example, goes so far as to suggest that it is the late poetry more than any actual or possible performance which realizes Artaud's concept of cruelty.

79. I base my remarks in this section on Helm Stierlin's *Adolf Hitler: A Family Perspective* (New York: The Psychohistory Press, 1976).

80. At the close of World War I, Hitler suffered from hysterical blindness following his temporary burial by a shell blast, at which time he had had a vision of the Virgin Mary beckoning him to redeem Germany, referred to by Hitler on the first page of *Mein Kampf*, for example, now as "fatherland," now as "motherland." He was thirty years old at the time of his vision and henceforward destined to tap into Germany's ventriloquism or indigestion in the wake of a defeat that would not be acknowledged. Stierlin even sees Hitler's efforts to recoup Germany's lost territories as an attempt to retrieve Klara's lost children, just as, according to Stierlin, Hitler's impulse to undo Germany's defeat in World War I through repeating warfare reflects Klara's doubling and incorporation of her triple loss through four years of infertility. That Hitler's father had been a customs inspector, whose very status rested upon the continued existence of that very boundary between Germany and Austria which Hitler would violate, further underscores this view of Hitler's identification of Germany with his mother.

81. See Paule Thévenin's reply to Bettina Knapp's queries about Artaud's last days in *Tel Quel* 20 (1965), esp. 33.

82. McLuhan, *Understanding Media*, 124.

83. *SE* 10:213–14; *SA* 7:77–78.

84. *SE* 10:205–6; *SA* 7:71–72.

85. *SE* 10:204; *SA* 7:71. In "Über analerotische Charakterzüge," in *Internationale Zeitschrift für ärztliche Psychoanalyse* 5 (1919), Jones elaborates the anal logic of specular inversion.

86. *SE* 10:175; *SA* 7:50.

87. *SE* 10:166; *SA* 7:44.

88. *SE* 10:164; *SA* 7:42.

89. *SE* 10:186; *SA* 7:57.

90. *SE* 10:235; *SA* 7:93.

91. *SE* 10:187; *SA* 7:58.

92. *SE* 10:205, 207n, 235; *SA* 7:71, 73n, 93.

93. *SE* 13:119, 128; *SA* 9:405, 412.

94. *SE* 10:215n.2; *SA* 7:79n.1.
95. *SE* 13:139; *SA* 9:423–24.
96. *SE* 10:233n.1; *SA* 7:91n.1.
97. *SE* 10:236; *SA* 7:94.
98. In her discussion of the shift from filth to defilement in *Pouvoirs de l'horreur* (Paris: Editions du Seuil, 1980), Julia Kristeva covers the mother's creation of the body organized around the anus, which in turn belongs to her. It is the mother who, through sphincteral training, shapes her child's body into a territory having orifices, areas, and lines where the differentiation between proper and improper, clean and dirty, possible and impossible is mapped.
99. Jones, *The Life and Work of Sigmund Freud* 2:183.
100. Jones, "The Madonna's Conception through the Ear," 276–78.
101. Jones, "Über analerotische Charakterzüge," 83.
102. Jones, "The Madonna's Conception through the Ear," 293.
103. Abraham, *Gesammelte Schriften* 1:236–39.
104. Abraham, *Gesammelte Schriften* 2:114.
105. December 4, 1896.

CHAPTER FIVE

1. Franz Kafka, *Gesammelte Werke*, ed. Max Brod (New York: Schocken Books, 1948–1958), 1: 602.
2. Friedrich Nietzsche, *The Wanderer and His Shadow*, § 109.
3. Cited in Herbert Anton, " 'Stille Grundtrauer.' Die Schwerkraft der Dichtungen Kellers," in *Invaliden des Apoll. Motive und Mythen des Dichterleids*, ed. Herbert Anton (Munich: Wilhelm Fink Verlag, 1982), 113.
4. Keller describes his "stille Grundtrauer" in a letter to W. Petersen dated April 21, 1881.
5. Walter Benjamin, "Gottfried Keller: Zu Ehren einer kritischen Gesamtausgabe seiner Werke," in *Gesammelte Schriften*, ed. Rolf Tiedemann and Hermann Schweppenhäuser (Frankfurt a/M: Suhrkamp, 1974), 2.1:287.
6. See Freud's 1927 essay "Der Humor."
7. Gottfried Keller, *Sämtliche Werke*, ed. Jonas Fränkel (Wien: Kunstverlag Anton Schroll & Co., 1924), 16:196. All Keller references are to this edition and are cited in the text.
8. Winfried Menninghaus, *Artistische Schrift. Studien zur Kompositionskunst Gottfried Kellers* (Frankfurt a/M: Suhrkamp, 1982), 70–71.
9. See the chapter on "Therese" in Gerhard Kaiser's *Gottfried Keller: Das gedichtete Leben* (Frankfurt a/M: Insel Verlag, 1981). See also Eduard Hitschmann, *Gottfried Keller. Psychoanalyse des Dichters, seiner Gestalten und Motive* (Leipzig: Internationaler Psychoanalytischer Verlag, 1919), 34.
10. Cited in Emil Ermatinger, *Gottfried Kellers Leben* (Zürich: Artemis-Verlag, 1950), 247.
11. Ludwig Feuerbach, *Sämtliche Werke*, ed. Wilhelm Bolin and Frederich Jodl, 2d ed. (Stuttgart: Frommann Verlag, 1960), 6:90–98.
12. Feuerbach, *Sämtliche Werke* 7:140–41.
13. Feuerbach, *Sämtliche Werke* 7:141.
14. Feuerbach, *Sämtliche Werke* 7:153.

15. Feuerbach, *Sämtliche Werke* 7:142.
16. Feuerbach, *Sämtliche Werke* 7:150; 1:102–3, 126–29, 218–19.
17. Feuerbach, *Sämtliche Werke* 1:230–31.
18. Norbert Haas, "Exposé zu Lacans Diskursmathemen, Teil II: Die Terme," *Der Wunderblock* 5/6 (1980): 9–34.
19. In Ottokar Fischer, "Die Träume des grünen Heinrich," in *Untersuchungen und Quellen zur germanischen und romanischen Philologie (Prager deutsche Studien* 9, 1908), 2:343.
20. Adolf Muschg, *Gottfried Keller* (Frankfurt a/M: Suhrkamp Verlag, 1980), 24–25.
21. Tobin Siebers, *The Mirror of Medusa,* 4–5.
22. Marie E. P. König, *Am Anfang der Kultur. Die Zeichensprache des frühen Menschen* (Berlin: Gebr. Mann Verlag, 1973), 214–18.
23. See the section of Claude Lévi-Strauss's *Tristes Tropiques* on "The Living and the Dead."
24. Menninghaus devotes a chapter to the drifting of "white cloud" in *Green Heinrich.*
25. Tausk, "Über die Entstehung des 'Beeinflussungsapparates' in der Schizophrenie," 281–82n.3.
26. Benjamin, *Gesammelte Schriften* 2.1:291.
27. Charles Sanders Peirce pointed out that both mirror reflections and photographs were indexical signs.
28. See Luzius Gessler, *Lebendig begraben. Studien zur Lyrik des jungen Gottfried Keller* (Bern: Francke Verlag 1964), 51ff.
29. Emil Staiger, *Die Zeit als Einbildungskraft des Dichters: Untersuchungen zu Gedichten von Brentano, Goethe und Keller* (Zürich and Leipzig: Max Niehaus Verlag, 149; and Albert Hauser, *Gottfried Keller: Geburt and Zerfall der dichterischen Welt* (Zürich: Atlantis Verlag, 1959), 23. See also Walter Höllerer, "Gottfried Keller: Die Zeit geht nicht," in *Die deutsche Lyrik: Form und Geschichte,* ed. Benno von Wiese (Düsseldorf: August Bagel Verlag, 1957), 2:201–16; and Roy C. Cowen, "More about Gottfried Keller's Concept of Time," *The Modern Language Review* 58 (1963): 537–40.
30. See McLuhan, *Understanding Media,* 174, 181. Jacques Derrida has discussed photography as an exchange of steps in step with notions of seriality. See his commentary to Plissart's photographs in *Droit de regards* (Paris: Editions de Minuit, 1985). The most stunning elaboration of the photograph as commemorative portrait remains Roland Barthes' *La chambre claire. Note sur la photographie* (Paris: Les Editions du Seuil, 1980).
31. *Gesammelte Briefe,* ed. Carl Helbling (Bern: Verlag Benteli, 1952), 1:397, 256; 2:36; 1:250, respectively.
32. Cited in Emil Ermatinger, *Gottfried Kellers Leben* (Zürich: Artemis-Verlag, 1950), 247.
33. The *cliché* of the death scene in Keller, including acts of playing dead, is that of the body lying *reglos.*
34. See Erwin Ackerknecht, *Gottfried Keller. Geschichte seines Lebens* (Leipzig: Insel Verlag, 1939), 10.
35. Muschg, *Gottfried Keller,* 100.
36. Abraham, *Gesammelte Schriften* 2:106; Jones, "Über analerotische Charakterzüge," 105–09, 121–22.
37. *SE* 13:22–23; *SA* 9:314–16.
38. *SE* 21:99n.1; *SA* 9:229n.1.

39. All details regarding Keller's relation to his sister can be found in Hedwig Bleuler-Waser's *Die Dichterschwestern Regula Keller und Betsy Meyer* (Zürich: Art Institut Orell Füssli, 1919).

40. Herbert Anton, *Mythologische Erotik in Kellers "Sieben Legenden" und im "Sinngedicht"* (Stuttgart: J. B. Metlersche Verlagsbuchhandlung, 1970). The reversal of the masculine and the feminine is Benjamin's premier example of mirror effects in Keller's works. Benjamin points out that not only are gender traits in flux in these works but they even enjoy a certain cohabitation, that of the *venus barbata*, in Keller's own visage.

41. Jones, "Über analerotische Charakterzüge," 122.

42. *Gesammelte Briefe* 3.1:142.

43. *Gesammelte Briefe*, 3:138–39.

44. Friedrich Theodor Vischer, *Über das Erhabene und Komische und andere Texte zur Ästhetik* (Frankfurt a/M: Suhrkamp Verlag, 1967), 83, 89–90. Freud had in his library a copy of Vischer's work on the sublime.

45. Friedrich Theodor Vischer, *Aesthetik oder Wissenschaft des Schönen*, ed. Robert Vischer, 2d ed. (Munich: Meyer & Jessen Verlag, 1923), 4:194. Vischer, *Über das Erhabene und Komische*, 65.

46. Vischer, *Aesthetik* 4:220, 289.

47. Friedrich Theodor Vischer, "Gottfried Keller. Eine Studie," in *Altes und Neues* (Stuttgart: Verlag von Adolf Bonz, 1882), 137.

48. Vischer, "Gottfried Keller," 240–41, 279–80.

49. Vischer, "Gottfried Keller," 281.

50. Vischer, *Über das Erhabene und Komische*, 69.

51. Vischer, *Über das Erhabene und Komische*, 116–17.

52. Vischer, *Aesthetik* 3:6–11.

53. Vischer, *Aesthetik* 1:369 and 6:38.

54. Vischer, *Aesthetik* 4:138.

55. Vischer, *Aesthetik* 4:220ff.

56. Vischer, *Aesthetik* 4:225–26.

57. Vischer, *Aesthetik* 1:368–69.

58. Vischer, *Aesthetik* 6:39.

59. Vischer, *Aesthetik* 1:370 and 6:39.

60. Vischer, *Aesthetik* 2:17–18.

61. Vischer, *Aesthetik* 2:202.

62. Vischer, *Aesthetik* 4:409–11.

63. Vischer, *Aesthetik* 6:16–19.

64. Vischer, *Aesthetik* 4:36.

65. Vischer, *Aesthetik* 1:523.

66. Muschg, *Gottfried Keller*, 184.

67. Gessler, *Lebendig begraben*, 60ff.

68. Nietzsche, *Genealogy of Morals*, 2, §18.

69. Muschg, *Gottfried Keller*, 87.

70. Cited in Gessler, *Lebendig begraben*, 93.

71. Gessler, *Lebendig begraben*, 92.

72. Cited in Gessler, *Lebendig begraben*, 79, 85.

73. Abraham, *Gesammelte Schriften* 1:10–11.

74. See Karl Weiss, "Vom Reim und Refrain. Ein Beitrag zur Psychogenese dichterischer Ausdrucksmittel," in *Imago* 2 (1913): 552–72.

75. See Victor Tausk, "Zur Psychologie des alkoholischen Beschäftigungsdelirs," in *Gesammelte psychoanalytische und literarische Schriften*, esp. 152–157.

76. Cited in Gessler, *Lebendig begraben*, 101.
77. Helen Keller, *The Story of My Life* (London: Hodder & Stoughton, 1905), 63–64. Further references are cited in the text.

CHAPTER SIX

1. Cited and discussed in Martin Selge, *Adalbert Stifter; Poesie aus dem Geist der Naturwissenschaft* (Stuttgart: Verlag W. Kohlhammer, 1976), 22ff.
2. See Derrida's text to *Droit de regards*. The quote is taken from the German translation: *Recht auf Einsicht*, ed. Peter Engelmann (Graz and Vienna: Hermann Böhlaus Nachf. Gesellschaft, 1985), xxi.
3. See H. G. Wunderlich, *Wohin der Stier Europa trug. Kretas Geheimnis und das Erwachen des Abendlandes* (Reinbek bei Hamburg: Rowohlt Verlag, 1972), 268–77.
4. *Sämtliche Werke*, ed. Gustav Wilhelm (Graz: Stiasny Verlag, 1960), 1:21–22. Future references are given in the text.
5. Max Mengeringhausen, "Die Entwicklung der Flugtechnik und die Mythen vom Fliegen," *Imago* 15 (1929): 313–24.
6. *SE* 21:90–91; *SA* 9:220–21.
7. *SE* 22:188; *SA* 9:450.
8. Abraham, *Gesammelte Schriften* 1:58.
9. *SE* 13:87; *SA* 9:375–76.
10. Letter to Leo Tepe, dated December 26, 1867. In his *Adalbert Stifter. Persönlichkeit und Werk. Eine tiefenpsychologische Studie* (Wien: Phönix Verlag, 1946), Alfred Winterstein documents Stifter's dread fear of thunderstorms (13, 29).
11. According to Emil Staiger, in "Adalbert Stifter. *Der Nachsommer*," in his *Meisterwerke deutscher Sprache aus dem neunzehnten Jahrhundert* (Zürich: Atlantis, 1943), 189–90, the delay in the disclosure of the protagonist's name in *Indian Summer* is as such without deeper significance; but it betokens that self-effacement of the protagonist which enables him to indicate, without calling attention to himself, "the things of this world, the way they gradually become visible to human gaze in the sequence determined by God," "like a well-formed pointer on the sundial of existence."
12. In regard to the connections between Friedrich Roderer and Stifter himself, see Fritz Novotny, *Adalbert Stifter als Maler* (Wien: A. Schroll, 1947); Karl Polheim, "Die Wirkliche Wirklichkeit. Adalbert Stifters *Nachkommenschaften* und das Problem seiner Kunstanschauung," in *Untersuchungen zur Literatur als Geschichte. Festschrift für Benno von Wiese*, ed. Vincent Günther, Helmut Koopmann et al. (Berlin: E. Schmidt, 1973), 385–417; and Ursula Mahlendorf, "Stifter's Absage an die Kunst?" in *Goethezeit: Studien zur Erkenntnis und Rezeption Goethes und seiner Zeitgenossen. Festschrift für Stuart Atkins* (Bern: Francke Verlag, 1981), 369–83.
13. See Winterstein, *Adalbert Stifter*, 35–37.
14. For a discussion of the role of grandparents as narrators and instructors in Stifter's works, see Franz Hüller's "Leitmotive aus Adalbert Stifters Dichtungen," *Festschrift zur 17. Hauptversammlung des allgemeinen deutschen Sprachvereins* (Reichenberg, 1912), 67–82, esp. 70–73. Referring to works by

Freud, Rank, and Jones, John T. Irwin, in his *Doubling and Incest/Repetition and Revenge: A Speculative Reading of Faulkner* (Baltimore: The Johns Hopkins University Press, 1975), 64ff., discusses the notion of grandchildren as doubles of their grandparents. With regard to this specular relation between grandparents and grandchildren in Stifter's works, see Winterstein, *Adalbert Stifter*, 11–13, 234–35, 302. Abraham points out, however, that disappointment with the parents always appoints grandparents as surrogate parents, a substitution which aims to punish the parents (*Gesammelte Schriften* 1: 32–35).

15. See Winterstein, *Adalbert Stifter*, 12–13.
16. *Gesammelte Schriften* 2:72. Winterstein already made the connection on p. 13, in n. 8.
17. *Gesammelte Schriften* 1: 110–13.
18. 1:114–15.
19. Rousseau draws all these connections in his treatise on the origin of language. Back in the German context Heidegger addresses the convergence of *Lesen* and *Sammeln*, which would place reading within the oral/anal circuit of melancholia, as elaborated by Winterstein in Stifter's case; in *Indian Summer* collecting is described as "something very consuming" (*etwas sehr Einnehmendes*). Winterstein's reading of Stifter's aesthetics of collecting in terms of coprophilia is most instructive in this regard (esp. 35–36, 238, 245, 248, 262–63). Both Winterstein and Michael Kaiser, in his *Adalbert Stifter: Eine literaturpsychologische Untersuchung seiner Erzählungen* (Bonn: Bouvier, 1971), 56–57, have charted Stifter's abdominal pains via his fear of wagons to his father's death as well as to his mother's pregnancies.
20. *SE* 13:152; *SA* 9:435–36.
21. See Winterstein, *Adalbert Stifter*, 20, 77, 103.
22. Walter Benjamin, *Illuminationen* (Frankfurt a/M: Suhrkamp, 1977), 77.
23. See Marie-Ursula Lindau's discussion of Stifter's distrust of language—his poetics of concealment (*Verschweigen*)—in her *Stifters "Nachsommer": Ein Roman der verhaltenen Rührung* (Bern: Francke Verlag, 1974), 9–40. Addressing an issue legislated in the Old Testament, Derrida has dealt with the double bind of translation underlying the tower of Babel—translation being, after all, both necessary and against the law.
24. In his "Stifters Erzählung *Nachkommenschaften*," *Sprachkunst* 6 (1975): 238–60, esp. 239 and 255, Friedbert Aspetsberger discusses the interrelation in the novella of doubling on the one hand, and the literalization of names on the other. See Werner Hamacher's exploration of Hegel's various *Male* and *Mahle* in his introduction to Hegel's "*Der Geist des Christentums*": Schriften 1796–1800, ed. Werner Hamacher (Frankfurt a/M: Ullstein Verlag, 1978), 11–333, entitled "Pleroma—zu Genesis und Struktur einer dialektischen Hermeneutik bei Hegel."
25. See Otto Jungmair, *Adalbert Stifter als Denkmalpfleger* (Linz: Oberösterreichischer Landesverlag, 1973), esp. 35.
26. See Freud's "A Childhood Recollection from *Dichtung und Wahrheit*."
27. Stifter cites Juliane's suicide note in a letter to Louise von Eichendorff, in which he goes on to give the following reason for Juliane's suicide: "As far as our researches (*Forschungen*) now extend, researches I unceasingly conduct wherever I can hope for even the slightest information, a transfer (*Übersezung*) of menstruation into the brain was most likely the cause" (19:157).
28. See Urban Roedl, *Adalbert Stifter: Geschichte seines Lebens* (Bern: Francke Verlag, 1958), 119.

29. *SE* 12:57–58; *SA* 7:181–82.
30. Stifter indeed owes the eventual rehabilitation of his reputation in this century to just such a reader, namely, Nietzsche, who singled out Stifter's *Indian Summer* as one of four or five German books which deserve to be mentioned alongside Goethe's works.
31. Winterstein, *Adalbert Stifter*, 22.
32. See Otto Rank's "Die Nacktheit in Sage und Dichtung," in *Imago* 2 (1913).

CHAPTER SEVEN

1. Gilles Deleuze, "Nomad Thought" in *The New Nietzsche*, ed. David B. Allison (New York: Dell Publishing Co., 1979), 142–49. Also see Deleuze and Félix Guattari, *Kafka. Pour une littérature mineure* (Paris: Les Editions de Minuit, 1975).
2. Franz Kafka, *Gesammelte Schriften*, ed. Max Brod (New York: Schocken Books, 1946), 1:17. All Kafka references, which unless otherwise noted will be given in the text, are either to *Gesammelte Schriften* or to *Gesammelte Werke*, ed. Max Brod (New York: Schocken Books, 1948–1958). Hereafter cited as *GS* and *KGW*, respectively.
3. Roland Barthes, "Kafka's Answer," in *Critical Essays*, trans. Richard Howard (Evanston: Northwestern University Press, 1972), 136.
4. Stanley Corngold, *The Commentators' Despair: The Interpretation of Kafka's "Metamorphosis"* (Port Washington: Kennikat Press, 1973).
5. See Henry Sussman, *Franz Kafka: Geometrician of Metaphor* (Madison: Coda Press, 1979), 99.
6. Cited in Hartmut Binder, *Kafka in neuer Sicht. Mimik, Gestik und Personengefüge als Darstellungsformen des Autobiographischen* (Stuttgart: Metzler, 1976), 55–56.
7. In addition to *Kafka. Pour une littérature mineure*, see Deleuze and Guattari's *L'Anti-Oedipe*.
8. Cited in Barthes, *La chambre claire*, § 22.
9. For the most thorough account of the K.s' way of seeing see Jörgen Kobs, *Kafka: Untersuchungen zu Bewusstsein und Sprache seiner Gestalten*, ed. Ursula Brech (Bad Homburg: Athenäum Verlag, 1970).
10. Heinz Politzer, *Franz Kafka: Parable and Paradox* (Ithaca: Cornell University Press, 1962), 212.
11. Theodor W. Adorno, "Aufzeichnungen zu Kafka," in *Versuch das "Endspiel" zu verstehen* (Frankfurt a/M: Suhrkamp Verlag, 1973), 142.
12. Gerhard Kurz, *Traum-Schrecken: Kafkas literarische Existenzanalyse* (Stuttgart: J. B. Metzlersche Verlagsbuchhandlung, 1980), 183.
13. See Günther Anders, *Kafka. Pro und Contra* (Munich: C.H. Beck, 1951), 41.
14. Adorno, "Aufzeichnungen zu Kafka," 143.
15. *SE* 2:296; *GW* 1:301–2.
16. Sándor Ferenczi, *Schriften zur Psychoanalyse*, 2:14.
17. Karl Abraham, *Gesammelte Schriften* 2:58.
18. *SE* 3:196, 206; *SA* 6:58, 66.
19. Adorno, "Aufzeichnungen zu Kafka," 138.

20. *SE* 13:203; *SA* Ergänzungsband: 235.
21. *SE* 5:399; *SA* 2:390.
22. Max Mengeringhausen, "Die Entwicklung der Flugtechnik und die Mythen vom Fliegen," *Imago* 15 (1929): 313–24.
23. Nicolas Abraham and Maria Torok, "Introjection—Incorporation. *Mourning or Melancholia,*" in *Psychoanalysis in France,* ed. Serge Lebovici and Daniel Widlöcher (New York: International Universities Press, Inc., 1980), 14–15.
24. Jacques Derrida, "Fors," trans. Barbara Johnson, *The Georgia Review,* 30 (1979): 103.
25. Ronald Hayman, *Kafka. A Biography* (New York: Oxford University Press, 1982), 248.
26. *SE* 13:81; *SA* 9:372.
27. Letter to Max Brod, mid-September, 1917. *Briefe. 1902–1924,* ed. Max Brod (New York: Schocken Books, 1958), 164.
28. *Briefe an Milena,* ed. Willy Haas (New York: Schocken Books, 1952), 246.
29. Julie Kafka's reference to her dead son is cited in Hayman, *Kafka,* 10. Her abandonment of her children was in a sense rehearsed when she was abandoned, at age three, by her dead mother. Kafka used up all his strength surviving what his brothers succumbed to and his sisters circumvented only because Kafka was by then old enough to help out: negligent, resentful servants unsupervised by the busy parents.
30. This "birth"—Kafka writes in his diary entry of February 11, 1913—is allegorized in the story in terms of the creation of the phantom friend out of the "circle of blood" linking father and son.
31. Gustav Janouch, *Gespräche mit Kafka* (Frankfurt a/M: S. Fischer Verlag, 1968), 54.
32. See diary entry of February 11, 1913.
33. See Bernhard Böschenstein, "Elf Söhne," *Franz Kafka: Themen und Probleme,* ed. Claude David (Göttingen: Vandenhoeck & Ruprecht, 1980), 136–51.
34. Adorno, "Aufzeichnungen zu Kafka," 165.
35. Günter Mecke, *Franz Kafkas offenbares Geheimnis. Eine Psychopathographie* (Munich: Wilhelm Fink Verlag, 1982).
36. *Benjamin über Kafka. Texte, Briefzeugnisse, Aufzeichnungen,* ed. Hermann Schweppenhäuser (Frankfurt a/M: Suhrkamp Verlag, 1981), 126–27.
37. For example: *SE* 18:136, SA 9:127.
38. See his letter to Brod, dated July 5, 1922.
39. *Briefe an Milena,* 199.
40. *Hochzeitsvorbereitungen auf dem Lande, Gesammelte Werke,* 216.
41. Ferenczi, *Schriften zur Psychoanalyse,* 1:185, 195.
42. *SE* 11:88, 116–18; *SA* 10:114, 139–41. For Kafka's reading of Freud, see Stanley Corngold, "Freud as a Literary Text?" *Diacritics,* March 1979, 84–94.
43. According to Freud, the bird is also phallic, a claim Eissler sought to substantiate, for example by pointing out that in Leonardo's day erections were still explained as the filling up with air of the penis, a theory with which Leonardo was familiar since he refuted it. In his quest to understand just how the bird (and, Eissler adds, the erect penis) overcomes gravity, Leonardo came to realize that his flying machine must be impervious to air. He thus modeled his designs no longer after bird wings but instead after the wings of bats, whose vampiric and bisexual activities were already legend. See K. R. Eissler's *Leo-*

nardo Da Vinci: Psychoanalytic Notes on the Enigma (London: The Hogarth Press, 1962), 166–74.

44. *SE* 11:133ff; *SA* 10:154ff.
45. Jacqueline Rose, "Paranoia and the Film Screen," *Screen*, Winter 1976/77, 97.
46. *SE* 11:99–106; *SA* 10:124–31; *SE* 19:43; *SA* 3:310; *SE* 18:231; *SA* 7:227.
47. Ferenczi, *Schriften zur Psychoanalyse* 1:189; Jones, *The Life and Work of Sigmund Freud*, 3:385.
48. *SE* 12:73; *SA* 7:196.
49. *SE* 12:55; *SA* 7:180.
50. See Ned Lukacher's "Schreber's Juridical Opera: A Reading of the *Denkwürdigkeiten eines Nervenkranken*," in *Structuralist Review* 2, 2 (1981): 3–24.
51. Cited in Lukacher, "Schreber's Juridical Opera," 16.
52. See Lukacher, who refers to the work of Marie Balmary. See also John Bowlby's section on Schreber in volume 2 of *Attachment and Loss*, and Samuel Weber's "Die Parabel," the introduction to his edition of Schreber's *Denkwürdigkeiten* (Frankfurt a/M: Ullstein, 1973).
53. *SE* 12:52n.1, 53; *SA* 7:176n.4, 177.
54. Peter Worsley, *The Trumpet Shall Sound. A Study of 'Cargo' Cults in Melanesia* (London: Macgibbon and Kee, 1957), 18.
55. Avital Ronell has been exploring this primal reach of rumor. See, for example, "Street-Talk," *STCL* 11, 1 (Fall, 1986): 105–31.
56. See chapter 4 of *Pour une littérature mineure*. See Hayman for details of Kafka's letter-writing pacts. Travel and correspondence enabled Kafka to traverse the post of German letters without succumbing to what Kafka termed, in his diary entry of January 31, 1912, Goethe's "horrific being." Following his trip to Weimar Kafka visited a nudist colony where he would contemplate corresponding with the tanned and well-constituted landsurveyor who sought to convert him to Christianity. A certain Dr. Schiller painted his portrait while, in a dream, Kafka heard Goethe recite "with an infinite freedom and caprice." Immediately upon returning from the colony Kafka gave birth to "The Judgment." The funereal zone covered by nudist culture—referred to in German as FKK—was briefly uncovered, in anticipation of "The Judgment," by another dream Kafka had while at the colony: he saw the nudists battling each other crying out "Lustron and Castron."
57. See Friedrich Kittler's *Aufschreibesysteme. 1800. 1900.* (Munich: Wilhelm Fink Verlag, 1985), 370–71.
58. *Benjamin über Kafka*, 48. Not only would Brod's own most successful publication turn out to have been the name "Franz Kafka," but Brod moreover claimed responsibility for having encouraged Kafka to keep a diary, and hence for having instigated Kafka's entire oeuvre, which, after all, largely grew out of his diary.
59. End of March, 1918.
60. Janouch, *Gespräche mit Kafka*, 36.
61. "Meditations on Sin, Suffering, Hope, and the True Way," § 32.
62. Deleuze, "Nomad Thought," 149.
63. Günther Anders develops this notion in *Kafka. Pro und Contra* (Munich: Beck, 1951).
64. In a letter of July 5, 1922, to Max Brod, Kafka describes *Schriftstellersein* as his dwelling outside of life. In his diary entry of August 21, 1913, Kafka transcribes his letter to his fiancée's father, in which he explains his strong doubts about the

union of married life and writing, since he is "nothing but literature and cannot and would not want to be anything else."

65. *Tagebücher* 1910–1923, ed. Max Brod (Frankfurt a/M: Fischer Verlag, 1967), 268.

66. Postcard to Felice Bauer, September 9, 1913.

67. "Die Aeroplane in Brescia," in Max Brod, *Über Franz Kafka* (Frankfurt a/M: Fischer Taschenbuch Verlag, 1974), 366. Kafka and Brod were, it turns out, engaged in a more involved competition. For there is in the periphery of Kafka's report an actual writer, the Italian poet D'Annunzio, in attendance. Yet D'Annunzio was not merely a witness to the meeting in Brescia, for it was in Brescia that D'Annunzio undertook his first plane flight, which was hailed throughout Europe as the first flight of a poet-pilot. D'Annunzio went on to write the first fictive artistic work devoted to mechanical flight and its technology, incorporating notes he had made while in Brescia. See Felix P. Ingold, *Literatur und Aviatik. Europäische Flugdichtung 1909–1927* (Basel: Birkhäuser Verlag, 1978), 28ff.

68. "Die Aeroplane in Brescia," 365.

69. *The Papers of Wilbur and Orville Wright,* ed. Marvin W. McFarland (New York: McGraw Hill, 1953), 1:469ff. Orville Wright's letters regarding warfare are to C. M. Hitchcock (June 21, 1917) and Major Lester D. Gardner (August 28, 1945), respectively.

70. See Robert Byck's Introduction to Freud's *Cocaine Papers* (New York: Stonehill, 1974).

71. *Cocaine Papers,* 85.

72. Avital Ronell, "Goethezeit," 171.

73. *Cocaine Papers,* 65–66, 73.

74. Kittler, *Aufschreibesysteme,* 183–210.

75. Kafka is thus contained in nuce in his airplane piece: see Elisabeth Plessen, *Fakten und Erfindungen. Zeitgenössische Epik im Grenzgebiet von fiction und nonfiction* (Munich: Carl Hanser Verlag, 1971), 35–41.

76. *Hochzeitsvorbereitungen auf dem Lande und andere Prosa aus dem Nachlass* (Frankfurt a/M: Fischer Verlag, 1953), 104.

77. *SE* 22:169; *SA* 1:595. Strachey translates *Phantom* as "anatomical model."

78. *SE* 22:164–65; *SA* 1:592.

79. *SE* 22:177–78; *SA* 1:604.

80. *SE* 5:357; *SA* 2:351–52.

81. *SE* 4:37; *SA* 2:63.

82. *SE* 5:385–86; *SA* 2:377–78.

83. *SE* 4:248n.1; *SA* 2:253n.1.

84. *SE* 5:393; *SA* 2:384–85.

85. *SE* 4:253–54; *SA* 2:258.

86. McLuhan, *Understanding Media,* 165. And before the introduction through telecommunications of outside central control whereby iconic simultaneity came to inhere in airplane flight, for example, such that all parts of the globe are in touch and can be touched in one spot, planes, like cars, had, McLuhan, continues, at first decentered what wheels and roads had centered. The first transgression against centered transport was the bicycle, which, McLuhan notes, "lifted the wheel onto the plane of aerodynamic balance, and not so indirectly created the airplane," a connection to which the Wright brothers, who were themselves bicycle mechanics, attest.

87. Vladimir Nabokov, *Lectures on Literature*, ed. Fredson Bowers (New York: Harcourt Brace Jovanovich, 1980), 259.
88. "Die Aeroplane in Brescia," 361.
89. *Briefe an Milena*, 199.
90. Hayman, *Franz Kafka*, 149, 175.
91. McLuhan, *Understanding Media*, 233, 240.
92. *SE* 12:298–301; *SA* 10:190–93.
93. Jones, *The Life and Work of Sigmund Freud*, 3:381.
94. *SE* 22:38, 42; *SA* 1:479, 482.
95. *SE* 19:138; *GW* 1:573.
96. *SE* 12:96; *SA* Ergänzungsband: 155–56.
97. *Gesammelte Schriften* 1:266–68. Translation by Hilda Abraham and D. R. Ellison.
98. *SE* 1:357. Cited in Rüdiger Campe, "Pronto! Telefonate und Telefonstimmen," in *Diskursanalysen I: Medien*, 88.
99. See Derrida, "Télépathie," in *Furor*, February 1981, 5–41.
100. *SE* 22:36, 55; *SA* 1:477, 494.
101. *SE* 12:115–16; *SA* Ergänzungsband: 175–76.
102. Michael Wetzel, "Telephonanie," in *Eingebildete Texte*, ed. Jochen Hörisch and Georg Tholen (Munich: Wilhelm Fink Verlag, 1985) 136–45.
103. Cited in Wetzel, "Telephonanie," 138.
104. Karl Jung, "Über die Psychologie der Dementia Praecox: Ein Versuch," *Gesammelte Werke*, ed. Franz Riklin, Lilly Jung-Merker, Elisabeth Rüf (Zürich and Stuttgart: Rascher Verlag, 1968), vol. 3. On p. 286 of *Aufschreibesysteme* Kittler points out that Jung overhears that he has become "the telephone."
105. Jung, "Über die Psychologie der Dementia Praecox," 142.
106. 140.
107. 169.
108. Walter Benjamin, *Gesammelte Schriften*, ed. Rolf Tiedemann and Hermann Schweppenhäuser (Frankfurt a/M: Suhrkamp Verlag, 1972), 4.1:242–43.
109. *SE* 21:88; *SA* 9:219. Freud argues that there is no *no* in the unconscious: instead, things are more or less cathected—*besetzt*. According to both Freud and Kafka, there is no *no* on the phone.
110. Nietzsche, *Genealogy of Morals*, vol. 3, §5. What follows argues for the continued applicability of the psychoanalytic prosthesis argument alongside recent conceptions of the development of new media always along the battle lines of escalation and acceleration. See Friedrich Kittler, *Grammophon/Film/Schreibmaschine* (Berlin: Bose & Brinckmann, 1987). The primal phone's incorporation of a dead ear—on which my discussion with Kittler turns and closes—receives its full cryptological feedback in Avital Ronell's *The Telephone Book* (1988).
111. *SE* 22:55–56; *SA* 1:494.
112. See Joan Copjec, "The Anxiety of the Influencing Machine," *October*, 23 (1982): 43.
113. *SE* 12:50n.1; *SA* 7:175n.1.
114. Karl Jung, "Ein Beitrag zur Psychologie des Gerüchtes," *Zentralblatt für Psychoanalyse* 1, 3 (1910/11), 81–90.
115. *SE* 15:85–86; *SA* 1:103.
116. Jung, *Flying Saucers. A Modern Myth of Things Seen in the Skies*, trans. R. F.

C. Hull (Princeton: Princeton University Press, 1978), 100. Subsequent references are to this edition and are given in the text.
117. Kittler, *Aufschreibesysteme*, 369.
118. See the *Diacritics* issue devoted to "nuclear criticism" (Summer 1984), in particular the contributions by Derrida and Frances Ferguson on the uninsurable referent.

CHAPTER EIGHT

1. This is from Benjamin's first version of "Das Kunstwerk im Zeitalter seiner technischen Reproduzierbarkeit," *Gesammelte Schriften*, 1.2:462.
2. Theodor W. Adorno and Max Horkheimer, *Dialektik der Aufklärung*, in T. W. Adorno, *Gesammelte Schriften*, ed. Gretel Adorno and Rolf Tiedemann (Frankfurt a/M: Suhrkamp Verlag, 1981), 3:267, 269.
3. Adorno, *Gesammelte Schriften*, 3:142-43.
4. "Prolog zum Fernsehen," Adorno, *Gesammelte Schriften* (1977), 10, 2: 507-517.
5. Adorno, *Gesammelte Schriften* 3:187ff.
6. Adorno, *Gesammelte Schriften* 3: 188.
7. Adorno, *Gesammelte Schriften* 3: 243-44.
8. See the section "Technische Medien" in Friedrich Kittler's *Aufschreibesysteme*.
9. Adorno, *Gesammelte Schriften* 3:147-48, 168ff.
10. See Frances Yates, *The Art of Memory* (Chicago: University of Chicago Press, 1966), 17, 26.
11. Adorno, *Gesammelte Schriften* 3:160.
12. Kittler, *Aurschreibesysteme*, 235.
13. McLuhan, *Understanding Media*, 181.
14. Adorno, *Gesammelte Schriften* 3:182.
15. McLuhan, *Understanding Media*, 263-64.
16. *SE* 19:31, 36ff; *SA* 3:299, 303ff.
17. *SE* 12:73; *SA* 7:196.
18. *SE* 14:96-98; *SA* 3:62-64.
19. McLuhan, *Understanding Media*, 263-64.
20. Adorno, *Gesammelte Schriften* 3:183.
21. *SE* 19:54; *SA* 3:321.
22. "Satzzeichen," in Adorno, *Gesammelte Schriften* 2:106-113.
23. *Die Sprache* (Munich: Kösel Verlag, 1954), 77.
24. *Untergang der Welt durch schwarze Magie* (Munich: Kösel Verlag, 1960), 101-2.
25. Roland Barthes, *Mythologies*, trans. Annette Lavers (New York: Hill and Wang, 1972), 150-51.
26. *Die dritte Walpurgisnacht* (Munich: Kösel Verlag, 1952), 163.
27. Manfred Schneider, *Die Angst und das Paradies des Nörglers* (Frankfurt a/M: Syndikat, 1977),
28. *Worte in Versen* (Munich: Kösel Verlag, 1959), 80.
29. *Worte in Versen*, 59.
30. *Worte in Versen*, 81.
31. *Die Sprache*, 358.

32. *Die Sprache*, 392.
33. *Die Sprache*, 413.
34. *Worte in Versen*, 81.
35. *Worte in Versen*, 450.
36. See Andreas Disch, *Das gestaltete Wort: Die Idee der Dichtung im Werk von Karl Kraus* (Zürich: Juris Druck & Verlag, 1969), 65ff.
37. Benjamin, *Gesammelte Schriften* 2.3:1101.
38. Walter Benjamin, *Ursprung des deutschen Trauerspiels* (Frankfurt a/M: Suhrkamp Taschenbuch Verlag, 1972), 254.
39. Walter Benjamin, *Angelus Novus. Ausgewählte Schriften* (Frankfurt a/M: Suhrkamp Verlag, 1966), 2: 24–25.
40. *Untergang der Welt durch schwarze Magie*, 205; and *Beim Wort genommen* (Munich: Kösel Verlag, 1955), 111.
41. *Untergang der Welt duch schwarze Magie*, 202.
42. *Die Sprache*, 149.
43. *Die Sprache*, 356. See also *Über die Sprache* (Frankfurt a/M: Suhrkamp Verlag, 1982), 13.
44. *Die Sprache*, 149–50.
45. *Die Sprache*, 150.
46. *Die dritte Walpurgisnacht*, 121. The final strophe of "Rückkehr in die Zeit" can be found in Disch, 34.
47. *Die Fackel*, 890–905: 71.
48. *Die Fackel*, 890–905: 97.
49. *Die dritte Walpurgisnacht*, 121.
50. *Die Fackel*, 716–721.
51. *Worte in Versen*, 434.
52. *Die Fackel*, 890–905: 160.
53. At the time Benjamin became familiar with Mickey Mouse, this talking rodent, who was competing with the Jazz Singer, had a sadistic disposition and bared sharp teeth whenever it laughed. The mouse thus shared with Ratman a certain "impertinent laugh." The totemic significance of the mouse name was obscured at the same time as it emerged: when Disney replaced with Mickey, the mouse's original first name Mortimer.
54. Benjamin, *Gesammelte Schriften* 2.3: 1102–1106.
55. Benjamin, *Gesammelte Schriften* 2.1: 362–363.
56. *Die Sprache*, 149.
57. *SE* 19:50n.1; *SA* 3:316–317n.1.
58. Also see *SE* 18:113ff; *SA* 9:106ff.
59. *SE* 19:166; *SA* 3:350.
60. *SE* 19:32ff; *SA* 3:300ff.
61. *SE* 20:232; *SA* Ergänzungsband: 323.
62. Abraham, *Gesammelte Schriften* 2:88–90.
63. *SE* 14:94–96; *SA* 3:61–63.
64. Adorno, *Gesammelte Schriften* 3:162.
65. Friedrich Kittler's *Aufschreibesysteme* opens with a reading of *Faust* in terms of the modern university.
66. Werner Hamacher pursues Faust's signature in "Die andere Übersetzung des Wortes," *Bernhard Minetti/Faust*, ed. Gerhard Ahrens (Wien and Berlin: Medusa-Verlag, 1983).
67. Guttmacher's introduction to I. P. Semmelweis, *Die Aetiologie, der Begriff und*

die Prophylaxis des Kindbettfiebers (New York: Johnson Reprint Corporation, 1966), xxix. Reprinted from the 1861 edition.

68. *Die Fackel* 400–403 (1914): 92–93.
69. *SE* 17:253n.2; *SA* 4:258n.2.
70. *Die Fackel*, 368–369: 1.
71. *Beim Wort genommen*, 323.
72. *Worte in Versen*, 337 and *Beim Wort genommen*, 334, respectively.
73. See Kittler's *Aufschreibesysteme*, 362ff. See also Kittler's longer study of *Dracula*, "Draculas Vermächtnis," *Zeta* 02 (1982): 103–33.
74. *Die Fackel*, 800–805: 28. Though various machines, including automobiles and radios, had made mankind ever more stupid, according to Kraus, he emphasized that he could not condemn himself to stay behind and converse with stupidity when he could flee in an automobile: "There is only one way to save oneself from the machine. And that is to use it. Only within the auto does one come into one's own" (*Die Fackel*, 323:17). See also *Die Fackel* 264–265: 27.
75. *Genealogy of Morals* 1, §10. On this score, see Avital Ronell, "Queens of the Night: Nietzsche's Antibodies," *Genre* 16 (Winter 1983): 405–22.
76. Kittler, *Aufschreibesysteme*, 365.
77. Is this only yet another cross-fire in which "vampirism," since it cannot be acknowledged close-range, is aimed, by each side, at the other side? Or: by naming Hitler the vampire was the legend finally put to rest?
78. Montague Summers, *The Vampire, His Kith and Kin* (New Hyde Park, New York: University Books, 1960), 34ff.
79. Cited in Gabriel Ronay, *The Truth About Dracula* (New York: Stein and Day, 1972), 15. In 1732 alone there appeared at German universities fourteen treatises on vampirism.
80. The seamen/semen cycle even as literary trope is discussed in that portion of *Dictations: On Haunted Writing* which Ronell anchors in footnote 15 to Peter Connor (in part 2).
81. Ernest Jones, *On the Nightmare* (New York: Liveright, 1971), 119.
82. Cited in Joseph S. Bierman, "Dracula: Prolonged Childhood Illness, and the Oral Triad," in *American Imago* 29, 2 (1972): 186.
83. *SE* 21:88; *SA* 9:219.
84. Bierman, "Dracula," 198. It is Lewin's "oral triad" which is being recycled here.
85. Bram Stoker, *Dracula*, (New York: Bantam Books, 1981), 235.
86. Cited in Jones, *On the Nightmare*, 100.
87. McLuhan, *Understanding Media*, 250.
88. Kittler, "Draculas Vermächtnis," 133.
89. This invisible circulation of blood in German films—in precise contradistinction to French film—has been linked by Paul Monaco to the "unanticipated and undigested" loss of World War I. See *Cinema and Society: France and Germany During the Twenties* (New York: Elsevier, 1976).
90. See Kristian Sotriffer, *Expressionism and Fauvism*, trans. Richard Rickett (Vienna: Anton & Schroll & Co., 1972), 15, 16.
91. *SE* 18:177; *GW* 17:30.
92. See Scholem's chapter on the Golem in his book on the Cabbala.
93. The career of Karl Freund embraces the transfer of phantoms from Babelsberg to Hollywood. Murnau and Lang, for example, employed Freund as cameraman; on another continent Freund pops up in Browning's *Dracula*, also as cameraman. He goes on to direct *The Mummy*.

94. This discussion can be found in Hannah Arendt, *The Origins of Totalitarianism* (New York: Harcourt, Brace, 1951), 56–67.
95. Friedrich Torberg juxtaposes the Golem with the Nazi "Enlightenment Project" in "Golems Wiederkehr."

CHAPTER NINE

1. See Jones, *The Life and Work of Sigmund Freud*, vol. 3, ch. 2.
2. *SE* 20:135–37; *SA* 6:276–78.
3. *SE* 14:87–90; *SA* 3:54–57.
4. *SE* 14:91; *SA* 3:57–58.
5. *SE* 20:138–39; *SA* 6:278–79. As is pointed out in a note in the Standard Edition, *Caesur* was first misprinted, in the 1926 German edition, as *Censur* (censorship).
6. Günter Grass, "Vom Stillstand im Fortschritt. Variationen zu Albrecht Dürers Kupferstich 'Melencholia I,' " in *Aus dem Tagebuch einer Schnecke* (Darmstadt: Luchterhand, 1972), 340–68.
7. Günter Grass, *Die Blechtrommel* (Frankfurt a/M: Fischer Verlag, 1962), 39–40. Future references are to this edition and are given in the text.
8. *SE* 14:269; *SA* 7:213.
9. *SE* 5:407; *SA* 2:396–97.
10. *SE* 21:232; *SA* 5:282.
11. Abraham, *Gesammelte Schriften* 1:30–31.
12. Abraham, *Gesammelte Schriften* 1:237.
13. Ferenczi, *Schriften zur Psychoanalyse*, 1:151.
14. See the chapter on the werewolf in Jones, *On the Nightmare*.
15. See Jones, *The Life and Work of Sigmund Freud*, 3:45–47.
16. Róheim, "Nach dem Tode des Urvaters," 120.
17. *SE* 14:89; *SA* 3:55.
18. *SE* 18:123; *SA* 9:115.
19. *SE* 12:54; *SA* 7:179.
20. See Derrida's *L'oreille de l'autre*.
21. *SE* 7:180; *SA* 5:87–88.
22. Grass described *The Tin Drum* as standing in ironic relation to the German *Bildungsroman* tradition—an observation corroborated by Enzensberger who entitled his early review "Wilhelm Meister, drummed out on tin." But Grass also maintained that his novel traverses the entire European tradition beginning with the picaresque, the picaresque conceived, that is, "with all its ruptures (*Brechungen*)." Cited in Eberhard Mannack, *Zwei deutsche Literaturen?* (Kronberg: Athenäum Verlag, 1977), 66–68.
23. For discussion of the origin of the picaresque novel as a forum for *conversos*, see, for example, Richard Bjornson, *The Picaresque Hero in European Fiction* (Madison: The University of Wisconsin Press, 1977), esp. 17ff.
24. See Gilles Deleuze, *Nietzsche et la philosophie* (Paris: Presses Universitaires de France, 1962), ch. 5, §12.
25. See Susan Stewart, *On Longing: Narratives of the Miniature, the Gigantic, the Souvenir, the Collection* (Baltimore: Johns Hopkins University Press, 1984), 61.

26. See Kittler's geneaology of the nuclear family (in German: *Kleinfamilie*) in "Über die Sozialisation Wilhelm Meisters," in Gerhard Kaiser and Friedrich Kittler, *Dichtung als Sozialisationsspiel*, 13–133.

27. See Leo Steinberg, "The Sexuality of Christ in Renaissance Art and in Modern Oblivion," *October* 25 (1983).

28. For discussion of the picaro as embodiment of "nonlife" (*sin vivir*), see Alexander Blackburn, *The Myth of the Picaro* (Chapel Hill: University of North Carolina Press, 1979), 20f.

29. Oskar's identification with Christ is not without precedent in the picaresque tradition. See Bjornson, *The Picaresque Hero*, 64, 130.

30. Barthes, *La chambre claire*. See Michael Halley's review in *Diacritics*, Winter 1982, 69ff.

31. Charles Sanders Peirce makes this point about photography as a sign or vestige that does not imitate but points in *Collected Papers*, ed. Charles Hartshorne and Paul Weiss (Cambridge, Mass.: Harvard University Press, 1932), 2:159.

32. Cited in Kittler, "Wie man abschafft, wovon man spricht: Der Autor von *Ecce Homo*," in *Literaturmagazin* 12 (1980): 161.

33. Barthes, *La chambre claire*, 179.

34. Bernard Pautrat, "Nietzsche médusé," *Nietzsche aujourd'hui* (Paris: 10/18, 1973), "Intensites": 9–30. See also Avital Ronell, "Hitting the Streets: Ecce Fama," *Stanford Italian Review* (1987).

35. Abraham, *Gesammelte Schriften* 2:72–73.

36. This is Kittler's argument in "Wie man abschafft, wovon man spricht." Also see Tracy Strong, "Oedipus as Hero: Family and Family Metaphors in Nietzsche," *Boundary 2*, 9, 3 and 10, 1 (1981): 311–335. See Rodolphe Gasché, "Autobiography as *Gestalt*: Nietzsche's *Ecce Homo*," *Boundary 2*, 9, 3 and 10, 1 (1981): 271–290.

37. Abraham, *Gesammelte Schriften*, 2: 270–71.

38. *SE* 22:72; *SA* 1:509.

39. *SE* 22:77; *SA* 1:514. For *registrieren* Strachey has "take note of."

40. *SE* 22:75–76; *SA* 1:513.

41. *SE* 19:25; *SA* 3:293.

42. *SE* 19:25; *SA* 3:294.

43. *SE* 22:62; *SA* 1:500.

44. *SE* 15:88; *SA* 1:106.

45. *SE* 5:536; *SA* 2:512.

46. See Derrida's *Droit de regards*.

47. See Abraham's letters to Freud dated March 13, 1922 and May 2, 1922.

48. See Abraham's letter to Freud dated October 27, 1918.

49. Jones makes this point in "The Problem of Paul Morphy."

50. In Jones, *The Life and Work of Sigmund Freud*, 3:388.

51. *SE* 12:264; *SA* 3:34.

52. *SE* 19:16n.1; *SA* 3:285–86n.2.

53. *SE* 5:430; *SA* 2:417.

54. *SE* 5:426–27; *SA* 2:413–14.

55. See Halley's review of *La chambre claire*, *Diacritics*, Winter 1982, 75–76.

56. *SE* 5:424; *SA* 2:411.

57. *SE* 23:126; *SA* 9:571.

58. Once again: Derrida, *Droit de regards*.

59. Thomas Mann, *Die Entstehung des Doktor Faustus. Roman eines Romans* (Amsterdam: Bermann-Fischer Verlag, 1949), 60.

60. 137.
61. 9. See Kittler's "Weltatem: Über Wagners Medientechnologie," where Wagner's dictum that music is the breathing of language finds full orchestration.
62. 126–27.
63. 108.
64. 101.
65. "Über den Fetischcharakter in der Musik und die Regression des Hörens," in *Gesammelte Schriften*, ed. Gretel Adorno and Rolf Tiedemann (Frankfurt a/M: Suhrkamp, 1973), 14:15.
66. Mann, *Die Entstehung des Doktor Faustus*, 34.
67. Adorno, *Gesammelte Schriften* 14:41.
68. Adorno, *Gesammelte Schriften* 14:41.
69. Adorno, *Gesammelte Schriften* 14:35.
70. Adorno, *Gesammelte Schriften* 14:39, 41, 42, 45.
71. *SE* 21: 116; *SA* 9: 244.
72. Adorno, *Gesammelte Schriften* 14:36.
73. Jones, *The Life and Work of Sigmund Freud* 1:18.
74. See the introduction to Theodor Reik's *The Haunting Melody* (New York: Farrar, Straus and Young, 1953).
75. Anton Ehrenzweig, *The Psycho-analysis of Artistic Vision and Hearing*, 99, 153ff.
76. Sándor Ferenczi, "Das unwillkommene Kind und sein Todestrieb," in *Schriften zur Psychoanalyse* 2:251–256. Freud establishes this connection in his study of Dora.
77. Hans Sperber, "Über den Einfluss sexueller Momente auf Entstehung und Entwicklung der Sprache," *Imago* 1 (1912): 405–453.
78. Ernest Jones, "The Madonna's Conception through the Ear," in *Essays in Applied Psychoanalysis* 2:320.
79. Ehrenzweig, *The Psycho-analysis of Artistic Vision and Hearing*, 165.
80. Jones, "The Madonna's Conception through the Ear."
81. *SE* 23:114; *SA* 9:560.
82. *SE* 6:106–7.
83. Christoph Ruths, *Experimental-Untersuchungen über Musikphantome und ein daraus erschlossenes Grundgesetz der Enstehung, der Wiedergabe und der Aufnahme von Tonwerken* (Darmstadt: Kommissionsverlag von H. L. Schlapp, 1898), 202–3.
84. Ruths, *Experimental-Untersuchungen über Musikphantome*, 151, 156.
85. Ruths, *Experimental-Untersuchungen über Musikphantome*, 163, 174, 207, 232, 243.
86. Ruths, *Experimental-Untersuchungen über Musikphantome*, 365–67.
87. Róheim, *Magic and Schizophrenia*, 173, 164, 165.
88. Róheim, *Magic and Schizophrenia*, 182.
89. Róheim, *Magic and Schizophrenia*, 176.
90. Róheim, *Magic and Schizophrenia*, 164–65.
91. There appears to be a point of agreement here with Jacques Attali's *Noise: The Political Economy of Music*, trans. Brian Massumi (Minneapolis: University of Minnesota Press, 1985). But Attali inserts Girard in the place of Freud, thus doubling Girard's own repression and abbreviated simulation of *Totem and Taboo*.
92. Róheim, *Magic and Schizophrenia*, 187.
93. For example: SE 15:153; SA 1:162.

94. Róheim, *Magic and Schizophrenia*, 151.
95. Peter Worsley, *The Trumpet Shall Sound*, 85. On "noise" see Theodore Schwartz, *The Paliau Movement in the Admiralty Islands, 1946–1954* (New York: Anthropological Papers of the American Museum of Natural History, 1962).
96. Róheim, *Magic and Schizophrenia*, 198.

INDEX

Index

Broser. Stephan. 28
Burton. Robert. 4, 66

Cabinet of Dr. Caligari, The (film).
   325–26, 327
Cargo Cult. *See* Melanesians. Cargo
   Cult of.
"Carmilla" (Le Fanu). 68–70
Carroll. Lewis. 158
Castle, The (Kafka). 285. 286
Christ. 344–45
Civilization and Its Discontents
   (Freud). 42. 200. 327. 364
Coleridge. Samuel Taylor. 158
"Condor" (Stifter). 219, 220
"Contribution to the Psychology of Ru-
   mor, A" (Jung). 289
Corngold, Stanley. 245
Country Doctor (Kafka). 271
Critique of Judgment (Kant). 100, 101

Da Vinci. Leonardo. 5. 40. 74. 263–66
Deleuze. Gilles. 244. 272
De Man, Paul. 100
Derrida. Jacques. 134. 219. 254. 283.
   339, 359
Despair (Nabokov). 144
Deutsch. Helene. 149
Dialectic of Enlightenment (Adorno
   and Horkheimer). 21. 295–97
Dichtung und Wahrheit (Goethe). 86
Diderot. Denis. 127. 128
*Divine Legation of Moses Demon-
   strated, The* (Warburton). 127
Doctor Faustus (Mann). 342. 362–63
Dr. Mabuse the Gambler (film). 310–
   11
Dora. case study of. 71–72, 73
Dostoevsky. Feodor M.. 30
Dracula (Stoker). 179. 318. 319–20.
   322–23, 362
Dracula (film). 323
"Dream, The" (Kafka). 259. 272
"Dream and Occultism" (Freud). 31
"Dream and Telepathy" (Freud). 29
Dreambook (Keller). 197. 198
Dreyer. Carl-Theodor. 146
Dymant. Dora. 292. 293

Ecce Homo (Nietzsche). 48. 49. 51. 55.
   341, 350

Education of Mankind, The (Lessing).
   75
Ego and the Id, The (Freud). 40. 116,
   154. 299. 301. 354
Ehrenzweig. Anton. 111. 366. 367
Elective Affinities (Goethe). 96. 97. 346
"Eleven Sons" (Kafka). 259
Emilia Galotti (Lessing). 60–64. 67.
   72–73. 75–79. 81–84. 85. 91. 96–
   97. 102. 178
Ende. Stuart. 115–16
Essence of Christianity, The
   (Feuerbach). 182
"Eugenia" (Keller). 201
Euphorion (Nietzsche). 51–52
Evans. Sir Arthur. 122–23

Faust (Goethe). 33. 35. 304. 312–13
Ferenczi. Sándor. 17. 77. 135. 137.
   168. 262. 266. 337. 354. 366
Feuerbach. Ludwig. 181–82
Fine. Reuben. 114
Flaubert. Gustave. 24
Fliess. Wilhelm. 26. 27. 28. 56. 170.
   275. 358
Frankenstein (Shelley). 16–17. 143
Frankenstein (film). 324
"Fratricide. A" (Kafka). 259
Freilingrath. Ferdinand. 178
Freud. Ernst. 7
Freud. John. 25. 26. 29. 30. 40
Freud. Julius. 12–13. 26–28. 40
Freud. Pauline. 25. 26
Freud. Philipp. 28
Freud. Sigmund. 1. 53. 68. 111. 112.
   121. 173. 199. 220. 221. 225. 227–
   28. 235. 257. 297. 314. 363. 364.
   367; on anal eroticism. 139–40.
   200; and analogy of archaeological
   excavation. 123–24; and analogy
   of open wound. 13. 27. 43; avuncular complex of. 25–26. 40. 275;
   and castration concept. 28–29. 30.
   31. 43. 89–90. 140. 360; on childhood narcissism. 361–62; cocaine
   research of. 274–75; concept of
   melancholia. 3–4. 5. 6; and death
   of sibling. 12–13. 26–30; on death
   wish. 359–61. 365–66; on doubling
   of loved one. 142–45. 253; dream
   theory of. 129–32. 151. 152. 275–

404

Laurence A. Rickels moved to the West Coast in 1981 after completing graduate training in German philology at Princeton University. While in California he earned a psychotherapy license. He has published numerous studies of the phenomenon he calls "unmourning," a term that inspired his trilogy *Aberrations of Mourning*, *The Case of California*, and *Nazi Psychoanalysis*. He has also written the coursebooks *The Vampire Lectures* and *The Devil Notebooks*. All of these books have been published by the University of Minnesota Press.